How to Ruin a Queen

Marie Antoinette, the Stolen Diamonds and the
Scandal that Shook the French Throne

JONATHAN BECKMAN

JOHN MURRAY

First published in Great Britain in 2014 by John Murray (Publishers)
An Hachette UK Company

First published in paperback in 2015

1

A CIP catalogue record for this title is available from the British Library

Paperback ISBN 978-1-84854-997-5

Typeset in Bembo MT Pro by Palimpsest Book Production Ltd, Falkirk, Stirlingshire

Printed and bound by Clays Ltd, St Ives plc

John Murray policy is to use papers that are natural, renewable and recyclable products and
made from wood grown in sustainable forests. The logging and manufacturing processes
are expected to conform to the environmental regulations of the country of origin.

John Murray (Publishers)
338 Euston Road
London NW1 3BH

www.johnmurray.co.uk

To the memory of my mother, *z"l*,
who I hope would have liked it

Contents

CONTENTS

Dramatis Personae

The Main Characters

Jeanne's Family

Jeanne de Saint-Rémy, comtesse de La Motte-Valois, *an adventuress*
Jacques de Saint-Rémy, *her father*
Marie Jossell, *her mother*
Jacques de Saint-Rémy *fils, her brother*
Marianne de Saint-Rémy, *her sister*
Marguerite de Saint-Rémy, *her sister*
Marquise de Boulainvilliers, *Jeanne's benefactress*
Marquis de Boulainvilliers, *her husband*

The Rohan

Louis, Cardinal de Rohan, *prince-bishop of Strasbourg and grand almoner of France*
Prince de Soubise, *his uncle*
Comtesse de Marsan, *his aunt*
Abbé Georgel, *Rohan's vicar-general*
Baron de Planta, *Rohan's major-domo*

The Habsburgs

Maria Theresa, *archduchess of Austria, queen of Hungary and Bohemia, Holy Roman Empress and mother of Marie Antoinette*

Joseph II, *her son, Holy Roman Emperor and co-regent*
Prince Kaunitz, *the Austrian chancellor*

The House of Bourbon

Louis XVI, *king of France*
Comte de Provence, *his brother*
Comte d'Artois, *his brother*
Madame Elisabeth, known simply as Madame, *his sister*
Louis XV, *his grandfather and predecessor*
Madame du Barry, *Louis XV's mistress*

Servants of the Crown

Duc de Choiseul, *Louis XV's chief minister*
Duc d'Aiguillon, *foreign minister after Choiseul's dismissal*
Comte de Calonne, *minister of finance*
Baron de Breteuil, *minister of the king's household*
Comte de Vergennes, *foreign minister*
Maréchal de Castries, *minister of the navy*
Marquis de Miromesnil, *keeper of the seals*

The Queen's Circle

Marie Antoinette, *queen of France*
Princesse de Lamballe, *a favourite*
Duchesse de Polignac, *another favourite*
Madame Campan, *a femme de chambre*
Comte de Mercy-Argenteau, *Austrian ambassador to the French Court*
Abbé de Vermond, *reader to the queen and a trusted counsellor*

Jeanne's Circle

Jacques Beugnot, *a lawyer*
Nicolas de La Motte, *a soldier, later husband to Jeanne*
Rétaux de Villette, *a messmate of Nicolas*
Rosalie Brissault, *Jeanne's chambermaid*

Marie de La Tour, *Jeanne's niece*
Père Nicolas Loth, *a Minim friar*

The English Connection

Chevalier O'Neil, *a friend of Nicolas*
Barthélemy Macdermott, *a Capuchin monk*
Nathaniel Jefferys, *a jeweller*
William Gray, *another jeweller*
Costa, also known as François Benevent, *a language tutor and spy*
D'Arragon, *a secretary at the French Embassy*
Comte d'Adhémar, *French ambassador to Great Britain*
Charles Théveneau de Morande, *a muckraking journalist*

The Jewellers

Charles Boehmer, *a Parisian jeweller, also crown jeweller and jeweller to the queen*
Paul Bassenge, *his partner*
Louis-François Achet, *a lawyer and friend of Bassenge*
Jean-Baptiste Laporte, *Achet's son-in-law, another lawyer*
Claude Baudard de Sainte-James, *a financier*

The Suspects

Nicole le Guay, later the Baronne d'Oliva, *a prostitute with a resemblance to Marie Antoinette*
Toussaint de Beausire, *her lover*
Comte de Cagliostro, *an alchemist and savant*
Seraphina, *his wife*

The Law Officers

Marquis de Launay, *governor of the Bastille*
Louis Thiroux de Crosne, *lieutenant-general of the Paris Police*
Quidor, *a police inspector*
Etienne François d'Aligre, *chief magistrate of the parlement of Paris*

François-Louis Joly de Fleury, *procureur-général of the parlement of Paris*

Pierre Laurencel, *Fleury's deputy*

Maximilien Titon de Villotran, *one of the investigating magistrates*

Dupuis de Marcé, *the other investigating magistrate*

Lawyers

Guy-Jean-Baptiste Target, *Rohan's lawyer*

Maître Doillot, *Jeanne's lawyer*

Why, such have revolutionized this land
With diamond-necklace-dealing!
Red Cotton Night-Cap Country, Robert Browning

Madame, il est charmant votre projet. Je viens d'y réfléchir. Il rapproche tout, termine tout, embrasse tout.
The Marriage of Figaro,
Pierre-Augustin Caron de Beaumarchais

Prologue

Before the Law

France, 31 May 1786

B EFORE PARIS AWOKE, before carriages troubled the streets, before
clerks unbolted their offices and barbers stropped their blades,
before hawkers tuned their voices and labourers sloped into town
with their kit upon their backs, as the cafes stood shuttered and
stray drunks bumped through the city, as the fishmongers and florists
and grocers laid out their wares, glossy with dew on the dew-damp
stalls, the kinsmen of the house of Rohan rose. In the Hôtel de
Soubise in the Marais, in the Pavillon de Marsan in the Tuileries,
in the Hôtel de Brionne nearby, they dressed in solemn black and
rode in silence to the Ile de la Cité, the larger of the two islands
on the Seine, to the Palais de Justice, where the highest court in
the land was to sit in judgement. At half past five in the morning,
while the light still shone cold, nineteen members of the Rohan
family drew themselves up in two lines near the entrance of the
palace to reverence the magistrates as they arrived. We have humbled
ourselves before you, spoke the bowed heads silently. We, the Rohan,
who stand above all the nobility of France, have humbled ourselves
before you. Let not your verdict be the wrong one.

This extraordinary performance was delivered in solidarity with
the family's golden boy, Cardinal Louis de Rohan, prince-bishop of
Strasbourg, provisor of the Sorbonne and grand almoner of France.
He stood accused not only of stealing one of the most valuable items
of jewellery in Europe – a 2,800-carat diamond necklace worth 1.6
million livres – but of invoking the name of the queen to lubricate
his criminal enterprise. This left him vulnerable to the charge of
lèse-majesté – offending royal dignity – an exponentially more serious

offence than theft. That Rohan should have claimed to represent the queen was one of the most prominent improbabilities in a story tattooed with them, for Marie Antoinette – as everyone knew – despised him. His gilded, feckless youth had slumped into a gilded, feckless middle age of pursuing stags and society ladies, before, thanks to political manoeuvrings by his family, he was appointed ambassador to Vienna. While in his post, he managed to offend the Empress Maria Theresa, Marie Antoinette's mother, so gracelessly that the French queen treated him from then on with silent contempt.

Rohan believed that Marie Antoinette's hatred prevented his appointment, like the great cardinal-politicians before him, to chief minister of the realm. His frustrated ambition turned sour, vinegaring his spendthrift days. He was overjoyed, therefore, to make the acquaintance in 1782 of the impoverished, alluring Jeanne, comtesse de La Motte-Valois. She had been born in Champagne to a family that claimed descent from an illegitimate line of the Valois kings. After her father had squandered her inheritance, she and her husband had decamped to Paris in an attempt to regain her ancestral domains. Rohan – intrigued, charmed, lusty – took the comtesse under his wing, but shortly afterwards found himself seeking her patronage. Jeanne told the cardinal that the queen had taken pity on her condition, had invited her into her private chambers, and had adopted her as a companion. She used the opportunity to tell the queen of the chagrin Rohan felt at his disgrace and of his wish to atone. Marie Antoinette proved open to a reconciliation, and they embarked on a correspondence, with Jeanne as go-between, of welling intimacy.

There were endless factional rivalries that needed assuaging and numerous political obstructions to be overcome before the rapprochement could be acknowledged openly, but Rohan was granted a brief interview with the queen late one night in the gardens of Versailles. True, the moon was obscured and Marie Antoinette's face could only be dimly made out; true, too, there was time only to exchange a single sentence before the assignation was abruptly terminated by the sound of nearby footsteps. But Rohan was convinced the press of Her Majesty's hand had absolved him of his misdemeanours, promised him, indeed, that the high office he deserved would soon be his. Soon enough an instruction arrived from the queen for a delicate mission – he was the only man she could trust to oversee it. She wished to buy the gargantuan necklace assembled by Boehmer and Bassenge, jewellers to the crown. They were delighted and relieved – having failed a number of times to sell their masterwork to Marie Antoinette, they were hanging on the verge of bankruptcy. An agreement was reached – the first instalment was to be paid six months later – and a copy of the terms returned from the queen signed 'Marie Antoinette de France'.

No money was forthcoming, however, at the beginning of August 1785 when the initial tranche fell due. Rohan explained to the jewellers that the queen was temporarily out of funds but would pay off a greater proportion in October. They tried to question Marie Antoinette in person; she, angered by their persistent importuning, refused to see them. Eventually, word reached the Court that Boehmer and Bassenge were seeking payment from the queen for the necklace. This was preposterous, she declared to the king and his ministers, she had never agreed to buy any necklace, certainly not a grotesque one she had rejected numerous times before. When Rohan was summoned to explain himself, he could barely stammer out a sentence, let alone construct a convincing explanation of the necklace's disappearance. He was arrested and imprisoned in the Bastille, while a police investigation was opened.

Paris was het up with speculation. Had the cardinal devised a lunatic scheme to pay off his debts? Or had he been the victim of another's deceit? Was the queen, whose extravagant behaviour had provoked envy and contempt, entirely uninvolved, despite her aggrieved denials? And what was the role of Jeanne? Was she pawn or player? The case was heard before the *parlement* of Paris, the country's supreme court, and nothing less than the reputation of the queen was at stake. For nine months the investigating judges sifted through evidence and interrogated the suspects, for nine months the citizens of Paris, France, Europe stood slack-jawed as they heard the fantastical defences of the accused. Never before had the expected conduct of a queen been debated so exhaustively by the public. The disputes would echo down through the Revolution – a *cri de guerre* to the rebellious, a taunting cacophony to the faithful.

The significance of the affair was evident to perceptive contemporaries. 'Watch out for this diamond necklace business,' wrote Talleyrand, 'it may well rock the throne of France.' Napoleon, pondering the caprice of history in exile, declared that 'the Queen's death must be dated from the Diamond Necklace trial'. The many nineteenth-century historians who wrote about this episode viewed it as a major staging post on the road to regicide. But the Marxist bent of much twentieth-century historiography on the Revolution, which sought out its causes in class conflict and the structural deficiencies of the French economy, considered the necklace business as so much froth lathered up by deeper-running historical currents. Another example of royal delinquency and incompetence, to be sure, but one of vastly less significance than the societal upheavals churning through the country.

Fashions change and the Diamond Necklace Affair now intersects with some of the most fruitful furrows of scholarly work on eighteenth-century France, yet it still merits only a footnote or glancing mention in many accounts of the pre-revolutionary years. Historians are now far more conscious of the effect of libellous literature, directed at elites, in desacralising the monarchy – once the king and queen had been removed from their pedestal, it was easier to pack them off in a tumbril. The Affair ought to be seen as a pivotal moment in this narrative, not simply because it produced sheaves of political pornography – it was also a defining pedagogic encounter for the French people in which they learned to discuss, interpret and judge the actions of their betters. They would apply these lessons, with often bloody consequences, in the years that followed the summoning of the Estates-General in 1789.

This book traces the fate of the necklace and hacks through the thicket of lies which flowered during the trial. It shows that the rule of reason supposedly established by the Enlightenment was fragile, assailed by occult beliefs and subsuming desires that would not be quelled by the evidence of one's eyes. It warns those who wish to reduce man to *homo economicus* that his motives and self-justifications are cloudy even to himself. It explores how history is comprised of the stories told by its participants, that learning to read these stories like a contemporary – to appreciate that their terrible influence in no way correlates to their adherence to the truth — is the foremost duty of the historian. Above all, this is such an improbable story — one which, were it offered up in a novel, would be condemned for violating the laws of plausibility — that I was compelled to retell it as soon as I came across it. Thomas Carlyle was too. He saw a romance more wondrous than a poet could ever compose, which broke through the crust of everyday life to partake in our Universal History. Here, away from the 'empty invoice-lists of Pitched Battles and Changes of Ministry', he heard the beat of humanity's heart in all its complacency and fear and exhilaration.

I

Princess in Rags

FREUD OBSERVED THAT many children fantasise that their real
mother and father are aristocrats – even royalty – and that they
were ripped from their true family and implanted into a lowlier, adoptive one. It is part of the process of growing up when a child, comparing
his parents to other adults, realises they are no longer 'the only authority
and the source of all belief'. But what if daydreams of a life among
the nobility are not simply the wishful denial of your parents? What
if they are coloured with regret at your belatedness, with disappoint-
ment and anger that your forebears squandered money and honours
you deserved? What if you lived in a tumbledown castle and had been
told from the moment you began to understand that one of your
ancestors had been, long ago, the king of France?

Jeanne de Saint-Rémy was born on 22 July 1756 in the chateau
of Fontette, a tiny village in Champagne about thirty miles to the
west of Troyes.* Her father, Jacques, the baron de Saint-Rémy, was
descended from Henri de Valois de Saint-Rémy, an illegitimate son
of the priapic Henri II, the Valois king who ruled France from 1547
to 1559 (the Valois dynasty preceded the Bourbons, who reigned
from 1589 until the French Revolution). Henri II left 30,000 écus
to his natural son, and gave permission to the Saint-Rémy heirs to
sport three gold fleur-de-lys – the emblem of the French kings – on
their escutcheons.

---

* Practically all we know of Jeanne's childhood derives from her own memoirs – and
they are hugely unreliable. The narrative here is based on them, though modified
where more trustworthy evidence to the contrary exists. Readers should be aware
that Jeanne's account is, in many ways, the one that she wished to tell about herself
– because it is emotionally affective; because of the aura of romance – and not
necessarily a comprehensive description of her early years.

But by the end of the seventeenth century the family's wealth had been decimated. French inheritance law generally allowed each child to claim a portion of their parents' estate, which meant that, without complex financial planning, a handsome patrimony could be pared down to slivers in less than a century. Despite protesting of her sole entitlement to her family's lands, Jeanne was only descended from the sixth and final child of the second baron de Saint-Rémy. Her grandfather, Nicolas-René, had served in Louis XIV's *garde du corps* for ten years but had moved back to Fontette to marry the daughter of a prominent local official in nearby Bar-sur-Seine. The Saint-Rémys had neither the inclination nor the money to buzz around Versailles in search of promotion and lucrative sinecures: local legend had it that, when Louis XIII asked one of Jeanne's ancestors why he avoided the Court, he replied 'Je n'y fait ce que je dois', which means 'I only do there what I ought to' and 'I only make there what I owe' – he was later discovered illegally minting coins.

The family's sullen and blocky chateau rose from within a tonsure of walnut trees, and was set among fields of oats and lucerne. In Champagne the Saint-Rémys lived as though their royal forebear had endowed them with limitless droits de seigneur, stealing from neighbours' property and cowing the local authorities into inaction. But by the middle of the eighteenth century, they could barely squeeze a living from their land. The debilitating famines which afflicted France in 1725 and 1740 ate into their capital, and they were forced to sell off parts of their acreage and chateau piecemeal.

Their plight was not unusual, especially in Champagne, one of the country's poorer provinces. While many members of the nobility had accrued vast fortunes, others needed to scrimp to maintain appearances. The most abject nobles were known as *hobereaux* ('little hawks'): over 5,000 families existed on less than 1,000 livres a year, which left them dangerously susceptible to slipping into poverty. They poached, fished and hunted game; some indentured themselves to the wealthy; all hoped their situation would pass unnoticed and they would escape *dérogance* – being forcibly submerged into the ranks of commoners should they fail to uphold the dignity of their estate.

Jacques's parents may have intended a respectable match for their son. They were certainly appalled when Jacques seduced or – more likely, given his general lassitude – was seduced by Marie Jossell, the family's illiterate and alluring housekeeper. She had 'fine blue eyes [that] appear[ed] through long silken lashes . . . her dark tresses [fell] in graceful profusion over her shoulder drawing out to the greatest advantage the natural whiteness of her skin'. Though Marie was evidently pregnant, Nicolas-René forbade their marriage. Jacques would not disobey his father but refused to abandon his lover. A son, also named Jacques, was born on 25 February 1755. Nicolas-René must have relented because the couple were married in Langres in July. Jeanne was born almost a year later; Marianne arrived in 1757; and Marguerite followed in 1759.

Jacques had a sweet temperament but, as a contemporary described him, he was 'weak, indolent, a man who amounted to nothing'. He spent most of his time and money on drink. Like many impoverished noblemen, he became indistinguishable from the peasants he lived alongside. His lack of resolve deliquesced into self-destructive generosity: if a neighbour slaughtered a pig, he would exchange a copse or a field for a share. While Jacques indulged his children, Marie treated them sternly. Scarcely had they left their cribs than she forced them to work. Jeanne, feisty from an early age, was frequently beaten by her mother for refusing to herd the cows. Both parents utterly neglected their offsprings' well-being. They were 'brought up like savages', wandering around naked and reliant for their food on charitable neighbours, who slipped them bowls of soup. What little money the family accrued was siphoned off by Marie for her relatives.

Between the prodigality of Jacques and the peculation of Marie, it was not long before the family was broke. 1759 was an especially hungry year. A poor harvest inflated food prices; money was already tight after tax obligations surged in 1756 to pay for what would become the Seven Years War against Britain and Prussia. By 1760 all the Saint-Rémys' property had been sold or mortgaged – and Marie was expecting another baby. The family's only option was to flee their creditors. Marianne, too young to travel and too heavy to be carried, was left hanging in a basket outside the window of the house of her godfather Durand, a sympathetic farmer who had quietly subsidised Jacques in the past. The family slipped out of the village by night and hurried down the road to Paris. Occasionally they were able to thumb a lift from a wagon, but Jeanne, still only four years old, trudged practically the entire distance – over two hundred kilometres – on foot. Adversity did not forge any familial solidarity: Marie beat Jeanne with a rod wreathed in nettles; when Jacques found out he pummelled his wife.

Migration was how the poor survived in eighteenth-century France. Some went in search of seasonal, agricultural work; others moved permanently from the country to town. Paris had swollen under the reigns of Louis XIV and Louis XV: by the middle of the eighteenth century, less than a quarter of its residents were native Parisians. A new city offered opportunities for reinvention. Vulpine cronies; debts like grenades fizzing towards explosion; even inveterate character traits – all could be abandoned. Jacques showed more application in the forced march north-west than he had ever done before. But well-advertised snares awaited newcomers to the metropolis: exploitation, robbery, and a life of beggary, prostitution and theft.

On arrival, the family split: the two Jacques took off together, while Jeanne remained with her mother. Marie had no desire to work if her perfectly healthy daughter could line her pockets, so Jeanne was sent out begging each morning (this was far from unusual – between a half and two-thirds of beggars in France at the time were children), her name supposed to inspire curiosity. She walked the streets, pipsqueaking 'ladies and gentlemen, take compassion on a poor orphan, descended directly from Henry II, of Valois, King of France', as Marie stood close by with an array of genealogical charts to further intrigue punters. Unfortunately the worldly citizens of Paris were sceptical of princesses in rags, and all Jeanne received for her pains were barrages of abuse and the occasional cuff round the ear.

Jacques had been planning to unearth legal support for the restitution of his lands but, his mind addled by drink, achieved nothing. The family moved to Boulogne where the parish priest, Abbé Henocque, agreed to help them petition the crown, yet the optimism did not last long, as Jacques was arrested by the police. The reasons for this are unclear, though it may have been because he bandied about his Valois title, which was believed to be extinct. Visiting her father in prison, Jeanne saw him 'extended on a bed of straw, his body emaciated, his complexion sallow and pinched, his eyes languid and sunken, yet a faint and transient gleam seemed to speak the joy in his heart and welcome our approach'.

Henocque agitated for Jacques's release, which finally occurred seven weeks after his arrest. By then, his constitution, already charred by alcohol, had crumbled under the strain of prison. He was taken to the Hôtel-Dieu, the paupers' hospital adjoining Notre Dame. The prospect of recovery there was minimal: up to six people were crammed in each bed, the infectious jostling against the convalescent, clammy with each other's sweat as the shudders of the dying sent tremors through the living. It did not take long for Jacques to expire, with Jeanne on hand to record his last words: 'My dear child! I fear my conduct will cause you much misery in the future; but let me beg you, under every misfortune, to remember that you are a VALOIS! Cherish, throughout life, sentiments of that name and never forget your birth! – I tremble . . . I tremble at the thought of leaving you in the care of such a mother!'

It is extremely unlikely that Jacques de Saint-Rémy ever uttered these words, doused in unctuous sentimentality. He failed to protect his eldest daughter from the violence of her mother during his life and, from the little that can be extrapolated of his character, upholding the reputation of the Valois was not his principal motivation. That should not, however, obscure the harrowing effect of Jacques's death on Jeanne and its reverberations over the course of her life. Her father may not have lived up to the family name, but Jeanne declaimed it every time she went out begging. From a young age, she would have marked the contrast between her lineage and the means to which she had been reduced to support her relatives. '[T]he noble blood of the Valois flowing within my veins oppos[ed], like an indignant torrent, such degradation,' she recalled. Jeanne's subsequent ambition can only be understood in the light of her wish to comport herself like a Valois.

In March 1762, three months after Jacques's death, Marie and her children moved to Versailles. Jeanne resumed begging, but pre-empted official harassment by ingratiating herself with the family of the chief of police, Monsieur Deionice. His wife and daughter lavished her with food, toys and spare change, though her success probably relied more on Deionice's regular visits to Marie's bedroom – when Marie took up with Jean-Baptiste Ramond, a handsome Sardinian soldier, Jeanne found herself no longer welcome in the Deionice household. The couple married and settled in a dosshouse in Chaillot, just to the west of Paris. The newlyweds shared the bed; the children slept on the floor on straw pallets.

In Ramond, Marie had found a partner more suited to her taste for violence. Jeanne, bearing Marguerite on her back, was instructed to bring back ten *sous* each day – and twenty on Sundays and holidays. This was a formidable target. A lacemaker or woolspinner could not expect to make more than eight *sous*, and an agricultural labourer no more than ten. When Jeanne failed to collect enough money, she was ordered to sleep in the streets. If she tried to evade her mother and stepfather, Ramond would hunt her down and drag her home, where Marie beat her with a vinegar-soaked rod which tore her back with splinters.

Ramond moved to Paris with Jacques, so that the children's profitability might be maximised. He appropriated the boy's titles and styled himself the baron de Valois, but was repeatedly arrested for begging. On the third occasion, the authorities decided to employ a more effective deterrent: he was sentenced to the pillory for twenty-four hours, then banished from the city for five years. On hearing of her lover's imminent exile, Marie hurried to join him for a final embrace, leaving her two young daughters with a bag of hazelnuts and a breezy promise that she would return within the week. They never saw her again.

It seems Marie eventually returned to Fontette, where she found no shortage of admirers prepared to buy her dinner. When her looks faded, she toiled in the vineyards. From the mid-1760s to the mid-1770s, harvests were lean. The freeing up of the trade in grain in 1763 and 1764 encouraged speculation and hoarding, exacerbating the scarcity and leading to a surge in food prices. At some point during these years, Marie ceased to be able to support herself. She left Fontette and wandered off the historical record – most likely working as a migrant labourer and intermittent prostitute until a penurious death.

There is more evidence, though less clarity, about the fate of the children. According to one account – written by a *champenois* who knew the family – the kindly priest Abbé Henocque took in Jeanne and her siblings and obtained the patronage of a wealthy noble family, who paid for their education in a convent. Jeanne's own account arrives at a similar destination, though by a more picturesque route. After Marie's disappearance, the little street rats scurried around as usual, badgering anyone they could find for a coin. Whatever trepidation they may have felt about their abandonment must have been alleviated by the disappearence of anyone likely to batter them with an improvised weapon at the slightest provocation.

Nearly a month had passed when a coach drew up beside a tiny, pale six-year-old girl, standing on the side of a country road and bellowing that she was the last relict of the Valois. The vehicle contained the marquis and marquise de Boulainvilliers, who asked Jeanne to explain herself. As she told her story the marquis's face torqued itself incredulously, but his wife told Jeanne, 'if you speak the truth, I will be a mother to you'. When the claims were corroborated by their neighbours and Henocque, Jeanne, Jacques and Marguerite were packed off to the Boulainvilliers' chateau at Passy, where they were washed, dressed, given proper beds with crisp linen sheets, and introduced to the marquise's daughters, whom they were told to regard as sisters.

Anne Gabriel Henri Bernard, marquis de Boulainvilliers, was a man of considerable distinction. He was *prévôt* of Paris, supervising the policing and legal administration of the city. Boulainvilliers's grandfather was Henri, comte de Boulainvilliers – astrologer, admirer of Mohammed and, according to Voltaire, the 'most scholarly man in the history of the kingdom'. In his historical works, the comte pined after a feudal age of seigneurial camaraderie, in which his caste was neither reduced to mummers in the spectacles of absolute monarchy, nor diluted by the admission of thousands of arrivistes who had purchased their rank. It was ironic, then, that his daughter – the marquis's mother – should marry the son of Samuel Bernard who, though elevated as the comte de Coubert, had been raised in the stolidly bourgeois household of a Dutch painter of portrait miniatures. Bernard was the richest banker in Europe and underwrote the French government during the War of the Spanish Succession. The Boulainvilliers' household combined staggering wealth with a pious, if hypocritical adulation of the old nobility – a combination that may have made them especially susceptible to the plight of the young Valois.

Jeanne herself had reasons to claim she had effectively been adopted by the Boulainvilliers, not just treated as a distant charitable project funded at the behest of a kindly old curate. Her entry into the family offered, as much as any official documentation, recognition of her deserts, and challenged the authorities to support her in comparable luxury. Though her story seems like a fairy tale, it has corroboration from other quarters. Jacques's petition to Louis XVI in 1776 spoke of how the 'Marquise de Boulainvilliers met them by chance on the road'; and Rose Bertin, Marie Antoinette's dressmaker, knew the Boulainvilliers' cook, who told her that the children had turned up at Passy with a little casket containing their title deeds.

The three siblings were sent off to boarding school. Jacques eventually joined the navy and Jeanne made 'rapid progress in every branch of female education, particularly in writing' – but Marguerite died during a smallpox outbreak. The Boulainvilliers fled Paris in fright and Jeanne would not see them again for another five years. Her schoolmistress, Madame le Clerc, took advantage of the marquise's seclusion to force Jeanne into servitude: 'I fetched water; I rubbed the chairs, made the beds; in short I did every menial office about the house . . . in the different occupations of washing, ironing, housekeeping, nursing.' She was eventually rescued by the marquise but her wish to be enfolded within the family was not granted. Soon she was apprenticed to a number of professionals – first to a seamstress, then to a maker of mantuas (loose-fitting gowns). It is evident that the marquise wanted Jeanne to learn a trade so she could support herself independently and with dignity, and needlework was the most promising profession for women without wealth.

None of this was congenial to Jeanne. Mademoiselle la Marcha may have been 'a mantua-maker of the highest reputation', but 'the urgency of her very extensive business was by no means suitable for a person of my condition'. She was moved elsewhere but chafed when taken on by a retired lady-in-waiting to the marquise de

Narbonne, 'compelled to carry water from the bottom of a house four storeys high, to prepare the bath which her indisposition obliged her to use' and 'reduced to the situation of *servant to a servant!*'.

During her teenage years, Jeanne frequently fell sick and returned to the Boulainvilliers. She claimed to suffer from 'putrid fever' – or typhus – but it's easy to see how, in her misery, she might have developed a hypochondriac sensitivity to the smallest somatic fluctuations, or have feigned illness. Her dreams of being waited upon by others were only fulfilled by the nurses at her sickbed. An insight into these fantasies might be found in the library she later accumulated: among the multi-volume editions of Rousseau, Crébillon and the *Hommes Illustres de Plutarque*, was shelved an obscure play called *L'Orphelin Anglais* (*The English Orphan*) by Charles Henri de Longueil. The rest of Jeanne's books seem to have been bought to furnish her rooms rather than her mind but, as there were no other individual play scripts in the inventory, *L'Orphelin Anglais* almost certainly held some specific sentimental value.

Set in medieval England, the play was first performed by the Comédie-Française in February 1769. Its two central characters, Thomas Frick and his son-in-law Thomas Spencer, are prosperous carpenters. The younger Thomas is admirably honest, fair and devoted to his wife and children. But one of their customers, Lady Lallin, seems determined that the family should spend a number of years travelling on the continent so that young Thomas can perfect his trade. First she offers to pay for their trip; when they refuse to go, she threatens to arrange for their expulsion from the kingdom. It soon transpires that Thomas was an orphan taken in by Frick. Lord Kitson, Lady Lallin's brother, informs him that he is, in fact, the heir to the earldom of Gloucester. His father had relinquished him when he had fallen into disgrace with the queen; and Lady Lallin is eager for the family to take a lengthy voyage abroad because she was granted the earl's confiscated property. Reclaiming the title, however, would mean the annulment of Thomas's marriage to Molly, a commoner, a fate that looks increasingly likely when Kitson fails to extract an exemption from the king. Only when Molly tearfully collapses before the throne is the king's decision reversed and the family saved.

At first glance there is little in common between the personalities of Jeanne and Thomas. He takes pride in craftsmanship, has no yearning for great wealth and refuses to sacrifice his marriage in exchange for an exalted rank. But this was probably not how Jeanne read the play. It fulfilled a number of hopes that her life with the Boulainvilliers failed to deliver. She saw an orphan who had been absorbed so fully into his adoptive family that he had married into it. She observed that the fate of the high-born is of great interest to kings, if only the opportunity could be found to arouse their pity. Most dramatically, the play offered a fantasy of instantaneous redemption – however tedious the endless prospect of life as a seamstress seemed, it could be escaped in the time it takes for a man with welcome news to walk through the door. Jeanne would grow to realise that intervention was required for fantasies to become real.

During the increasingly lengthy stretches of time Jeanne spent recuperating in the Boulainvilliers' home, she began to attract the attention of the marquis. He was deeply concerned about the state of her body – more for carnal than medical reasons. In her auto-biography, Jeanne records how the marquis would visit her alone, conduct a number of vital diagnostic tests and palliatives (taking her pulse, rubbing her temples, stroking her stomach), offer her money and diamond-encrusted jewellery, before telling her that she must not mention any of this to the servants. 'Although I deemed this conduct very indelicate,' she wrote, 'yet, under the specious pretence that he disguised it, it would have appeared unreasonable to remonstrate.' (It is questionable, given Jeanne's pliancy towards powerful men throughout her life, whether Boulainvilliers's approaches were entirely unwelcome or without encouragement.)

When the marquis's daughters found out about these tête-à-têtes they understandably grew frosty towards Jeanne. The marquise concealed her in a hospital, 'not wishing to expose my youth and innocence to such temptations as the Marquis, availing himself of his station and circumstance, perhaps might offer', though Jeanne, finding that the accommodation lacked the plushness of the Boulainvilliers' town house, bravely risked her chastity by returning home.

Despite Jeanne's despondency about her prospects, the

Boulainvilliers had been pressing her cause. Bernard Chérin, the royal genealogist, known to be 'painstaking in his investigations and unbending in his judgements', confirmed that Jacques and Jeanne were descended from Henri II. In December 1775, Jacques, now twenty, was presented to Louis XVI by the chief minister, the comte de Maurepas. No monarch takes pleasure in being reminded of the existence of the tenacious offshoots of a previous dynasty, but the king granted Jacques and his sisters pensions of 800 livres a year. Jacques was commissioned as a lieutenant in the navy and departed for Brest in April 1776.

The pension meant Jeanne was no longer reliant on the beneficence of the Boulainvilliers. Not that she was grateful. She dismissed the amount as 'trifling' (in a way, it was – the king's brother the comte de Provence received 2.3 million livres from the crown each year, and in 1783 was given a separate grant of 7.65 million livres to pay off his gambling debts). The 800 livres would allow her to live modestly, but if she'd wanted to live modestly, she would have applied herself to needlework. The discontent at receiving such a derisory sum was sufficient to snap her brittle health: 'I was frequently attacked by convulsions, probably brought on by the concealment of what was passing in my breast.' Soon her new family would be in no position to help her any further.

In early December 1776, Jeanne, lying feverish in bed, was tormented by a sulphurous reek. She interrogated the servants about the smell – all of them replied evasively. But she was not the only person suffering; a crowd, beset by the stench and curious about its origin, had gathered outside the Boulainvilliers' house, where it was ineffectually marshalled by a small detachment of police. It was soon established that the marquis had been running an illegal distillery in his cellars, and there had been insufficient ventilation to disperse the fermented gases unobtrusively. Though a secretary had attempted to flood the cellar, enough evidence remained to prove that the marquis had been illicitly manufacturing alcohol. This was not the kind of hobby expected of Paris's chief legal officer. The Boulainvilliers retired to the country in disgrace, and Jeanne's hopes of establishing herself at Versailles and increasing her pension were punctured.

A little consolation arrived when the marquise engineered a

reunion between Jeanne and her sister Marianne, who had last seen each other fifteen years previously. The two girls moved briefly into a Benedictine convent before they were shuffled, in March 1778, to the Abbaye Royale at Longchamp, an entirely different sort of foundation. Longchamp served as an aristocratic finishing school. It had gained particular notoriety in the middle of the eighteenth century when the opera star Nicole Le Maure retired from the stage to become a novice there. Services were transformed into concerts as Le Maure sung with the backing of an orchestra. Thousands crammed in to hear her, and people began to note that the Mother Superior seemed to have recruited her choristers more for their coloratura than their religious calling.

By the time Jeanne arrived, Longchamp was no longer a permanent party and she bucked at its strictures. The abbey was not intended, she realised, to polish her up in preparation for breaching Court society with the Boulainvilliers at her back; it was, instead, the culmination of the marquise's generosity, a place where she would be genteelly preserved. But Jeanne had little appetite to spend her life among the dog-eared memories of spinsters past marriageable age. When the abbess began to pressure her into taking the veil, she and Marianne planned their escape.

In the autumn of 1779, Mademoiselle de Valois (Jeanne) and Mademoiselle de Saint-Rémy (Marianne), with twelve livres between them, checked into the Tête rouge in Bar-sur-Aube, 'the most miserable inn, in a town where there was not a decent one'. Bar-sur-Aube is one of the oldest settlements in Champagne, dating back to the Celts, if not further. The inhabitants were conscious of the place's antiquity: every New Year they greeted each other with sprigs of juniper, crying 'to the new wood' as, they believed, the druids had done. 'Its situation is pleasant; the air you breathe there is healthy; they live there for a long time', wrote a visitor in 1785.

Fontette lay just over ten miles to the south-west, and Jeanne had persuaded the marquise de Boulainvilliers that moving to Bar would allow her to pursue her claims on her father's property. The marquise consented to the sisters' departure and wrote to an acquaintance, Madame de Surmont, the wife of the town's provost, asking her to look after Jeanne and Marianne. The girls were convinced that, as the protégées of a great lady, they would be met with flutings of admiration, yet despite the marquise's endorsement, Madame de Surmont was wary of the new arrivals (perhaps because of their father's blasted reputation). She was reluctantly persuaded to call on them, and was surprised to find them demure and winsome. Jeanne made a striking impression on everyone she met, especially the men. Jacques Beugnot, a newly qualified lawyer, was one of those who mooned after her. Later, after being ennobled by Napoleon and serving in the government of Louis XVIII, he remembered her rough charm:

> [She] was not what one would call beautiful. She was of medium height, but svelte and compact. She had blue eyes full of expression, under high-arched black eyebrows, a slightly elongated face, a wide mouth but full of excellent teeth and, as is proper for someone like her, her smile was enchanting. She had beautiful hands and very small feet. Her complexion was remarkably white. By a curious circumstance, nature, in making her throat, had stopped halfway through the business, and the existing half made one long for the rest. She was lacking in any kind of education, but she had a great deal of wit, which was lively and astute. Struggling since her birth with the social order, she had defied the law and hardly respected morality much more. One saw her toying with both of these entirely instinctively, as if she didn't have a clue about their existence. All this created a frightening whole for the observer, which was seductive for the class of men who did not look too closely.

Marianne, in contrast, was blonde, chubby, placid and markedly stupid – and volubly insistent on being treated with deference. Initially Madame de Surmont was so taken with the pair that, over the objections of her – as it turned out, perceptive – husband, she invited them to stay for a week while they searched for lodgings. The girls all too easily made themselves at home: the day after their arrival, Madame de Surmont lent them a couple of dresses; the next morning she discovered that they had stayed up all night altering them. Jeanne and Marianne long overstayed their welcome – Madame de Surmont told Beugnot that 'the worst year of her life was the one she spent in the society of this demon [Jeanne]'. Beugnot, however, found himself utterly captivated: her 'brazen spirit . . .

contrasted particularly with the timid and strait-laced character of the women in the town'. But his father, though sympathetic towards the orphaned girls, was terrified of the social complications that might arise if his son, a mere bourgeois, should marry a Valois. He shooed Jacques off to Paris under the pretext of furthering his law studies.

Another suitor had more success. Nicolas de La Motte was Madame de Surmont's nephew. His father, an army quartermaster, had been killed in 1759 at the Battle of Minden during the Seven Years War, and his mother maintained herself on a small pension. At the age of fifteen, and despite standing at only four feet nine inches, Nicolas joined his father's regiment and was garrisoned at Lunéville in Lorraine. France was no longer at war, so Nicolas diligently applied himself to the peacetime occupations of idle military officers – duelling and gambling. At the age of twenty-seven he returned to Bar to live with his mother.

Short, stocky and dark-skinned, Nicolas was lively and good-humoured, if not endowed with the sharpest of minds. Even Beugnot, who thought Nicolas ugly, admitted that, 'despite [this] his face was friendly and sweet'. He met Jeanne when they performed together in an amateur production of Voltaire's *The Prodigal Son*. As so often in the theatre, onstage passions led to backstage entanglements. Jeanne discerned in the comparatively worldly Nicolas a more expansive way of living than the one on offer in Bar. He 'possessed', she wrote 'a sincerity of heart seldom found but in the country, blended with those polished manners which are not often excelled in the metropolis'. This probably means he was a flashy dresser with an arsenal of crude chat-up lines.

They carried on their affair in private but matters were complicated when Marianne, after falling out with the Surmonts, flounced off to live in a convent, enabling Madame de Surmont to train all her powers of surveillance on Jeanne. The couple, however, saw enough of each other for Jeanne to fall pregnant, and there was no option but to get married – though this solution had little appeal to the interested parties. Nicolas's mother had hoped that her son might snare a wealthy wife to pay off his debts; Jeanne must have realised that a good marriage offered one of her only chances of scaling the social ladder. Nicolas, penniless and thoroughly common, would not help her ascent at all. Nonetheless, Jeanne was not one to sacrifice immediate benefits to long-term considerations: the wedding would shield her from some of her neighbours' opprobrium, and offer an escape from the provincial pettiness that was beginning to grate. Nicolas, for his part, saw that the respectability of having a wife might win him a promotion.

Nicolas and Jeanne were married on 6 July 1780 at midnight, in accordance with local custom. Jeanne had mortgaged her royal pension for two years in order not to stint on the celebrations. After the ceremony, the couple, without any justification, minted themselves the comte and comtesse de La Motte (there were, in fact, noble La Mottes living in Bar who were unrelated to Nicolas). Such appropriation of titles was widespread; one jurisprudent griped that 'usurpers are operating without restraint . . . persons well known to be commoners are having themselves announced as marquesses, counts, barons, and viscounts'. In 1788 the royal genealogist Antoine Maugard estimated that, at most, a quarter of noble titles were genuine.

There was little point adopting a title if you couldn't support yourself in style – but the La Mottes had no source of income. Shortly after the wedding, Jeanne bore twins, baptised Jean-Baptiste and Nicolas-Marc, who died within a few days. Whatever grief she must have felt would have been tempered by relief at not having to feed two more mouths. It is possible, too, that the deaths caused her some resentment: she had been funnelled into marriage with Nicolas to legitimate her children; when they didn't survive, she may have regretted lashing herself to an oafish man who hampered her quest for acceptance. It's striking that Jeanne, despite her carefree and eclectic sex life, never conceived again, as though the double abandonment – by her parents and her children – left her wishing to be accountable to no one.

Nicolas was unable to justify his absence from his regiment any longer and in April 1781 returned to Lunéville. Jeanne billeted with the local Benedictines, though not through a sudden reflux of piety – it was an ineffective attempt by Nicolas to stop her flirting with his fellow officers. Even in the convent Jeanne 'delivered herself up to all pleasures', including those administered by the garrison commander, the marquis d'Autichamp. Humiliated and suffocated by debts which no amount of renegotiation would postpone, Nicolas left Lunéville for good, with his wife and without any idea what to do next.

Help arrived from the Beugnots. Jacques's father retained sentimental memories of Jeanne as a ragged child, and his concern was reignited now it was impossible for his son to marry her. He loaned the La Mottes 1,000 livres, which they decided to use to fund a campaign to reclaim the land that Jeanne's forebears had whittled away. Nicolas would head to Fontette to investigate first-hand; Jeanne went to Paris where she would 'put her husband's discoveries to good use'.

Jeanne took rooms at the Ville de Reims on the rue de la Verrerie, a busy thoroughfare on the edge of the Marais. It was the nearest inn to the coach stop at which travellers from Champagne alighted and its reputation glowed about as brightly as the Tête rouge's in Bar. Jacques Beugnot had agreed to provide any legal assistance Jeanne required. He drew up for Nicolas a list of archives near Fontette in need of examination, while he himself rummaged through the papers lodged at the *chambre des comptes* in Paris, the court that dealt with financial matters. Though the documentary record was scrappy, Beugnot established that most of the Saint-Rémy lands now belonged to the king. This offered a measure of hope: it was possible that Louis, who had already proved himself well disposed to the family, could be persuaded to return the property.

Nicolas, meanwhile, ignored Beugnot's instructions entirely. He was not the kind of man to spend days scouring deeds of conveyance in cobwebbed muniment rooms. Instead he spent all his money on 'a kind of triumphal entry into the places that had witnessed the extreme misery of his wife's first years', as if coins strewn like seed would somehow sprout of themselves into golden sheaves. On arrival in Fontette he ordered a *Te Deum* be sung in his honour, and left the church sprinkling money on the bemused but grateful villagers. He rapidly drank his way through the rest, then dashed off a letter to Paris, detailing the names of three or four lawyers Beugnot could write to if he wished, 'but with whom a man of his quality could not possibly enter business'. So concluded Nicolas's research trip.

Jeanne, too, soon ran out of money. She relied on Beugnot to buy her dinner a couple of times a week and lend cash to tide her over. She probably went without food for much of time: when Beugnot took her to a cafe, she would eat three dozen *madeleines* in a sitting. Jeanne became increasingly frustrated with what she saw as Beugnot's pettifogging adhesion to legal protocol. She saw things simply: the lands had belonged to her family; now they belonged to the king; surely the king would see the righteousness of her claim and return them to her gladly? Wouldn't he undoubtedly have done so already had he realised that he owned them? She would be doing Louis a favour by repossessing them herself. All that remained, then, was for Nicolas to stake their claim; and if Beugnot would not instruct him to do this, she certainly would (Beugnot later recalled 'trembling in fear, because I knew her capable of issuing these mad directives').

The lawyer managed to pacify Jeanne as he completed an accomplished petition, urging the Bourbons to discharge their 'natural debt' to their Valois predecessors. But he was dissuaded from having it printed and distributed – it was the norm for lawyers to appeal to the public – by more experienced heads who advised that any overt campaigning risked alienating the king. Jeanne remained optimistic that she would soon be the chatelaine of Fontette; but Beugnot knew that to succeed she would need 'credibility, powerful friends and money', none of which were in ready supply. By the end of the summer of 1781, the La Mottes were harried by their creditors and they turned to the one person who possessed the means and inclination to help them – the marquise de Boulainvilliers. They understood her to be in Strasbourg, but Nicolas and Jeanne learned on arrival that she was thirty miles away, staying at Saverne with the local bishop, Cardinal Louis Réné Edouard de Rohan.

2

The Man Who Never Grew Up

Fʀᴇɴᴄʜ ꜱᴏᴄɪᴇᴛʏ ᴅᴜʀɪɴɢ the Ancien Régime, according to its most acute observers, was drenched in a *cascade de mépris*, a cataract of disdain. Everyone was struggling to clamber up to a niche from where they could peer with satisfaction at those beneath them; those above struggled to fend off the inundation of scrabblers from below. Wealthy bourgeois could purchase ennobling offices in the judicial system or as king's secretaries (who numbered in the thousands), which scrubbed them clean of the grime of commonness, as well as offering enormous exemptions from tax. In the army, in the Church and at Court, many of the most senior roles were reserved for the most ancient clans (though the government itself was comparatively meritocratic). At the pinnacle, surveying all the arduous mountaineering further down the slopes, perched the Rohan.

They were an old Breton family, though their superiority was disputed. Saint-Simon, that policeman of precedence and chronicler of life at Louis XIV's Court, thought that 'without having origins that were any different to the rest of the nobility, nor without having ever been particularly distinguished within it, they held themselves, however, far above the ordinary nobility and were able to speak of their most elevated rank'. The Rohan themselves traced their lineage back through the ancient kings of Brittany to the mythical founder of the kingdom, Conan Meriadoc. Their motto, 'Roi ne puis, prince ne daigne, Rohan suis' – 'I cannot be a king, I won't deign to be a prince, I am a Rohan' – defiantly proclaimed their Celtic independence. Membership of the family granted a unique distinction that no conventional hierarchy of dukes and princes and kings could accommodate.

Alongside a few select Houses, the Rohan were treated in France as *princes étrangers*, inferior only to the royal family and the princes of the blood (though both the Valois and Bourbon dynasties had Rohan nesting on branches of their family trees). Unlike other foreign princes who did not stand upon ceremony, the Rohan flaunted the privileges of their caste as a matter of principle. They guarded them more carefully than their own limbs – maintaining a spartan room at Versailles; sitting on a wobbly stool in the presence of the queen. When, in the 1760s, ministers plotted to reduce their status, the Rohan fought back furiously and successfully. The 'courtesy of the Rohan' was renowned, primarily as a means of softly strong-arming allies and waverers in the little treacheries of court life, but also to hold at a distance those who had become overfamiliar.

In the middle of the eighteenth century, the Rohan were coiled round the heart of the Court. Charles de Rohan, prince de Soubise was a favourite of Louis XV and his *maîtresse en titre*, Madame de Pompadour. Soubise was not popular – Voltaire called him 'a snivelling little brat in red heels' – nor was he particularly accomplished: after the disastrous Battle of Rossbach during the Seven Years War, he supposedly wandered the battlefield with a lantern searching for the remnants of his army. But he shared with the king a profound concern for the mattress education of teenage opera singers and, despite his military embarrassments, was granted the title of marshal of France and elevated to the king's council. Soubise's religiose sister, the comtesse de Marsan, had been appointed governess of the children of France, in charge of the education of Louis XV's grandchildren (the future Louis XVI, Louis XVIII and Charles X). When the Dauphin – the children's father – died of consumption at the age of thirty-six in 1765, Marsan became responsible for moulding the character of the country's next king.

Prince Louis de Rohan was born on 25 September 1734, the sixth child of the intermarriage of two branches of the Rohan family, the Guéméné and the Soubise. His father, Hercule Mériadec, prince de Guéméné, was described as 'the darkest and most brutal animal that one might encounter', and had unwound into insanity by the time Louis emerged. The young prince was destined for a career in the Church: at the precocious age of nineteen, he was created a canon in the cathedral chapter of Strasbourg, thanks to the patronage of his great-uncle, the bishop. One fellow pupil at his Parisian seminary, the *philosophe* Abbé Morellet, remembered him as 'haughty, inconsiderate, unreasonable, spendthrift, not very sharp, fickle in his tastes and his friendships'. Morellet was prone to exaggeration – Voltaire nicknamed him Abbé Mords-les (Abbé Bite'em) because he was so relentlessly caustic – and Louis was considerably more intelligent than his critic gave him credit for. But neither at the Oratorian seminary of Saint-Magloire nor later at the Sorbonne were piety or chastity cultivated. When Louis's uncle, Louis Constantin de Rohan, was anointed bishop of Strasbourg in 1756 he immediately requested that Louis be appointed coadjutor, a kind of ecclesiastical crown-prince whose succession to the see was guaranteed. Louis stood to be the fourth successive Rohan to wear the mitre in Alsace.

Impeccably polite, still slim, with carefully coiffed blond hair and full, dark eyes that shone under gently drooping eyelids, Louis glided through Parisian society. Even when his hair grew whiter and his forehead rose higher and gleamed like a billiard ball, his face never lost its ruddy, plump, boyish openness. He charmed everyone he met, and accumulated a pantheon of lovers, including his own cousin. Madame de Genlis, mistress of the future duc d'Orléans, thought that 'he was about as personable as it's possible to be'. The post-revolutionary memoirists, for whom Louis was always a fool, retrospectively diffracted his character through the incident that sealed his notoriety. Throughout most of his life, however, Louis was regarded as intelligent if superficial and unwilling to apply himself seriously – clever enough to grasp immediately the nub of a matter and therefore bored with pursuing it any further. It is understandable how an ambitious man who occupied no position of responsibility until middle age might harden into flippancy in order to reconcile himself to his lack of advancement; how frustrated ambition might lead him to snap at an opportunity, outlandish though it may seem, hanging low before him.

At Madame Geoffrin's salon, one of the most glittering in Paris, Louis mingled with writers, philosophers and politicians in ascendancy. He was not cowed by the flashing minds around him, even if he showed no particular brilliance of his own. The *encyclopédiste* and historiographer of France Abbé Marmontel remembered him as 'risqué, absent-minded, good-natured, quick-witted in competition with those of a station comparable to his'. In these circles he discovered the materialism of Diderot and Helvétius, though later allegations that he was an atheist were misguided: Louis was fascinated by scientific experiment and became the patron of Masonic theists, but he equally felt the tug of his family's tradition as defenders of the One True Church, and objected to the publication of Voltaire's complete works as a 'forge of impiety in which one might weld new arms against religion'.

Louis also acquired a more democratic interest in men and women of wit, irrespective of their birth. The salons nourished an atmosphere of convivial sociability among the *honnêtes hommes* gathered there. 'My warmth was only for my opinion, and never against my adversary,' wrote Morellet in his *Mémoires*. But affability carried dangers – it might be feigned to exploit another's trust. Louis's weakness for diverting company would lead him, disastrously, to equate spark with honesty.

During the 1760s the Rohan formed part of the *dévot* party – the Devouts – that coalesced around the Dauphin and sought to undermine Louis XV's chief minister, the duc de Choiseul. The faction had existed, in various guises, since the seventeenth century, when they pressed for a government directed by religious principles (France was the pre-eminent Catholic power in Europe). They were motivated, in part, by a puritanical distaste for Choiseul, who was as debauched as Louis XV, and the struggle against the dissolution of the Jesuits in France (which ultimately occurred in 1764), an episode in the contest for supremacy between the French Church and the Vatican, which had run for much of the century. Like all opposition groups, godly or otherwise, they were primarily discontented with not being in power. The alliance brokered by Choiseul in 1756 with Habsburg Austria, France's historic enemy, ought to have been a cause for rejoicing, as Europe's two great Catholic powers were now conjoined, but the *dévots* could not wholeheartedly endorse it, since it had been accomplished by their political enemies.

It is unlikely that Louis himself felt strongly about these developments. His own morals were more akin to Choiseul's than the dauphin's; and he did little more to help local Jesuits than occasionally send them some hares he had caught (he also appointed to his staff a defrocked Jesuit, Abbé Georgel, whose memoirs provide one of the most detailed accounts of the Diamond Necklace Affair). But following the family whip was the duty of the Rohan, and Louis helped cultivate the king's new mistress, Madame du Barry, as a possible ally. And, despite their differences, Louis and the Dauphin enjoyed each other's company. 'An amicable prince, an agreeable prelate and a dashing rogue,' was the latter's generous assessment.

On 7 May 1770, the fifteen-year-old Marie Antoinette entered France for the first time. Her marriage to the heir to the French throne – the now-dead Dauphin's son also, confusingly, called Louis – was the capstone of Choiseul's foreign policy, the clasp which would hold French and Austrian interests in alignment. She had been stripped down to her shift on an island in the Rhine, in symbolic repudiation of her motherland as she prepared to meet her husband-to-be.

Three companies of teenagers dressed as Swiss Guards lined her route into Strasbourg; juvenile shepherdesses garlanded her with flowers; the daughters of the town's leading burghers sprinkled petals before her. The whole city gorged itself in celebration. Oxen were roasted; fountains spumed with wine; loaves of bread were heedlessly kneaded into the cobblestones by the feet of the surging crowd. The houses on one side of the river were transformed to look like the Habsburg palace at Schönbrunn. The day after the festivities, Louis de Rohan addressed Marie Antoinette in Strasbourg Cathedral. His speech was unmemorable diplomatese about a new golden age and flourishing peace (the future queen welled up during it, though homesickness or the sting of a passing bank of incense may have been the cause). There was consternation when Marie Antoinette left the church the moment Louis finished, leaving no opportunity for him and the other canons to accompany her. It was unclear what lay behind the hurried exit: innocent confusion, a deliberate snub to the insincerity of an anti-Choiseulist, or the first instance of Marie Antoinette's bridling at protocol? For the rest of the visit, the dauphine found Louis's attempts at ingratiation too cloying. She later wrote to her mother that Rohan's way of living 'more resembled that of a soldier than a coadjutor'.

Choiseul did not see out the year by the king's side. He was dismissed on Christmas Eve when Louis XV refused to support him in declaring war with Britain over the Falklands. The new foreign minister, the duc d'Aiguillon, appointed Louis de Rohan as ambassador to Vienna. This was the most prestigious ambassadorial appointment, with the onerous responsibility of maintaining good relations with France's chief ally. Louis had no diplomatic experience, was a noted anglophile and belonged to a family that had intrigued against Austrian interests for the last fifteen years. The comte de Mercy-Argenteau, the Austrian ambassador to Versailles, called the appointment 'as odd as it is improper'. But d'Aiguillon selected Louis precisely because he was so inappropriate: the foreign minister, more devoted to advancing his own cause than his country's, wished to loosen his dependency on the Rohan, who had helped him to power. How better than by priming one of their sprigs – who was being groomed by his family for high office – to fail?

Louis himself expressed no enthusiasm for the position. Vienna was a shabby replacement for Paris; and he regarded a mere ambassadorship as demeaning. Eventually, he was reconciled to the job by an ample allowance and a promise to pay off his debts. It was agreed, too, that he would succeed the decrepit cardinal de La Roche-Aymon as grand almoner (the head of the French Church and the Chapel Royal – one of the great offices of state).

Anyone looking on as Rohan entered Vienna on 10 January 1772 might have wondered what business the Queen of Sheba had in town. Rohan had brought with him two state coaches and fifty horses, marshalled by a chief equerry, a sub-equerry and two grooms. Seven pages, drawn from the Breton and Alsatian nobility, followed with their tutors. There were two gentlemen of the bedchamber, a major-domo, a steward, a bursar and a chamberlain in scarlet uniforms squirted with gold braid; two postilions rode on his coach, four heralds in liveries embroidered with gold and sequinned with silver trumpeted his arrival, six *valets de chambre* and twelve footmen waited upon him, two Switzers – who stood like heavily armed tropical fish in their particoloured uniforms – guarded him, and a ten-piece orchestra was on permanent stand-by for emergency musical entertainment. Though the embassy in Vienna was fully staffed, Rohan was accompanied by four further ambassadorial assistants, who would also be credentialled at Court, as well as his secretary Georgel and four undersecretaries.

Vienna was a tangled city seeped of colour – tall, white-stuccoed buildings cast their shadows across the narrow streets. Because of the paucity of space – on average eighty people lived in each house – the wealthy compensated for what they lacked in frontage with their interiors. 'Nothing can be more surprising', wrote Lady Mary Wortley Montagu, 'than the apartments. They are commonly a *suite* of eight or ten large rooms, all inlaid, the doors and windows richly carved and gilt, and the furniture such as is seldom seen in the palaces of sovereign princes of other countries'. The city had neither the intellectual vitality nor commercial bustle of Paris, but was sustained by the expanding bureaucracy of the Habsburg monarchy. Its stifling atmosphere was heightened by the intrigues of its citizens to acquire and retain state office.

Rohan immediately presented himself to Prince Kaunitz, the Austrian Chancellor, and Joseph II, the Holy Roman Emperor and Maria Theresa's son and co-regent. The empress herself kept Rohan waiting ten days for an audience. She was, she claimed, indisposed with a cold, though everyone recognised the delay signalled her disapproval at Rohan's appointment. She had written to Mercy-Argenteau six months previously to express her 'displeasure at the choice that France has made of such a wicked subject as the coadjutor of Strasbourg . . . I would have refused if I had not been held back by consideration of the unpleasantness that could have rebounded onto my daughter'.

Maria Theresa had ruled the Habsburg Empire since 1740, having acceded to the throne at the age of only twenty-three. The unseasoned queen was fettered by shiftless advisors, and the European powers slavered in anticipation of dividing up her lands. But she had mastered statecraft through sheer force of will, replenishing her treasury, establishing a standing army and holding together her centrifugal territories. A reformer but no radical, she stalwartly, sometimes hysterically, defended religious and social proprieties.

By the time that Rohan arrived in Vienna, Maria Theresa was a tetchy, stout, ageing woman with the stouter opinions of an autodidact. Encased in a bombazine sarcophagus (she had lived in permanent mourning since her husband's death in 1765), she could be obtuse, bloody-minded and imperious towards her children and courtiers. She was prone to tantrums and, on occasion, threatened to abdicate and wall herself up in a convent. And she nursed decidedly firm views about moral behaviour, especially that of clergymen (in 1747 she had, briefly, established a Chastity Commission empowered to enter people's houses and arrest anyone suspected of being an opera singer). A combination of flattery and deference would be required for Louis to win her over.

Maria Theresa spent their first meeting trying to needle him. She listed those predecessors she had known and, coming to Choiseul – to whose dismissal Louis owed his job – she wistfully remarked, 'whom I will never forget'. The French ambassador smiled silently and remained complaisant. 'He had . . . an air of composure,' Maria Theresa reported to Mercy-Argenteau, 'his manners are utterly smooth and his appearance is extremely plain . . . he is very polite towards everyone'. Though, she added distrustfully, 'perhaps this is only in order to require a complete reciprocation of attentiveness and respect'. The initial cordiality soon drained away. A little more than a month after his arrival, the empress was writing to Mercy-Argenteau that Louis 'was a great tome stuffed full with wicked words, that are little in keeping with his position as a cleric and as a minister. He talks carelessly in all sorts of company . . . always in a tone of superficiality, presumption and flippancy.' Louis was 'a very wicked subject: without talent, without discretion, without morals'.

Rohan refused to behave like a pious churchman. He hunted constantly and flirted outrageously: 'nearly all of our ladies, young and old, beautiful and ugly are still enchanted by this wicked genius,' despaired Maria Theresa. His men smuggled contraband in diplomatic bags and, on one occasion, cudgelled the empress's servants. Louis also hosted extravagant dinner parties that flouted protocol by sitting guests at small, round tables rather than the long tables normally employed for official dinners, where placement was dictated by minute discriminations of rank. Maria Theresa divined in this a plot to deflower the ingenuous virgins of Vienna. When she asked Louis to desist, he replied that he 'did not depart from the rules of the most scrupulous decency'; indeed, unwarranted suspicion would be cast upon his guests were he to suspend his suppers.

But Louis's transgressions went beyond a cavalier disregard for punctilio. Like all good diplomats he had a taste for gossip; like bad ones he had penchant for gossiping. He had mocked Maria Theresa's fond memories of Choiseul to his aunt, the comtesse de Marsan, who had then disparaged the empress at Versailles. It did not take long for one of Rohan's enemies to brief Mercy-Argenteau. To Maria Theresa, Rohan did not simply appear as a braggart: he was the ambassador of a faction conniving against her daughter. She began to pray for the bishop of Strasbourg's death to hasten Louis's recall.

Chancellor Kaunitz and Joseph II found Louis more congenial. The two Austrians could be companionable but they were keenly conscious of their own superiority – in Kaunitz's case intellectual, in Joseph's social – and frequently disdained members of their own class (Joseph remarked that 'if I conversed only with my equals, I should have to spend my days in the imperial vault'). Louis's chumminess, which so affronted Maria Theresa, was welcomed by her son. The coadjutor and the emperor shared a sense of frustration: both were middle-aged men who had been waiting too long for the death of an elderly, bed-blocking relative.

Though Louis's lack of self-effacement undoubtedly stymied his embassy, he was, when he concentrated on business, far more prescient on the most important diplomatic issue of the day than his more experienced colleagues. Austria was looking fearfully to the east. In 1764, the Russian empress, Catherine the Great, had imposed a discarded lover, Stanislaw Poniatowski, on the Poles as king. This had provoked a rebellion by the Polish nobility, which was tacitly supported by the French, who sent hundreds of military advisors (France had a longstanding involvement in Polish affairs and Louis XV's queen, Marie Leszczyńska, was a Pole). Russian victories over the Ottoman Empire threatened to molest Austrian lands in south-eastern Europe and Austria pondered war to deter Russia's destabilising advances. But Russia's ally Prussia, still recuperating from the battering it received in the Seven Years War, had no desire to be dragged into a conflict over a patch of Europe of little concern to her. The Prussian king,

Frederick the Great, devised a plan to maintain the equilibrium in Europe – the tripartite division of Poland. Negotiations were conducted through the winter of 1771 and, a month after Louis took up his post, Austria, Prussia and Russia concluded a secret compact.

Louis knew nothing of the bargain, but his first dispatch to the foreign minister d'Aiguillon contained a lengthy and passionate case for limiting the alliance with Austria and expressed unease at Kaunitz's evasive blandishments. D'Aiguillon's reply was slicked with contempt: 'We strongly feel that your arrival in Austria is too recent for you to have anything to add to the reports of Monsieur Durand [the Minister Plenipotentiary].' The foreign minister refused to divulge Louis XV's own views on policy and even forbade Louis from probing Kaunitz's intentions. D'Aiguillon – who had 'neither strategy, steadfastness or money', as the Prussian king brutally remarked – simply believed that 'bit by bit they [the Austrians] will warm towards the Poles'. The minister regarded Louis's repeated warnings about partition in the spring of 1772 more as a nuisance than a source of intelligence: 'We cannot claim to believe any rumour that spreads,' d'Aiguillon responded. In August 1772 the agreement was officially declared. 'The king can only wail at the fate of Poland,' was Versailles' fatalistic response.

Whether d'Aiguillon had genuinely failed to grasp the severity of the situation, or simply lacked the nous to defuse it, he refused to take responsibility. Most of his constipated intelligence was devoted to deflecting the blame for his failures onto others. 'Your previous reports . . . had not prepared us for such a sudden turn of events', he told Louis, as though his ambassador had been expressing himself for the past six months in subjunctive equivocations. The pair's professional relationship was sundered by mutual recriminations and undermining (d'Aiguillon had already angered Louis by welching on his agreement to pay his expenses).

The spat with d'Aiguillon curdled Louis's enjoyment of Viennese hospitality; but the leak of a dispatch which ridiculed the empress was far more prejudicial to the coadjutor's aspirations. In a letter to the foreign minister about the Polish crisis, Louis wrote, 'I have indeed seen Maria Theresa cry over the misfortunes of the oppressed; but this princess, experienced in the art of revealing nothing, appeared to me to have tears at her command. In one hand she held a handkerchief to dry her eyes, in the other she seized the sword of negotiation in order to be the third partitioning power.'* (Louis's characterisation is not entirely fair. Maria Theresa had tenaciously opposed Kaunitz and Joseph over the abrogation of Polish independence until it became clear that the only alternative would be war with Russia.) The letter, intended only for d'Aiguillon, was read out at one of Madame du Barry's dinners, where the company chortled at the empress's sanctimonious hypocrisy. Word of the mockery soon reached Marie Antoinette and she never forgave the slight to her mother. The offence taken would have perilous consequences for Louis and the future queen.

The days of Louis's ambassadorship were numbered, even though it gasped on for nearly two more years. The Austrian ambassador Mercy-Argenteau had extracted assurances from du Barry, who held immense sway over the king, that Louis would be replaced. Louis's poor health – he may have suffered from venereal disease – and his commitment to work rapidly sapped his energies. What strength remained was devoted to hunting: when Louis stayed with the prince of Auersperg, his party bagged over 2,000 partridges and hares in forty-eight hours.

Because of the standing of the Rohan, appearances needed to be saved. Towards the end of March 1774 Louis was granted permission to leave Vienna. Joseph II was due to travel to France at Easter – if Louis went with him, everyone would assume he was required to coordinate the visit. But Louis was paranoid about machinations against him in Versailles. 'I will strap on my shield against them,' he wrote to a friend. 'Oh villains! How I despise them! How they have acted wickedly to persecute me!' He was still in situ at the end of May when news arrived of the death of Louis XV. The king's smallpox-scuttled body had, over the course of a fortnight, rotted

---

* Louis Hastier, author of *The Truth about the Affair of the Necklace*, has argued that this letter was apocryphal. But Georgel and Madame Campan – whose accounts of other parts of the story diverge dramatically – are in agreement on this point and clearly received their information from independent sources (Rohan and Marie Antoinette respectively).

itself to expiration; the burnt-copper scabs on the suppurating pustules which armoured his skin made him appear 'like . . . a moor, like a negro, swarthy and swollen'. The funeral was hurried and without pomp, the Court having fled Versailles to escape the contagion.

In mid-June Louis finally wrote to d'Aiguillon's replacement, the comte de Vergennes, taking up his predecessor's offer of leave. The precise reason for his change of heart is uncertain. Given the labile political situation in France, he may have felt that his presence at Versailles was needed to cement his position. Maria Theresa, though elated by his departure, had grown a little fonder of Louis in recent weeks. 'I wish that the king would grant him some sign of favour,' she wrote to Mercy-Argenteau, 'since he has a good heart and his behaviour has improved for some time now.' She also asked her daughter to grant Louis an audience on his return.

The Rohan welcomed the appointment of the *dévot* Vergennes, who was personally indebted to them. The new king, Louis XVI, moved quickly, however, to establish his independence. He particularly wished to escape the asphyxiating sense of obligation that Marsan – the governess he used to address as 'my dear mama' – attempted to stoke. His public frostiness towards her became the chatter of the Court. Louis was noisily eager to resume his duties, but his re-immersion in the Parisian beau monde had dimmed his enthusiasm for diplomacy. 'In actual fact,' Mercy-Argenteau wrote to Maria Theresa, 'the prince de Rohan does not wish to return to Vienna, but he asks to in the hope that he will receive some wealthy abbey in compensation.' In August that year, Louis XVI named a replacement.

Marie Antoinette received Louis, as instructed by Maria Theresa, though solely, it seems, out of filial deference. Within a few days Mercy-Argenteau reported that 'she treats him very coolly and no longer speaks to him'. Was the new queen simply less magnanimous than her mother? Or had Louis yet again preferred raillery to discretion?* The baron de Besenval writes in his memoirs that Louis

---

* Louis was unable to stifle his compulsion for gossip, however stale, even in tranquil recollection at the writing desk. On one occasion he wrote to Marie Antoinette of his sincere belief in the discredited rumour that Choiseul had poisoned the old Dauphin.

had vulturously remarked of the queen that she displayed 'a coquet-
tishness that prepared the way for an accomplished lover to succeed
with her' and later gabbed about Marie Antoinette conducting an
affair with her brother-in-law, the comte d'Artois. The queen, when
she heard he had maligned her, refused to exchange another word
with him. It is difficult to comprehend why Louis would take such
risks – if he did indeed make such statements – since he was desperate
to ingratiate himself with Marie Antoinette. He may have viewed
infidelity as a staple of life at Versailles, a sign, in fact, that the queen
had been comfortably absorbed into the French Establishment. In
tightly circumscribed environments such as the Court, rumour-
mongering was a token of power – a flash of one's membership of
exclusive networks of information. Someone as conscious of status
as Louis might have felt the impulse to gossip in order to assert his
importance, especially during the unresolved flux after the death of
Louis XV, when it was unclear which faction would triumph.

Whatever the reason for his disgrace, Louis found the finality of
Marie Antoinette's rejection impossible to sublimate. He had thought
no woman impervious to his allure. The queen's refusal even to
acknowledge him was a bruise to his self-worth – and it also corked
his ministerial ambitions. While in Vienna Louis had boasted that
he would replace d'Aiguillon. His tactlessness, sloth and inexperience
made him wholly unsuitable for the highest offices, but he believed
that, as the standard bearer for his generation of Rohan, he would
inevitably be summoned. Now his only occupation was to wait for
his uncle's death. His creditors pestered him; his fellow clergymen
despised him for his rapacious acquisition of lucrative benefices; and
the queen's hatred presented a steepling bulwark against his dreams.

Louis's redundancy and lack of influence became increasingly
apparent. The princesse de Guéméné, the new Rohan incumbent
as governess of the children of France and a favourite of Marie
Antoinette, tried to broker a reconciliation with the queen, but was
easily parried by Mercy-Argenteau. There was even a tussle over
Louis's appointment as grand almoner of France, which had been
promised to him by both Louis XV and Louis XVI. Despite these
guarantees, Marie Antoinette advocated an alternative candidate, and
attempted to foil Louis and placate the Rohan by nominating Louis's

brother Ferdinand, archbishop of Bordeaux, instead. It required a dawn ambush of the king by the comtesse de Marsan to wring out an assurance of Louis's succession. Louis XVI relented 'with regret' but refused to nominate him to the ex-officio cardinalate, which was normally bundled in with the position. Not that Louis minded – the king of Poland proposed him instead.

On 11 March 1779, the near-blind, gout-rouged, dropsy-bloated Louis Constantin died, and Louis, after twenty-three years of expectation, was finally elevated to Principality-Bishopric of Strasbourg and became known as cardinal de Rohan. The diocese straddled the Rhine and so was under the suzerainty of both France and the Holy Roman Empire, though it maintained a degree of fiscal and judicial independence which Rohan strove to preserve against the centralising aspirations of successive French finance ministers.

Rohan desperately needed the one million livres of income the province provided each year – he had debts dating back to his embassy in Vienna and no intention of trimming his expenditure. The early years of his rule show Rohan at his most trivial and self-interested: designing new uniforms for his counsellors; ineptly meddling in church politics; and, though a seasoned spendthrift himself, vigorously and publicly pursuing those who owed him money. Petty despotism came naturally.

The bishop's seat at Saverne was a doll's-house royal court, with its own chamberlains and equerries and Grand Huntsman. The chateau itself, built by the first cardinal de Rohan between 1712 and 1728, was admired as the Versailles of Alsace. For weeks after Rohan's installation, dinners were thrown each night for dozens of guests. The new bishop did not enjoy the palace for long: six months after his election a fire broke out under the mansard roof, when an abandoned candle ignited drying linen. He was woken only when his smoke-maddened dog tried to throttle his valet. Rohan escaped in his nightshirt but the chateau was consumed in the conflagration; all that was left was a crusty wing at the back. Rohan's response to the destruction of his home was phlegmatic – 'Yesterday, I had a chateau; I was deprived of it today. I offer it as a sacrifice to the Lord' – perhaps because he viewed the destruction more as an opportunity than a loss.

Though Rohan had two other palaces in the province – the similarly proportioned Palais Rohan in Strasbourg, and a dinkier one in Mutzig – he was intent on rebuilding an even more imposing edifice at Saverne, to the horror of his bookkeepers. The acquisition by the cardinal of the wealthy Abbey of Saint Vaast merely replaced two-thirds of his diplomatic pension of 157,000 livres, which was to be terminated in 1780. So furniture in other residences was auctioned off; a tax rise of 15 per cent and a substantial contribution by the clergy were announced; the Jews were squeezed; and large tracts of Alsatian forest were hewn for scaffolding and joists. Rohan was determined that the palace should be furnished sumptuously: he gathered a magnificent collection of Chinese porcelain – urns camouflaged with cobalt foliage; a pair of prancing, grimacing terracotta lions; a foot-wide basin glazed with stag-antlered, ox-eared, camel-headed, vulture-taloned dragons; and a pair of miniature pagodas whose awnings furled upwards like riffled newspaper. The chateau's architect, Nicolas Salins de Montfort, also designed a t'ing in the gardens that combined neoclassical colonnades, a pair of squatting buddhas and a belvedere surmounted by a rhubarb-and-custard parasol.

It took eleven years to complete the new palace, and there was widespread resentment at the burden the population shouldered to underwrite Rohan's titanic architectural fantasies (the finished building's muddy red facade is so monotonously extended that it looks as though the builders began unfolding it from the middle and forgot to stop). When Rohan's reputation was perilously poised later on, he received no support from his cathedral chapter or local politicians. But it was at an optimistic, purposeful building site that Jeanne and Nicolas de La Motte arrived one September day in 1781.

3

Faith, Hope and Charity

SOMEONE IN NEED of succour could not hope to meet a more suitable person than Rohan. Not only was he personally generous – indeed, he was pathologically incapable of thrift – but, as grand almoner, he had been charged with disbursing alms on behalf of the crown. At Jeanne's interview, however, the cardinal was not in a giving mood. He responded to her tale with shopworn sympathy and buttery promises of assistance when he was next in Paris. Immediate respite came from the well-thumbed generosity of Madame de Boulainvilliers. This allowed the couple to return to Lunéville, where Nicolas paid off his debts and obtained a *certificat de service*, discharging him honourably and terminally from the Gendarmerie.

By the time the La Mottes returned to Paris, they found Madame de Boulainvilliers parlously ill with smallpox (one of Jeanne's less charitable early biographers suggested that she rushed back in order to snatch as much of the Boulainvilliers' bounty as she could). In her autobiography, Jeanne depicts herself as a medical and moral heroine: nursing the marquise herself, soothing and poulticing at risk to her own health, while fighting off the marquis who, though his wife lay blotchy and shivering, was shameless enough to persist with his overtures. Jeanne's ministrations were initially successful: the marquise recovered sufficiently to ask her son-in-law, the baron de Crussol, captain of the *garde du corps* of the comte d'Artois, to obtain a commission for Nicolas in the regiment.

Whether the strength of the disease grew irresistible or Jeanne's attentiveness wandered once Nicolas had been gratified will never be known, but the marquise soon relapsed. She died, according to Jeanne's self-dramatising memoirs, in the embrace of her adopted daughter, rather than her natural ones. 'Live, live, my dear mother, or I am ruined for ever! You are my soul, my support, my life,' pleaded Jeanne as she was dragged away delirious from the dying woman's bedside. It is noticeable that, while wishing to portray herself as selfless, Jeanne's worry over her own future muscles out any pity for her stepmother. This concern was well grounded – the spurned marquis was unlikely to prove as benevolent. It is also hard to believe that the loss of a maternal figure was devoid of emotional repercussions. Jeanne writes about the marquise with a tenderness that she rarely extends to the rest of her acquaintances. It would have taken little effort to vilify someone who, by Jeanne's own account, had established her adopted daughter in the kind of menial life she abhorred, as another of those who frustrated Jeanne's justifiable ambitions. Instead, Jeanne refused to blame her, even though they disagreed.

Grief and the hours of watching sapped Jeanne to exhaustion. She raved feverishly for four days, then fell into convulsions at every stabbing memory. Her adopted sisters, who had digested their mother's death less intemperately, tried to console Jeanne. But neither they nor the marquise's doctor could 'raze the written troubles in her brain'. The most effective medicine, it transpired, was the carriage put at her exclusive disposal by the baron de Crussol, at which point Jeanne rapidly reacquired the strength to venture abroad.

Sympathy and carriages were provided for a limited period only, and Jeanne was forced to flee the unshackled marquis and the trivial revenges he exacted for refusing his bed (intercepting her letters, substituting tallow candles for wax ones). There may have been, in actuality, a less Gothic sequence of events: Jeanne may have taken revenge in her autobiography for the marquis's less lucrative concern by portraying him as a figure of unquenchable lechery. In Jeanne's account of the first meeting on the road to Passy, there is a marked attempt to contrast the two Boulainvilliers: the marquis responds incredulously to her family history while the marquise is enthused by it. Perhaps, as Jeanne grew older, the marquis baulked at her demands to be treated as a princess and resented the way she grafted herself onto his wife's affections. After the marquise's death he may simply have dismissed her.

In early spring 1782 the La Mottes moved to Versailles so that Nicolas could join his regiment. They took a *chambre garnie* in what is now the Place Hoche, seconds away from the front of the chateau. *Chambres garnies* tended to be grimy and draughty, the dry-rotted attics of wigmakers and wine-sellers wanting to make a bit up above. They were favoured by footpads, prostitutes, debtors lying low, and unwitting foreigners who thought that a 'furnished room' sounded comfortable.

A hundred thousand people lived in Versailles, a thrumming colony of worker bees that supplied and serviced those hived off in the chateau. There were more than two hundred innkeepers who housed the servants of courtiers; running repairs to liveries and the continual demand for new outfits – Marie Antoinette led a permanent revolution in fashion – inflated the numbers of mercers and haberdashers, dressmakers and tailors; weather-stiffened soldiers grumbled about their emaciated pensions and the pusillanimity of the country's foreign policy. At the town's western edge stood the palace – the original, modest stone and faux-brick building enveloped on three sides by vast marble wings the colour of a smoker's teeth – which was approached through the yawning maw of the Place d'Armes. Jean-Baptiste Colbert, Louis XIV's minister who reluctantly supervised his master's grandiose designs, thought the building 'an architectural monster' – 'a little man with big arms and a large head'. At the rear, the groomed gardens sloped in a series of groves down to the cruciform canal; bronze and marble figures from classical mythology disported themselves within them. Louis XIV had devoted over forty years to transforming his father's hunting lodge into a magnificent, domineering, hideous residence, the architectural condensation of absolutist principles of kingship into stone and silver and gilt. The Court swelled at its apogee at the turn of the eighteenth century to 20,000. The stables could house 12,000 horses and the palace was stuffed with thousands of servants. There was a horologist whose sole duty was to wind the king's watch each day and a man whose job was to deliver a copy of the newspaper to each member of the royal family.

The lustre of the Court dulled through the eighteenth century. During the regency of Louis XV, Versailles had been abandoned, and even though the new king returned in 1722, the palace never gleamed as it had under the Sun King. Both Louis XV and Louis XVI were socially awkward and tongue-tied; neither had the personality nor the bearing to sustain a perpetual display of regal glory. The culture instituted by Louis XIV demanded that the king sacrifice his private life to live publicly as an incarnation of royalty. But Louis XV preferred to spend time with a handful of cronies or in the embraces of a low-bred mistress or procured dancing-girl; and Louis XVI was too slovenly to master the ceremonials. At his *coucher* – the ceremonial retiring to bed – he would grin like a gargoyle as he tried joshingly to avoid being divested of his shirt. Louis XIV's successors renovated the *petits appartements* and *petits cabinets* to which they increasingly escaped from the dumbshow of court ritual; these were painted in pastels in contrast to the blare of gold and mirrors in the staterooms. To conservative courtiers, the tendency of the royal family to cultivate their privacy threatened the integrity of the absolutist state. 'This inner disorganization of the Court', wrote the Prince de Montbarey, 'created an easiness in relations that soon led to familiarity and, confusing everything, destroyed the respect and veneration which Louis XIV . . . thought necessary to his own person.'

As monarchical belief in the formalities weakened, the national importance of Versailles dwindled. It 'had become', said the duc de Lévis, 'nothing more than a little provincial town, to which one only went with reluctance and from which one fled as soon as possible'. The road to Paris grew clotted with courtiers trundling to perform their duties at the palace before escaping home. One could be a 'man of the Court' – living in town, nipping down to Versailles to hunt with the king or dine with the queen – without being a courtier.

Versailles was in a constant state of excitement yet fundamentally static, like a weathervane on a squally day. The business of government was transacted; ambassadors came to negotiate treaties; everyone exhaled rumours as they breathed. Yet the symptoms of boredom could be identified everywhere – the days spent hunting; the fortunes lost in hand upon hand of lansquenet; the listless, exiguous balls. Many campaigned for entry into exclusive coteries, such as that of Marie Antoinette's favourite, Madame de Polignac, only to find the conversation bland and lukewarm. The baronne d'Oberkirch remarked that these gatherings were 'actually like a mousse that vanishes and leaves nothing after, but the taste of which is very pleasant. Having tasted it once, the rest appears to fade and is tasteless.'

Nonetheless, Versailles remained the most lucrative spigot of patronage in the country. The palace itself was permeable and anyone could drift around without being troubled, as long as they were smartly dressed – but the physical proximity only intensified the sense of estrangement that a newcomer might feel. Versailles had its own jargon – the smallest solecism would identify the speaker as an interloper. '*Sac*' was pronounced '*sa*', and '*tabac*', '*taba*'. One asked for 'wine from Champagne', not 'champagne'. One went to 'Paris' and not 'the capital', in one's coach ('*voiture*') not one's horse and carriage ('*equipage*'). The oldest families, whose genealogy had been unsullied by common blood since 1400, received the Honours of the Court, which entitled them to be presented to the king, to ride with him to hounds and to be invited to feasts and galas. For the majority, the only way to petition the king – apart from the very few who possessed an entrée to the king's private suite – was to accost him politely as he wandered through the palace.

Otherwise the importunate jogged governmental ministers – who saw the king frequently and, with his signature, were allowed to spend unlimited amounts – to intercede on their behalf. This entailed firm calves and much patience. 'A courtier aged eighty is a reborn Simon Stylites,' wrote Louis-Sébastien Mercier, 'in that he has spent a good forty-five of them on his feet in the antechamber of the king, of princes and of ministers.' Even after gaining admittance, one was likely to be received by a minister with a tightened smile and inconsequential pleasantries, who did not look up from his scribbling as he grunted non-committally. Everyone at Versailles was waiting – for a promotion, for an assignation, for an increased stipend or a favour for a relative. The La Mottes joined the queue.

Jeanne probably had a brief affair with the king's rakish brother, the comte d'Artois. The language of her memoir – she caught the comte's eye 'in a particular manner'; he 'honoured her with a distinction she had not sought' – seems to confirm suspicions. But the fling was too fleeting for Jeanne to extract any useful introductions

– or even sufficient booty to supply her for the foreseeable future. By the early summer of 1782, again running short of money, Jeanne wrote to Rohan and asked to meet with him. The delay of nearly a year between her introduction to the cardinal and her return to him for help indicates that even Jeanne – who could be as obtuse as anyone – had realised that the cardinal's promises were vacuous. At least, perhaps, she could present herself as worthy of the alms that he was entrusted to distribute. Jeanne ordered Beugnot to lend her his horse and trap – 'there are only two ways in this country of demanding charity', she told him, 'at the doors of the church and in a carriage'.

The Hôtel de Rohan-Strasbourg stands on rue Vieille du Temple in the Marais, on the eastern side of a quadrangle of Rohan residences. The complex was a statement of the Rohan's princely independence. One entered the main palace, the Hôtel Soubise, through a narrow archway in the stout, concave exterior wall that seemed to clasp visitors inwards. The gate widened onto a large cobbled courtyard – the biggest in Paris – surrounded by a horseshoe colonnade which led up to the neoclassical facade mounted with allegorical representatives of Might, Wisdom, Knowledge, Renown, Watchfulness, Glory and Magnificence. Within this enclave, the Rohan ruled supreme. The Hôtel de Rohan-Strasbourg, lent to the bishops of Strasbourg by their Soubise cousins, was narrower and more austere, though it had stables large enough to house a string of fifty-two horses. Its interior was plushly furnished: the bedsheets were of crimson damask; tapestries from the Gobelins factory and paintings by Boucher hung on the walls. The Cabinet des Singes, where piquet was played and tea sipped, had been painted with ludic freshness by Christophe Huet. The decoration combined two of the eighteenth century's obsessions: the Orient and humanoid monkeys. Frolicsome Chinamen bounced on stilts and seesaws in pastoral contentment and smartly dressed simians walked tightropes blindfolded, performed tricks with dogs and twanged musical instruments. A small oratory was concealed behind a panel, giving a clear sense of the relative importance that the Rohan cardinals placed on private prayer.

Any anxiety Jeanne may have felt in approaching Rohan was well concealed. His secretary Georgel recalled that Jeanne did not possess 'striking beauty' – a consideration that held sway with the cardinal – 'but she found herself adorned with all the graces of youth: her face was lively and attractive; she spoke with ease; an air of good faith in her stories placed persuasion on her lips'. This time, Rohan was moved by Jeanne's account of her childhood ordeals and irked by the cursory attention which Louis XVI had given a Valois. For the first time in her campaign to insinuate herself at Court, Jeanne received some practical counsel. Obtain an interview with the queen, Rohan advised, though he frankly admitted that he could not fix one himself because she so detested him. He also suggested approaching the *contrôleur-général* (the finance minister), and promised to draw up a memorandum in her cause.

The cardinal kept his word, and rapped on doors on Jeanne's behalf. But the French treasury had far greater worries than whether Jeanne had the money to quilt the walls of her apartment. There were four *contrôleurs-général* between 1781 and 1783: Jacques Necker, Jean-François Joly de Fleury (a decrepit, unpleasant man who, wits remarked, was neither delightful nor flourishing), Henri d'Ormesson and Charles Alexandre de Calonne.* The rapid turnover testifies to the unmanageable nature of the task each was presented with. The rickety state of the exchequer compelled officials to arrange the mirrors so the state finances, flabby with accrued debt and tax receipts mortgaged in advance, appeared more attractive to lenders. The American War of Independence, in which France had supported the rebels, had drastically unbalanced the country's spending; nearly a third of all borrowing during this period had been spent on the navy. Necker deployed a combination of money raised through annuities, the pruning of venal offices, administrative reform and increased oversight of departmental spending to keep the state solvent. In February 1781 he published the *Compte Rendu du Roi*, which purported to show a budgetary surplus of 10 million livres, but was immediately attacked for prestidigitation (when Joly took office he discovered that the

---

* Necker was technically director-general of finances because, as a foreigner and a Protestant, he could not be appointed *contrôleur-général*. Nonetheless, he was the government's chief finance minister.

state was actually 50 million livres in the red). Necker, Joly and d'Ormesson were all forced out because of the hostility to their attempts to centralise spending and revenue collection. Jeanne extracted nothing from successive ministers bar the money to redeem some pawned possessions – but she became soon a frequent guest at Rohan's table.

Jeanne appealed to Rohan by reconciling contrary impulses: the cardinal, who regarded himself as enlightened, felt the imperative to embrace ecumenically men and women of intelligence and wit; but, like the rest of his family, he was a stickler for the claims of heredity. Jeanne's verve and pluckiness – her will to establish herself – seemed animated by her Valois pulse. She was imperially confident, shared Rohan's reverence for genealogy, yet was déclassée enough to rouse his magnanimity. Jeanne was more than a mere charity case.

And then there is sex. The exact parameters of the affair between Rohan and Jeanne will never be known, but it would be surprising if one did not occur. The cardinal was a confirmed womaniser; Jeanne had shown herself willing to fall into the beds of potential benefactors. Much of the positive evidence for their liaison, however, is of doubtful value. Jeanne told her friend the comte Dolomieu that she and Rohan were lovers, but Jeanne's modus operandi relied on her claiming more intimate relations with persons of influence than actually existed. Rétaux de Villette, who will shortly enter this story, alleged in his memoir of the affair that, in the very first meeting, the cardinal 'laid his hands on her, his eyes gleaming with lust; and Madame de la Motte, gazing at him tenderly, made him know that he could dare all'. Villette, though, had an intermittent acquaintance with the truth. The most reliable testimony comes from the man unseated by Rohan – Jacques Beugnot.[*]

With Rohan on her case, Jeanne no longer required Beugnot. 'One cannot deal with a cardinal as one does with a lawyer,' she

---

[*] Beugnot's memoirs, written many years after the Diamond Necklace Affair, also present problems of interpretation. He misdates events and inserts himself into episodes from which he was provably absent. But Beugnot was being marginalised at this juncture and he does not – as he clearly does elsewhere – embellish his memories by insisting on his importance. It is significant too that, during the trial, the cardinal, for all his growls of outrage, never explicitly denied an affair with Jeanne.

told him, deprecating all his exertions on her behalf. But she could not resist showing him the letters she exchanged with the cardinal in which, remembered Beugnot, 'an ardent ambition became mixed up with tender affection . . . they were all fire; the clash, or rather the movement of the two passions was frightening'.

Beugnot does not say how long the conflagration lasted. Most likely it rapidly burnt itself out. During the trial it emerged that the baron de Planta, Rohan's aide-de-camp, had spent eleven months trying to seduce Jeanne – he would surely not have risked his master's displeasure had the cardinal himself still taken an interest. Rohan, unlike the comte d'Artois, did not discard Jeanne once his sexual attraction had waned; he took pleasure in her company and provided financial support, though to what extent would later become a matter of fierce public controversy.*

Whatever charity Rohan provided could not fund a sustainable mode of living. For the next six months, the La Mottes lived in a room on the rue de la Verrerie, prioritising the purchase of a cabriolet over settling their bills or even buying food. They left in October 1782, owing over 1,500 livres in unpaid rent, after Jeanne had hurled

---

* Rohan claimed that he occasionally gave Jeanne two or three louis (each of which was worth twenty-four livres). He sent her vermouth when she was ill, and the odd bottle of wine or haunch of venison. According to Jeanne, however, the cardinal gave her a pouch full of louis during their first meeting. He rented and furnished her apartments, subsidised her sister's medical bills, paid off thousands of livres of debt and would think nothing of dropping by with 15,000 livres in cash in case her purse needed replenishing. In total, she claimed, she received more than 80,000 livres.

Jeanne's calculations are hyperinflated – for much of the period in which she was supposedly the object of generosity she lived on the hem of poverty. Rohan, whose own expenditure was in need of retrenchment, could not have afforded such sums even had he desired to dispense them. But Rohan was more munificent than he let on. He acted as Jeanne's guarantor on a 5,000-livre loan (which he paid when Jeanne defaulted). Later, during his interrogations, Rohan would suddenly remember an occasion when he gave 600 livres to Jeanne without offering any explanation for his actions. A member of Jeanne's household – who had been turned by Rohan's lawyers and might have been expected to comply with their narrative – testified that Rohan supplied Jeanne with a regular weekly stipend. Despite his own financial travails, Rohan had access to the royal almonry and could easily have skimmed off funds to support this worthy cause.

their landlord's wife down the stairs. Nicolas and Jeanne then took a six-year lease on the top floor, coach house and stables of 10 rue Neuve-Saint-Gilles in the Marais, and in May 1783, once they were able to afford the furnishings, finally moved in. The apartment was literally down the road from the Hôtel de Rohan-Strasbourg.

During the seventeenth century the Marais had housed the ancient noble dynasties and ennobled magistrates and bureaucrats. By the end of the eighteenth century, many had migrated westwards to the new *faubourgs* and the district acquired a reputation as a redoubt of pious reaction, full of crotchety old-timers who referred to the *philosophes* as 'people for burning' and in high summer remained indoors to play cards. (This helps explain Rohan's prolonged friendship with Jeanne – she may have been the most entertaining company around.) Abandoned mansions were dissected into tenements and workshops, as a sludge of petits bourgeois seeped up through the *quartier* from the riverbank.

The La Mottes' financial situation had in no way ameliorated – the need to maintain a foothold in both the capital and at Court consumed every penny. They regularly travelled to the palace: Nicolas for his regimental duties and Jeanne to wait and grovel, wait and grovel. But to be treated seriously one needed servants, even if one's wardrobe was spartan and there was no bread for the table. Jeanne regularly pawned her best clothes. At the end of each week, she and her maid would wash by hand her two muslin skirts and two linen dresses. Nicolas, a threadbare dandy, remained in bed for days on end because he had nothing suitable to wear. The cook ordered food on credit – when it ran out, everyone went hungry. They borrowed silver tableware and pretended it was their own. When their goods were threatened with seizure, they stashed their furniture with neighbours and placed mirrors and curtains in pawn. The bailiffs arrived to naked rooms and blank faces, but the belongings still needed to be redeemed. On one occasion Jeanne wrote to her adopted sister, the baronne de Crussol, that 'the greater part of my things are at the Mont de Piété [the pawnbrokers] . . . if by Thursday I do not find six hundred livres, I shall be reduced to sleeping on straw'.

★

The La Mottes followed the Court. October 1783 found them in Fontainebleau: Nicolas spent each day wandering through the heated rooms of the chateau to stave off the cold; Jeanne kept herself warm and solvent with a succession of gentleman visitors. From Fontainebleu the La Mottes switched back to Versailles, to a greasy inn on the Place Dauphine, where they dined on cabbage, lentils and haricot beans.

Then, after two years of chivvying and pleading and loitering and dreaming, Jeanne struck a potentially lucrative seam: she obtained an interview with Madame Elisabeth, the king's sister.* On meeting her, she fainted. The sense of occasion may have been overwhelming, but it is more likely that her swoon was premeditated. Jeanne had bored even herself with the legal intricacies of her own petition. Her claims were so self-evident, she believed, that their acknowledgement would be determined merely by the level of sympathy she induced. How better to reinforce them than by showing herself on the point of collapse, by demonstrating that she was so sensitive to the mysterious power of royalty that, in its presence, her spirit left her body and flew towards it? When Jeanne came to, having been whisked home, she instructed her servant Deschamps that 'if Madame sends one of her people to ask after me, tell them that I've had a miscarriage [and] that I was bled five times'. Madame did send her doctors to enquire after Jeanne's health, along with a gift of ten louis, but that was the extent of her concern.

Despite not being invited back to Madame Elisabeth's, Jeanne acted as though she were now a bosom friend of the princess and the recipient of her patronage (in practice this meant that whenever she told her landlady that she was going to 'visit Madame', she sat in the Hotel Jouy around the corner for a few hours). In January 1784, Calonne, the *contrôleur-général*, doubled Jeanne's pension to 1,500 livres and gave her a one-off grant of nearly 800 livres. The reason for the change of heart is unclear, but the timing suggests that word of the princess's interest may have been a consideration. Not that Jeanne was grateful: 'the king', she confidently told Calonne,

---

* In her autobiography Jeanne claimed to have been presented as a child to Madame Elisabeth by the Boulainvilliers.

'gives more than this to his valets and footmen', and she dismissed the minister's apparent generosity as a bribe to withdraw her claims for the restitution of her estates.

The new spurt of money instantly whirled through the rusty drain-grate of accrued debt. By February all of Jeanne's possessions, including her dresses, had been pawned. She would not countenance finding a job and, shackled to her husband, could no longer hope for a transformative marriage. Inspired by the modest success of her collapse in front of Madame Elisabeth, Jeanne rustled up a somewhat desperate plan. Perhaps another damsel display of keeling over would prick the heart of someone with even greater influence and a reputation for whimsical concern. And so it was on 2 February 1784, the feast of Candlemas, that Jeanne, hugging her petition, found herself in the mirrored gallery of Versailles, as the winter light dustily reflected, awaiting the approach of the queen.

4

Antoinette Against Versailles

FERTILITY WAS NOT just a symbol of a royal dynasty's magnificence. It expanded a family's influence – the more children, the more alliances could be sealed in marriage. And the Habsburgs, sitting plumb in the middle of Europe with acquisitive powers on either side, were in need of all the support they could secure. Marie Antoinette, known to her family as Antoine, was born on 2 November 1755: she was the fifteenth child, and the twelfth who survived. Her father, Francis Stephen, a Lorrainer, was an indulgent and affectionate parent; Maria Theresa less so. Maria's domineering attitude towards her children – which would continue through Marie Antoinette's time in France – was exacerbated by the strain of the Seven Years War and the sudden death of her beloved husband in 1763. Though Marie Antoinette strove to please her mother, it was difficult to earn her affection – the empress was always distracted by her other children and affairs of state. When she was noticed, it tended to be in the form of admonition. 'I love the Empress,' she later wrote after she had left her homeland, 'but I am frightened of her.'

She was an attractive young woman, once her splayed teeth had been straightened on a wire, with blue eyes and a slender neck. A high, pale expanse of forehead was mounted by a tower of gunmetal, powdered hair (its natural colour was a dirty blonde). Her first family heirloom was the Habsburg lip, the protruding lower jaw that could make her appear surly to the uninstructed onlooker, but she delighted everyone she met. Even her mother, a severe judge, praised her 'affability'. Hester Thrale, Samuel Johnson's friend and biographer, visited France in 1775 and reported that Marie Antoinette was 'the prettiest Woman at her own Court'.

The archduchess's education focused on the refinements expected of a young princess. The Habsburg Court was filled with music – by Haydn, Gluck and Mozart, an exact contemporary of Marie Antoinette whom she heard perform when they were both six. She was taught to play the harpsichord and the armonica, and her deportment and dancing were universally admired. The more academic aspects of schooling received less sustained attention: Marie Antoinette's first governess, the Countess Brandeis, preferred coddling her charge to instructing her – she took far longer than normal to learn to read and write. Eventually the abbé de Vermond was appointed as her tutor – he scrubbed up her French in time for her marriage, and would remain her counsellor during her life in France.

Marie Antoinette was not the only princess under consideration for the hand of the Dauphin of France – she wasn't even the only member of her own family. Her older sister Charlotte had been suggested, but was snapped up by the king of Naples after the death of another sister, Josepha. Siblings were fungible in the politics of dynastic marriage; their value lay in locking together ruling houses and deterring the breaking of an alliance – which would mean not just tearing up paper, but families too. The intense mutual suspicion that persisted among the political elite of France and Austria required the two nations to be firmly lashed together, and Marie Antoinette was the fourth of Maria Theresa's children to marry a grandchild of Louis XV. Her wedding was conducted under the gothic vaulting of the Augustinian Church in Vienna on 19 April 1770, with her older brother Archduke Ferdinand serving as a proxy husband. Two days later a convoy of fifty-seven carriages accompanied the new dauphine on her journey to France.

At his birth, no one considered that Louis Auguste would be Dauphin at the age of eleven, but the deaths of his father and older brother in the space of four years left him, by 1765, the heir to the kingdom. He did not appear magisterial, being bulky, costive, gauche, introverted and short-sighted, which led him to lour down on people as he struggled to identify them. His sense of humour, for what it was, tended towards slapstick. His diary, most of which devoutly itemises his daily game bag, shows, in the words of his biographer John Hardman, 'the mind of an accountant'. The entry for 13 March 1767 read simply 'Death of my mother at eight in the evening' – though, to be fair, the hand is noticeably scraggier than usual.

As a child Louis showed a preference for geography and science, for the empirical above the imaginative. His faith was orthodox, his tastes were middlebrow and his belief in absolute monarchy was as unreflective and firm as that of his predecessors. Like all Bourbons – apart from, ironically, the Grand Huntsman of France, the duc de Penthièvre – his first love was hunting. His second love was picking apart locks. Occasionally Louis would retreat to the turret above his private suite, from where he would observe through a telescope the to-and-fro of Versailles, and snipe at cats, a species he could not abide, with his musket. (Even a sceptic of Freud might wonder whether all that riding to hounds, keyhole surgery and gunning down of felines might have been symptomatic of a psychosexual problem.) Louis had no interest in the conventional amusements of noble life. The controller of the king's Menus-Plaisirs, which organised royal entertainments, was effectively made redundant when Louis told him that 'my Menus Plaisirs are to walk about the park. I do not need you.' Louis was personally parsimonious and refused to indulge or rescue courtiers – apart from his wife and brothers – who had sunk into unpayable debt. Refreshingly he did not stand on ceremony – he used to shave himself every morning – though he earned a rebuke from his chief minister when he entered a party so unobtrusively that none of the attendees noticed his arrival: it was disgraceful for the king not to be acknowledged.

Louis's shortcomings were particularly acute in comparison to his two younger, more companionable brothers, the porky but ready-witted comte de Provence and the lean, raffish comte d'Artois. His natural lack of confidence had been exacerbated by his tutors, who continually compared him to his pedestalled older brother, and left him with a repulsion of any form of dispute. Provence compared Louis to 'a set of oiled billiard balls you are trying vainly to hold together', not because he was duplicitous but because he would stew silently rather than risk confrontation. When Louis, in his first days as king, decided to dismiss one of his grandfather's ministers but could not bring himself to summon him, the comte de Maurepas, the new chief minister (in practice if not in title), refused to leave the room until the matter had been settled.

Louis knew that he was naturally ill-suited to the role for which he had been bullied into by fate – on becoming king he said 'I feel the universe is going to fall on me' (a not inaccurate prophecy) – and his accession to the throne mellowed him little. He was known at Versailles as 'the butcher' because of his terse, unsentimental manner: when the *contrôleur-général* Henri d'Ormesson apologised for a poorly planned *travail* – his one-on-one weekly conference with the king – because his son lay mortally ill, Louis replied 'that's a bother', leaving it unclear whether he was put out by his minister's indolence or gruffly commiserating. But he grew more confident as a king over time and could be solicitous towards favoured minis-ters, such as the comte de Vergennes, whom he begged not to damage his health by working too hard.

From the beginning of his reign, Louis was determined to dedicate himself to the business of government, and worked far more conscien-tiously than his grandfather. In the early days his taciturn demeanour enabled his ministers to manipulate him: they continually fired off questions and readily supplied the answers they wanted. But he soon became adept at using silence to convey disapproval and to prey on a minister's fears of dismissal. This maintained his influence in a system where it was quite possible for the king to be marginalised, but it did not make for healthy government. Louis's distaste for contention prevented the compromises needed between his territorial ministers: his solution to interdepartmental quarrels was to sack one of the ministers involved, rather than attempt to reconcile the disputants.

Louis was not an easy man to love, and his marriage to Marie Antoinette struggled from the start. Louis's anti-Austrian tutor, the duc de La Vauguyon, had instilled him with a distrust of his new wife. The couple also lacked common interests: 'My tastes', she wrote to her mother, 'are not the same as the King's, who is only interested in hunting and his metal-working.' More troubling, from a political perspective, was Louis's performance in the bedroom. Seven years passed before the marriage was properly consummated, and the pressure on Louis was increased by agitators who wished the marriage annulled. (Maria Theresa's unhelpful advice was for the queen to tempt him with 'redoubled caresses'.)

It has been suggested that Louis suffered from phimosis, which would have made his erections painful, though he was examined on numerous occasions by doctors who found nothing to inhibit them, and there is no evidence that he ever went under the knife. Marie Antoinette's brother, the Holy Roman Emperor Joseph II, left a description of the king's curious sexual technique: 'he has strong, perfectly satisfactory erections; he introduces the member, stays there without moving for about two minutes, withdraws without ejaculating but still erect, and bids goodnight'. Marie Antoinette, for all the later depictions of her as a ravenous nymphomaniac, seemed to have been equally uninterested in sex (Joseph II thought that his sister was 'prudish'). The frustrations that the queen expressed in her letters to her mother are more social than physical: she was embarrassed at being regarded as frigid and unwomanly, and failing in her primary duty as queen, which was to provide a male heir to the French throne. Eventually in 1778 she gave birth to a daughter, Marie Thérèse; a sickly Dauphin, Louis Joseph, followed in 1781.

But Marie Antoinette's discomfort at the French Court was not simply a result of marital incompatibility, and Louis had reason to be wary of his wife. The role that Maria Theresa had envisaged for her was distorted by an inherent contradiction. Marie Antoinette had been supposed to consecrate a new era of friendship between the Habsburgs and the Bourbons and conciliate, through her natural charm and adoption of French manners, those who disdained the alliance. But she was also expected to promote Austrian interests when they clashed with French ones – as they increasingly did after the fall of Choiseul – and thwart those whom she most needed to mollify, inevitably leading to increased resentment at her political interference.

Marie Antoinette's closest advisors at Versailles were Vermond, whose self-importance ballooned so much that he would receive ministers while soaking in the bath; and the ambassador of the Holy Roman Empire, the comte de Mercy-Argenteau. A bachelor though no monk, Mercy-Argenteau was an elegant and experienced diplomat who adopted the role of exasperated parent towards the queen. He wrote detailed reports to Maria Theresa about her conduct; the empress would then rebuke her daughter in the next post. Historically, the king's official mistress typically held tremendous influence over the nation's affairs. Since Louis had no interest in taking one, Marie Antoinette's position ought to have been strengthened – and Mercy-Argenteau browbeat her into speaking to the king on matters of policy. But Marie Antoinette had neither any interest in the detail of politics – the comte de La Marck spoke of her 'repugnance for the whole subject' – nor any finesse. During the Bavarian Crisis of 1778, when the Austrians wished to incorporate Bavaria into their empire, her efforts to persuade her husband to support Joseph II's tenuous claim to the duchy were ineffective; Louis was able to deflect her with one of his studied silences, faintly lit by a thin smile.

The queen showed greater zest for meddling in the disbursement of offices and honours, though her handling was equally clunky. She failed to restore her friend, the Choiseulist comte de Guînes, to his position as ambassador to the Court of St James, after he was caught in a scandal involving the sale of classified information. She spluttered through a tantrum aimed at obtaining the dismissal of the foreign minister Vergennes to no effect. And when Vermond suggested that Loménie de Brienne, the archbishop of Toulouse – a man more arch than bishop, and his patron – be appointed to the king's council on Maurepas's death, Louis worked himself up into 'a towering rage', and bellowed that 'the one [Brienne] must be confined to his diocese, and have his revenues confiscated and the other [Vermond] must be sent away from the queen' (neither happened). Yet Marie Antoinette's influence did grow over the course of the reign, and by 1783 there were three ministers on the king's council who, at least in part, owed their appointments to her.

Politics was not the only royal activity that Marie Antoinette found tiresome. She was little more than fourteen when she arrived at Versailles – when Louis XV first met her, he found her 'spontaneous and a little childish' – and she struggled to find stimulation in court life. It took a great deal of cajoling before she would even deliver a few words in the vague direction of Louis XV's mistress, Madame du Barry ('there are a lot of people here at Versailles today', ran the deathless opening gambit). Marie Antoinette felt the rituals of the Court were humiliating and claustrophobic – and with good reason: on one morning she was left naked and prickled with goose-pimples as three noblewomen, each more senior than the last, arrived in succession and demanded the privilege of handing the queen her chemise. When she ate in public in the Grand Couvert, she scarcely tasted her food. She jibbed against the strictures of her *dame d'honneur*, the comtesse de Noailles, whom she dubbed 'Madame Etiquette'. Having fallen down once when riding, she told her companions not to help her up: 'We must wait for Madame Etiquette. She will show us the right way to pick up a Dauphine who has tumbled off a donkey.' One of the reasons that she enjoyed the company of children so much, especially her young sister-in-law Elisabeth, was their emotional transparency and lack of artifice. Marie Antoinette was sentimental in the best sense of the word – her feelings had not been juiced out of her by the estrangements and cynicism of the sclerotic Court. She has been unjustly and inaccurately maligned for remarking of starving peasants during the Flour War of 1775 'let them eat cake' (a comment only attributed to her in the nineteenth century). In fact, she was conscious of her duties to her adopted people: 'It is quite certain that in seeing people who treat us so well despite their own misfortune,' she wrote to Maria Theresa, 'we are more obliged than ever to work hard for their happiness.'

It must have been particularly frustrating for Marie Antoinette to have arrived in France just as she emerged from childhood. The infant-ilising nature of court protocol prevented her from being treated by adults as an equal, because the regimen was designed to make her exceptional. She couldn't perform the simplest tasks without prompting disapproval, and was once reprimanded for acting like a servant when she passed food around at a picnic. Trapped between the wagging finger of Madame Etiquette and the unblinking gaze of Mercy-Argenteau, it is unsurprising that she developed a craving for privacy and simplicity. The most delicate aspects of her life became subject of public chatter: when the comtesse d'Artois gave birth, Marie Antoinette was heckled by the fishwives of Versailles, asking when she would pop a sprog. After she became queen, she ordered the construction of a secret passageway between her apartments and the king's, so she would not be seen en route.

She developed an instinct for secrecy – papers were carefully locked away in her bureau – as she was confused by how well informed her mother seemed to be and assumed the French were spying on her too, a presumption that only heightened her sense of isolation. Versailles was the kind of place where behind every door stood a man with his ear squeezed against it – on one occasion a footman's departure revealed to Louis and Marie Antoinette the figure of the duc de La Vauguyon crouched on the other side of the threshold, who reacted as though he had been caught fondling himself.

Marie Antoinette established a parallel life in which she could behave as a friend and companion, rather than a royal consort. She held exclusive dinners in her rooms where the guests were allowed to wear less formal clothes. Her pastimes tended toward the louche: they were permitted though not embraced by her husband, who perhaps saw that obstructing them would give rise to grievances not worth the bother. She frequented the opera in Paris – she kept her own box in all the main theatres – where she chatted amiably and unaffectedly with theatregoers.

Her frivolity was in part an attempt to avoid confronting her difficult and ambiguous predicament. It was also motivated by the wish to carve out a sphere for herself in which she could escape the passivity that life at Versailles imposed, even if she could act with abandon only in the most minor matters. With the assistance of her couturier Rose Bertin – 'the Minister of Fashion' – she dedicated herself to style. In 1776, she spent 100,000 livres on accessories alone (the budget for her entire wardrobe was supposed to be 120,000 livres). In her early years in France, Bertin and the queen's hairdresser Leonard assembled *poufs*, teetering smokestacks on the top of the head, in which the natural tresses were bulked up by horsehair and cloth. These were adorned with ribbons, flowers, feathers, and bejewelled objets d'art, including on one occasion a neck-straining model of a frigate.

Marie Antoinette gambled prodigiously at the racetrack and on the baize – in 1777 she lost nearly 500,000 livres. Louis had no interest in cards – his older brother had cheated him when they played as children – but his wife's predilection meant that they spent an increasing number of evenings apart, as the queen played canasta or faro with her set. Her male friends were raddled, charismatic womanisers, such as the baron de Besenval and the duc de Coigny, whose company, though entirely chaste, lent support to the prevailing view that her marriage was disintegrating. The women who became her favourites – first the princesse de Lamballe, then Yolande de Polastron, the comtesse, later duchesse de Polignac – were distinguishable by their extreme vapidness: Lamballe was famed for her stupidity and was so sensitive that she once reportedly passed out on encountering a sprig of violets; Polignac was a winsome young woman with a gleaming pallor, entirely bereft of 'avidity or egotism', in whose pleasantly mind-numbing company the queen could relax.

Marie Antoinette's closest friendship was with the Swedish count, Axel Fersen – blade-nosed, sharp-cheeked and lean, with an air of wistfulness – who spent long stretches of time at Versailles from 1774 and fought with French troops during the American War of Independence. There was speculation that he had an affair with the queen, though contemporaries had no proof or confession by either party. To keep such a liaison hidden for years would have required a talent for logistics and discretion well beyond Marie Antoinette. Irrespective of whether they slept with each other, their mutual ardour was beyond doubt.

In 1775, Louis gave Marie Antoinette the Petit Trianon, a small, clean-lined caramel-coloured palace at the far end of the gardens of Versailles, which Louis XV had commissioned for Madame du Pompadour. Here, with the painter Hubert Robert, Marie Antoinette planted a *jardin anglais* – artificial arcadian landscapes of undulating terrain, studiedly haphazard planting and the odd neoclassical temple – that repudiated the trimness of Versailles's classical horticulture. She also built a *hameau* – a hamlet – containing twelve cottages, a mill, a dovecot, an aviary, a henhouse and a farm with a working dairy. The village was quilted in flowers that filled hundreds of faience pots stamped in blue with the figure of the queen, along with bushes and trees stooping with apricots, gooseberries, raspberries and strawberries. The *hameau* was another of the fandangles for which Marie Antoinette was taxed. But it should also be seen as an attempt, however remote and patronising, to understand something of the lives of her more lowly subjects, to whom she had shown sympathy and affection on the occasions she had encountered them (for example, when 130 people had been killed in a stampede in Paris at a fireworks display to mark her marriage, she had given generously to the bereaved). In a similar vein, Louis XVI had, as a child, been taught how to plough a field.

The queen's retreat into a Shangri-La of her own fashioning was accompanied by a turn in public opinion against her. She had been genuinely adored on her arrival in France; in 1773, she and Louis were mobbed by so many well-wishers at the Tuileries that their progress was stalled for forty-five minutes. When the chorus in Gluck's *Iphigénie en Aulide* sang 'Let us sing now, let us celebrate our Queen' there was vigorous clapping and cries of 'Vive la Reine'. Marie Antoinette knew how fickle such adulation was: 'How fortunate we are', she wrote, 'given our rank, to have gained the love of a whole people with such ease.' She was aware that her privileges might as easily breed resentment.

Little in her conduct, however, seemed directed at preserving the respect of her subjects, and her disavowal of much of her public role led to malicious speculation about what went on behind closed doors. When her first child was born, numerous potential fathers were listed by the satirists. These libels were not necessarily being produced by fervent republicans (who, at this point, existed only in tiny numbers); they were commissioned and distributed by courtiers who felt excluded from the queen's coterie. She was also accused of acting as a fifth columnist for Austrian interests – during the Bavarian crisis, sporadic applause for her at the opera was stifled by other spectators. And her extravagant expenditure caused consternation; it was believed, for instance, that Trianon contained a wall of diamonds. In 1784 the king bought for her the chateau of Saint-Cloud for 6 million livres from his cousin the duc d'Orléans; the palace was to be the queen's personal property and all orders there were given in her name. There was suspicion about the purchase – objections were raised in the *parlement* of Paris, where the king's edicts needed to be ratified – much of which was justified; the deal had been orchestrated by the baron de Breteuil, a ministerial supporter of Marie Antoinette, against the objections of the finance minister, Calonne, as a staging post in his project to let the queen rule (*'faire regner la Reine'*). Saint-Cloud marked the confluence of disgust at the queen's excess and distrust of her political aspirations. From then on, both would fret harder and deeper.

5

In My Lady's Chamber

A T MIDDAY, SPECTATORS, drily whispering, gather as the king
and queen make their way to Mass. The queen strides down
the gallery, ringed by her ladies-in-waiting and her *garde du corps*.
As she passes, Jeanne topples like a felled sapling. Perhaps the queen
is too enveloped in conversation to notice; perhaps she glances at
the falling woman but presumes that she will be looked after.* But
Marie Antoinette does not halt, does not seek to discover who
Jeanne is or why she was taken ill. No royal doctors arrive to diag-
nose the malady; no coin-stuffed purses are delivered to Jeanne's
lodgings.

Jeanne's ambush had guttered out dismally, but failure did not
deter her. She told everyone who would listen that the queen had
taken a profound interest in her health, actually. She had been invited
to the queen's private rooms, Jeanne said, where she had told Marie
Antoinette about her family and its misfortunes. The queen was
deeply touched and had proffered her money. Jeanne's story gained
plausibility because in May 1784 she received permission to sell both
her and her brother's pensions for 9,000 livres. She claimed this
money flowed from the queen.

One of Jeanne's closest friends would later argue that Jeanne
concocted this grand lie as she was simply too 'vain' to admit her
stratagem had failed. Jeanne was indeed sensitive to others' opinions
because of her dubious and dilute royal heritage. But she had also
learned from her time at Versailles that the regard in which one was

* Jeanne may have been encouraged in her plan by the story of *le beau* Dillon – the
queen had pressed a hand to her admirer's chest when he fainted in her
presence.

held – and the material benefits which flowered from this – was proportionate to one's perceived closeness to the royal family. Those who had hitherto dealt with you frostily would become open-eared and amenable at the merest snip of a rumour that you were welcome in the private quarters of a princess. Jeanne's boasts of proximity to the queen could be leveraged with others desperate for advancement and recognition – but mortal danger awaited if her deceit was exposed and those who were not convinced were summarily excised from her company: Madame Colson, a relative of Jeanne who had been lodging with the La Mottes, was exiled to a convent for voicing doubts.

Jeanne began to solidify a scheme by which she could transmute her blossoming 'friendship' with the queen into hard coin. She had been brooding on this for some time. A begging letter written to d'Ormesson, the finance minister, in 1783 was pregnant with menace: 'You will without doubt find me, Monsieur, very extravagant; but I cannot stop myself from complaining since the smallest favour has not been granted to me. I am no longer surprised if a great evil is done and I can only say again that my faith has held me back from doing evil.' Her plotting was energised by the arrival in Paris of a potential accomplice of far greater nous that her plodding husband: Rétaux de Villette, an old messmate of Nicolas's from Lunéville.

Villette had been born in 1754 in Lyons, where his father was a tax collector. After his father's death, he and his mother moved north to Troyes. Villette was educated at the artillery school in Bapaume before joining the Gendarmerie, where he and Nicolas squandered many undisturbed hours at cards. He later served in the Maréchaussée, the regional police force, but was chased from 'a small provincial town . . . having received a blow at a ball where he had had the brazenness to insult a young lady of quality before her mother and father'.

Out of money and on the make, Villette arrived in Paris in January 1784. In May, just as Jeanne received the windfall from her mortgaged pensions, he renewed his acquaintance with his old comrade. Beugnot described Villette as 'smooth and insinuating': he shared with Jeanne a crafty intelligence and a greaseless plausibility. Most historians of the Diamond Necklace Affair have presumed that Villette and Jeanne became lovers, which seems reasonable: Villette had a reputation for caddishness and Jeanne, who had previously deployed her body for pragmatic ends, may have felt that giving herself to Villette was necessary to dissuade this man – in whom she saw her own duplicity reflected – from double-crossing her. Nicolas was either past caring whom his wife slept with, or was too dull to notice.

Without realising it, Rohan had shown Jeanne a tempting chink in their very first meeting, when he told her that, because of the queen's hatred for him, he could not arrange an audience. The cardinal made no attempt to hide the chagrin he felt at the disgrace into which he had fallen: it was, wrote Georgel, 'a habitual bitterness that poisoned all his most beautiful days'. Rohan's malcontent was both personal and political. He was humiliated when celebrating Mass for the royal family – as was his duty whenever he stayed at Versailles – to feel the prick of the queen's disdainful gaze and to slouch out afterwards without the slightest acknowledgement. As grand almoner Rohan sat snugly at the centre of the Court; but his juxtaposition to the royal family made him feel all the more peripheral when ignored by them. Grand Duke Paul of Russia had visited Versailles in 1782, and Rohan, uninvited to the ball thrown by Louis and Marie Antoinette at Trianon in the duke's honour, had persuaded a porter to let him into the party as soon as the queen had retired for the evening. Rohan, whose ardour to see the queen overpowered his discretion, sneaked out of the lodge too early. His impenetrable disguise was a greatcoat draped over his cardinal's regalia. A pair of scarlet stockings was visible to all – including Marie Antoinette. She made her displeasure known.

Rohan was also nagged by frustrated political ambitions. He believed he ought to be prime minister, a defunct office the Bourbon kings had deliberately avoided filling. It did not matter that the comte de Vergennes, an ally of the Rohan, was the king's closest counsellor and would remain so until his death in 1787; or that Rohan's diplomatic career had been limited to a few controversial years in Vienna, and he lacked experience of civil or military administration. He was self-deluded enough to overlook his failure to cultivate those character traits – tact, discipline, fiscal prudence – needed to govern successfully.

He imagined himself as a worthy successor to the all-powerful cardinal-ministers the crown had called upon during the previous two hundred years: Richelieu, who had tamped down Habsburg aggrandisement during the Thirty Years War; Mazarin, effectively co-regent of France during Louis XIV's minority and vanquisher of the Fronde; and Fleury, Louis XV's tutor who became chief minister at the age of seventy-three and ruled unchallenged for a further seventeen years. Armand-Gaston-Maximilien, the first Rohan bishop of Strasbourg, had sat on the Council of Regency before Louis XV came of age. Rohan believed that the queen's hatred was the sole impediment to his destiny – once his sin had been absolved, his purified talent would float unobstructed to the king's right hand. On numerous occasions, Rohan confided in Jeanne his stunted aspirations and his fruitless assays to soften the queen's unforgiving rigour.

Jeanne proceeded patiently. She disseminated hints of a deepening friendship with the queen while coyly refusing to confirm or deny anything. It was not long, however, before she broached the subject with Rohan. The story she told him differed slightly from the narrative she had dreamt up after the fainting episode. It is possible that she did this to probe the limits of Rohan's credulity and test the viability of her plan, but Jeanne never placed any value in consistency and probably improvised the entire conversation.

The queen, Jeanne told the stupefied Rohan, had found her with Madame Elisabeth, recounting her troubles. Marie Antoinette was intrigued and invited Jeanne to call on her. This would have been a most unusual introduction. Women traditionally required a formal presentation to the queen: bare-shouldered in their court dress, the initiates would remove their glove and make to kiss the queen's hem before being stopped with a flick of the hand. The presentation was inscribed in a register and published in the government's official newspaper, the *Gazette de France*. But Jeanne's story had some purchase with Rohan, because people of insufficient nobility were introduced on the sly and the queen was widely known to scorn formality.

Marie Antoinette, Jeanne continued, soon took her into her confidence, receiving her in a room reserved for private relaxation. This would have been the *cabinet doré*, which the queen had remodelled the previous year. The white wooden panels were decorated in gilt, cornucopias bound up by strings of pearls, fleurs-de-lys and winged sphinxes. Jean-Baptiste Oudry's painting of a potted pineapple tree suspending a single fruit hung on the wall. It was here that the queen sang, gossiped with her closest friends and sat for Elisabeth Vigée-Lebrun's portraits. In the main, however, the queen's penetralia were more like a bunker than a palace: 'a mass of small rooms . . . the majority [of which] were dingy [and] simply furnished, nearly all with mirrors and panelling'. These were unexplored by even the most experienced courtiers, which enabled Jeanne to claim without fear of contradiction that she had interpolated herself into the queen's *cabinet*.

Rohan was initially incredulous but, with persistence, Jeanne managed to batter through his amazement. That Marie Antoinette should have adopted Jeanne may have seemed outlandish but it was not entirely impossible to believe. The queen was given to spasms of generosity: once, she came across an orphan being trampled by horses and, even though he sprung up unhurt, she vowed to support him and his five siblings. Mercy-Argenteau noted that 'it was already a flaw in her character in Vienna to press the cause of all sorts of people to the hilt, without examining their worthiness'. How much more likely, then, that her heart would have wept for Jeanne, an orphan of distinguished lineage, whose state of indigence would have moved anyone who valued royal dignity.

Jeanne – voluble, contentious and brash – was the antithesis of the placid, unchallenging women in Marie Antoinette's circle. But the cardinal was too preoccupied imagining how, allied to Jeanne, he might restore himself in the queen's estimation and resuscitate his political career to ponder this. With his early doubts overcome, Rohan urged Jeanne to mention him to the queen at every available opportunity, but Jeanne insisted that their friendship was still too fragile for so unwelcome a subject to be broached. This was the first example of the accomplishment Jeanne showed in managing and manipulating Rohan's expectations. When Rohan began to express doubts, Jeanne produced letters, supposedly from Marie Antoinette, addressed to 'My cousin, the comtesse de Valois'; she flourished 1,000 écus which she said were a gift from the queen (they were actually the proceeds of her liquidated pension). The La Motte household began to look less dowdy. Jeanne bought – on credit, naturally – three dozen sets of silver cutlery, a large silver soup ladle, two dozen silver coffee spoons and two crystal salt cellars. Nicolas and Jeanne sported new bracelets and rings worth thousands of livres. The couple chatted openly about the source of their wealth; Jeanne told the abbesse of Longchamps, her alma mater, that she received now an annual stipend of 45,000 livres from the king. The La Mottes still had to scrimp and hustle to find the money for less conspicuous consumption such as rent and food; despite the windfall of 9,000 livres from the sale of the pensions, Nicolas borrowed 300 livres in June 1784 to pay the landlord. And the only way that they could maintain their pied-à-terre in Versailles was by purchasing a bolt of satin in Paris – again on credit – then pawning it as soon as they stepped off the coach.

It is unlikely that Jeanne had planned her deception precisely. She was not a naturally strategic thinker, but she did understand the necessity of advancing carefully to the point where Rohan was utterly dependent on her. And Jeanne's motivations must have been more complex than just exploitation. She was buoyed up by the surge of attention. Doors, once locked against her, were now held respectfully open. Toadies and place-seekers courted her. People sprang forward to seek her assistance: a Madame de Quinques gave Jeanne 1,000 écus, believing that she had sufficient influence with the queen to obtain a sinecure for a friend. She experienced, on the cheap, the life she had long desired, dispensing patronage and basking in sycophancy. She knew that it was painted on pasteboard but, an actress herself, she enjoyed playing the part.

Her relationship with Rohan had reversed itself. Now he was in need of her good offices, he had to vie for her attention, had to discard his lordliness and beg. For Jeanne's pretence was, indirectly, a form of revenge. Revenge at Marie Antoinette for disregarding her; and revenge at Rohan for treating her like just another poor girl. If their esteem would not be granted freely, then it would be counterfeited. With Marie Antoinette, the subject of her story, and Rohan, her rapt audience, Jeanne had become, as authors do, a kind of absolute monarch, determining the fates of her characters and toying with the expectations of her readers. It was as though she had been crowned the last Valois queen.

Once Jeanne had seen Rohan grow accustomed to her anecdotes of afternoons at the palace, she told him that she had spoken to Marie Antoinette about the cardinal's concern for her. 'Above all,' said Jeanne, 'I generously extolled the good that you do in your diocese and the prodigious good deeds the gratitude for which I hear about every day.' The queen had not blenched at the mention of Rohan's name, so Jeanne had informed her that Rohan's 'health was visibly altered' because he had exhausted all means of persuading her of his remorse and continued devotion. She convinced Marie Antoinette to allow the cardinal to justify himself in writing.

Rohan must have already written such a letter a thousand times in his head. The one he committed to paper does not survive, but, if other examples of his correspondence are any guide, it would have been elegant and direct: an apology for any offence caused, perhaps a brief defence that he had been misrepresented by his enemies, a declaration of his respect for his queen and a request for an audience.

A few days later, Jeanne delivered a response. According to Georgel, it ran: 'I have read your letter. I am delighted to find that you are not guilty. I am not yet able to grant you the audience you desire. When the circumstances permit it, I will let you know. Be discreet.'*

Now began a series of letters between Rohan and the person he believed to be the queen. Each letter was, in fact, dictated by Jeanne to Villette – presumably because Rohan was familiar with her own hand – who wrote on blue-bordered paper bought by Jeanne from a stationer on the nearby rue Sainte-Anastase (this was a relatively restrained choice: paper edged with gilt or bordered with flowers or dusted with gold was highly fashionable). No attempt was made to procure a sample of the queen's handwriting and imitate it, even though this was probably not the first time that Jeanne had adopted

---

* Georgel wrote his memoirs at least twenty-five years later and without access to the cardinal's correspondence, so the language is certainly not exact; but he was well-acquainted with the details of the affair and this message's tenor is of a piece with subsequent events.

such a method (at the end of 1783, she had been accused of forging letters of recommendation).

Later, many people would express disbelief that Rohan failed to realise the letters were not in the queen's hand. But there had been no contact between the cardinal and the queen – in person or in writing – for a decade, and there is no good reason why, during that time, he should have encountered an extended example of Marie Antoinette's script (though he must have scanned her signature in the registers of the Chapel Royal). It was clear from the outset that the correspondence was, if not illicit, at least secretive. From the refusal to grant an immediate audience and the order to 'be discreet', Rohan would have deduced that there were powerful figures who objected to his reconciliation: perhaps the Polignacs and other members of the queen's circle, protective of their election; perhaps the king's approval needed to be carefully coaxed out. Even had Rohan noted something amiss with the handwriting he may well have reasoned – and Jeanne could have argued – that a disguised hand was a necessary precaution in the event of the letters being intercepted.

This was not the first occasion in Louis XVI's reign that the queen's confidence, her gestures or her handwriting had been exploited: Madame Cahouet de Villers, the wife of the treasurer-general of the king's household, was a repeat offender. In the twilight years of Louis XV's reign, she had boasted of being the king's mistress. After Louis XVI ascended to the throne, Cahouet de Villers took as a lover an *intendant* of the queen's finances, whose principal attraction was that he offered access to the queen's rooms on Sundays. At first, Cahouet de Villers made a genuine if deluded attempt to befriend Marie Antoinette. She commissioned a portrait of the queen, which the latter refused to accept, objecting to the quality of both the picture and its donor.

Cahouet de Villers then resorted to craftier measures. Her lover provided her with a sample of the queen's handwriting, which she copied over and over until her own hand matched it. Cahouet de Villers then composed a number of letters to herself from Marie Antoinette 'in the tenderest and most familiar style', as evidence of the queen's favour. Jewellers received orders from the queen, instructing them to send Cahouet de Villers their wares. In 1776 Cahouet de Villers alighted on Jean-Louis Loiseau de Bérengar, an immensely wealthy tax collector who hankered after respectability to complement his riches. She told him the queen desired a loan of 200,000 livres – the queen's debts were well known – and needed to keep it secret from Louis. Bérengar was eager to comply, but demanded the go-ahead from the queen in person. Impossible, said Cahouet de Villers, that was not how the queen did business. Instead, she promised that the queen would signal her approval, with a smile and twist of her head, as she walked to Mass. Cahouet de Villers spread word that two women would be sporting particularly elaborate headdresses, and arranged for two friends of hers to be suitably scaffolded and decked out. When the queen noticed them, she reacted as predicted. Bérengar's money was spent furnishing the Cahouet de Villers' *hôtel* with chandeliers of Bohemian crystal and paintings by Rubens and Titian.

But Bérengar grew suspicious and informed the police, whose investigation uncovered a skilful forgery – the only difference between the queen's handwriting and Cahouet de Villers's counterfeits was 'a little more regularity in the letters'. The case was reported in the newsletters: some speculated that Cahouet de Villers had been framed by the queen, who had genuinely asked her to arrange a loan on the quiet. The comte de Maurepas acted decisively, exiling the false scrivener to a convent and preventing the poisoning of the queen's reputation had the case been sent to trial (as some argued it should).

Rohan's own lack of wariness is strange, since he had come close to being hoodwinked in a similar manner. A number of years previously, Rohan had briefly been involved with a Madame Goupil, who convinced him she could engineer a rapprochement with the queen. Though Madame Goupil was once a close companion of the queen's friend, the princesse de Lamballe, Rohan ought to have been sceptical, since her husband had died in the Bastille.* Rohan's

---

* A police officer charged with suppressing libels against the monarchy, Goupil had discovered that there was a profit to be turned in printing them himself, bringing them to the attention of royal officials, then asking for money to buy off the supposed blackmailers.

fling with Madame Goupil was brief and inconclusive – but this scrape did not make him any more circumspect when beckoned by a flirtatious young woman dangling the keys to Marie Antoinette's boudoir. The cardinal would later argue in his defence that doubting Jeanne's motives was unimaginable: from his perspective, he had generously patched up her rackety finances. To distrust her would have meant believing she was a 'monster'.

Jeanne supplemented the forged correspondence with non-epistolary evidence of her familiarity with the queen's household and movements. She predicted to Rohan the days that Marie Antoinette would arrive or leave Trianon – having been tipped off by a concierge dazzled by Jeanne's family history – and the cardinal would crouch behind a bush to observe the comings and goings. On one occasion, Villette was kitted out in royal livery and introduced to Rohan as the queen's valet.

Not one of the letters sent to or by Rohan survives. During the subsequent investigation, the suspects – including Rohan – squirmed away from discussing their contents. But it is possible, with careful and duly tentative reading, to reconstruct some of the topography of the correspondence by examining two fictional collections of letters, one published five years after Jeanne started her deception, the other two years before.

6

Notes on a Scandal

THE EIGHTEENTH CENTURY was built on letters. State-run postal services had expanded their reach and efficiency over the course of the 1600s. Rising levels of literacy enabled more and more families, dispersed across the globe by the scattergun dynamics of war, colonisation and commerce, to communicate with each other. Letter-writing manuals furnished the newly literate classes with exemplars from which they could fashion their own correspondence and, through it, themselves as cultivated and urbane citizens.

The possibilities of the letter – it could be structured or rag-tag, cool or effusive, conversational or declamatory, focused or miscellaneous – meant it became the template for a wide variety of literary genres. It could turn, as it does in Diderot's *Letter on the Blind*, towards philosophical speculation; or towards social criticism like Montesquieu's *Persian Letters* and Graffigny's *Letters of a Peruvian Woman*, in which a faux foreigner, explaining to his or her countrymen the goings-on of an unfamiliar land, looked aslant at French mores. Newsletters, most often printed in the Low Countries or England to avoid the censor, collated reports and gossip from their correspondents. With the immense success of two books – the Abbé Prévost's translation of Samuel Richardson's *Clarissa* in 1751 and Jean-Jacques Rousseau's *Julie, ou la Nouvelle Héloïse* ten years later – the epistolary novel became the epoch's defining fictional form.

The letter is a slippery and paradoxical thing. While polite society demands affectation and hypocrisy, it appears to offer an unfrosted vitrine into the human heart. It is a safehouse into which secrets that one cannot speak of in public for fear of others overhearing are admitted. Yet the letter is both crafted and crafty. Conversation is improvisatory, rough-edged and risky; its punctuation is fluffing and hemming and pausing for thought. You can read in the quiver of a voice, the blush of a cheek or the damp of an eye a truth that runs counter to the speaker's words; and the tumbling momentum of speech can barrel you into revelations which you had intended to keep hidden.

A letter might be scribbled down in the gyre of emotional confusion, but hyperventilations, effusions, aposiopeses can also be composed in tranquillity (many letters of the period were written for circulation beyond their intended recipient: Madame de Sévigné's correspondence with her daughter was published from 1734 onwards, but copies had been passed around for decades previously). A letter admits none of the scrutiny or contradiction that can be interjected in company; it is never nonplussed by the recipient's objections or suspicions, because these can be reflected upon when they are received in their turn and parried at leisure. The only voice capable of rebutting a letter's argument is the reader's conscience, and that may be weak or changeable or willing to believe anything it hears. While protesting honesty, the accomplished letter-writer can speak poison.

The appendix to Jeanne's *Mémoires Justificatifs*, the apologia published in 1789, contains thirty-one letters exchanged by the cardinal and Marie Antoinette, which Jeanne claimed to have transcribed when acting as their intermediary. There is plentiful evidence – both internal and external – to discredit their authenticity, even in the eyes of those inclined to believe Jeanne. One letter, for example, implies that Marie Antoinette and Rohan had known each other in Vienna, though Rohan's embassy began a year after Marie Antoinette arrived in France.

Nonetheless, the mind that devised these letters also dreamt up the queen's half of the original correspondence and read Rohan's responses, so one should expect some overlap of form, style and characterisation. In the 1789 letters, Jeanne revels in the clandestine aspect of the exchange. The letters are dabbed with obscure acronyms ('M.B.S.T.C.B.' and 'J.T.R.T.B.A.V.C.S.'); transparent ciphers ('T' for 'Trianon' and 'P' for Polignac); and theatrical aliases – Marie Antoinette is 'The Master', Rohan 'The Slave', Louis 'The Minister' and the baron de Planta 'The Savage'. Marie Antoinette appears as a woman easily roused and quickly placated. She immediately accepts Rohan's justification and expresses her indignation at being duped into hating him by her enemies. And she is devoted to politicking: 'I have weighed up', she writes to Rohan, 'all the situations which will infallibly lead to the outcomes that I desire.'

Marie Antoinette confesses the peril posed by her coterie: 'I am in a wood surrounded by all the most dangerous and poisonous creatures on the earth's surface', and admits that her own 'imprudence' has left her exposed to blackmail by the Polignacs. But she also expresses full confidence that she can scupper their intrigues and boasts of her power over the king, of having on previous occasions 'chained the lion and made him see and believe everything that I want'. A similar funambulist reasoning must have been invoked in 1784, as Jeanne needed to keep Rohan alert with expectation while compelling him to accept that his reunion with the queen would be delayed. Villette confessed that in the letters from Rohan which he read, the cardinal grumbled about the elevation to the ministry of his enemy, the baron de Breteuil, and the nefarious power that the Polignacs held over the queen.

The 1789 letters attributed to the cardinal seem written by a lover rather than a loyal subject. The very first one, in which Rohan begs for an audience, concludes: 'When your beautiful mouth declares yes, then you will see your slave at your feet and this day will be the happiest of his life.' By the twentieth letter in the correspondence, Rohan is *tutoying* Marie Antoinette.

It is impossible to calculate how far Rohan risked any amorous sentiments in the letters he actually sent. Beugnot, who claimed to have seen them, observed the

> madness of love intensified by the madness of ambition . . . such were the times when a prince of the church did not hesitate to write letters . . . to a woman whom he knew so little and so badly, which in our days a man who wished for the smallest amount of respect would be able to begin reading but would not finish.

There are reasons to doubt Beugnot's testimony: he reported the existence of thousands of letters, when other sources point to far fewer.* But Rohan's situation bore a resemblance to that of a man wooing his mistress out of sight of her husband. He had embarked on a form of courtship – political, if not romantic – and there may have been instances where flattery of the queen could have over-balanced, or deliberately contorted itself, into protestations of affection, desire, even love.

The reigning ideology – the belief in the king's quasi-divinity – conjured forth an extravagance of language that could easily slide from devotion to the queen as the crowning glory of France to admiration of her person, her figure, her lips, to effusions that would sit neatly in a billet-doux. Strait-laced contemporaries compared Marie Antoinette, quite innocently, to the classical goddesses Flora and Venus, but such comparisons might edge into flirtation.

Any letter from a man to a woman, especially in secret, is stamped with an erotic seal. In Fragonard's paintings, the mere presence of writing paper, even if illegible, serves as evidence of an affair. *The Love Letter* (c.1770) shows a young woman with her head pertly turned towards the viewer holding a bunch of flowers out of which a note protrudes; has she bent forward to conceal or to tantalise? Is she teasingly drawing the paper out or coolly slipping it in? The secrecy surrounding Rohan's correspondence inevitably suggested that political bargains might be thrashed out in the queen's bed.

A second gathering of fictional letters caused sputters of fascin-ation, condemnation and hypocrisy on nearly the same scale as the Diamond Necklace Affair. In April 1782, a collection of 175 letters was published in Paris by the bookseller Durand. Together, they told the story of the debauching of a virtuous married woman and the rape-seduction of a teenage girl by an incorrigible yet charming womaniser. Its editor claimed to have sifted the printed selection from a much larger cache – though a publisher's note warns that 'we cannot guarantee its authenticity' – and been forbidden by its owner from amending any stylistic flaws.

The book was Choderlos de Laclos's *Les Liaisons dangereuses*, one of the most popular and notorious novels of the eighteenth century. The

---

* Jeanne claimed that there were two hundred; the baron de Planta testified that most of the queen's responses were conveyed verbally by Jeanne.

modest initial print-run of two thousand copies sold out instantaneously, and between sixteen and twenty further editions were printed in 1782 alone. The review in Grimm's *Correspondance littéraire* called it 'dazzling'. The critic Jean-François de La Harpe said that the book was 'without morality'. Moufle d'Angerville, who admired the novel's construction, denounced its contents as 'very black, it is indeed a pack of horrors and infamies'. Laclos, a provincial artillery officer, was treated like the god Dionysus – one journalist wrote that he 'is feared, admired, celebrated' – and his book, if you believed the stories, infected all who read it: the novelist Rétif de la Bretonne reported that when a mother confiscated a copy from her fifteen-year-old daughter, the girl told an older acquaintance that he could do whatever he wanted with her, so long as she got to finish the story.

Les Liaisons dangereuses is an epistolary novel of great artistry: the letters do not simply recount events but are themselves vectors of the plot – concealed, discovered, expected, exchanged. Cécile Volanges, just out of her convent school, falls in love with the Chevalier Danceny, even though her stern mother has betrothed her to the comte de Gercourt. The marquise de Merteuil – who, despite a reputation for probity, discreetly and voraciously entertains a series of lovers – wishes to exact revenge on Gercourt for jilting her once. So she entices another of her former inamoratos, the vicomte de Valmont, into deflowering Cécile before the marriage, and weasels herself into the young girl's confidence. Valmont's energies are primarily devoted to 'the most ambitious plan I have yet conceived', the seduction of the pious présidente de Tourvel. Valmont treats Merteuil to involved descriptions of his investment of the redoubtable Tourvel, whose resistance, nonetheless, slowly buckles. He also serves as mentor to the chevalier and go-between with his beloved; and the obduracy of the présidente is made more endurable by a diversionary dalliance with – or rather the sexual assault of – Cécile. Merteuil, in turn, enjoys herself with Danceny. Eventually Valmont's cajoling relieves Tourvel of her chastity. The maxim 'revenge is a dish best served cold' is frequently misattributed to the novel – but it is certainly a story in which just desserts are consumed lukewarm.

The Diamond Necklace Affair is shadowed by *Les Liaisons dangereuses*: in the novel, the credulous are entrapped through letters;

intermediaries and confidants exercise a stealthy dominion over those reliant on them; the book even ends with the theft of jewellery. The fictional story twines itself around historical events – inverting, reflecting, distorting. Rohan employs the language of courtship to advance his own political ambitions; Valmont and Merteuil discuss their sexual exploits in the vocabulary of politics and war (which, as Clausewitz would point out a few decades later is 'merely the continuation of policy through other means'). In Ancien Régime France, love and statecraft were more than metaphors for each other. Matters of the heart were of interest to the government, not solely because alliances were soldered together by marriage. It was possible, for example, for a family to obtain a *lettre de cachet* from a minister to lock away an errant child. Merteuil tells Valmont that she rescued her chambermaid from her parents, who had threatened to incarcerate their daughter for a 'folie d'amour'.

The lexicon of the anguished lover – banishment, pardon, captivity – speaks of politics in extremis. The most highly charged term – one that bursts frequently out of the pages of *Les Liaisons dangereuses* – is 'slavery' and its cognates. It encompasses both the successful lover, who demeans himself before his mistress and will cater to any whim in order to retain her affection; and the failed one, reduced to the status of a 'timid slave'.

Valmont's own invocation of the trope is rhetorical, a sham weakness to gain admittance to a woman's affections so that he can lead an insurrection once her guard drops. Slavery had more troubling resonances in Rohan's political courting of Marie Antoinette, as it touched upon the two great popular fears that would express themselves so violently during the French Revolution: dominion by a foreign power and despotism. In a certain light, Rohan strove for a double usurpation: he wished to replace the king in the queen's affections; and, since his elevation to prime minister would be at the instigation of the woman already known as *L'Autrichienne* ('The Austrian bitch'), he would have to accommodate himself to her, displacing French interests with Habsburg ones. The 1789 correspondence manifested a disloyalty not just to king, but to country – the cardinal was willing to become an Austrian cat's paw.

The ideological justification of the Bourbon monarchs rested on a fine – some would argue non-existent – distinction: absolute rulers were not despots and subjects were not slaves. As long as a king ruled within the limits set by the law, his monopoly on power could not be equated with tyranny. Of course, the idea that Louis XVI was able to act without restraint was a fiction – the confidence of the money markets, for example, determined his ability to raise loans – but the exercise of authority had few constitutional checks. In screening Rohan's conduct through *Les Liasions dangereuses*, an allegory of a society ripe for despotism emerges.

There is no direct proof that Rohan actually referred to himself as 'the slave' in his correspondence with the queen. However, in a memorandum he drafted in 1785, he referred to the queen as 'the master' – the same epithet used in the letters which Jeanne attributed to them in 1789 – so it is reasonable to infer he did abase himself. In this, he is akin to Valmont, whom Merteuil compares to 'the Sultan, you have never been either the lover or the friend of a woman, but always either her tyrant or her slave'. Before a conquest the suitor is indentured, his sense of self-worth contingent on the outcome; afterwards, he is triumphant. The vision of politics pursued by Rohan similarly mingles despotism with dependency. While exercising his authority over the rest of the country in his dreamed-of ministry, Rohan would become a lickspittle to the queen, anxious that her support might be removed at any moment. The passing fancies of an individual replace the law at the source of sovereignty. Here lay the horrible future many saw presaged in the Diamond Necklace Affair.

One aspect of the Diamond Necklace Affair confounded contemporaries and still troubles historians today: how could Rohan have believed that the letters he received were written to him by the queen? It seems so implausible that a number of historians have concluded that the cardinal was in some way party to Jeanne's machinations. *Les Liaisons dangereuses* cannot, of course, offer evidence for the defence; but the novel expands upon the manifold ways that letters can misdirect us and invigorate our self-deceptions. Infatuation – with another, in the case of the novel's young lovers; with oneself, in the case of Rohan – creates a holographic universe, in which everything genuflects towards the object of desire. 'Even when the distractions of society carried me far out of your sphere,' Danceny write to Cécile, 'we were never apart . . . In company and in the street I would seize upon the slightest resemblance to you.' The world becomes a parade of semblances or, to put it slightly differently, a series of confirmations, in which likenesses are emphasised at the expense of distinctions, in which the particular carriage of a queen's head can seem like a private signal.

Letters intensify these hallucinations because they purport to offer a landscape of the emotional hinterland while, either deliberately or unintentionally, playing upon the preconceptions of the recipient. The ingenuous Danceny admits as much without realising it: 'A letter is a portrait of the heart, and, unlike a picture, it has not that coldness, that fixity which is so alien to love; it lends itself to all our emotions; it is in turn lively, joyful, at rest.' The slackness of the phrasing – to whose emotions does a letter lend itself? – suggests that a letter's plasticity does not simply lie, as Danceny supposes, in its responsiveness to the writer's mood. The recipient needs to write himself into a letter – or translate it into his own terms – yet this can lead him to blind himself to what was intended, or seize upon particularly suggestive elements that have been laid for him. Rohan thought that he was Valmont – a masterful tactician – while actually being Tourvel, manipulated by Jeanne, who knew him better than he knew himself. What he took for the queen's effusions were transcripts of his own soul.

Merteuil is wise to this fallacy. She advises Cécile that, when writing to her beloved, she should

take more care of your style: You still write like a child . . . you say what you think, and never what you don't believe. You will agree, I am sure, that when you write to someone it is for his sake and not yours. You must therefore try to say less what you think than what you think he will be pleased to hear.

Letters are written for the most specific audience possible and, like any performance, strive for appreciation. The generous language of compliment abuts the insidious language of flattery, and sifting one from the other – or even wanting to – was beyond Rohan's billowing vanity.

Rohan had no reason to doubt the identity of his correspondent, since most letters are composites of previous ones – the same mildewed usages, the same recycled sentiments. Merteuil writes to Danceny:

> I might well say, for example, that it would be a great pleasure to see you, and that I am cross to find people around me who bore me, instead of people who amuse me, but you would translate the same sentence into 'teach me how to live where you are not', so that, I suppose, when you are by your mistress's side you will not know how to live there unless I make a third . . . This is what comes of using a language which nowadays is so abused that it means less even than the jargon of compliment. It has become no more than a set of formulas, and one believes in it no more than one believes in 'your very humble servant'.

The hyperbole of the love letters in *Les Liaisons dangereuses*, which may have been echoed in the correspondence between Rohan and the queen, is a currency. It forms part of a ritual that has been conducted many times before, to which the participants must knowingly conform, in order to consummate their desires. Merteuil felicitously touches upon the rattling inanity, 'your very humble servant', since that was the very part Rohan played before the queen. An abnegation was needed to wash clean the sins of his past, but it was a requirement of etiquette rather than the movement of genuine humility.

A correspondence also nurtures an intimacy that would be precluded in person. Cécile is happy to write to her confidante, Sophie, about her burgeoning love for Danceny, but adds 'perhaps, even with you, to whom I tell everything, if we were to talk about it I should be embarrassed'. An amorous relationship may smoothly develop because barrages of wit can be traded as more sincere feelings incubate. The physical distance gives an impression of safety, makes it easy to imagine that escape is a simple matter should you begin to feel uneasy. But it is harder to wriggle away than you suspect. The tragic predicament of Madame de Tourvel, the reason she is ensnared by Valmont, is that she is too well-mannered to simply break from him: 'While you do everything in your power to oblige me to discontinue this correspondence, it is I who am put to finding some way of sustaining it,' she writes.

Most dangerously, the isolation that letters create is easy to ignore, because the presence of the other writer is felt so intensely through the written word. The touch of a letter, its near-corporal intimacy, is evoked in Fragonard's *Love Letters*. In a glade enclosed with snaking flowers in the foreground and the kissing boughs of two trees, a woman sits upon a pedestal reading a letter. Her lover nuzzles her neck and lays his arm across her waist, though she seems as oblivious to his presence as she is to her propped-up parasol, its erect shaft parallel to the man's slouching spine. To the right of the canvas stands, on a higher pedestal, a statue of Cupid waving at Friendship for attention. But Friendship, looking over the lovers, overlooks the scamp at her feet. This is a garden of absorption. Fragonard's painting crisply clarifies the illusions which letters deliver: your correspondent may seem so close that they are draped across your shoulder, but a letter does not simply resurrect the absent writer. It drags you deeper into yourself, stimulates your own imagination so you may not realise that your lover – or someone more dangerous – is at your back.

It is not known whether Rohan read *Les Liaisons dangereuses*. The chances are that, like most other fashionable and broad-minded cosmopolitans, he did. If so, he failed to absorb its lessons. The book is a compendium of the dangers in sending and receiving letters. In the novel's very first letter, Cécile tells Sophie she is 'sitting as I write at the prettiest desk to which I have been given the key so that I can lock away whatever I wish'. Soon she will be banished to the country after her mother breaks it open and discovers Danceny's love letters. Merteuil, more worldly wise, lists among the precautions she takes to preserve her respectability 'never writing letters' to her lovers. Valmont is grudgingly admitted by Tourvel into her home, where she finally breaks her marriage vows, on the pretext of returning the letters she wrote to him.

Letters are hostages. They contain confessions that we are only willing to reveal to a select group of people. Secrets are divulged in the hope that our confidant will offer advice or incline more favourably towards us. But ink and paper are durable. Our most emotionally naked moments, when we have offered ourselves up unprotected by irony or restraint, can be turned against us if our hazards fail or our trust is betrayed. Rohan's greatest quandary in the spring of 1784 was not deciding whether his correspondent was actually the queen but whether, should things turn sour, his letters might be the death of him. The gamble was large, the potential reward almost without measure.

The exchanges sharpened Rohan's appetite for meeting the queen in person. Jeanne was able to fend him off for a number of weeks with a variety of petty excuses, like the real Marie Antoinette had done after the cardinal returned from Vienna. But as June wore into July, Rohan sensed a discord between the warmth of Marie Antoinette's sentiments and her evasions. Jeanne realised that there was great danger if the cardinal's suspicions proliferated, but her fundamental problem seemed insoluble – she could not produce the queen. With courage forged in desperation, Jeanne hit upon a stratagem so audacious that if it misfired it would, at the very least, expose her deceit to Rohan and cut off his trickling patronage, and might lead to her arraignment, trial, imprisonment or worse. But if, somehow, it succeeded, the cardinal would be unshakeably convinced that Marie Antoinette was his friend, ally and redeemer.

7

To Play the Queen

O N A SUNNY afternoon in July 1784, a woman of thirty-two – blonde-haired, blue-eyed, long-necked and full-figured – sits basking in the gardens of the Palais-Royal. A gentleman, smartly dressed and of distinguished bearing, settles down next to her wearing an expression of determined thoughtfulness, as though worried it might fall off. The man jangles with nerves, looks the woman up and down like a dressmaker during a fitting, then leaves without uttering a word. For a number of days the man returns, each time staring at the woman intently, each time saying nothing.

The Palais-Royal was a free state in the middle of Paris, a sem-inary of sedition and licentiousness, a Bacchic democracy where morality was tossed aside. It had been acquired in the middle of the seventeenth century by the Orléans, the cadet line of the Bourbons, who brooded resentfully over their cousins' supremacy. The complex had been developed during the early 1780s by the duc de Chartres, the Orléans' heir: he erected in its arcades boutiques and cafes, a theatre, a Roman circus where races were held and a waxworks exhibit. It was a lotus-eating paradise, known as 'the capital of Paris', a place, wrote the journalist Louis-Sébastien Mercier, where you would gladly be confined as a prisoner. It was a temple to consump-tion, from disposable gewgaws to bejewelled telescopes, where the vendors would tell you that bronze was gold and paste diamonds were the real deal. In the Caveau, idlers would congregate to eat ice cream and prattle about literature and politics – because the municipal police were forbidden from entering the Palais, you could voice radical opinions here louder than in the rest of the city. Young libertines came to the Palais to graze and brassed-up courtesans mingled indistinguishably with duchesses. There were few hours of the day where an attractive young woman could promenade without a leer or a grope.

When the man finally addresses the woman, he asks permission to accompany her to her apartment and to 'woo her' (the wooing was to be very brief and transactional). The woman agrees – she is an archetypal denizen of the Palais-Royal – and the man becomes a frequent visitor.

Nicole le Guay was born in the parish of Saint Laurent in Paris on 1 September 1751 into a hard-working but poor family. Her mother died when she was young and the savings she had put aside for her daughter's upkeep were stolen by her executors. Even though some of the money was recovered, Nicole ran up debts with loan sharks and was forced, at least temporarily, to turn to prostitution. Earlier in 1784, she had obtained a moratorium against her creditors. She was young, pretty and broke, and with her broad forehead, her straight, chiselled nose and her small, protuberant mouth, she resembled no one so much as Marie Antoinette. And the man Nicole welcomed into her rooms? Well, he was Nicolas de La Motte.

Nicolas described himself as a high-ranking officer, with good prospects for promotion and numerous influential patrons. On his ninth visit, he arrived with an air of 'satisfaction and joy'. 'I have come', he said, 'from a house, where a person of very great standing has spoken much of you. I will take you there this evening.' Nicole was bemused, her only acquaintance with noble gentlemen being quick and carnal: 'I do not know who that could be,' she replied. 'I do not have the honour of knowing any person at Court.' Leaving the mystery hanging in the air, Nicolas left.

He returned that evening and announced to Nicole, who had been fretting all afternoon, that the secret admirer would arrive presently. His wife walked in a moment later. 'You might be a bit surprised by my visit since you don't know me,' said Jeanne, bluntly anticipating Nicole's confusion. Nicole, who had no inkling of the woman's identity, replied politely that 'this surprise can only be agreeable'. Jeanne – at no point giving any indication that she was married to Nicolas – sat down next to Nicole and, smiling, simpering, caressing her hand, looked at her 'with an expression at once mysterious and trusting'; she threw me 'a glance in which', Nicole later remembered, 'I thought I saw the interest and informality of friendship.'

'You can be confident, my dear, in what I am about to tell you,' continued Jeanne. 'I am a respectable woman and well-connected at Court.'

She handed Nicole letters, which she said had been sent to her by Marie Antoinette. The younger woman, who half-realised that perusing the queen's correspondence was as sacrilegious as seeing her naked, could barely bring herself to look.

'But, madame, I don't understand any of this. It is an enigma to me,' said Nicole.

'You will understand me, my dear. I have the queen's total confidence. She and I are as close as two fingers of a hand. She has just given me new proof of this, in charging me to find a person who could do something that will be explained when the time comes. I saw you. If you want to do this, I'll give you 15,000 livres: and the present you'll receive from the queen will be even better. I cannot reveal who I am at the moment, but you'll soon find out. If you don't take me at my word, if you want guarantees for the 15,000 livres, we will go straight away to a lawyer.'

Nicole was thoroughly disconcerted at being asked by the queen for a favour. Turning her down would be unimaginable. Who could refuse to serve their queen? And those 15,000 livres obliterated any lurking qualms: 'I would give my blood, I would sacrifice my life for my sovereign,' she said. 'I could not refuse a demand, whatever it may be, which I believe to have been made in the name of the queen herself.'* It was arranged that Nicolas would collect her the next day.

On 11 August 1784, Nicolas and Nicole left Paris in a remise. They arrived in Versailles at ten o'clock in the evening (Nicolas airily

---

* This conversation was published in Nicole's legal *mémoire* during the trial, in which Nicole was accused of the crime of *lèse-majesté*. Though the conversation must have followed this course, she had an obvious interest in foregrounding her devotion to the queen. This particular outburst is unlikely to be authentic: the hyperbole about laying down her life is out of character; even more damning is the very careful formulation – 'which I believe to have been made in the name of the queen herself' – that seems to have been crafted in hindsight to mitigate her actions.

promised the coachman that someone would be sent to him with the fare – no one ever came). Jeanne greeted them and instructed Nicolas to take Nicole to their rooms on the Place Dauphine, where he left her with Jeanne's chambermaid. Two hours passed in tentative conversation and stagnating silence. The La Mottes returned, glowing with good cheer, at around midnight, and told Nicole that the queen was delighted with her safe arrival and looked forward 'with the most lively impatience' to what was planned. Unable to rein in her curiosity any longer, Nicole asked what was going to happen. 'Oh, it's the smallest thing in the world,' Jeanne replied dismissively. To divert the girl's curiosity, Jeanne now revealed that she and Nicolas were the comte and comtesse de Valois. It was unacceptable, said Jeanne, that Nicole should meet the queen without a title of her own – so she peremptorily dubbed her the baronne d'Oliva.

The next day, Jeanne groomed and dressed d'Oliva. The newly anointed baroness put on a *gaulle* (a dress of white, flecked linen), gathered at the waist by a ribbon, with a translucent ruffle at the neck and sleeves puffed like piped cream. Her head was snugly rimmed with a demi-bonnet. Jeanne handed d'Oliva a tiny letter, saying: 'I will lead you this evening to the park, and you will hand over this letter to a very noble seigneur whom you will meet there.' The outside of the letter was blank and no clue was given as to its contents.

As midnight approached, d'Oliva was taken towards Versailles by Jeanne and Nicolas. Louis XIV had devoted thirty years of his life to modelling the gardens at the rear of the palace, and was so obsessed with his creation that he wrote the first guidebook to them, the *Manière de montrer les jardins de Versailles*. An area extending over 230 acres had required draining, flattening, terracing, planting and irrigating. From the gravelled parterre on the central axis, the Sun King looked down to the fountain of Apollo, the Sun God, which stood at the tip of the Grand Canal. Flanking this vista stood a number of *bosquets*, densely planted with espaliered trees – hazels and maples, sycamores, elms and hornbeams – that were accessible only by narrow paths, in the middle of which an explorer might find platoons of statuary, an Arc de Triomphe firing off bursts of water or, in the case of the Salle de Bal, an amphitheatre.

Once on the parterre, Jeanne gave d'Oliva a rose. 'You will hand over the rose with the letter to the person who introduces himself to you, and the only thing you will say will be "You know what this means",' instructed Jeanne. 'The queen will be there to see how your interview goes. She will speak to you later. She is there. She will be behind you. You yourself will get to speak to her very soon.' D'Oliva's skin itched with awe. 'I don't know how to address a queen,' she said. 'Just call her Your Majesty,' replied Nicolas, as though she were about to visit the doctor or go to confession. Suddenly, a man loomed into view. 'Ah, there you are,' he said and, having confirmed their arrival, strode off into the black. Tacking south-west, the three figures descended to the Bosquet de Venus, named after the bronze cast of the Medici Venus which stood there (in theory the gardens were for the use of the royal family alone, but it was easy to obtain a key if you knew the right people). A snaggle of trails writhed around a clearing at its centre, where the royal family picnicked during the summer. Once they had settled d'Oliva in position, Jeanne and Nicolas darted back the way they had come. The darkness was absolute, the moon buried by clouds. A citric tang, drifting down from the Orangerie, played at the girl's nostrils. D'Oliva heard only the hoots of the owls and the rapid tread of her heart, as her eyes, adjusting to the darkness, searched out the hidden queen.

As d'Oliva and Nicolas were driving to Versailles, another carriage had bounced in the same direction. It contained Jeanne and the baron de Planta, who had been summoned by Rohan to assist on a very delicate mission. For a number of weeks, Jeanne had tantalised Rohan with the prospect of a meeting with Marie Antoinette. 'If you just happen to be in the park at Versailles,' she told him, 'perhaps some day you will be fortunate enough to meet the queen, so she can confirm herself the consolatory change in circumstances that I foresee for you.' Rohan spent a number of fruitless evenings mooning through the garden's walks and poking around bowers.

But then, on 12 August, he received word through Jeanne that the queen was willing to see him. The tête-à-tête could not happen in the palace itself, as the queen was not yet ready to reveal their concord to the world, but something more discreet was on offer. So, trying to look unobtrusive in a plain, black soutane and a drooping, broad-brimmed hat, the cardinal was to be found late that evening on the palace terrace, loitering nervily with de Planta by his side. Up scurried Jeanne, masked in a black domino and hyper-ventilating. 'I have just left the queen,' she said as she shuffled the cardinal towards the grove, 'she is very upset. She will not be able to extend the interview as she wanted. Madame' – Louis XVI's sister – 'and Madame d'Artois have suggested a walk with her. She will escape them and, despite the short window, she will give you unequivocal proofs of her protection and benevolence.' Jeanne took Rohan to the Bosquet de Venus and left him at the opening of the clearing.

He would have seen her first, the solitary, female figure whose dress glowed grey against the leaves. She would have heard his muffled tramp on the sward before she saw his outline. The regal features looked familiar to him, as did her clothing. She had no idea who he was. A drunken priest lost on the way home? An emissary from hell? He didn't look much like a mighty lord. He kneels at her feet in submission. Dumb with fear of the unknown man and her exalted audience, she thrusts the rose towards him – as though a rat had materialised in her hands – unable even to look him in the eyes. She raises her fan to hide her face (he thinks she is flicking away a frond of hair). Words scratch around her dry throat. Perhaps she says, 'You know what this means.' But she's not thinking clearly any more. He will later claim that she said 'You may believe that the past will be forgotten.' But that might just have been what he wanted to hear.

A rustle of bushes. Footsteps. Voices. Jeanne hurtles into the grove, whispering urgently 'quick, quick, go' (maybe you're allowed to drop 'Your Majesty' in an emergency). Madame Elisabeth and the comtesse d'Artois are close by. At least, someone is. Villette, for instance, stomping about, the foliage his castanets. Nicolas peels d'Oliva away, Jeanne returns Rohan to Planta on the terrace, the cardinal still muttering angrily about the curtailment. It was only on the way home that d'Oliva realised that she had forgotten to hand over the letter. Jeanne did not care. 'The queen could not be more happy than with what has just been done,' she told her. The table was laid, wine poured, and Nicolas, Jeanne and d'Oliva drank and joked through the night.

In the morning, Jeanne showed d'Oliva a letter that she had received from Marie Antoinette: 'I am very happy, my dear countess, with the person you procured for me. She played her role to perfection and I beg you to inform her that she is assured a satisfactory arrangement.' Jeanne then ripped up the letter – it was 'not the sort of thing to carry around with you'.

The purpose of the scene in the *bosquet* – to lock Rohan irredeemably in the prison-house of his fantasies – is easy to comprehend. But its interpretation by Rohan, its complex meaning for Jeanne, and its political undertones need careful teasing out. First, the name. As historians of the affair have noted, 'Oliva' is a near anagram of 'Valois' (it is sometimes spelt 'Olisva', in which case it is a perfect one). But why did Jeanne choose a name that would make it harder to cut herself loose from her accomplice, if her fraud were later exposed? The answer may be found in the Janus-faced signification of the performance – for Jeanne it fulfilled not merely a pragmatic need, but also a psychological one. She did not merely regard herself as the queen's equal, but her equivalent. The romance of her Valois ancestors led her to imagine that she could – perhaps ought to – be a queen herself. This was a fantasy of which, perhaps, she was only partly aware. But she contrived ways in which she could play the queen. In the letters to Rohan, Jeanne spoke in the queen's voice. And in the Bosquet de Venus, on that night of doubles, Jeanne herself performed a double doubling, hovering above the genuflecting Rohan within the scrambled name she had accorded her lead actress; and secreted among the leaves, where d'Oliva believed the true queen watched on. Jeanne spectrally wore the crown, while travestying Marie Antoinette: if she and her cronies refused to admit a Valois into their society, Jeanne would show that the only difference between a prostitute and a queen was a clean dress and a dark night.

D'Oliva's outfit had not been unthinkingly thrown together. In 1783, to much consternation, the queen's favoured artist, Elisabeth Vigée-Lebrun, exhibited *La Reine en gaulle* at the Salon. The picture showed the queen wearing a straw hat with a wide, sinuous brim that sunk on the left-hand side under the weight of a blue-grey plume, ponderous as a rain cloud. Her uncombed hair hangs loose. She is dressed in a muslin *gaulle*, cinched at the waist with a ribbon of gold silk, the only regal flash in the painting. In her left hand she holds a bouquet of roses, which she is tying together. There was not an architectonic hairpiece or a silken gown in sight – *La Reine en gaulle* is the closest extant representation of the milkmaid queen.

The queen had begun to wear *gaulles* in 1780. They were cool in summer – the trend had been inspired by the wives of colonists in the West Indies – and did not require rigging on a whalebone cupola. Visitors to the Salon, however, thought the get-up at best unbecoming to her station – one said she was 'dressed like a serving-maid'; another that she was 'wearing a chambermaid's dust-cloth' – and at worst indecently sluttish. Many believed she had been painted in her underwear. Others were more concerned about the geopolitical implications of the painting. Were the Habsburg rose and the muslin from the Austrian Netherlands signals that the queen inclined more towards Germany than France? On that summer night, Rohan did not simply see the queen. He saw a woman of loose clothes and looser morals, a woman with sufficient political independence to raise him up. When he encountered d'Oliva, he may also have wondered whether he would be rehabilitated with benefits. Why else did she press a rose in his hand? Why else did she arrange to meet him in the grove dedicated to the goddess of love?

The royal gardens were trysting places – there were plenty of nooks in which petticoats were shifted and giggles evaporated without detection. Police arrested numerous prostitutes trawling the grounds: in 1784 Gervais Mausard, one of the queen's coachmen, was caught in a 'most indecent position' with Catherine Godroi. How the queen behaved there was the subject of fervid speculation. During her pregnancy in the summer of 1778, she found the daytime heat too oppressive for promenading, so would sit on the terrace during the evening. Dressed casually and with her face obscured by a slouchy hat, she strolled incognito – so she thought – among those gathered to take the evening air. Young gallants approached her, inured from reproach by her efforts at disguise. The gentle flirtation was innocent but the queen's informal clothes and the whispered conversations gave a risqué impression. Her night walks, wrote Mercy-Argenteau to Maria Theresa, 'provoked a lot of criticism in Paris'. Her behaviour was distorted into something more sordid by those who felt excluded – a private concert on the colonnade led to jokes about which kind of instruments were played. One pamphlet, *Le Lever de l'aurore*, twisted an innocent jaunt to see the sun rise above the gardens of Marly into an orgy in which the queen rolled around the turf, copulating indiscriminately with courtiers. By staging the reconciliation in the gardens of Versailles, Jeanne heightened the sexual piquancy of the occasion.*

Rose Bertin, Marie Antoinette's dressmaker, called the masquerade a 'story that would barely be credible in a bad novel'. It reminded her of La Fontaine's fable, 'Le Magnifique', in which a young blade wishes to make love to the wife of a jealous miser, Aldobrandin (it was dramatised by Antoine Houdar de La Motte – no relation – in 1753, and turned into an opera by one of the queen's favourite composers, André Grétry, twenty years later). Le Magnifique offers to sell his horse to Aldobrandin in exchange for fifteen minutes with his wife – which Aldobrandin will supervise at a distance, so the pair can be seen but not heard. Aldobrandin agrees but, cunningly, forbids his wife from uttering a word to Le Magnifique. Once Le Magnifique twigs that the woman will not reply, he takes up her part in the conversation, agreeing to meet himself later that evening at the bottom of the gardens. After Aldobrandin goes to the country to train the spirited horse, Le Magnifique and the wife spend an enjoyable few days in the garden lodge.

La Fontaine's tale comprehends how the confidence bred by a lover's past successes enables him to seize control of the dynamics of court-ship; to narrate the story, not merely participate. Rohan was easily

---

* A number of historians, such as Louis Hastier, have suggested that the queen herself actually organised the performance to mock the cardinal. The only evidence on offer is a snippet from a letter from Marie Antoinette to Mercy-Argenteau written on 19 May 1786 – during the trial – that reads: 'I say nothing to you of the great affair; the baron will tell you my thoughts, especially about not speaking of the meeting and the terrace, and he will explain my reasons.' It is not obvious that the 'great affair', as these historians assume, refers to the affair of the necklace. And a grove, rather than the terrace, was the stage on which the gulling was played out. These events were by this time well known and had been so for a number of months, so why would Marie Antoinette only now have instructed Mercy to hold his tongue, if she had in some way been involved?

beguiled by Jeanne because the assignation in the *bosquet* tallied with the fables he told himself: it confirmed his own seductive prowess, but it also cast him as the hero of a romantic adventure. What seems to us and seemed to his contemporaries incredible – that he believed he had met the queen under these circumstances – was swallowed smoothly in the thrill of self-dramatisation. The story being written for him meshed with the one he believed he was writing for himself, and the satisfactions that arose from it – the secret preparations, the surmounting of obstacles, the flirtation with danger – left him furiously dreaming the tale's conclusion, not attending to the implausibilities and inconsistencies of the present. You are never more unwittingly in peril than when you think you're the author of your own fate, but are in fact a character in someone else's plot.

There are also parallels in two fine plays, one of which may well have provided Jeanne with her inspiration. That summer, the Comédie-Française was staging its most successful production ever. *The Marriage of Figaro*, the sequel to the popular *Barber of Seville*, had suffered a protracted gestation – nearly a decade had elapsed before it reached the public. Five censors quashed it, and Louis XVI, after reading the play himself, forbade its performance or publication, abhorring its broadsides against the justice system, the prisons, venality and the state-run press. 'The man mocks everything that should be respected in a government,' said the king of its author – and sometime government agent and gunrunner – Pierre-Augustin Caron de Beaumarchais. Most troubling was the indictment of aristocratic decadence and abuse. Count Almaviva, Figaro's employer, claims to have given up the feudal privilege of droit de seigneur, but does not relent from pursuing Suzanne, Figaro's intended, and threatening to stop the couple's marriage if she denies him a tumble. Despite this unflattering portrait, the play had a number of noble supporters, especially among the light-headed companions of Marie Antoinette – the Polignacs, the comte d'Artois, the comte de Vaudreuil – who thought that outrage at Beaumarchais's wit was a terribly common reaction. Vaudreuil organised a private performance, and in 1784 a sixth censor finally approved the play and the king withdrew his objections.

In *The Marriage of Figaro*, Suzanne arranges to meet Almaviva at night in a grove of chestnut trees in the gardens of his castle. Her mistress, the countess, tricks herself out like Suzanne and takes her place, in order to catch her husband misbehaving. But Almaviva is no Rohan. Where the cardinal is too eager to believe, he is tetchy with suspicions. Like a tyrant, he threatens his family and staff with exile and imprisonment, but much of the play's comedy derives from the feisty disregard with which he is treated – doors are locked on him, servants talk back, orders are ignored.

Jeanne may have found in *Figaro* a moral justification for her actions, albeit in a roundabout way. While Figaro arrives first at the scheme of replacing Suzanne with a double, it is the countess who later suggests to Suzanne, without Figaro's knowledge, that she herself plays the role. By aligning herself with the irrepressible and inventive Figaro – who, in his famous soliloquy, enumerates the Establishment's successes in suppressing his endeavours – Jeanne became the scourge of the order that had refused to embrace her, deriding its foibles and its pretensions to authority. But she also, perhaps, saw her scheme as a last resort. Just as the countess used deception to recall her husband to the noble values he had cast aside, Jeanne's staging brought to a head a process in which, at least in the theatre of Rohan's mind, she had re-established her family in its rightful position – among royalty. *The Marriage of Figaro*, which ends indulgently – as comedies do – with the characters forgiving each other, reconciled the conflicting impulses which were the inheritance of Jeanne's generation: a thoroughly modern sense of aspiration that wished to break free from the restraining privileges of the aristocracy; and a nostalgia for a time where true nobility would be immediately recognised through its innate virtues.

A young lady cut adrift from her family, a great woman who secludes herself, an official who believes that his mistress is in love with him, dressing up, forged letters and trickery in a garden – all these are found in Shakespeare's *Twelfth Night* too. The play was not well known in eighteenth-century France. It seems there was no professional production before the Revolution – its tonal ambiguity, its swerving from tavern talk to tenderness to a kind of sadism make it a prime example of the lack of taste for which detractors like Voltaire condemned Shakespeare. Pierre-Antoine de La Place's *Le Théâtre Anglois*, an eight-volume work published between 1745 and 1748, contains a brief precis that, with a concern for purity of language and plot, omits any reference to any of the comic characters: Malvolio, Sir Toby Belch, Sir Andrew Aguecheek, Feste and Maria. The play is relegated to the nineteenth volume of the first ever translation into French – by Pierre Le Tourneur – of the complete plays of Shakespeare. A 'Monsieur Lamotte' is listed among the subscribers who funded the project, though the name is a common one. The cardinal, however, was a subscriber – he is listed as the Prince de Rohan – so it is possible that Jeanne, during a visit to the Hôtel de Rohan-Strasbourg, may have glanced through the translation, which appeared in 1783 as *La Soirée des rois*, the year before she began her machinations.

One aspect of the affinity appears to stretch the bounds of coincidence. 'D'Oliva' is not only a shuffling of 'Valoi': it is also an exact anagram of Viola, the heroine of *Twelfth Night*, and is contained within the names of Olivia and Malvolio. Each of these characters is the fictional counterpart of the players in Jeanne's drama: Viola transforms herself into Cesario by disguising herself as a boy, just as Nicole le Guay becomes the queen with a change of clothes; Olivia, the reclusive countess, mirrors Marie Antoinette, whose aloofness enables Jeanne's plan to succeed; and Malvolio, Olivia's steward who, finding a letter planted in her garden, convinces himself that the woman he serves loves him, shadows Rohan. Anagrams are a particularly appropriate wormhole into Shakespeare's play. The letter Malvolio finds is addressed to 'M.O.A.I'. He worries that the order differs from his own name, but concludes that 'to crush this a little, it would bow to me, for every one of these letters are in my name'. 'If this falls into thy hand, revolve,' the letter continues. Annotators gloss 'revolve' as 'consider' or 'contemplate' (Le Tourneur translates it as 'médite-la'). But it is also an instruction to rearrange the letters and to revolutionise his comportment, to smear a rictus across his face in place of his stern demeanour, and prance about 'in yellow stockings, and cross-gartered'. 'Revolution' was still, in 1784, an innocent word but, by the end of the century, a thread would be traced from that night in the garden to the guillotine. We will never know if Jeanne read *Twelfth Night* and cast the cardinal as Malvolio; Rohan should have. Had he done so, he would have seen that Malvolio, having obeyed the letter's instructions, is deemed mad by his mistress, thrust into 'a dark room and bound', and leaves the stage swearing his revenge 'on the whole pack of you'.

8

Diamonds and Best Friends

L IKE SO MANY of the La Mottes' friendships, d'Oliva's began with sugared compliments and ended with an acrid taste. After d'Oliva returned to Paris, she dined regularly with the couple, and they attended a performance of *The Marriage of Figaro* together to celebrate their triumph. But Jeanne was less forthcoming where money was concerned. Eventually d'Oliva received nearly 4,000 livres, about a quarter of the promised amount. She, however, had moved into more expensive rooms in anticipation of a greater wind-fall. But who would believe her if she complained that the queen owed her money for giving a rose to a lord on a summer's evening in Versailles? Her lamentations made it simple for Jeanne to distance herself. They no longer ate together; when they did meet, Jeanne's tone became 'formal and grave'; and by the beginning of October the La Mottes had stopped seeing d'Oliva entirely.

How did Jeanne find 4,000 livres? Shortly after the midnight meeting, once Rohan had returned to Saverne, Jeanne offered him the opportunity to impress Marie Antoinette further. The queen was worried about a poor family in urgent need of 60,000 livres. Unfortunately, she did not have ready money available. Could Rohan help her out? This was the stress test of Jeanne's plan; if Rohan refused, then he must have seen through her charade. Strung out, Jeanne waited for the courier. When he arrived with a full purse, Jeanne celebrated, 'drunk with joy'.

It's a strange kind of poor family that needs 60,000 livres, though one leading French family had recently required assistance on an even larger scale. Two years previously, Rohan's cousin, the prince de Guéméné, the grand chamberlain of France, had been declared bankrupt with debts of 32 million livres. He had run an ill-conceived scheme, selling annuities and funding them with credit. When rumours about his financial position deterred his lenders, thousands of ordinary Frenchman lost their investments. The princesse de Guéméné who, as a close friend of Marie Antoinette and governess of her children, was the most influential Rohan at Court, resigned from her office in shame. The cardinal led the family's efforts to consolidate the debts, negotiating doggedly and impressing his uncle Soubise with 'his decisiveness and industry'. He even felt a leap of pride in the vast scale of the indebtedness: 'It is only a king or a Rohan who could make such a bankruptcy.' The prince's disgrace left the cardinal the undisputed leader of his generation of Rohan (he and Guéméné had been frostily jockeying for position). But his own wealth, already depleted, crumpled under the burden – over 300,000 livres were siphoned down the Guéméné sump.

Rohan needed to take out a loan for the 60,000 livres. Nonetheless, he instructed de Planta to draw on the funds in his treasury, even sell valuables, should Jeanne make further demands. Rohan felt reassured that the queen's embrace was genuine, yet the syrupy pace of developments continued to vex him. The brief exchange in the *bosquet* only exacerbated his sense of the queen's remoteness, day on day, and worries over his still-unsecured promotion to prime minister plucked at him. An inveterate gossip, Rohan was frustrated at being forbidden from sharing his reversal of fortune; there was always another reason – potential allies in need of convincing, the king's tidal moods, the intrigues of his enemies – that precluded a public acknowledgement of his return to favour.

Jeanne's reassurances were deftly improvised. Having noticed that the queen bobbed her head in a curious fashion each time she wandered through one of the doorways in Versailles, Jeanne – as Madame Cahouet de Villers had done – stationed Rohan in her line of sight and told him that the queen would silently signal her good wishes. As the queen walked past, the man standing next to the cardinal remarked that the queen's attentiveness seemed overt: 'I don't know why they say that there is bad blood between you and the queen, for she appears to be looking at you with great kindness.' But tricks like this were single-shot – Rohan's angst still needed managing. So early in September, the cardinal received a letter from Marie Antoinette ordering him to Alsace, while final preparations were made, so she intimated, for his unveiling.

Had you popped into the La Mottes' place on the rue Neuve-Saint-Gilles in the late summer of 1784, you would have noticed that the apartment looked considerably sprucer than normal. The furniture no longer moulted; a new clock supervised the salon; Jeanne's wrists and fingers were now armoured with gold jewellery. Though Jeanne maintained a facade of indigence towards Rohan – he still sent her a spill of money every now and then – she paraded her wealth to everyone else, and made clear that it flowed from the cardinal and Marie Antoinette.

Jeanne's profligate invocation of the queen's name quickly reverberated among people who knew she was lying: 'You boasted of seeing the queen,' a friend warned her, 'of often spending time with Her Majesty, of chatting with her. Leonard, the queen's hairdresser, who heard you do it, said that he would only need to say a word to the queen, and you would be locked up for the rest of your days. He said that you've never approached the queen. If you bragged about this, and it is not the case, you will be doomed.' Jeanne replied with provocative ingenuousness: 'I don't boast of speaking to the queen. I see Her Majesty and mention it to no one.' But she took care to make sure that Leonard was sufficiently satisfied not to report her. Most people were happy to believe her; the rest could be bought off.

Money bred more money, fraud more fraud. A consortium of Lyonnaise businessmen approached Jeanne with a project they thought might be of interest to the government. Could Rohan facilitate an introduction? Jeanne would not arrange a meeting with the cardinal unless her palm was crossed with gold, though she was not, they should understand, mercenary: the cardinal insisted on it, since she was always doing good to others without any thought for her own welfare. A gift of gorgeous silks worth 12,000 livres arrived from Lyons. Strangely, Jeanne showed no more interest in the scheme.

Jeanne enjoyed the fawning which attended the influx of riches. But she still yearned, more than anything, for recognition from her own people in Champagne. She wished to replace their memories of the uppity, penniless youth, who had married because she could not keep her petticoats on, by returning as a wealthy and esteemed lady. On 8 September 1784, heralded by two outriders, the La Mottes set off to Bar-sur-Aube with a fleet of new carriages – a cabriolet, a coach and a berlin drawn by five horses. Jeanne had insouciantly written to her old friend Beugnot, informing him that she had sent her things ahead, and asking him to make arrangements for her accommodation. Beugnot was astounded to see an enormous wagon, wheezing like a consumptive under the weight of so many furnishings, draw up in the centre of Bar.

Jeanne insisted that a woman of her standing needed a country residence. Beugnot recommended a modest property but Jeanne bought the biggest house in town for double its value, then instructed architects to make further improvements. Chandeliers were hung, crystal polished, Sèvres vases stood guard. Gemstones dripped from Jeanne's garments like sweat, and a battalion of servants was costumed in liveries threaded with gold. These adornments required more than the cardinal's fat purse, but Jeanne was able to leverage her ostentatious wealth into credit with the town's merchants.

For the most part Jeanne was received cordially. Even the duc de Penthièvre, a prince of the blood – his father was the legitimated son of Louis XIV – and a man who hauled up the drawbridge to *nouveaus*, welcomed her. Some, though, had longer memories. Respectable women, worried that their daughters' heads might be filled with fanciful ideas, sought reasons to turn down invitations to her soirées. Jeanne, in turn, resented being shunned. She had wanted to take her place at the summit of society, to be admired but also loved by those whose charity she had lived off, but a number of her former friends regarded her more as a flash, condescending Parisian than a native girl done good.

When funds ran low in November 1784, Jeanne returned to Paris. Another note was sent by Marie Antoinette to Rohan in Saverne, with a request for 100,000 livres. Planta rode hard from Alsace to deliver the sum in person. Jeanne's aspirations for her siblings bloomed under the shower of Rohan's munificence: her brother Jacques ought to leave the navy – 'a thankless and boring service in peacetime' – for a position in a prestigious regiment; her sister would become a canoness; her husband, a captain at least, if he couldn't obtain a colonelcy. In the Marais, the La Mottes kept open table, and were so generous that friends were invited to dine there even if they were absent. 'Coquettes, kept girls, conniving monks, ruined officers, idle lawyers [and] tradesmen' was one cynical contemporary's epitome of the company you would expect to find. But judges, generals and senior royal officials also made an appearance, enjoying the demi-mondaine frisson that arose from mixing with carnivorous sharpers and women whose reputation was certainly not in doubt.

The La Mottes were finally hauling themselves into society, but their marriage, never bursting with love, grew increasingly strained. 'If I had married a man with a name and position at Court, as would have been easy for me,' Jeanne grumbled to Beugnot, 'I would be rising faster; but my husband is an obstacle to me rather than of use. In order to achieve anything I must put my name above his, and that flies in the face of social conventions.' They were repeatedly unfaithful to each other, though Nicolas was particularly shameless, bringing his mistress home for dinner. Jeanne reacted to her husband's infidelity histrionically – once she stormed off to the convent at Longchamps, swearing she would become a nun (she returned soon enough). She threatened suicide at least twice: on one occasion Nicolas grabbed her as she reared onto the windowsill; on another, he knocked a pistol out of her hand with a well-aimed book. The pressures multiplied beyond marital disagreement. She always had to wear a mask – of poverty to the cardinal, of carefree wealth to everyone else – yet her income was insufficient to sustain her opulence. The fear that Rohan would discover her deception squatted on her, especially since the longer a second meeting with the queen was delayed, the more difficult sustaining the pretence became. With exquisite timing, a business opportunity arose that would, if successful, dispel any worries about money for ever. All Jeanne needed was a dupe of prodigious credulity. Luckily, she knew exactly where to find one.

The necklace comprised 647 diamonds weighing 2,800 carats. Seventeen shallot-sized diamonds formed a choker round the neck, from which three festoons lolled. Two rows of smaller stones ran crosswise like bandoliers from the shoulders, meeting at the breast-bone. Two frills of diamonds hung from this knot, pawing at the waist like withered forearms. Down the back hung two streamers which counterbalanced the weight of the necklace and prevented the wearer from toppling forwards. Grotesque and almost literally unbearable, it more resembled an item of chain mail or something a monk might wear in penitential self-chastisement than a coveted piece of jewellery. But some contemporaries were complimentary: the marquis de Bombelles described it as 'one of the best possible examples of its type, due to the size, purity, regularity and sparkle of the stones'. It had been compiled by two Saxons, Charles Boehmer and Paul Bassenge, whose business had flourished under Louis XV: Boehmer, the senior partner, held the offices of crown jeweller and jeweller to the queen. The style was known as a *collier d'esclavage*, a necklace of slavery – an apt name, since it threatened to ruin its artificers' business.

Why the Boehmers, as the firm was known, chose to invest so much money in a single piece is unclear, though by the time the necklace acquired its notoriety it was widely assumed to have been commissioned by Louis XV as a gift for his mistress, Madame du Barry. Though the king inconveniently died before the Boehmers had completed it, they were confident they could sell their handi-work to the new queen. Since arriving in Court, she had spent nearly one million livres on jewellery: a set of earrings, each with three pear-drop diamonds; diamond bracelets; a fan barnacled with rocks. It seemed like a done deal. But Marie Antoinette despised shoulder-cracking parures of the kind the Boehmers had created; she rarely wore necklaces at all, since they detracted from her neck's sinuous grace; and, in addition to her purchases, she had inherited a vast quantity of gems from her late mother-in-law. As early as 1776 she had told Boehmer she had no interest in buying any more jewellery.

The Boehmers considered this denial little more than a coquettish tease by a woman with a reputation for extravagance. At the beginning of 1782, the prospect of a sale recrudesced when the king retained the necklace with a view to acquiring it, but considerations of greater magnitude confounded matters: on 12 April, the French

Caribbean fleet was defeated by the British in the Battle of the Saintes, losing five vessels. When the jewellers finally asked the queen whether she intended to buy the necklace, she reportedly replied that 'we stand more in need of ships than jewels'.

The jewellers' business was suffocated by the interest payments. Boehmer tried hawking the necklace around the courts of Europe – a paste model was sent to the Spanish Court for the Princess de Asturias to examine – but no sovereign was prepared to meet the asking price. In despair, he sought an audience with Marie Antoinette, who did not suspect that her jeweller would hurl himself on the floor weeping, wring his hands and declare: 'Madame I am ruined and disgraced if you do not purchase my necklace. I cannot outlive so many misfortunes. When I leave here, I shall throw myself into the river.'

Queens do not expect to be emotionally blackmailed by tradesmen, and Marie Antoinette scolded Boehmer for his outburst:

> Rise Boehmer, I do not like these rhapsodies. Honest men have no need to fall to their knees when making their petitions. If you were to kill yourself, I should regret it as the act of a madman in whom I have taken an interest, but I would not hold myself responsible in any way for that misfortune. Not only did I never order the article that is the cause of your present despair, but whenever you have talked to me about that fine collection of jewels, I have told you that I should not add four diamonds to those which I already possess. I told you in person that I refuse to buy the necklace; the king wished to give it to me, but I refused him also. Never mention it again to me. Divide it and try to sell it piecemeal, and do not drown yourself. I am very angry with you acting out this scene of despair in my presence and before my child.* Never let me see you behave in this way again. Go.

Boehmer would not countenance dismembering the creation he saw as the pinnacle of his professional career, and flogging the diamonds individually might pay for the interest but would reflect poorly on his commercial acumen. In its safebox the necklace continued to

---

* Her daughter was in the room.

hang like a halter, blistering the partnership. All the while the Boehmers' creditors circled, pecking away with enquiries about repayment.

Optimistic to the point of delusion, Boehmer convinced himself that the crown's financial retrenchment would be abandoned once peace with Britain was concluded at the end of the American War of Independence. Then, he was certain, the king or queen would be disposed towards buying the necklace. By the end of 1784, nearly two years after the treaty was signed, the queen's pregnancy was evident to all, and the jewellers knew that a royal birth meant presents for everyone. But, having exhausted all their goodwill with Marie Antoinette, they sought a more acceptable paraclete.

Bassenge hoped that a friend of his, Louis-François Achet, a lawyer who held an office in the comte de Provence's household, might know someone – or at least know someone who knew someone. In December 1784 Achet told the jewellers that his son-in-law Jean-Baptiste Laporte, another lawyer, was an acquaintance of the comtesse de La Motte-Valois, who everyone knew – didn't they? – was a bosom friend of the queen. Laporte agreed to broach the matter with Jeanne.

Jeanne was initially coy, ducking away from any commitment. She did agree to examine the necklace, which gave the jewellers hope of convincing her to intervene, and Jeanne time to ponder how she might inflect this opportunity to her advantage. On 29 December, Bassenge, Achet and Laporte escorted the necklace from the jewellers' atelier to the rue Neuve-Saint-Gilles (Boehmer, who had a feeble constitution, was laid up in bed). Bassenge dropped the small talk. As soon as he was introduced to Jeanne, he implored her to speak to the king and queen on his behalf. Tell them, he said as he raised the lid on the necklace's case, that they would secure the Boehmers' happiness 'if they deigned to unload such a heavy burden'.

Jeanne affected a polite lack of interest: 'I desire greatly to be useful,' she said, 'but I don't like to embroil myself in these sorts of affairs' (something of a surprise to Laporte, who knew all about the Lyonnaise merchants). But the meeting was not entirely fruitless for the jewellers – if the chance arose, Jeanne promised, she would speak to the queen of their concerns.

Anyone would have been astonished by the sheer quantity of gems in the *collier d'esclavage*, by the sheer amount of crystallised money bound up in it, by its unsold dead weight. The image did not lie inert in Jeanne's mind. The necklace unlaced itself, stones spun loose, each diamond splintered into thousands of hard specks; these flattened into gold coins, flashed into silk and taffeta, ormolu and marble, carriage clocks and music boxes and firedogs and rose-wood cabinets, a motte of horses and houses and coaches and bobbing servants, and at the summit of this profusion, drunk on riches, Jeanne and Nicolas sat, surrounded by more money than they could ever squander.

On 5 January 1785, the last day of Christmas, the cardinal de Rohan was summoned from Saverne to Paris by an enigmatic note from Marie Antoinette. She was still not in a position to recognise publicly their reconcilement, but spoke of 'a secret negotiation' for which she needed his assistance. The comtesse would explain everything. On his arrival, Jeanne presented Rohan with another letter from the queen, in which Marie Antoinette declared her wish to buy the Boehmers' necklace and, not wanting to bargain in person, asked the cardinal to negotiate on her behalf. It was a mark of her high regard, the queen added, that she had entrusted him with such a delicate task.

Rohan was eager to assist, but needed some time to consider the matter. It was unclear from the queen's note if he was expected to advance the money himself and, if so, when he would be paid back. Saddled with the Guéméné debts, and with the restoration of Saverne ongoing, he was not in a position to tap the amount required – the baron de Planta was horrified Rohan was even contemplating involvement. Yet at no point did Rohan pause over the queen's decision to buy the necklace secretly – her well-known debts and prodigality led him to surmise that she needed to hide the acquisition from the king.

For three weeks the jewellers heard nothing, eventually assuming that Jeanne had decided to remain aloof. Bassenge told Achet that his anxiety over the necklace was overwhelming and he was prepared to offer 1,000 louis to whoever could engineer a sale, an enticement which convinced Achet it was worth supplicating Jeanne just one more time. Before he had an opportunity to call on her, however, she summoned him to dinner, where she announced that she needed to speak with the jewellers as soon as possible.

On the next day, 21 January, Bassenge and Achet returned to Jeanne's apartment. She informed them that, within a few days, they would have 'heartwarming news' about the necklace. The queen desired it but, for reasons which could not be revealed, would not deal directly with the jewellers. A 'distinguished nobleman' had been instructed to settle all the arrangements. Jeanne warned, at the same time, that all necessary precautions should be taken with this man. Bassenge, with a jig of relief, offered to reward Jeanne for her brokerage, but she refused – the only gratification she needed was the pleasure which came from helping those in difficulties.

Had you looked out of a glacial window on the rue Neuve-Saint-Louis early in the morning of the 24 January 1785, you might have noticed two figures scuttling up the road. If you were suspiciously minded, you would have seen that the cloaks hugged tightly against the frost served also to mask their faces. They were headed to the Boehmers' shop on the rue de Vendôme, now the rue Béranger, in the north-eastern corner of the Marais. Wary of being spotted, the pair slid in through the coach door. The jewellers, who lived on the first floor, were still in bed. Bassenge, his mind still lumbering with sleep, told his servant that whoever had arrived must come upstairs if they wished to speak to him. He crackled awake when Jeanne and Nicolas entered. They informed him that the distinguished nobleman would arrive shortly to discuss buying the necklace. Jeanne reiterated that it was Bassenge's responsibility to ensure due diligence was carried out; she also asked that her name and the necklace should never again be mentioned together.

As soon as the La Mottes had left, Bassenge dashed into Boehmer's room and shook his ailing partner awake. Boehmer had barely dressed when Rohan entered the shop, fifteen minutes after Jeanne's departure. Both parties hummed with nerves, both were wary of raising the matter of the necklace, as though mentioning it might break it. The Boehmers showed Rohan some other pieces of jewellery; Rohan cooed politely. Finally, Rohan asked to see the 'item of great importance', the 'unique specimen' of which he had heard so much.

The jewellers produced the necklace, indicating 'the unprecedented arrangement of stones'. 'How much is it?' Rohan asked. Only 1.6 million livres, they replied, the estimated price six years previously.

Boehmer, never one to rein in his self-pity, now spewed out the whole saga: he would have sold the necklace had the king not so inconsiderately declared war on Britain; he had crafted it to adorn a queen but Marie Antoinette seemed utterly uninterested; his life's work was crushing his business. Rohan responded coolly to the blethering. He did not know if a sale would take place but, if it did, he was certain they would approve of the buyer and her terms. Whether he would be allowed to name the person he was acting for, he could not yet say; if he wasn't, the purchase would be made in his name. The Boehmers, who knew perfectly well whom Rohan represented, were amenable to any suggested payment plan, so long as a proportion of the cost was deposited upfront.

When Rohan recounted his conversation with the jewellers to Jeanne, he added, as a frank and loyal friend of the queen, a word of advice. It was an 'act of folly' to spend so much on a single piece of ugly and unfashionable jewellery. Buying the necklace was 'madness' as Marie Antoinette 'had no need for it in order to appear glamorous'. Perhaps, underneath, lay an unformed worry about the exposure – financial and political – he risked: he was well aware he was collaborating with Marie Antoinette to deceive the king. Presumably these objections were dismissed because he never raised them again. Every command, however misguided, had to be endured if Rohan was to become prime minister.

On 29 January, Rohan told the jewellers that he had been author-ised to strike a deal – but absolute secrecy needed to be maintained. The price of 1.6 million livres was provisionally accepted, though the necklace would have to be revalued independently. Once the price had been agreed, the first payment of 400,000 livres would fall after six months, with further instalments following at half-yearly intervals. The Boehmers, with no other prospective buyers, had no option but to agree, even though no deposit was offered. The neck-lace was to be delivered on 1 February, the eve of Candlemas, the first anniversary of Jeanne's staged fit in front of the queen. Rohan scribbled down the conditions of sale, which the jewellers signed.

This was not a formal contract – it was not notarised, nor did the Boehmers retain a copy – but the jewellers, knowing the buyer's true identity, may have thought such a document unnecessary, or felt it improper to demand one. They were desperate to conclude the transaction as soon as possible, even if the terms were not ideal: only a few weeks previously they had told another potential intermediary, the comte de Valbonne, they would prefer to sell to the king, since they doubted the queen had sufficient funds, and worried, were she to die in childbirth, that they would be left unpaid.

Rohan handed the terms of sale to Jeanne, asking that the queen sign them. Jeanne returned the deed unmarked. 'It is utterly unnecessary', she said, 'as the queen will pay shortly.' But Rohan insisted on a signature. The Boehmers had placed enormous faith in him. It was their interests that needed protecting, he emphasised, not his. This time the document was returned to Rohan with the signature 'Marie Antoinette de France' affixed to the bottom. Each article was neatly tagged with the word 'approuvé'. Accompanying it was a snippy letter from the queen: 'I am not accustomed to dealing in this way with my jewellers. You will keep this document at your house and you will arrange the rest as you see fit.'*

The cardinal moved swiftly to finalise the exchange. On 1 February he wrote to the jewellers: 'I would like Monsieur Boehmer and his partner to come as soon as possible to my house this morning with the object in question.' Only now did Rohan show the Boehmers the signature, telling them 'it was only right that you should know to whom you have sold the jewels'. It is strange that Rohan should have done so without authorisation. He may have convinced himself that secrecy was required only during the course of negotiations; once the deal had been completed, he was free to talk. He had shown, and would continue to show, genuine concern for the vulnerable position in which the jewellers had placed themselves: later that month Rohan wrote on the deed that 'in case of death, this document should be handed over to Monsieurs Boehmer and Bassenge'. But perhaps there was another, less altruistic motivation.

* The existence of this letter is disputed. Rohan denied ever having seen it but, during the trial, Bassenge claimed to have been shown it by the cardinal.

Finally, here were two people to whom he could speak about his friendship with the queen – and they had a commercial incentive not to gossip about it. Here was a valve through which Rohan could safely vent his pride and hope for the future, feelings he had bottled up for nine months.

Rohan forced the jewellers to take an unsigned copy of the terms of sale, though they protested that this was unnecessary. He also wrote to Boehmer, clarifying that interest on monies owed would start to accrue only after the first payment in August. Again, Rohan explicitly mentioned the identity of the purchaser: 'the queen has made known her intentions to me', a phrase that would be scrutinised intensely in the coming months.

Rohan travelled from Paris to Versailles on the same day. Hugging the necklace case like a sick child, he climbed the cold stairs to the La Mottes' rooms, where he and Jeanne chatted amiably. Then, a rap at the door. 'It's someone from the queen,' whispered Jeanne, bustling the cardinal, like an adulterer caught in flagrante, into a niche curtained with a strip of paper. A slim, pale man with a long face, dressed entirely in black and looking not dissimilar to Rétaux de Villette, entered and handed a letter to Jeanne, who unsealed it, asked the man to wait outside, then crept over to Rohan. She told him the queen wished that the necklace be handed over to the bearer of the letter. 'Do you know this man?' Rohan asked. 'He is a member of the queen's household – one of the queen's musicians,' Jeanne replied. Rohan retreated to his alcove. The man in black was readmitted, picked up the case and left.

Later that evening, on the terrace of the chateau, Jeanne told the cardinal of the queen's delight at her new acquisition, and the pleasure Rohan's tact and efficiency had given her. The queen would not wear the necklace, Jeanne said, until she had broached the matter with the king. The cardinal assumed this would be a matter of hours. The following day, Rohan spotted Boehmer and Bassenge as he left chapel. Gesticulating as forcefully as discretion permitted, the cardinal silently attempted to ask them if they had seen the queen wearing the necklace. The jewellers did not appear to understand his flapping so, when he arrived home, Rohan sent two of his servants to watch the king and queen dine and scrutinise the queen's neck. They reported it was unadorned, but Rohan presumed that Marie Antoinette had simply not yet found Louis in the right mood to break the news that she had dropped a million and a half livres on something pretty.

The Boehmers were also disappointed their necklace was not on show, but were assuaged somewhat when Rohan explained why. He hoped that the day of revelation would not be long coming. In the meantime, they should write to the queen thanking her for her gracious purchase; the Boehmers agreed to do so. A few days later, Rohan bumped into the Boehmers in one of the corridors of Versailles. 'Have you thanked the queen?' the cardinal demanded – they had not. Rohan reproached them for their disrespect and insisted they rectify the situation as soon as possible. Boehmer gave dilute assent but still ignored the cardinal's instructions. He had already been scorched by the queen's temper and was mindful that she had directly ordered him never to mention the necklace again: an injunction, he supposed, that still stood, especially since she had bought the necklace through such circuitous means.

Jeanne's comportment towards the jewellers was typically contradictory and extemporised. The Boehmers wished to reward her. At first Jeanne chastely refused the offers; she had striven throughout to minimise her role, so that, were her plan to unravel, Rohan would appear the more deeply implicated. Soon, however, demands reached Laporte from cronies of the La Mottes for jewellery worth tens of thousands of livres. When he showed one of the shopping lists to Jeanne, she pleaded ignorance. Yet shortly afterwards he received one of Jeanne's rings for measurement.

Exasperated, Laporte visited the La Mottes and told them if they wanted an emolument, they would have to speak directly to the Boehmers. Jeanne wore a wilted, silent smile; Nicolas, who had played no direct role in scamming the necklace, thought it bizarre to turn down a present, and with a bovine snort declared that 'if my wife has the delicacy not to wish for anything, I would happily receive a gift on her behalf because her service was important enough to deserve a gift'. He drew up a modest list of demands: 'four earrings, the most fashionable diamond girandoles; two gold watches with diamond chains, two solitaires in diamonds, and enough diamonds to encircle a portrait medallion'. Jeanne was content to receive the Boehmers' bounty, so long as she was not seen to beg for it herself. The jewellers gladly gave Nicolas all he wanted, but expressed concern that they were still yet to see the queen wear the necklace. She would only wear it once it had been fully paid off, Jeanne now explained, in order to avoid a public outcry. At this, even the hypertensive Boehmer calmed down – for the time being, at least.

9

The Greatest Man in Europe

An Interlude

S OME SAID THAT he was an English spy; some a Jesuit agent. Was he simply a Neapolitan coachman or a Portuguese Jew? Or was he the illegitimate son of an Arabian prince? An Egyptian raised in the pyramids? An amphibian born of the foams of the sea? He was revered as a prophet, another John the Baptist, the Son of Man returned, a demi-god who transcended fractured religions. He was excoriated as a Moravian schismatic come to corrupt the souls of good Christian men, as the Wandering Jew, as the Antichrist. He was rumoured to be five thousand years old; to have travelled through time and witnessed Alexander the Great give battle; to have communed with Socrates and Caesar; to fly through the air on the wings of angels. He could turn hemp into silk, scrap metal to gold and cure men doctors had abandoned.

So much of what we know about Count Cagliostro, the greatest European celebrity of the late eighteenth century, is garbling, exaggeration and slander. The details of his earliest years are especially uncertain, since the first biographies were written either by hagiographers or calumniators, but we know that Giuseppe Balsamo was born on 2 June 1743 in a slum in Palermo in Sicily. His father, a jeweller, died shortly after the birth and Giuseppe was brought up by his mother and older sister. As a child he was a tearaway: he robbed his own uncle and terrorised the authorities and anyone else who unwisely strayed into his parish. According to the word on the street, he had stabbed a priest to death, but no one was brave enough to testify against him.

Giuseppe was given a comparatively extensive education, both from private tutors and at a seminary for orphans, and excelled at chemistry and art. For a short while he enrolled as a novice in a community of country friars, though he had little inclination for monkish disciplines

– he was supposedly expelled from the order for intoning the names of local prostitutes when leading the company in prayer. Afterwards he lived off his wits, his penmanship and his sense of theatre. He was an exceptional counterfeiter, forging everything from wills to theatre tickets. And he cultivated a reputation as a magus, a conductor of the ghosts and djinns that haunted Sicilian folk memory. He manufactured amulets and read as widely as he could about Neoplatonic philosophy, alchemy, astrology and the Kabbalah. At the age of twenty he skipped town after he had extracted sixty pieces of silver from a local silversmith, whom he had promised to lead to a hidden treasure trove, having vanquished the jealous spirits guarding it (the jealous spirits turned out to be a gang of hired heavies lying in ambush).

Giuseppe's initial movements after this point are uncertain. He may have headed to Rhodes; he may have travelled to Egypt on one of the trade routes that laced together the shores of the Mediterranean. By 1766 he had shipped up in Malta, where he became a lackey of the Knights Hospitaller, the rulers of the island, and was provided with a laboratory to experiment with medicinals and alchemy. Two years later he travelled to Rome with letters of introduction provided by the Knights, and snagged a job as a secretary to Cardinal Orsini. Giuseppe was not a natural bureaucrat. He still hankered after the street – the patter, the wary companionship, the clink of coins slipped into your purse – and set himself up in the piazzas as a hawker of philtres, face creams made out of salad leaves and remarkably convincing knock-offs of Old Masters. Giuseppe also married Lorenza Feliciani – a beautiful, illiterate fourteen-year-old. The Balsamos moved into Lorenza's parents' pokey home, but Giuseppe could not abide his parents-in-law's religiosity, and found his ambitions stultifying.

The couple escaped in the train of the Marquis Agliata, a doubtful nobleman of doubtful character, whom Giuseppe served as a confidential secretary, forging banker's drafts and military commissions, and as a pimp for his own wife. Agliata soon disappeared with all Giuseppe and Lorenza's money, so they hit the road. It was the start of a peripatetic two decades, a vagabond Grand Tour, which began in mendicancy and ended in acclaim and notoriety across the continent. The couple begged their way through northern Italy and southern France – holy pilgrims, they said, seeking alms to pay their way to Santiago de Compostela. In Aix-en-Provence they encountered Casanova, whom Giuseppe presented with an imitation Rembrandt which the old goat pronounced finer than any original.

The Balsamos soon struck upon a formula for survival. They pretended to be Italian nobles: Lorenza, now renamed more grandiloquently Seraphina, would insinuate herself into the bed of a nobleman, while Giuseppe thunderously hinted that he would gladly overlook his wife's infidelity if a position could be found for him as an artist or an apothecary. Whenever their debts loured too threateningly, the Balsamos slipped out of town towards another European metropolis, where Giuseppe would adopt a different title: Colonel Pelligrini, comte Fenix, comte Harat, marquis d'Anna.

London, 1771: Giuseppe sets himself up as a broker of Brazilian gemstones and moves into rooms in Compton Street in Soho, an Italian neighbourhood. But his business flops: he does time in a debtors' prison and works as a tough for a crim called the Marquis Vivona – as much of a marquis as Agliata – blackmailing respectable bourgeois who inexplicably found themselves locked in a bedroom with the naked Seraphina. Paris, 1772: Seraphina leaves Giuseppe for a Monsieur Duplessis, a wealthy lawyer she is only supposed to be sleeping with for the money. Giuseppe accuses Duplessis of trying to kill him with a rotten egg and a poisoned glass of wine. He despatches Seraphina to a convent for four months, as punishment for trying to escape a life of perpetual motion and enforced prostitution. London, 1776: Giuseppe establishes an alchemical laboratory in Whitcomb Street and runs a racket selling winning lottery numbers. He is terrorised by a Mr and Mrs Scott who first try to cajole and bribe him into revealing his secrets, then, when he refuses, frame him for robbery and sorcery.

Giuseppe's second stay in London was significant for two reasons: for the first time, he called himself Count Cagliostro; and he became a Freemason. Modern Freemasonry first appeared in Scotland during the seventeenth century, having emerged when guilds of stonemasons – medieval in origin – began to admit non-masons to increase their income. During the eighteenth century, it became one of the most vibrant elements of the European public sphere, combining

Enlightenment ideals – fraternity, disinterested scientific and philosophical enquiry, the perfection of human nature, opposition to censorship and religious persecution – with mystico-architectural rituals and a mythology that traced its origins back to Solomon's temple. Behind the arcana, Masons enjoyed like-minded company and joined with each other in charitable works. Members of lodges took their places in a strict hierarchy but the organisation was, in theory at least, underpinned by an ethos of equality: Protestants and Catholics, deists and pantheists, atheists and Jews were all admitted and conversed with each other without hauteur or obsequiousness. King Gustav III of Sweden was a Mason; one Parisian lodge had a 'Negro trumpeter' on its books.

In practice, many lodges were organised along class lines. Cagliostro was not inducted into the Grand Lodge of England, which the year before had purchased two houses on Great Queen Street that would become Freemason's Hall. His lodge was altogether more common, comprising, for the most part, working-class immigrants – its members included 'a hairdresser, a ladies' shoemaker, a pastry maker, a waiter, a musician, and a couple of painters' – who met above a pub in Gerrard Street in Soho. At his initiation, Cagliostro was blindfolded, trussed up, raised to the ceiling on a block and tackle – at which point the haulier accidentally let go of the rope and Cagliostro plunged to the floor, bruising his hand. He was then handed a pistol and ordered to shoot himself in the forehead – the gun was loaded only with powder – before swearing to obey his superiors and never reveal Masonic mysteries.

Cagliostro immersed himself in Masonic esoterica. He discovered a manuscript that argued Freemasonry had been founded in ancient Egypt by a hierophant called the Great Copt, who had lived for thousands of years. Cagliostro devised his own rite from a bricolage of sources that ecumenically traversed the Bible – Jesus was 'the first and greatest magician who ever lived', though Moses was admired less because of the plagues he had viciously inflicted upon the Egyptians – Zoroastrianism, Norse Sagas, Rosicrucianism and Pythagorean and Neoplatonic teachings. He had been sent, he said, from the Great Copt himself to spread enlightenment through the world, and fight off the necromancers, evil spirits who sought to tempt mankind from the way of truth and righteousness.

Cagliostro promised communion with the godhead and immortality to those who applied themselves to his rule. A number of ascetic practices, so extreme that no one could ever have actually attempted them, were devised for physical and moral rebirth: devotees who wished to live for ever had to spend weeks on end in the forest, subsisting only on water and grass, until their hair and teeth fell out and their skin peeled away. He performed telegnosis through child mediums, correctly predicting what was simultaneously happening miles away (he informed friends of the death of Maria Theresa five days before the news reached town). He carved magic circles in the air with a fling of his sword – people crossed them at their peril. Sometimes he babbled in tongues, sometimes he thrashed on the ground as though possessed, cranking his legs and arms. Despite these bizarre ceremonials, the Egyptian rite was profoundly unrevolutionary: though Cagliostro himself preferred 'the simple and pure cult of natural religion', he welcomed anyone – Jews and Muslims included – provided they maintained faith in a supreme being; and he ordered his followers to respect the established Church, the king and the laws wherever they were.

Freemasonry offered Cagliostro an opportunity to direct his mountebank speciousness, his quicksilver talents as a thespian and huckster, at an audience that might lift him out of the gutter. Masons were respectable figures who had vowed to help their brethren in any way they could, but they had a weakness for fanciful tales that burnished their order's prehistory. In whatever town he arrived, Cagliostro was welcomed hospitably by the brothers; in The Hague they formed an 'arch of steel' with their swords to salute his departure. Physically, he was unprepossessing: medium height, podgy, tanned and with an upturned nose. What drew the eye was his hair: braided into dreadlocks and tied at the back in a ponytail. His furious charisma, his strange mode of speech that flickered between languages, the blast of his voice like a 'trumpet muted with a crepe veil', fascinated all who met him, even those whose scepticism was barricaded and entrenched.

He was careful to ration his prodigious charm, which kept his acolytes eager to ingratiate: effusive one moment, he could rapidly turn cold and would speak only in elliptical pensées. He was canny when taking money from his eager, often immensely rich supporters, ostentatiously refusing payment for his services on a number of occasions, in order to bolster his reputation for selflessness. The further Cagliostro travelled in time and space from Palermo, the more aristocratic endorsements he rustled up, and the easier it became to convince people of his outlandish cosmology.

A number of nobles in the duchy of Courland, a small Germanic state in present-day Latvia, were so taken by the man they saw transmute mercury to silver that they wished to make him duke in place of their Russian-imposed ruler. Cagliostro travelled to St Petersburg, hoping that Catherine the Great would join the Egyptian Rite (in the event, Catherine, who believed that Masonry was a dangerous harbinger of democracy, wanted nothing to do with him). While there he cured sufferers from cancer, insanity and other severe ailments, employing only a 'delicious distilled water' – otherwise known as water – and exorcisms. But Cagliostro's rampant belief that he had been chosen started to alienate his fellow Masons. In the summer of 1780 he was forced out of Warsaw after accusations of legerdemain during his alchemical demonstrations. Travelling westwards, he arrived in Strasbourg in September that year, foppishly dressed in an outfit of Turkish taffeta, Artois shoes with diamond buckles and a musketeer's hat quiffed with white feathers.

Strasbourg's Franco-German cosmopolitanism made it fertile territory for Masonry – the city contained twenty-nine lodges. But the native Masons shunned Cagliostro, who by now had decided that he was not merely the Great Copt's plenipotentiary but the Great Copt himself – he made out, if not explicitly, that he was an immortal being who conversed with the angel of light and the spirit of darkness. Cagliostro offered free healthcare to the poorest members of society, which incurred the enmity of the doctors' guild, irate that their business was being undercut, and the suspicion of the authorities, who worried about the radicalism inherent in any individual who attracted the adulation of the masses.

You only read of unlikely recoveries in the works of Cagliostro's advocates, though there must have been many cases for which he was unable to offer any remedy. But it is worth considering why this self-anointed healer had any success at all. His medicines, whose recipes he guarded fiercely, were, for the most part, utterly innocuous: tinctures, herbal laxatives, cough mixtures. More importantly, he placed great emphasis on two aspects of treatment then ignored by the medical profession – nutrition and pastoral care. Cagliostro ran a soup kitchen alongside his practice, which meant that the malnourished could regain the strength to defeat their illnesses through their own resources. And he spent many hours talking to and consoling his patients, counselling them against despair and, with his effervescent confidence, firing their belief that their health would be restored.

The most important reason why Cagliostro's treatments sometimes worked, however, was simply because he was not a doctor. Even by the late eighteenth century, medical theory had not progressed significantly beyond the Galenic suppositions of Ancient Greece, in which disease was considered to be the result of an imbalance of humours. The primary means of treatment for a wide range of conditions was bloodletting, a deleterious procedure that sapped the sufferer and hurried him towards death. Only since the beginning of the twentieth century have doctors healed more than harmed.* Cagliostro had no formal medical training and lacked the anatomical expertise to tap veins. Any patient was, therefore, more likely to recover if treated by Cagliostro than by the most experienced doctor in Strasbourg.

The energy which Cagliostro expended on tending his impoverished charges suggests he had begun to believe he was truly the saviour of mankind. But his efforts were not entirely altruistic. He was accompanied by an apothecary who was the sole custodian of Cagliostro's patent cure-all, which his patients were encouraged to buy. When he healed the wife of the Swiss banker Jacques Sarasin, who was dying from an undiagnosed illness that had necrotised her flesh, Sarasin, in gratitude, gave Cagliostro permission to draw on his bank's funds at will. Cagliostro's clinic was a very public bid for patronage, and within weeks of arriving in Strasbourg in September 1780, he had attracted the interest of the greatest magnate in Alsace: the cardinal de Rohan.

* As the historian David Wootton has noted, this meant that only since 1950 did medicine 'acquire a genuine capacity to extend life'.

Rohan invited Cagliostro to Saverne. Cagliostro declined with disdain: 'If the cardinal is ill, then he should come and I will cure him; if he's well, he has no need for me, nor I of him.' Rohan travelled up to town to have his asthma treated and was instantly convinced on meeting Cagliostro that he was in the presence of the greatest man alive: he saw in him 'a dignity so imposing that he felt himself penetrated by religious awe'. After compelling the cardinal to pay court, Cagliostro recognised Rohan as a 'soul worthy of mine'. Rohan considered the comte 'his oracle, his guide, his compass'; Saverne and its servants were placed at Cagliostro's disposal, and Rohan encouraged his research into a panacea that would 'cure illness and prolong life', and experiments which would fatten small diamonds into larger ones. While at the cardinal's, Cagliostro continued to live like an anchorite, refusing to sleep in a bed – he used a sofa instead – and eating only cheese.

There is a continuity between Rohan's belief in Jeanne's stories of her influence with the queen and his reverence of Cagliostro; when you have lived a life of such privilege that practically everything you've wished for has been granted, it is easy to slump into trusting those who offer to fulfil your remaining desires – greater wealth, higher office. Rohan's upper-crust enervation meant he gladly welcomed enthusiasts willing to expend their energy on his behalf. But there were more impersonal cultural forces which sustained his faith.

Many of the idols of superstition may have been smashed during the Enlightenment, but simply positing a materialistic explanation of nature – in which the hand of God was no longer a final explanatory resort – did not bring philosophers any closer to understanding its mechanics. From the detritus of older certainties, scientists were as likely to build blind alleys and false walls as durable monuments of knowledge. In an environment where understanding of the universe was underdeveloped, lacking in evidence and theoretically flawed, many people seized upon scientific language to varnish their gimcrack schemes. Particularly celebrated were those who flexed their mastery over the physical world, usually in theatrical demonstrations, as the evidence to the eye was evidence enough to the scientifically illiterate – the water dowser Barthélemy Bléton and

Léon the Jew, who cured the sick using mirrors, briefly captivated the French public. But one figure exemplifies more than anyone the involution of science with pseudo-science, a man whose fame was as great as Cagliostro – Franz Anton Mesmer.

Mesmer practised 'animal magnetism', a form of healing in which he directed the 'agent of nature', an invisible fluid that suffused the universe. The body, he claimed, comprised a number of small magnets, the poles of which could be manipulated to remove any blockages to the fluid's flow. He treated patients using a number of dramatic techniques that entertained spectators: inducing fits and trances, arranging mirrors to reflect the fluid, and submerging patients in a bath of iron filings and 'mesmerised' water, while resting iron bars on crucial organs: the stomach, the liver, the spleen.

In the way it related the health of the human body to the harmony of the heavens, Mesmer drew on Renaissance ideas of the inter-dependence of macrocosm and microcosm. But the emphasis on the transmission of invisible forces chimed with more recent research: Newton's discovery of gravity, and Franklin and Galvani's experiments with electricity. To the interested though scientifically unsophisticated layman, one invisible force seemed just as plausible as another. And not just to laymen – the medical faculty of the University of Paris split over his controversial methods.

The case of Mesmer shows how deeply entangled the reasonable and the fantastic were in the late eighteenth century. It was a period characterised not so much by fixity of knowledge as febrility – a frogspawn of ideas, some of which evolved over subsequent centuries and some of which were buried stillborn. Rohan's faith in Cagliostro's dominion over nature was not an aberration. It was as symptomatic of his milieu as Diderot's atheism or Linnaean taxonomy. In eras of uncertainty, false beliefs can thrive because their challengers are still unproven. Like Jeanne, Cagliostro provided ocular proof for his boasts. Like Othello, Rohan would discover that ocular proof was no proof at all.

Not everyone at Saverne was as smitten with Cagliostro. Georgel was especially disgruntled, since the comte had displaced him as Rohan's most trusted advisor. 'I do not know', he wrote 'which monster, enemy of the happiness of honest souls, vomited onto our land an enthusiast empiric, a new apostle of the religion of Nature, who despotically seized his proselytes and subjugated them.' And Cagliostro was rapidly accumulating other detractors among the medical profession and sceptical dignitaries.

Though three ministers wrote letters of support to the provincial notables, Cagliostro and Seraphina were forced out of Strasbourg in 1783. They went first to Bordeaux, then Lyons, establishing lodges in each town. On 30 January 1785, two days before Rohan was due to hand over the necklace to the queen, the Cagliostros arrived in Paris. They were greeted as though they had lifted a siege. Any object with a printable surface – fans, buckles, scarves, snuffboxes – was stamped with his portrait. 'The best of men is now in Paris,' said the writer Breffroy de Reigny. Cagliostro took a spacious house in the Marais, set back from the rue St Claude and screened by trees, not far from Rohan's *hôtel*.

The cardinal dined regularly with the newcomers – Rohan supplied the food, cooked in his own kitchens – and through him Jeanne became acquainted with Cagliostro. They had met briefly, five years earlier, when she had travelled to Saverne in pursuit of the Boulainvilliers. Now they became friends, 'hand in glove' according to Beugnot. There is no evidence that Cagliostro suspected Jeanne of wielding a malign power over the cardinal. And though Jeanne may have realised Cagliostro was a charlatan, it was not in her interest to expose him and place Rohan on his guard. She knew that Rohan looked unfavourably on those who did not share his admiration for the comte.

It was difficult to hold a conversation with Cagliostro since he chirruped in a melange of Italian and mangled French, interspersed with declamations in cod Arabic that he refused to translate (one doubter said that 'he is taken for an oracle because he has the obscurity of one'). He repeatedly asked if he was understood, while staring ferociously at his interlocutor to ensure that the answer was yes. A typical encounter comprehended discussion of 'the sky, the stars, the Great Mystery, Memphis, hierophancy, transcendental chemistry, giants, huge animals [and] a city in the middle of Africa ten times the size of Paris'.

Cagliostro's presence in Paris provided Rohan with a further opportunity to serve the queen. Marie Antoinette was in the last stages of pregnancy and, Jeanne told the cardinal, terrified of dying in childbirth. Could she consult the Great Copt so that the queen's perturbations might be settled? Raising the prospect of the queen's death was dangerous, since it risked stirring Rohan's worries about his possible liability for the necklace. But Jeanne may have been planning for the future – at some point it would no longer be possible to maintain the fiction that Marie Antoinette possessed the necklace – and by intimating a profound shift in the queen's emotional state, she tenderised the cardinal for a potential break.

It is hard to tell how seriously the participants treated the ensuing seance, since their accounts are integrated within accusations and counter-accusations over culpability for the necklace's disappearance. But it is likely that Cagliostro was more serious and Jeanne less sceptical than they would later claim. Rohan treated the proceedings with the utmost solemnity. Foretelling the future required a virginal child, the younger the better (blue eyes and favourable star signs enhanced the results). Fortuitously, Jeanne's niece, Marie de La Tour, had been living with the La Mottes since November (though Cagliostro was taken aback when presented with a fifteen-year-old, rather than the five-year-olds he normally worked with – teenagers are much less biddable, and there's a good chance they're less virginal than they admit).

In a room in the Hôtel de Rohan, Cagliostro arranged a screen behind which stood a glass vase filled with water, in which spirits would appear. Two smouldering candles in silver candlesticks were arranged on a table covered in a black cloth decorated with Kabbalistic symbols. Vials of lustral water, crucifixes and Egyptian figurines were placed about the candles. Marie was dressed in a silver apron and swaddled with four sashes – blue, green, black and white. From the bottommost hung a silver cross.

Cagliostro laid an unsheathed sword across the table and intoned to the young medium: 'Recommend yourself to God and to your innocence. Put yourself behind this screen, close your eyes, and wish for the thing you want to see. If you are innocent you will see what you want to see. But if you are not innocent you will see nothing.' He made a number of curious hand movements, as though conducting an orchestra, and plunged into an invocation of the archangels Raphael and Michael, imploring them to 'drive out any demons' who were lurking in the victim.

'Stamp on the ground with your *innocent* foot, and tell me if you see anything,' said Cagliostro.

Marie saw nothing.

'Stamp again, stamp, stamp,' insisted Cagliostro. 'Don't you see a woman, dressed in white, lying on her back. She's blonde and has a large stomach.'

'Yes, sir,' said the girl amenably.

'Who is it? Don't you see the queen? Do you recognise her?'

Marie may have been innocent but she was not an idiot. 'Yes, sir,' she said, 'it is the queen.'

Cagliostro asked Marie to ask the queen's phantasm if her labour would run smoothly. The well-informed apparition said that it would.

'Say it again: in the name of the Great Copt, I order you to make me see all that I want,' said Cagliostro, roaring like a bull. 'Stamp. What do you see, darling? Don't you see an angel on your right who is coming to hug you? Don't you see it?'

Marie, worried that this was a test of her chastity, denied being groped by an angel. Cagliostro again called upon the higher powers.

'Do you see them now?' Cagliostro asked.

Marie realised that an angelic embrace was a vital element to the proceedings.

'Yes, sir.'

'Kiss it hard.'

The soft squelch of puckering lips concluded the ceremony. Rohan had been praying fervently throughout, and everyone was satisfied apart from Marie. Cagliostro told her she would dream of the visions in the vase; when she later mentioned that she had not, he said this was absolute proof that she was not a virgin.

10

Follow the Money

O N 8 FEBRUARY 1785 – Shrove Tuesday – Jacques-Christophe Paris, a silversmith on the Place Dauphine, was visited by a gentleman who pointedly carried with him a book about valuing diamonds. The man produced a pouch containing sixty-four diamonds and demanded 50,000 livres. Too expensive, Paris said, and refused to buy them.

On the following day, a smartly dressed figure tried to sell three lots of diamonds for 20,000 livres to Israel Vidal-Lainé, a Jewish broker on the rue Neuve-Saint-Eustache.

'What is your name?' asked Vidal-Lainé.

'Villette – I am a soldier,' said Villette, with a redundancy of information that the nervous are prone to supply.

'And where do you live?'

'That's none of your business.'

Vidal-Lainé refused to negotiate further unless a reputable person vouched for the customer. He never saw him again.

Other merchants approached the authorities. On 12 February, Inspector Jean-François de Bruginères of the Paris Police was told by a jeweller that someone called Rétaux de Villette had offered him diamonds at irrationally low prices and was rumoured to be preparing to travel to Holland, intent on selling them there. Bruginères tracked down Villette to his apartment on the rue Saint-Louis and asked him to explain himself. At first Villette was 'reticent'.

'If you're not doing anything dubious, you can tell me exactly what's going on,' said Bruginères. 'But if you don't fancy speaking, I could alway bring you before a judge.'

Villette admitted he had been given diamonds to sell by 'a relative of the queen, the comtesse de Valois de La Motte', but, since he had been unable to strike a reasonable bargain, he had returned them. He had only been reluctant to mention this to the police officer because the comtesse had explicitly requested that she not be named. Bruginères checked if there had been any reports of stolen diamonds – as there were none, he closed the case.

It is indicative of Jeanne's naivety that she believed she could sell such large quantities of diamonds in Paris without rousing suspicion. The La Mottes were actually more successful than Villette's gauche approaches suggest: 70,000 livres-worth were exchanged for cash, and more for clocks and jewellery. Pierre-Auguste Regnier, the couple's regular jeweller, was commissioned to make a sweet box with a portrait of the queen embedded in the lid, girdled with forty-nine brilliants. But it is impossible to eat bracelets or live inside a bonbonnière. The La Mottes ran through money like blight, and Villette's brush with the law had demonstrated that they needed to sell the remainder of the stones outside the capital. Jeanne, with some trepidation, turned to her husband.

In the middle of April, Nicolas rode north, accompanied by Laisus, his valet, and the Chevalier O'Neil, a captain in the Irish Brigade, who had been cajoled by Nicolas into accompanying him to London on what, he had been told, was a business trip. Nicolas took with him a pouch full of diamonds, a credit note for 6,000 livres and all his brusque charm.

London, along with Amsterdam, was the major centre of the gem trade in northern Europe. Its jewellery shops, according to one foreign visitor, made 'a most brilliant and agreeable shew . . . which is productive of an air of wealth and elegance that we do not see in any other city'. Nicolas arrived in London on 17 April and sought recommendations of trustworthy dealers. He was directed towards Nathaniel Jefferys, jeweller to the Prince of Wales and the Duke of York, and William Gray, who worked out of New Bond Street.

Nicolas went first to Jefferys but considered his offer for eighteen diamonds insufficiently generous. A few days later, Jefferys asked the Runners at Bow Street if there was news of a theft in Paris. He did not believe that Nicolas could have acquired his jewels through legal means, his suspicions having been aroused by the Frenchman's decision to sell the diamonds in London, where, because of the large quantity in circulation, prices were considerably cheaper than in Paris. The police had nothing to report, but Jefferys still refused to do business with Nicolas.

Meanwhile Nicolas had opened negotiations with Gray, telling him the jewels originated from a stomacher he had inherited from his mother. After protracted bargaining, Nicolas sold most of his hoard for 240,000 livres, significantly less than the diamonds' nominal value of 400,000 livres – partly because, in their haste to remove the diamonds from their settings, the La Mottes had scratched them; partly because of Nicolas's eagerness to conclude a deal; and partly because of the poor exchange rate. Of the total, 130,000 livres-worth were paid in silver coin, some with bankers' drafts and the rest in kind. So greedily did Nicolas seize upon Gray's merchandise that he ended up paying back the jeweller over £5,000: his trove included diamond medallions, a diamond brooch in the shape of a star, a diamond rose, diamond earrings, a diamond ring, a pearl bow, a pearl necklace, over £1,800-worth of loose pearls, a gold watch, a watch chain, two steel epées, two toothpick boxes, a pair of jewellery balances, a carving knife, a strong box, four razors, two thousand needles, a silk briefcase, a snuff box and some asparagus tongs.

Early in May, O'Neil was summoned to his regiment. Before he left, he introduced Nicolas to Barthélemy Macdermott, a 55-year-old Capuchin friar, who offered to act as an interpreter in O'Neil's absence. Previously Macdermott had served as chaplain to the French ambassador; he was also a spy in the pay of at least two French ministers. Macdermott was worldly and politic, a fixer whose first piece of advice to his new friend was how best to smuggle the pearls past English customs.

Macdermott had lived in a friary not far from Bar-sur-Aube and knew Nicolas's family. As they grew closer, Nicolas confided in him the reason he had so many diamonds. He told the familiar story of Jeanne's initiation into the queen's circle: his wife, Nicolas said, had been unwilling to take advantage of the queen's goodwill; he had no such qualms. At the time they could not even afford bread, so he had insisted that Jeanne appeal to Marie Antoinette for support (there is something pitiful in Nicolas's insistence that he was the decisive spirit, a symptom of the redundancy he must have felt in Paris as Jeanne and Villette conspired without him). The queen foisted upon them unwanted necklaces and bracelets. He had come to England to sell them, even though he would receive a lower price, so that those who had originally bought the jewellery for Marie Antoinette would not be put out by happening upon their gift in a Paris showroom.

Towards the end of May, Nicolas received a letter from Jeanne telling him she was in urgent need of money. He left sixty diamonds with Gray to set into a necklace and a pair of earrings – Macdermott was entrusted with delivering the pieces when they had been completed. Nicolas hurried back to Paris, arriving on 2 June, and immediately cashed the bankers' drafts and sold the pearls. No money was saved, invested or even guarded with particular care – one of Jeanne's friends saw 40,000 livres in notes simply lying around, and Jeanne spent 100,000 livres on a jewellery case alone.

Tapestries, marble, crystal and silk replaced the worsted upholstery, the tin candlesticks, the stained and tatty dresses. Sometimes the La Mottes paid for items with the remaining diamonds – a mechanical bird was exchanged for a single, plump sparkler. In the twelve months that followed d'Oliva's performance at Versailles, the La Mottes spent something in the order of 400,000 livres, more than most of the country's leading nobles (the Prince de Robecq, who was renowned for the state in which he lived, spent less than 200,000 livres each year). To explain their upswell in fortune, the La Mottes gave out that Nicolas had won big at the races. They were generous enough to dissuade their neighbours from probing too deeply. Every neighbour, that is, except Rohan: he still sent his servants to Jeanne with small gifts of money; when he visited, he was received in a scratchily furnished room, its walls dour and peeling.

Managing Rohan's hopes of advancement was proving increasingly fraught. The cardinal's presence, in Paris and Versailles, disquieted Jeanne: he repeatedly professed his desire to speak to the queen. She also worried that Nicolas's extended absence would arouse suspicions. But in order to convince Rohan to depart, she needed to dangle before him the promise of imminent reward. On 12 May, Jeanne delivered a letter from the queen which dispatched Rohan to Saverne. The letter explained that 'your absence will be necessary to decide on the measures which I believe have to be taken, in order that you are promoted to a position you deserve'. At the end of May Jeanne travelled to Saverne disguised as a man (not to deceive anyone in particular, but simply to impress the need for secrecy). Nicolas's return was imminent – his absence no longer needed masking – and Jeanne knew that unless she maintained the initiative in managing Rohan's expectations, the cardinal might strike out rashly by himself. She told Rohan to return to the capital – the queen would receive him soon after.

Rohan arrived in Paris on 7 June but no meeting was scheduled, and his confidence in Jeanne began to fray. He harped on the queen's unwillingness to wear the necklace. Its conspicuous absence chilled him, and he felt the pulse of destiny weakening. These worries were bound to have arisen ever since Rohan handed over the necklace, but Jeanne saw no need to plan ahead. Her improvisation was bold, if risky. The queen, she told Rohan, believed that the necklace was too expensive and was now uncertain whether she would keep it: she wanted either the price reduced or an independent estimate made, as she had originally requested. If the jewellers had opted for the restitution of the necklace, Jeanne's story would have rapidly unravelled. But Jeanne, having heard Boehmer's plaintive confession of the despair, believed they would concede the demands.

On 10 July, Rohan asked the Boehmers to reduce the price of the necklace by 200,000 livres, to 1.4 million. This placed the jewellers in a painful position. They had already given the queen a discount and did not wish to absorb any further losses; but they abhorred the thought of being lumbered again with an object that had nestled among their stock like a squid, secreting its poison. They were terrified, too, of angering the queen and losing any future business.

They had passed up the opportunity to send the necklace to the Spanish Court, the Boehmers told Rohan, where it had been greatly in demand (a brass-necked exaggeration). More pressingly, they had reached accommodations with their creditors based on the agreed timetable of payments. Rohan returned with a compromise: the overall price would still fall to 1.4 million livres, but the first instalment, due on 1 August, would be 700,000 livres, rather than 400,000 livres. The jewellers grudgingly agreed.

A day or two later, Rohan summoned the Boehmers and asked them again whether they had thanked the queen yet for deigning to buy the necklace. They mumbled something about not yet having found the right occasion (Boehmer had actually spurned a number of opportunities). Rohan seethed at their evasiveness and demanded that they immediately set down their appreciation for the queen's generous request for a discount. Bassenge retorted that a letter would have more weight coming from the cardinal.

'As my letters pass through the hands of a third party,' said Rohan, 'it would be better if you yourselves write it and take it to the queen. Indeed, as I'm worried that you'll delay again, write it now.'

Rohan shoved Bassenge towards his desk and, standing at his shoulder, supervised the jeweller as he drafted the letter. Bassenge's first attempt – Boehmer's French was too poor to compose official correspondence – was hideously contorted, like a man tripping himself up while attempting an over-elaborate bow:

> The terror in which we live of not being able to be happy enough to find the moment to express in person to Your Majesty our respectful gratitude obliges us to do so by this note. Your Majesty today has crowned our wishes in acquiring the parure of diamonds that we have had the honour to present to her. We have eagerly accepted the latest arrangements which have been proposed in Your Majesty's name. These arrangements being agreeable to you, we regard ourselves as fortunate in seizing the occasion to prove to Your Majesty our zeal and our respect.

Rohan gagged at all the wriggling and fawning – he must have been privately relieved that the Boehmers had not tried to thank the queen by themselves – and briskly dictated a more elegant response:

> Madame, we are filled with joy to dare to hope about the latest arrangements that have been proposed to us, which we have accepted with respect and devotion to the orders of Your Majesty, and we have genuine satisfaction in thinking that the most beautiful diamond parure that exists will be worn by the greatest and the best of queens.

The letter's opening communicates a subtle remonstrance from Rohan for being kept in limbo – should the emphasis fall on 'to dare', the Boehmers' pro-forma expression of respect? Or on 'to hope', which might, from some angles, suggest capriciousness on the queen's part? The jewellers, on whom such nuances were lost, agreed to deliver the letter to the queen immediately.

Boehmer had an audience with the queen on 12 July, in which he handed over the letter; but before the queen could respond, the *contrôleur-général* entered and he was obliged to leave. The jeweller might as well have left behind a vial containing the drool of a lunatic. According to Madame Campan, her *femme de chambre*, the queen saw 'nothing in it but proof of mental aberration'. She lit one of its corners and tossed it into the grate. 'Tell Boehmer the next time you see him,' said Marie Antoinette to Campan, 'that I do not like diamonds now, and that I will buy no more as long as I live. If I had any money to spare, I would rather add to my property at Saint-Cloud.'

When Boehmer was told of the queen's perplexity, he immediately took to his bed with a fever brought on by an attack of nerves. It was left to Bassenge to break the news to the cardinal. Rohan was agitated – 'I am very surprised at your calmness,' he said to Bassenge – and expressed amazement that Boehmer had not battered down the queen's doors and demanded an explanation. But he also rationalised the queen's response: because the purchase of the necklace had been kept secret from even her closest attendants, Marie Antoinette was forced to feign bemusement when opening the letter in Campan's presence. The cardinal ordered Boehmer to return to Versailles and clarify the queen's disposition. Marie Antoinette, however, did not wish to hear the witterings of her jeweller any longer, and Boehmer was indefinitely barred from her presence.

A second sickening flinch of uncertainty was brought on by a new revelation: the cardinal received a letter from Marie Antoinette, which revealed that she had spent the 700,000 livres she had set aside for the necklace (on what, she did not say, though the profligate in Rohan may have quietly admired such dedicated dissipation). The payment of the first instalment would have to be delayed until 1 October, but the queen graciously insisted on paying the interest due in August, as if not to do so would display the most abject impropriety. Jeanne suggested that Rohan touch Claude Baudard de Sainte-James, the treasurer-general of the navy, for a loan to the queen.

Sainte-James's business interests were diversified and extremely lucrative. He had made money in sailmaking in Angers and an arms foundry in Charleville; he had stakes in the Parisian waterworks, the national discount bank, coal mines, crystal manufacturing, the Company of the North, which traded in the Baltic, and sugar plantations in the Caribbean. His income from his governmental post alone was 500,000 livres. He was the ideal man to approach, since he was the only other person who knew the secret of the necklace. In March, the Boehmers had asked the cardinal whether he could confirm to Sainte-James, their largest creditor, whom they owed 800,000 livres, that the necklace had been sold (they wanted to delay servicing their debt until the queen had delivered the first instalment). Rohan not only told Sainte-James that the queen had bought the necklace, he also showed him the bill of sale with Marie Antoinette's signature.

At a party in early July, the cardinal snatched a word with Sainte-James in the cool of a terrace. His thrust was that the queen no longer had – or would not have for much longer – the 700,000 livres. The prattle of the guests littered the air; the pair's conversation was muffled by discretion; and the exact language used by Rohan would later be disputed by Sainte-James with baleful implications. In a further exchange between the two, Rohan emphasised the advantages of the situation, 'since it would commit her [Marie Antoinette] to have recourse to you to secure the necessary funds for the payment of the necklace'. Eager for the validation that would arise from Her Majesty's gratitude, Sainte-James was receptive, but did not commit himself. He was rightly cautious of any financial imbroglio involving Rohan and, once he had heard of the queen's difficulties, considered circumventing the cardinal entirely. He only wished 'to show his zeal and willingness to serve'.

Rohan told the queen in a letter that Sainte-James was willing to lend her money. Before he received a response, news reached him that clotted his heart: Boehmer had been summoned to Versailles by the baron de Breteuil, minister for the king's household and the man to whom the crown jeweller reported. Rohan had especial reasons to worry about this particular minister's interest. Breteuil was a career diplomat, and in the final months of 1770, he had been chosen by the duc de Choiseul to serve as ambassador to the Habsburg Court. When Choiseul was rusticated by Louis XV, Rohan was sent in his stead. Breteuil, who had already shipped out his furniture, was furious to learn that he would not be joining it and nurtured an animus against the cardinal from that day on that did not smoulder out. Eventually, in 1774, Breteuil was named as Rohan's successor, and on taking up his post he poured out his bitterness to Georgel: 'I know one day I will revenge it. I will be his minister and will make him feel the weight of my authority.'

The strong bond Breteuil formed with Maria Theresa while in Vienna recommended him to Marie Antoinette, who propelled him into government in 1783. Superficially Breteuil was an unattractive character: he cut a portly figure, with contemptuous eyes and a nose which protruded like a rudder, and treated even his closest friends curtly. His enemies considered him impetuous, ignorant, pompous, arrogant and slapdash, lacking the social grace, tact and clarity of mind required of a successful politician, but his admirers praised him as an effective administrator of practical intelligence.

Boehmer presumed the baron would demand an explanation of the letter he had handed to the queen and applied to Rohan for advice. The cardinal calmed the jeweller's anxieties, but his own apprehensions over the minister's interest in the matter would not be shaken off. At some point between 22 and 25 July, he drafted a memorandum – partly guidance for Boehmer, partly for self-motivation – which offers the only contemporaneous insight into his thinking during those anxious summer months. This gives us a clearer view than any other record of the Diamond Necklace Affair of the compound of bluster and hopefulness that muddied Rohan's mind and dictated his conduct:

B sent for, who suspects that it is to speak to him about that object. He asked me how he must reply. I said to him that he must keep himself from mentioning it at all, and to say only that he has sent the object in question abroad, and I requested again the strictest secrecy and that he not mention it at all.* He insisted and repeated several times that his life was no longer anything but torture, especially since he took the liberty to write to . . . and after what had been said to him by C that the master did not understand what these men intended – it was making his head spin. This coincidence of circumstances could, I believe, make mine spin too, if I was not confident that the proposed plan sorts everything out for the present and the future. Rather, the person I suggest knows about everything because, as a debtor, he could not do otherwise. Thus, this changes nothing in the scheme of things and, on the contrary, gives rise to peace where there is, at the moment, worry and despair.

'B' is Boehmer; 'C' is Madame Campan; 'the person I suggest' is Sainte-James; and 'the master' and the ellipsis signify the queen. The tone here is scumbled and evasive, perhaps because Rohan feared the note falling into the wrong hands, but also, one senses, because he believed that directly confronting his mind-conceived monsters might summon them into existence. The triumphant sense of security with which the minute ends is not earned by its argument – it's the bravado of man straining to patch up and reinflate his burst confidence.

There had been a lengthy wait for a response from the queen to Sainte-James's overtures as Villette was in Bar, and could not, therefore, take down a letter. Jeanne mentioned to Rohan that Marie Antoinette, not wishing to take advantage of Sainte-James, had been trawling for succour in more familiar waters – but eventually the queen admitted that her efforts had been fruitless. This would be the only occasion, she stated, when she would rely on Sainte-James, and she vowed to repay him promptly.

By the time Rohan transmitted the news to Sainte-James, however, the navy treasurer was in a less bountiful mood. He would only lend the money if he could speak to the queen in person, a favour not even granted to Rohan himself. There are two possible explanations of Sainte-James's change of mind. He may, on reflection, have realised the inadvisability of doing business with Rohan. It must have seemed

---

* In the event, the jeweller gabbled to Breteuil about some unspecified jewels he had wanted to show the queen.

curious, if not outright suspect, that a man whom the queen was known to despise should cajole him into lending her money. There were more secure means of earning the queen's gratitude.

Rohan's secretary Georgel offers a more sinister interpretation (to be taken advisedly since he is prone to conspiracy-theorising). In his version, Sainte-James, agitated by doubts, approached Breteuil and Marie Antoinette's confidant Vermond, confirming their own suspicions that the cardinal had invoked the queen's name in some kind of scam. Breteuil took a deposition from Sainte-James and warned him not to lend the money. There is no positive evidence for Georgel's accusations, but it is clear that by mid-July the minister was ferreting around the edges of Boehmer's business.* Boehmer, a man of violent oscillations of mood and confidence, may have revealed to Breteuil more than he was willing to admit to Rohan; and the minister could have nudged Sainte-James into withdrawing his offer. In Georgel's account, Sainte-James, retracting the offer of the loan, asks Rohan: 'Are you sure about the intentions of the queen? Are you mistaken or has someone tricked you?' These were questions the cardinal was already asking himself.

* Georgel was convinced that Breteuil had been planning Rohan's downfall from July, when he instructed the Paris Police to investigate. However, the memoirs of Lenoir, the lieutenant-general of the Police, make clear that his officers received no instructions to investigate either Jeanne or Rohan in connection with the necklace's disappearance during that month.

11

Days of Reckoning

I T MAY HAVE been the promptings of Sainte-James, or the circling Breteuil, or long-hibernating fears which stretched themselves awake as awful spectres and seized Rohan's mind, expanding, louring, sprouting sharp teeth. With his associates, the cardinal breezed confidence. When Bassenge admitted his own worries and asked Rohan whether he had complete confidence in his intermediary, he replied: 'I have no doubts and the queen has the necklace.' But his actions ran contrariwise. At the end of July he procured a sample of Marie Antoinette's handwriting and was astonished to find that it bore no resemblance to the sale agreement in his possession. 'I'm tricked,' cried Rohan, alone in his study, with the two sheets of paper lying alongside each other, resisting all comparison.

Rohan rushed to Cagliostro and showed him the bill of sale. Cagliostro immediately lighted upon the signature: 'Marie Antoinette de France'.

'The queen does not sign her name like this,' he said. He was right – the queen signed herself simply as 'Marie Antoinette'.

'As grand almoner, you ought to know that. I'd wager you have been tricked.'

But the cardinal was seeking reassurance, not confirmation of his own suspicions, and dismissed Cagliostro's instinct.

'Surely you are tricked,' Cagliostro persisted. 'You have no alternative but to throw yourself at the king's feet and tell him exactly what has happened.'

'Alas, if I do that, this woman will be destroyed,' said Rohan.

The exchange offers a remarkable insight into the strength of Rohan's feeling for Jeanne. Through his paternalism, he had fashioned himself into a surrogate father: however prodigal his daughter was, he could not himself condemn her, could not do anything that might bring her to suffer. But the cardinal's pride was also talking here: there could be little more humiliating for a Rohan than to prostrate himself before a Bourbon king, a man he regarded as his equal. His concern for Jeanne was coupled with an impulse to stave off the day of his humbling.

Cagliostro, hoping to save Rohan from himself, suggested that 'if you don't want to do it, one of your friends will do it for you'.

Again, Rohan demurred.

Nonetheless, the cardinal was not entirely inactive. Jeanne was ordered to Rohan's *hôtel* to explain herself. With amazing forcefulness, she dismantled the evidence of Rohan's own eyes:

'Monseigneur, you affront me at the moment when I have just persuaded the queen to tear the veil that she believed ought to be maintained between her feelings and her conduct! Soon you will be ashamed of your suspicions.'

The necklace was with the queen, Jeanne insisted, and the signature on the document was genuine (due to her belated education, Marie Antoinette retained a childishly formed hand throughout her life, which might have enabled Jeanne to defend the lack of consistency in the penmanship).

Marie Antoinette would be in a position to pay the first instalment in September or October, Jeanne assured the cardinal. In the interim, she would hand over 30,000 livres, the amount of interest owed. Faith in Jeanne was reaffirmed at least partly because Rohan still believed that she lived in straitened circumstances, reliant on his intermittent charity, and could not raise such a large sum of money herself.

Jeanne's excuses bred their own difficulties. She had thrown out the figure of 30,000 livres, like gravel in the face of an assailant, but she did not have anywhere near that amount at home. Nicolas, who had more cash to hand, was in Bar. Jeanne scrabbled round her acquaintances, trying – and failing – to raise the requisite funds. In a bind, she stuffed the diamonds still lying around her house into her jewellery case, pawned the lot for 35,000 livres, and delivered the money to Rohan. Villette immediately rode to Bar to summon Nicolas back to Paris to redeem their nest eggs.

Rohan had known for nearly a month that the queen would be unable to pay the first instalment on 1 August, but it was only on 31 July that he told Boehmer all she would pay was the interest. Boehmer, atypically phlegmatic, accepted the queen's new proposal but insisted that the sum offset the capital owed. It appeared that the matter would not come to a head for at least another two months.

The cardinal's confrontation of Jeanne with the forged agreement had alerted the La Mottes. They realised it would serve their ends best if the ultimate revelation of their deceit – which would inevitably emerge when either the Boehmers' patience abraded entirely, or the cardinal's concerns grew insupportably heavy – occurred on their own terms. They almost certainly had not begun their heist with the endgame planned: they were opportunists, and Jeanne was more comfortable extemporising than calibrating a strategy. Certain preparations, however, had been made. As early as 15 June, the La Mottes had begun to transport their furniture to their house in Bar. Jeanne spread rumours that Rohan had been seen making large gifts of diamonds to the Cagliostros. At the beginning of August her apartment swarmed with activity; Jeanne and her servants were spotted entering and leaving with their heads burrowed furtively in their cloaks. Then, silence: the house had been stripped of its contents, its lights extinguished. The time for reckoning had arrived.

Jeanne asked Bassenge to call upon her on 3 August. He agreed to drop by at ten o'clock. Beforehand, he visited the cardinal. Rohan asked whether Marie Antoinette had yet mentioned the necklace to him or his partner. No, replied Bassenge. The cardinal expressed his astonishment that the queen was so unwilling to break her silence. He promised to write to her himself, explaining the difficulties in which the Boehmers had been placed by the postponement of the first instalment, and begging her to allay their worries.

Bassenge then went directly to Jeanne's house and found her rooms bare apart from a solitary bed in the bedroom. Jeanne asked if he had seen Rohan recently. I've just come from him, said Bassenge. Did he have anything important to declare? asked Jeanne. No, said Bassenge. Jeanne now revealed that Rohan was in a position of exquisite embarrassment. People, she insinuated, were bent on destroying the cardinal (who these were remained unspecified). It transpired that the signature on the sale agreement was forged, though Jeanne insisted – gratuitously – this had nothing to do with her. On the day before she had given the cardinal authentic samples of the queen's handwriting for comparison. (She showed Bassenge some scraps of paper and asked if he recognised the queen's hand – Bassenge did not.) Jeanne did not know how Rohan intended to proceed, but she warned the jewellers to 'take precautions' in case he fled.

The queen had been deeply offended, Jeanne continued, by the thank-you note that Rohan had insisted the jewellers write. Had they consulted her, she would have strongly advised against it. Now Jeanne became more precise about the enemies ranged against Rohan. She had 'certain knowledge that the queen sought to destroy the cardinal and she would refuse to declare that she had received the necklace'. When Bassenge asked how she knew this, Jeanne did not answer directly. Instead she began to decry Cagliostro's malevolent ascendancy over Rohan: her own niece had even been forced to participate in one of his satanic seances. And where, she wondered aloud, did all of the shaman's diamonds come from? 'I repeat,' said Jeanne, 'force the prince to take clear measures with you. He has a huge fortune. He can pay you.'

Jeanne's revelations were wandering and incoherent. What was the great crime? The forgery of the signature or the impolitic letter to the queen? Were they related? Who was intent on the cardinal's downfall? A rival faction at Court? The queen herself? How, exactly, was Cagliostro involved? Clarity was unnecessary: Jeanne banked on her intelligence so discombobulating Bassenge that he would not question its design. She was correct in her judgement, especially since her revelations were compounded by worse news that Boehmer had received the day before.

On 2 August Boehmer had visited Madame Campan, the queen's lady-in-waiting. For nearly three weeks, the failure of the queen to respond to his letter had lacerated the jeweller's nerves and he could bear the silence no longer. Agitated to learn the queen had no message for him, he asked Campan:

'But the answer to the letter I presented to her – to whom must I apply for that?'

'To nobody,' replied Campan. 'Her Majesty burned your memorandum without even comprehending its meaning.'

'Madame,' said Boehmer, 'that is impossible: the queen knows she owes me money.'

'Money, Monsieur Boehmer? Your last account with the queen was settled long ago.'

Boehmer, aching with frustration, snapped haughtily: 'Madame, you are not in on the secret. A man who is ruined for want of the payment of 1.5 million francs cannot be said to be satisfied.'

'Have you lost your senses? For what can the queen owe you so extravagant a sum!'

'For my necklace, madame.'

'What! That necklace again, which you have nagged the queen about for so many years! Did you not tell me you had sold it in Constantinople?'

'The queen desired me to give that answer to all who asked me about that subject.'

Boehmer now divulged that Rohan had acted as the queen's intermediary. Campan was astounded: 'You are deceived, the queen has not once spoken to the cardinal since his return from Vienna; there is no man at Court she looks less favourably upon.'

'You are deceived yourself, madame,' Boehmer responded with equally passionate certainty. 'She sees him very much in private. She gave 30,000 francs to His Eminence, which were paid to me as an instalment. She took them, in his presence, out of the little *secrétaire* of Sèvres porcelain next to the fireplace in the boudoir.'

'And the cardinal told you all this?'

'Yes, madame, himself.'

'What a detestable plot!'

'Indeed, to tell you the truth, madame, I am beginning to be much alarmed, for His Eminence assured me that the queen would wear the necklace on Pentecost, but I did not see it upon her, and it was that which induced me to write to Her Majesty.'

Campan advised Boehmer, for his own safety, to tell everything to Breteuil immediately. He had been 'extremely culpable' since, as 'a sworn officer it was unpardonable for him to have acted without the direct orders of the king, the queen or the minister'. Boehmer insisted he had done nothing wrong – he had several letters pertaining to the sale in his possession, signed by Marie Antoinette.

This exchange is drawn from Madame Campan's memoirs. The reliability of the account – like other of Campan's recollections – is in doubt, due to the preponderance of provably inaccurate details. For example, Boehmer did not write a memorandum, but a brief thank-you letter; and he did not possess any letters from Marie Antoinette on the subject of the necklace. The most significant claim – that Rohan was handed 30,000 livres by the queen herself – should be treated with severe scepticism. Perhaps Rohan might have told Boehmer that the queen had given him the money in person, in order to reassure him. However, given that Boehmer never mentions this crucial incident in his testimony during the trial, Campan's report of it should be discounted.

At this point, it is reasonable to question whether anything of substance can be drawn from Campan's account – or whether, indeed, the conversation happened at all. Writing retrospectively, tangential characters have a tendency to insert themselves more prominently into events of historical moment (both Beugnot and Georgel do so in this story). But despite all the caveats, the diary of the maréchal de Castries, the navy minister, written contemporaneously, records that 'it appears that on 2 August the queen for the first time suspected that someone had bought the diamonds in her name'.* The only people able, and possibly willing, to confirm the purchase, were the jewellers. Since they could not obtain an audience with the queen, they would have approached a member of her entourage, and it seems reasonable that this would be a person acquainted with the matter.†

That Boehmer spoke to Campan is of greater significance than the exact words they exchanged. This was the first time someone close to Marie Antoinette learned of the nexus linking the jewellers, the cardinal and the queen. From this point, events would veer in directions neither Rohan nor Jeanne could have anticipated. Still, Madame

* Campan gives the date of her conversation with Boehmer as 3 August, but the odd day, when writing thirty years later, is not significant.
† Bassenge's deposition mentions it had been Campan's husband who had told the jewellers in July that the queen was baffled by the letter they had sent her.

Campan did not immediately inform her mistress; nor, despite the advice he had been given, did Boehmer confess all to Breteuil.

Instead, he returned to his partner to discuss their predicament, and they were compelled to acknowledge they may have been victims of a swindle. The Boehmers needed to elicit from Rohan the extent of his involvement and complicity; and they would also have to grovel before the queen for absolution for any inadvertent wrongdoing and – hope beyond hope – her intervention to rescue them from bankruptcy. Bassenge remained distrustful of Jeanne's frisky evasions. He had always supposed that Jeanne was the intermediary between Rohan and the queen (her instruction that her name never be mentioned in conjunction with the necklace's sale raised his suspicions). She knew more, he believed, that she had admitted. And the cardinal, though he appeared to have orchestrated the deception, may in fact have been its victim.

Jeanne realised that a reckoning between the jewellers and Rohan was imminent, but she thought that when the latter understood he had been duped, he would stump up for the necklace to avoid disgrace. He would not have been able to raise the money himself; but the Rohan had mobilised to bail out the prince de Guéméné, and could be relied on to take all measures necessary to preserve their turgid pride. Rohan himself later admitted he would have tamped down the affair had he been granted the chance.

Nonetheless, Jeanne took further measures to insulate herself in case the disappearance of the necklace were to become the subject of criminal investigation. She needed to bind herself tightly to the cardinal so it would not appear, in hindsight, that she had spent the previous months distancing herself from him, concealing her opulence, leaving him to dangle alone. Paris was thick with police informants and Jeanne herself had been of interest to the police – on unrelated matters – since June, if not earlier.* She probably suspected that during any inquiry the authorities were likely to take

---

* Alan Williams in *The Police of Paris* has calculated that there could have been no more than 340 full-time spies. This is still a large number for, geographically, a relatively small city. And there were many more informants who were paid on an irregular basis.

an interest in someone who had so rapidly and inexplicably leapt from pauper to profligate. But stool pigeons could be bamboozled. They reported gossamer gossip, on visitors, on movements. False rumours could be seeded, guests paraded, strolls taken like catwalks. You just had to know the story you wanted to tell.

The La Mottes held an uproarious dinner party on the evening of 3 August – they would not see their Parisian friends again for some time. After the guests had left, Jeanne sent Rosalie Brissault, her *femme de chambre*, to Rohan's *hôtel* with an urgent message: she was unable to leave her house; he must visit her immediately. Rohan found Jeanne maddened with panic and streaming with tears. She told the cardinal she had been accused before Marie Antoinette of boasting of the favour shown to her by her royal patron. Despite her pleading that these lies had been fomented by jealousy, the queen had sided with her accusers. Her only option was to retreat to the countryside – this explained her denuded house – and wait for the queen's anger to subside.

Yet she was not quite ready to depart and, while she completed her business, felt exposed and threatened. Had the cardinal not seen the undercover officers circling her house, a garrotte ready to snap round her? Jeanne begged Rohan to protect her and Nicolas in his home until they were able to leave Paris. Despite an uneasy feeling that this was a charade, Rohan agreed to take her in. As he later told Georgel, 'if this woman had not acted in good faith, would she have come and handed herself over to me like this?'

Early in the morning of the 4 August, in the stifling darkness, Nicolas, Jeanne and Rosalie were smuggled into the cardinal's palace up the road. Rohan offered her practical assistance: a safe haven in his sovereign lands on the east bank of the Rhine, outside the jurisdiction of the French authorities. Jeanne, for whom flight and exile were never a consideration, insisted on sitting out her ostracism in Bar.

Rohan's serenity at this juncture is hard to fathom. He did not interrogate Jeanne about the details of her contretemps or express any anxiety about how future payments from the queen for the necklace might be winkled out. Perhaps, after a few hours of brooding over Jeanne's tale of grief, Rohan had finally accepted he had been deceived, but did not wish to accuse Jeanne for fear of provoking some unpredictable rashness. But the opposite is equally plausible. The dismissal of Jeanne had severed the single ligature that connected Rohan with the queen. With their intermediary dispatched, Marie Antoinette would be compelled to receive Rohan in person and avow her esteem for him. The day he had anticipated for so long was now imminent. Cagliostro, flitting through the palace, knew exactly what was required of Rohan: turning over the La Mottes to the police and confessing all he knew to the king. Rohan again refused. 'In this case', said Cagliostro, 'you have no one to turn to apart from God. He must expedite the rest.'

Another uninvited guest arrived at seven o'clock in the morning: Bassenge, truffling for clues. He apologised in advance for the presumptuous question he was about to pose.

'Don't worry,' said Rohan.

'Monseigneur, are you entirely confident in the intermediary whom you have employed in the business of the necklace with the queen? I ask you this question because you informed me on a few occasions that there was an intermediary employed in this business.'

Rohan paused: 'If I hesitate, it is not because I am untruthful, but to tell you only what you need to know.' Raising his hands to the heavens, the cardinal declaimed, 'See us, hear us, I have said nothing to you that is not completely true,' and waved the jeweller towards the door.

After thirty-six hours of Rohan's hospitality, the La Mottes announced they were leaving to stay with relatives. They returned to their apartment and burned all their papers. At two o'clock in the morning on 6 August, Villette rode east from Paris, his destination unknown. That evening, the lights in the apartment on the rue Neuve-Saint-Gilles were snuffed out, the door bolted, and a coach bearing the La Mottes drove towards Bar-sur-Aube.

12

'I Will Pay for Everything'

ROHAN'S PLATITUDES LEFT Bassenge dissatisfied – and the jeweller remained suspicious of Jeanne too. Just before she abandoned Paris, he called again at her house. Only Nicolas was around: his wife, he said, was at Versailles, owing too many personal obligations to the cardinal to abandon him now. Nicolas claimed to have only recently learned about the necklace. As far as he knew, it had been sold on to an unknown party.

Apart from admitting to theft, there was nothing else Nicolas could have said that would have alarmed Bassenge more. The necklace had always been intended to adorn the queen; now she would never be seen wearing it. But financial calculations shouldered out sentimental regrets. If Marie Antoinette had indeed sold the necklace, then she ought to be in a position to pay the first instalment. Why, then, had she postponed it until October? There was only one person left to question. On 5 August, Boehmer went to Versailles, seeking an audience with the queen. He was turned away. 'He is mad,' Marie Antoinette said. 'I have nothing to say to him and will not see him.'

None of the cardinal's actions during this period suggests any anxiety. No family councils were convoked; no efforts to borrow money were made; no further mollifications of the jewellers attempted. As late as 10 August, Rohan told Sainte-James he was going to encourage the Boehmers to ask the queen again about her debt. His vacillating trust in Jeanne seems to have settled into security. Whatever misgivings had sedimented within him were suppressed by a belief in his own invulnerability – events would defer to him like footmen. He still had in his possession the purchase agreement signed by the queen. True, its authenticity was in question, but at least it proved he had conducted himself in good faith.

Two or three days after the La Mottes' departure, Marie Antoinette and her close circle began rehearsals at Trianon for a production of Beaumarchais's *The Barber of Seville*. Marie Antoinette was to play Rosine, the ward of Bartholo and Count Almaviva's beloved. During a break, the queen berated Campan, somewhat unfairly, for having sent Boehmer to her (Campan had actually told the jeweller to speak to Breteuil). Now, the lady-in-waiting pleaded with Marie Antoinette to speak to Boehmer: 'It was of the utmost importance for her peace of mind. There was a plot afoot, of which she was unaware . . . it was a serious one, since documents signed by herself had been shown to people who had lent Boehmer money.' The queen, though outraged, moved discreetly. A letter survives from one of Marie Antoinette's lackeys to Boehmer, dated 8 August. It is marked 'very urgent', and the bearer was given the incentive of a tip of 18 sols if it was delivered before three o'clock. The note inside asks the jeweller to examine 'a belt buckle that had lost some diamonds' – hardly the most pressing of matters – but the mention of lost diamonds winked at the true reason for the summons.

The journey by coach to Versailles, early in the morning on 9 August, gave Boehmer plenty of time to muster his thoughts. On arrival, Boehmer mapped out to Marie Antoinette the relationship, as he understood it, between the cardinal and the queen, and refused to accept the queen's denials. 'Madame, there is no longer time for feigning,' he implored. 'Condescend to admit that you have my necklace, and let some help be given to me, or my bankruptcy will bring the whole business to light.' Frustrated, the queen sent him away.

Like so many critical moments in this affair, Marie Antoinette's reaction to her conversation with Boehmer is disputed. In a letter to her brother, the Emperor Joseph II, she wrote that the first person she spoke to was her husband. According to Madame Campan, however, the queen closeted herself with her confidant, Abbé Vermond, and Breteuil. Their advice, Campan would later decry, was coloured by their loathing of Rohan. Rohan's conduct was so egregious, the pair counselled, that it required exemplary punishment. The queen declared 'hideous vices must be unmasked, when the Roman purple and the title of Prince cloak a money-grubber, a fraudster who dares to compromise the wife of his sovereign – France and all Europe shall know it'.

On the 12 August, the jewellers gave Breteuil a written statement: Rohan had approached them to buy the necklace in secret on behalf of a third party; he only told them that the queen was their customer after the deal had been concluded; and there was little further contact with Rohan until the queen demanded a reduction in price. At no point was Jeanne's name mentioned. Now, for the first time, Louis XVI was informed.

The king and queen asked the maréchal de Soubise, the patriarch of the Rohan clan, to obtain a response to the Boehmers' deposition from the cardinal. But when they sent for him on 14 August – a Sunday – he was not to be found at home. Louis was insistent that the cardinal should be presented with the accusations as soon as possible but, mindful that he and his wife were interested parties, he secured witnesses to the confrontation. On Monday morning he requested the presence of Breteuil and the marquis de Miromesnil, the keeper of the seals (the minister of justice). Miromesnil, tapped on his shoulder while still at Mass, feared that an unexpected royal audience meant only one thing: his imminent sacking. The king asked the ministers for their advice on how to proceed. Miromesnil peevishly remarked that had Madame Cahouet de Villers, who had also forged the queen's handwriting, been chastised publicly, future malefactors would have been deterred. Breteuil, for the time being, merely reiterated his belief in Rohan's culpability.

Monday 15 August was the Assumption of the Virgin Mary, Marie Antoinette's patronal feast day. The gallery of Versailles, filled with primped court folk and city folk, pullulated with neck-craning and inconsequential talk:

'Have you seen the king?'

'Yes, he smiled.'

'It's true. He did smile.'

'He appears happy.'

'Woman! What's it to you?'

Rohan was dressing in his regalia, a white rochet underneath his scarlet mozetta, preparing to celebrate Mass for the royal family. At ten o'clock one of Louis's *garde du corps* arrived to escort him to the king. Louis disapproved of the cardinal, quite apart from his wife's loathing, and always avoided speaking to him whenever possible. Rohan must have known that he was not being invited for coffee and cake before the service.

As the queen could not even bear to look at Rohan, he was questioned by the king alone.* Louis asked the cardinal whether he had bought the necklace in the queen's name.

'It is true, sire,' Rohan immediately confessed. 'I have been tricked.'

Rohan read the Boehmers' statement and did not contest its contents. This time addressing the queen directly, he again admitted he had been deceived. A copy of a letter written by him, which confirmed the authenticity of the signature and requested delivery of the necklace, had been attached to the jewellers' deposition.

'I don't remember having written this letter, but I must have done since they have given you a copy,' said Rohan, judging that compliance was wiser than contradiction. 'I will pay,' he added.

'Do you have anything to say to justify this conduct and the guarantee you gave [about the signature]?' said Louis. Rohan was, by now, visibly shaking, so Louis, Marie Antoinette and the two ministers left the room to allow him time to regain his equanimity and produce a written response. With Rohan in solitary contemplation, Louis

---

* The two best-known chronicles of the skirmishing that occurred in the king's council chamber were written decades after the event, by people who were not present and who were each fierce partisans of one of the participants – Madame Campan and the Abbé Georgel. Their accounts are vivid, dramatic and – festooned with an implausible quantity of reported speech – entirely unreliable. Fortunately, four more objective sources, all written contemporaneously, allow us to reconstruct the disputation before the king and the queen. The navy minister, the maréchal de Castries, kept a diary during his time in office. Though he was not in the room, he remained in constant communication with his colleagues and was involved in questioning the cardinal during the early stages of the investigation. He was of neither the king's nor the queen's faction (in fact, he was desperate to leave government and had tried to resign – and failed – a number of times). Diplomatic dispatches also exist from Jean-Baptiste Rivière, the chargé d'affaires of the Saxon legation at the French court; and the Swedish ambassador, the Baron de Staël-Holstein. Staël-Holstein maintained firm friendships with Axel Fersen, his countryman, and the duchesse de Polignac, both boon companions of the queen. Finally, there is a report of the meeting by Louis Thiroux de Crosne, who had just been appointed as lieutenant-general of the Paris Police.

canvassed opinion on how best to proceed. He and Breteuil agreed that Rohan ought to be arrested. Miromesnil objected: it would be inappropriate to seize the cardinal while he was dressed in his pontifical vestments. The king shrugged dismissively.

Fifteen minutes later, Rohan brought them his justification: it contained a few scrawled lines restating his admission and his plea that he had been duped. Now, however, he mentioned Madame de La Motte, who had persuaded him that the queen wanted the necklace.

'Where is this woman?' asked the king.

'I don't know,' said Rohan.*

'Do you have the necklace?'

'The woman has it.'

Breteuil was instructed to have her arrested.

'Where are the supposed letters of authorisation, written and signed by the queen?' continued Louis.

'I have them, sire,' replied Rohan. 'I now realise that they are forged. I will bring them to Your Majesty at Versailles.'

Louis was in no mood to trust Rohan: 'Sir I can do nothing in a circumstance such as this other than seal your papers and take you into custody' – the sealing of papers was standard procedure in a criminal case, to prevent the accused from destroying evidence. 'The queen's name is precious to me. It had been compromised and I must not neglect that.'

'I beg Your Majesty', said Rohan desperately, 'not to make a scene over this, especially on a day like today, out of consideration for my family. I will pay for everything.'

'I will try to console them as much as I can,' responded Louis, unmoved. 'I want you to have the chance to justify yourself. You will not pay anything. But I cannot, as either a king or a husband, let this matter drop, for the queen has been compromised in it. I am warning you that you will be arrested as you leave my rooms.'

---

* According to Staël-Holstein, Rohan claimed he had only ever met Jeanne once. But it would have been bizarre to risk such a blatant and easily refutable lie, and one that undermined his case. After all, would Rohan have bought such an expensive item for a woman he believed despised him if asked by someone he barely knew?

Finally, the queen spoke: 'It is extraordinary, monsieur, that you could have imagined for an instant that I would have charged an unknown person with a matter of this importance. Moreover, my opinion about you has been established for a long enough time – you should have known that I would never have given you an order like this.'

As Rohan strained to answer, the queen visibly lost patience (she later told a friend that she almost fell ill with horror and anger). The king, pained at his wife's distemper, demanded that Rohan leave immediately. In almost the same breath he ordered Breteuil to apprehend him.

Outside the king's apartment, the crowd, waiting for the royal party, rippled with something more than restlessness. From the way that Rohan had been briskly marched in and the length of time he had been kept, they concluded that his business was extraordinary. The cardinal lingered in the Salon de l'Oeil de Boeuf, a gilt and stucco antechamber that was overseen by a large, oculate window. Veronese's *Judith with the Head of Holofernes* hung ominously on one of the walls. As Breteuil emerged, Rohan asked if they could remain there until the gawkers had dispersed; or, he suggested, Breteuil could personally guard him as they walked through the palace, as though discussing some affair of state, so that he might be spared the shame of detention in public. While he was pestering the baron, the pair emerged in the gallery, where the greatest number of onlookers had assembled. Without answering, Breteuil turned to the nearest guard and, his voice snapping for attention, declaimed: 'The king orders you, monsieur, to arrest the cardinal.'

13

Arresting Developments

FROM MIDSUMMER ONWARDS, a fleet of wagons, distended with furniture, had trundled down the road from Paris to Bar-sur-Aube. Twenty craftsmen toiled on improving the La Mottes' house, lacquering it in the most fashionable oriental taste. Ceiling-high mirrors and a riot of ormolu made the rooms swell and glint. Stuff jostled everywhere: busts of Rousseau and Voltaire, statues of Flora and Hebe, vases balanced on plinths, stucco columns surmounted with bronze candelabra, a litter of card tables, an ostrich egg. One display case was filled entirely with diamonds; two mechanical canaries twittered in harmony; golden music boxes sang; the clocks were decorated with marionettes that danced when the hour struck. Novels by Riccoboni and Crébillon, Rousseau's collected works in thirty volumes and Père Anselme's *Genealogical and Chronological History of the Royal House of France* filled the bookshelves. In the dining room, two gargantuan dressers shouldered silver plate and porcelain; twenty capacious copper pans hung in the kitchen. Jeanne's bed alone cost more than 6,000 livres: a canopied *lit à la polonaise* with a coverlet of crimson velvet, embroidered with sequins and gold lace and pearls.

On the evening of 6 August, having left Rohan and the jewellers floundering, the La Mottes arrived in Bar. They had given no thought to fleeing abroad. Jeanne did not desire to live in comfortable exile. Her father's dying words were indelibly stamped upon her conscience. Remembering that she was a Valois was not an exercise in nostalgia or a goad to moral nobility: it meant acquiring the resources, by any means necessary, to live according to her station. For all her success in the shark pool of the capital, Jeanne ultimately wished to return home, to be reverenced by the folk among whom she had been raised.

One of those surprised to see the La Mottes was their lawyer, Jacques Beugnot, who had returned to Bar in July. When he had seen Jeanne before leaving Paris, she had told him she would remain there until October (an indication that Jeanne was forced to activate her escape plan earlier than anticipated). Beugnot saw something melancholy in the couple's relentless expenditure: they acted, he thought, like 'people that are bored of money and feel the urge to throw it out of the window'. On their last visit, many had been awed by their ostentation; now they were disgusted by it. Jeanne was a courtesan who got lucky, the townfolk sniped. Few people attended their soirées and fewer still invited them.

On 17 August, Jeanne dined with Beugnot at the Abbey of Clairvaux. It was the feast of St Bernard, the monastery's founder, and the Abbé Maury, one of the most popular preachers in the country (and, later, Napoleon's archbishop of Paris) was due to address the assembled dignitaries. He was delayed, however, and dinner began without him, the abbot treating Jeanne like a 'princess of the church', presuming she was Rohan's lover.

At 9.30, Maury dashed in: 'There is a piece of news', he declared, 'that astonishes, that confounds all of Paris. The cardinal de Rohan, grand almoner of France, was arrested on Tuesday, on Assumption Day, in his pontifical robes when leaving the king's *cabinet*.'

'Do you know what for?' Maury was asked.

'No, not precisely,' he replied. 'They speak of a diamond necklace that he should have bought for the queen, which he didn't buy. But people don't believe that, for such a trifle, they would have arrested the grand almoner of France in his pontifical robes – you understand, in his pontifical robes and leaving the king's *cabinet*.'

Jeanne dropped her napkin and, for a moment, stared palsied at her meal. Her face blenched. She had never envisioned that Rohan would be arrested; she had expected him to pay what was owed, shamefaced. Then, awakening to the company, she dashed out of the room. The more generous guests believed that she was overcome with concern for her friend; others wondered why she did not interrogate Maury further. Beugnot followed her after a few minutes. She was already waiting in the coach.

'I was perhaps wrong to leave so abruptly, especially in the presence of the Abbé Maury,' said Jeanne.

'Not at all,' Beugnot reassured her. 'Your relationship with the cardinal is well known and, for all intents and purposes, acknowledged. His life is at stake in this, perhaps. Your duty is to stay ahead of letters, couriers, news. You would have been guilty of losing time by having supper at Clairvaux. But can you explain this arrest?'

'No, unless it is some sleight of hand by his Cagliostro. The cardinal is obsessed with him. It is not my fault. I haven't stopped warning him.'

'That's in your favour. But what is this story of a necklace that the cardinal had to buy for the queen? And why was a cardinal commissioned to buy a necklace? And how could the queen have chosen Prince Louis for this, whom she openly hates?'

'I repeat that it is entirely Cagliostro,' said Jeanne, her voice tightening.

'But you have entertained this charlatan. Are you not compromised yourself at all by him?'

'Not in the least, and I am completely relaxed. I was very wrong to leave dinner.'

'It was not wrong. If you were at ease on your own account, you oughtn't to be for your unfortunate friend's.'

'Ah, you do not know him. When he is in trouble, he is capable of saying a hundred idiocies to extract himself from it.'

Jeanne's touchy manner, her defensiveness, the way she veered from forced serenity to angst, warned Beugnot that she was not being open. Yet, stirred by the same wilfulness that had originally attracted him and wishing to save her from it, he suggested a decisive course of action.

'Madame de La Motte, you are saying much more than I would have wanted to hear. I have one final thing to propose to you. It is ten o'clock at night; we are approaching Bayet. I will leave you in the care of a friend, whom you should know that I can answer for. I will return in your carriage to Bar-sur-Aube. I will warn Monsieur de La Motte, who, in one hour, can come to fetch you in a post-chaise drawn by your two best horses. He'll bring along your most precious valuables and both of you, tonight, will take the road to

Châlons, for the Troyes road is not safe for you. You will reach the Picardy coast or the Normandy one. Don't show yourself at Boulogne, Calais or Dieppe, or you might be spotted. But, between these ports, there are twenty places where, for ten louis, you can get across to England.'

But Jeanne had no intention of fleeing the country like a smuggler.

'Monsieur, you are tedious to the end. I have let you carry on like this because my mind was on other things. Must I tell you ten times that I have nothing to do with this? I will say it again. I'm very angry to have risen from the table, as though I was an accomplice in the madness of the cardinal.'

The Champagne night was untroubled by any more rancour. At Bar, they discovered that Nicolas had still not returned from hunting. Beugnot begged Jeanne to burn her papers. She agreed, but insisted on sifting them first. As Beugnot rummaged through the large sandalwood box which Jeanne had filled with her correspondence, the letters composed a poem of Rohan's beguilement by Jeanne. 'The madness of love was heightened by the madness of ambition . . . A prince of the church did not hesitate to write, to sign, to address a woman whom he knew so little and so badly.' (Beugnot leaves ambiguous whether the woman was Jeanne or Marie Antoinette.) Jeanne vacillated over what to keep – there were bank drafts, bearer bonds, title deeds mixed in; Beugnot stood shovelling armfuls of documents into the fire. It took until three in the morning to immolate the lot; the room stank of burnt paper and wax.*

At ten o'clock the next morning Inspector Subois of the Paris Police arrived with an order for Jeanne's arrest. Jeanne's maid told them that her mistress was still in bed. 'I don't care what state she's in,' said Subois, 'I have to speak with her. Take me to her

---

* The only account of what Jeanne did on the night she heard of the cardinal's arrest is found in Beugnot's memoirs, which are not entirely reliable. He also claimed that there were letters in Jeanne's chest from the Boehmers, setting out the payment dates for the necklace, though Rohan was the only person who retained such documents. Nonetheless, we do know that all Jeanne's correspondence was destroyed and this is the likeliest occasion for it.

room.' Once inside, he drew back the curtains and prodded Jeanne awake. Bleary-eyed, she was taken into custody. What papers remained in the house were placed under seal. Nicolas, by now returned, volunteered to accompany his wife, but hastily withdrew his offer when he learned, if he wished to join her, he, too, would have to travel manacled. Don't worry, Subois told Jeanne, you'll soon return home.

Once the baron de Breteuil had pealed the order for the cardinal's arrest, he did not linger long. Rohan, keenly perceiving the danger he was in, asked his guard for permission to write a brief note. The guard, as embarrassed as anyone, could hardly refuse a prince of the Church and the Holy Roman Empire so piddling a request, and even lent him a pencil. Rohan jotted down a few words and stowed the scrap of paper in his hat. Swearing volubly, he was then escorted by the captain of the king's *garde du corps*, the duc de Villeroi, to his room in Versailles, where seals were affixed to his papers. Unobserved, he slipped the message, scribbled in German, to a servant. Though it does not survive, its tenor is easily inferred: ride to Paris as fast as you can and burn my correspondence. Rohan then travelled to the capital under guard to rejoin Breteuil.

Fortunately for the cardinal, his servant was fleeter of foot than the minister, who journeyed at a languid pace. Rohan's valet had spurred his horse on so violently that it collapsed and died on his arrival at a quarter past two. He himself fainted, the note falling from his hands as he fell to the floor. Georgel struggled to read the cardinal's frantic handwriting, but the young man, hastily revived, conveyed the instructions. Soon, practically all the letters from Marie Antoinette were ash in the grate. Georgel, thinking that a couple of examples might come in useful later on, stashed them far from inquisitive eyes.

Rohan arrived at his palace at three o'clock. Breteuil had prohibited him from speaking to anyone until his own arrival, but his guard, the comte d'Agoult, permitted a short conversation with Georgel, in which Rohan was reassured that his orders had been followed. 'You must be very surprised,' he said to the abbé, 'but you should be certain that I'm not a fool, and that I have been authorised to do what I have done. I have proof of it. Be calm. Perhaps we will see each other this evening.'

An hour later, Breteuil, in the company of the police chief, de Crosne, walked into the house 'with the air and tone of a conqueror who had defeated his enemy'. Rohan, gathering his dignity, handed over the forged authorisation. His papers were sealed and Breteuil permitted him to remain at home under d'Agoult's watch. Throughout the evening, distressed and confused relatives visited; Rohan greeted them all with 'a serene countenance'. Was he confident that something would be done to clear up the mess? Or did his embarrassment limit his social interaction to beatific grinning?

The maréchal de Soubise, the godfather of the Rohan clan, creaked out of bed in the pale hours of the morning after. He thought a brief discussion at the palace ought to straighten out this little misunderstanding. The cardinal had not been particularly forthcoming, but Soubise struggled to imagine a crime severe enough to warrant the measures Breteuil had taken. He found the king in implacable mood. 'I don't wish for his downfall; but it is for his own sake that I must arrest him,' said Louis, who conveyed Rohan's own account of the sale of the necklace.

Louis directed the investigation with a purpose few believed he had in him. On the same day as he received Soubise, he appointed a ministerial committee to interview Rohan and examine his papers. Breteuil, the minister hitherto most involved and head of the department responsible for the police, was an obvious choice. His known detestation of the cardinal was balanced by the presence of the experienced foreign minister, the comte de Vergennes, who had long-standing ties to the Rohan. A diplomat from a young age, Vergennes had served across Europe from Portugal to the Ottoman Empire. A gravel-dry workaholic, he was the most durable minister in Louis XVI's reign, holding office from the king's accession in 1774 to his own death in 1787. Even his enemies respected his political cunning. He was the king's most trusted advisor and his supremacy in council was unchallenged.

The third member of the commission was the unaffiliated maréchal de Castries, a veteran of the Seven Years War, who had commanded the garrison in Lunéville where Nicolas de La Motte had enlisted.

From the outset, the inquiry was prejudiced by the king's conviction that there 'is excessive proof that he [Rohan] used the name of the queen in forged signatures to obtain from a jeweller diamonds worth 1.6 million livres'. The ministers' task was limited to discovering 'if there are not other people mixed up in this crime'. Louis himself was driven more by grief than revenge. 'It is the saddest and most horrible affair that I have yet seen,' he wrote to Vergennes: sadness at the pain caused to the queen; horror at the grand almoner's betrayal, but also in the burgeoning awareness that the cardinal's slip may have splashed acid over his wife's reputation.

Rohan spent all of 16 August instructing his family about his predicament, the men of the king's *garde du corps* clinging to his walls like stuccoed columns. He appeared at a window, playing with his monkey, to reassure the world he was still cheerful. At eleven o'clock, he retired to bed. Scarcely had he fallen asleep than he was roused by d'Agoult. Breteuil had personally delivered a *lettre de cachet* ordering his immediate transfer to the Bastille.

Lettres de cachets were more than simply arrest warrants. They were issued in the name of the king and could command the imprisonment or exile of the recipient for an indefinite amount of time. Regarded as arbitrary in their employment, and immune to appeal, they were the clearest exemplar of absolute rule's tendency to despotism, though their prevalence was exaggerated by their detractors. Most, in fact, were issued at the request of families to restrain delinquent relatives. Even though the use of *lettres de cachets* had been restricted in Louis XVI's reign, the public's detestation of them was lit by a number of excoriating indictments. The future Jacobin Billaud-Varenne, in his catalogue of ministerial atrocities published in 1789, called the *lettre de cachet* 'the Arm of Despotism' at the service of 'the horrors of tyranny'; the comte de Mirabeau's *Des lettres de cachets et des prisons d'état*, written after he had been shut up in the dungeons of Vincennes, argued that only a transformation in government – 'a body of representatives freely elected from the greatest part of the nation' – could preserve liberty from such abuses. Rohan had expected, at worst, to be banished to his diocese, not boarded up like an enemy of the state. He gathered a few possessions and stepped into the carriage of the marquis de Launay, governor of the prison.

The Bastille is remembered as the architectural embodiment of all that the Revolution upended – a bleacher of beards, a scarifier of brows, a candlesnuffer of men's lives; a medieval edifice that seemed to draw the light out from the capital of the Enlightenment. It had been built during the Hundred Years War as a fortress to defend Paris from the English – its blackened walls designed to repel invaders, not deter escapees – and had welcomed nobles and prelates many times before, along with the overweeningly ambitious, intriguers against the kingdom, sexual and religious deviants, as well as dozens of writers whose pens had scribbled too freely. The dank subterranean *cachots*, in which it was easy to forget a man, had been withdrawn from active service, though the *calottes* in the attic were still in use, leaking with rain, blasted by the heat.

In general, however, the detainees, the vast majority of whom were held in the eight octagonal towers that framed the castle, lived in circumstances which, while not plush, were far superior to the rest of Paris's prisons. The cells were sprucely furnished – a bed hung with green baize curtains, a fireplace or stove, a table, a smattering of chairs. Some had mattresses for valets, latrines and armchairs, and residents were allowed to accessorise their rooms. The marquis de Sade installed a wardrobe for his numerous outfits, tapestries and paintings, and 133 books. Prisoners could read books from the lending library or play billiards. Some were allowed visitors (though, most frequently, it was rats who breezed through), consultations with doctors, and took constitutionals on the battlements and the inner courtyard. For many years, none of the doors had bolts. A staff of 110, including a doctor, an apothecary, a midwife and a chaplain, served, on average, fewer than 40 *bastillards*.

Bread, cheese, wine and some kind of potage formed the basic ration, though the higher class of prisoner was fed more handsomely. Marmontel remembered 'an excellent soup, a succulent side of beef, a thigh of boiled chicken oozing with grease, a little dish of fried, marinaded artichokes or of spinach, really fine Cressane pears, fresh grapes, a bottle of old Burgundy and the best Moka coffee'. The luckiest were permitted luxuries: tobacco, mussels and gooseberry jam.

The Bastille's dread reputation was due, above all, to the work of Simon Linguet. After two years inside, Linguet wrote his *Memoirs of the Bastille*, a work made popular by its account of his eye-watering deprivations. The torments were perennial: lice, loneliness, the fear of poison. Linguet was Jonah inside the whale, a coffined man counting down his breaths. He was most troubled by the overwhelming sense of being engulfed – the 'empty existence more cruel than death' – and the slow obliteration of personality that comes with the severing of companionship. The Bastille deprived inmates not just of their liberty, but their humanity; the state did not protect its children, it consumed them. Linguet's account may have been exaggerated, but its Gothic horrors appealed to the public's cultural tastes. In the absence of countervailing narratives – ex-prisoners who had enjoyed superior treatment were not inclined to praise the amenities – the Bastille became the kingdom's heart of darkness.

Rohan was welcomed like an honoured guest. The rooms of the lieutenant-governor were given over to him, and he was waited on by three valets and permitted to receive visitors. Every evening he dined at the governor's table. On 17 August, he returned to his *hôtel* under escort to witness the unsealing of his papers. Georgel had given them a thorough gutting. Breteuil seethed; Vergennes and Castries, who took no pleasure in the disgrace of a fellow nobleman, were visibly delighted. Georgel gleefully told Breteuil, when questioned about the empty files, 'I am only fulfilling my duty, as you do to the king, when His Majesty gives you an order.' Then on to Versailles, Rohan chirruping all the way that he had been tricked and deserved only a fool's cap. Again, nothing pertinent was found.

On 20 August Rohan requested a meeting with Vergennes and Castries, hoping to parlay their personal sympathy into an intervention with Louis on his behalf. His opening gambit was gauchely direct: 'Should I treat you as the king's men or as friends?' he asked, instantaneously raising Castries's hackles.

'We are acting as ministers,' replied the navy minister. 'Otherwise we would be unable to give the king advice.'

'You're right,' said Rohan, 'I was about to act wrongly. But what do you suggest I say to you? And what is my duty if my admission could compromise someone?'

'I would speak the truth. We're going to record what you say in writing. It will serve as the basis for the investigation of this affair.'

'Alas,' sighed Rohan, 'I will tell you everything.'

Once the cardinal had finished expanding on the sketchy chron-ology he had presented to the king, Castries asked if there was 'any receipt, any letter, that might support what you say'.

'No, I have burnt everything,' said Rohan, as though expecting a round of applause for his nifty thinking.

'But what if she denies everything you claim?' asked Castries.

'She will not dare when we are brought together. But you will soon be able to learn what she has to say for I gather that she has been arrested and will be brought here this evening,' said Rohan, eager to show that imprisonment had not left him any worse informed. 'Is this true?'

The ministers pleaded ignorance, though Jeanne was already in the Bastille, having arrived at four o'clock that morning.

14

Hotel Bastille

JEANNE HAD BEEN cordially welcomed in the early hours of 20 August by de Launay in his dressing gown, who promised 'we will take great care of you'. Though assured an airy cell, the one she was led to was 'wretched'. A complaint resulted in the delivery of 'an excellent feather-bed with fine sheets and curtains'. The rest of the room was spartan: 'bare walls, no cabinet . . . nothing but a stove and a small chimney'. Like so many prisoners through the years, her immediate instinct was to try to make contact with whoever was roomed close by. 'I opened the window, to see if I could discover anybody or make myself sufficiently conspicuous for anybody to see me. I climbed up to the highest part of the window, holding my face close to the bars, but could discover nothing. As for the people, it was impossible to distinguish them.'

Soon she had company: later that morning, de Crosne, dressed austerely in flowing black robes, and another senior police officer, Pierre Chénon, arrived. The pair interrogated Jeanne for hours; she neatly parried their lines of questioning. Jeanne admitted introducing Rohan to the jewellers but denied taking any role in the necklace's sale. She had heard nothing more of it until July when an agitated Rohan confided that he believed he had been tricked by the comtesse de Cagliostro, who had become such 'an intimate friend of the queen, that they saw each other often together in private and conducted a correspondence'. 'I'll pay these unfortunates [the jewellers],' Rohan had said. 'What I'm utterly fearful of is the case reaching the courts.'

Rohan's troubles, Jeanne suggested, stemmed from his infatuation with Cagliostro, whom he revered as a 'great man', even a 'god'. Cagliostro conducted a seance with a small child – Jeanne did not mention that it had been her niece – where 'Rohan was on his knees, he was in ecstasy, he looked on tenderly, cried, raised his hands to the skies and lost his temper with me for not displaying the admiration that I ought to have done'. When questioned about an inventory of diamonds and receipts for their sale found among her papers, Jeanne replied that she and Nicolas had been given the gems by Rohan to sell on his behalf.

Jeanne's approach in her initial interrogations would remain consistent throughout the trial: admitting facts which could be independently verified; reverting blame onto the Cagliostros, who were suspiciously foreign and inexplicably wealthy; and arguing that her actions were not those of a rational criminal. Had she wanted to steal the necklace she would not have simulated a friendship with the queen that would surely have been exposed. Had she stolen it, why did she retire to Bar – a move intended to staunch her husband's profligacy, she claimed – rather than flee the country?

On the basis of Jeanne's testimony, the Cagliostros were immediately arrested. The prospect of a quick release dwindled when the police lifted the seals on the comtesse de Cagliostro's effects and discovered a number of diamonds and 'several papers that appeared suspect'. Cagliostro tried to ingratiate himself with his interrogators: he was a true Catholic, he said, who 'only wants to do good through medicine', though his claims to be an ordinary citizen were rather undermined by his insistence that he had been raised in Egypt until the age of eighteen.

Though the records of the ministerial investigation only partially survive, Jeanne's story emerged as the stronger one, especially as other suspects-cum-witnesses were interrogated. Nicolas's sister, Madame de La Tour, told the police that the La Mottes were not rich and had a measly jewellery collection. The baron de Planta mentioned the meeting with the queen in the gardens of Versailles, but his memory was too porous to supply any details. Rohan refused outright to be questioned by de Crosne, due to the latter's inferior rank. The cardinal nourished his faith that an Establishment fudge would see him released soon, without even having to relinquish the grand almonership – but his unwillingness to comply merely allowed Jeanne's testimony to pass unchallenged.

Marie Antoinette had been heartened by the king's protectiveness during the confrontation with Rohan. 'I am extremely moved by the reason and firmness that the king displayed in that difficult encounter,' she wrote to her brother. 'I hope that this affair will be finished soon; but I don't yet know if it will be sent to the *parlement* or if the guilty person and his or her family will throw themselves at the mercy of the king. In any case, I want all the details of this horrible event to be completely cleared up in the eyes of everyone.'

The queen referred to the 'event' in the most abstract of terms, in part to disinfect this disgusting intrusion into her life; but also because the affair itself was poorly understood – even she, as well briefed as anyone, incorrectly reported that 'the [forged] signature is by the aforementioned Valois de la Mothe. They have compared the letters, which are certainly in her hand.' A vindication was required precisely because the lack of established facts encouraged the public, many of whom were ill-disposed to the queen, to draw conclusions based on their prejudices.

On 25 August, Louis summoned his council, in the presence of his wife, to discuss the cardinal's fate. Marie Antoinette spoke first. 'I am accused; I am talked about in public as having received a necklace and not having paid for it. I want to know the truth about an incident in which someone dared to make free with my name. The relatives of the cardinal wish that he should be dealt with according to normal legal procedures. He appears to feel the same way. I want the affair to be sent [to the courts].'

Awkward silence. A shuffling of papers. Bowed eyes endlessly fascinated with toecaps. Vergennes, Miromesnil and Castries, all experienced ministers, knew that a lengthy trial could have uncontrollable repercussions – the queen's reputation, far from being repaired, might be singed further. Finally Castries spoke: 'Since the investigation has been conducted so far down an extrajudicial route, it appears that we could still pursue it in the same way and arrange a confrontation [between those arrested], in order to throw the necessary light on things.* I am sure . . . that the relatives, though not afraid of the courts, have not yet demanded [a trial].'

Miromesnil, on the other hand, felt Rohan had already been

---

* In the French legal system, confrontations between suspects tested disputed facts.

handled too brutally: 'These are shameful measures to take with a cardinal, and it would go too far to arrange a confrontation in order to establish what happened.'

'Why?' responded Castries. 'There have already been a number of confrontations.* It is against my own interest to make this suggestion, for the moment that the affair is taken up by the court, we will have nothing more to do with it. But I believe that the most moderate step is the one that should be preferred.'

Vergennes, the king's most trusted advisor, kept his counsel, careful not to say anything that might anger the queen – Marie Antoinette detested his influence over her husband – or betray the slightest favouritism towards Rohan.

'Well then,' said the queen, 'in my opinion a choice should be given to the cardinal. He should assemble all his family, he should discuss the matter, and he should choose whether to continue the case extrajudicially or through the courts. He should present his request, which should be endorsed by his family, to the king in writing, and the investigation should be conducted quickly for I have been compromised.' The proposal seemed reasonable, but had in fact been weighted to ensure the outcome she desired: Marie Antoinette calculated that Rohan would rather risk a trial than leave his freedom to her and Louis's discretion.

The triumvirate returned to the Bastille and told the cardinal that Jeanne de La Motte had denied ever receiving a necklace or speaking of a friendship with the queen.

'Oh my God,' he cried. 'If I could be granted a confrontation I am sure that I could confound that woman.'

This was refused: Rohan was given three days to choose whether to be tried or to appeal to the king's magnanimity. To Georgel, Rohan fumed at being cut adrift by Jeanne: 'This is an infernal wickedness! How does she have temerity to deny the truths for which her conscience ought to rebuke her?' Then his anger slackened and he wished for death rather than a life of pity and ridicule.

In the quiet of his cell, as he rolled his memories around his mind to examine their undercarriages, Rohan began to accept that he had

* There had not – he may have meant interrogations.

been deceived by Jeanne. He was still unsure whether she had acted on her own initiative or at the behest of his enemies. One enormous uncertainty complicated his decision-making – had Jeanne preserved the letters he had written to Marie Antoinette? If they were produced during a trial, because of the indiscretions contained within them, his punishment might not merely be disgrace but execution.

Rohan had appointed a formidable team of lawyers, headed by the pre-eminent barrister of the age, Guy-Jean-Baptiste Target. Target was an advocate of firm liberal credentials: he had challenged *lettres de cachet*, campaigned for religious toleration and led the opposition to governmental attempts at limiting the courts' authority. Like Rohan, he was a member of the Académie Française and his prose style was admired for its fluency, if not for its concision. The involvement of Target inevitably led to the politicising of the trial, and the perception that this was yet another intervention by the lawyer against the excesses of absolute monarchy.

Both of the choices presented by the ministers bristled with dangers. Placing himself at the king's mercy was, Rohan felt, a tacit admission of guilt. As the king was the source of all justice in the realm he could, theoretically, judge any matter himself. Previous monarchs had; some sent men to their deaths. Alternatively the king could convoke a special tribunal, hand-selecting the judges with only one verdict in mind. There was no guarantee that Louis, inflamed by the vengeful baying of his wife and Breteuil, would act mercifully or even justly. Many royal adversaries had pickled indefinitely in the Bastille. But the courts appeared no friendlier, as Rohan had been involved in a long-simmering dispute with the *parlement* of Paris regarding his autocratic administration of the Quinze-Vingts, a hospital for the blind.

Two of the lawyers, Tronchet and Collet, argued against the judicial route. The shame of an adverse verdict would cling longer than shame of seeking clemency; and the king would surely stack the *parlement* against him. Rohan's relations tearfully begged him to follow the advice of the two lawyers. But Target, while not recommending a specific course, presented a more balanced choice: 'If the means of showing your innocence can be found, the *parlement* is preferable, even if it possibly means being subjected to the lengthy humiliations of a criminal investigation. If measures taken by your enemies will prevent you from making your defence, you must choose the smallest of two evils – in that case it's worth placing yourself at the mercy of the king.'

Rohan had no evidence in his possession capable of convincing a court of his innocence: there were no independent witnesses to corroborate his case; no proof of who wrote the forged signature; no inkling of whom he had knelt before in the gardens of Versailles. Nonetheless, in the teeth of his family's misgivings, he chose a court trial.

Rohan composed a brief letter to the king, which angled for indulgence while refusing to deliver himself up to Louis without the near-certainty of merciful treatment:

> Sire, I was hoping by means of a confrontation [with Jeanne] to obtain the proofs that would have convinced Your Majesty of the truth about the fraud of which I have been the pawn, and in such a case I would have aspired only to your justice and your goodwill as judges. As the refusal of a confrontation deprives me of this hope, I accept, with the most respectful gratitude, the permission that Your Majesty grants me to prove my innocence by judicial means and, in consequence, I beg Your Majesty to give the necessary orders that my affair should be sent and allocated to the entire body of the *parlement* of Paris.
>
> However, if I could hope that the explanations that have been given, and which I am unaware of, might have led Your Majesty to judge that I am guilty only of having been tricked, I would then dare to beg you, Sire, to give judgement according to your justice and goodwill.

The decision surprised the king. He had assumed that Rohan wanted to avoid a scandal, and had only suggested a trial to placate his wife. Marie Antoinette bullishly told her brother that Rohan would regret his decision: she remained convinced he was a 'vile and clumsy forger' who, 'pressed by a need for money . . . believed himself able to pay the jewellers at the time indicated without anything being discovered'. More perspicacious thinkers worried about the unpleasantness which might condense around the case. As Georgel wrote, 'it was to strip himself [Louis] of sovereign power to fight in the judicial arena against one of his subjects'. The king could not be both the source and final arbiter of the law, and a partisan in his wife's defence. Doubt would be cast over the fairness of the trial, if he who held the scales of justice also stood in one of its pans. The king's stature would be diminished by his embroilment in a public quarrel over the queen's dignity. And Louis had also submitted not just his wife but himself, his reign and the monarchy to another fickle judge, one swayed more by well-wrought tales than facts, whose sympathies, like spring weather, shifted unpredictably – public opinion.

Of more immediate concern to Louis was the allegiance of the *parlement* of Paris itself. It was not a parliament in the English sense, but a court. Similar provincial ones existed across the country, though the jurisdiction of Paris, covering about a third of the country, was the largest, and the capital's *parlement* heard the nation's most serious cases. It also played an important constitutional role, though its exact significance was a matter of dispute between the court and the crown. Royal edicts needed to be registered there. Magistrates, if they objected, could issue a remonstrance. There were few practical consequences, since the king, in the ceremony known as the *lit de justice*, was able, through his very presence, to silence objectors and enforce his legislation. But the *parlement* nonetheless styled itself as the custodian of France's ancient constitution, the representative of the French people and guardian of their liberty against despotic incursions.

The *parlement* of Paris had served as a safe haven and breeding ground for opposition for two hundred years. The leaders of the Fronde, the rebellion against Louis XIV, emerged from it. In the eighteenth century, it had protected Jansenists, the sect of austere Augustanians suspected of being crypto-Protestant; and had led the campaign against the unfair taxation demanded by bellicose ministries. The *parlement*'s disputatiousness led to muscular restatements by the crown of absolutist ideology, and in 1771 Chancellor Maupeou lunged to assert the king's supremacy: he accused the *parlementaires* of treason, exiled them, confiscated their offices and appointed compliant judges in their place. Polemicists castigated Maupeou's coup as a rent in the very fabric of the nation, and the ensuing debate to define despotism would rumble through to the Revolution.

The banished *parlements* were only reinstated when Louis XVI ascended the throne and sacked Maupeou. Maurepas, the new chief minister, cultivated a pro-government faction in the *parlement*, the *parti ministériel*. Yet even loyalists among the magistrates had mixed feelings towards the crown, and guarded against moves to extend its power. After Maurepas's death the crown's leash on the *parti* had slackened. By the autumn of 1785 the first president of the court, Etienne François d'Aligre, could not bring himself to exchange a polite word with Miromesnil, the minister responsible for justice – and Miromesnil's own loyalty to his king over the cardinal's trial was vacillating.

In turning the case over to the *parlement* there were perils for both sides: it was possible that the magistrates might treat the imprisonment of the cardinal as an assault on noble prerogatives and yet another example of monarchical overreaching. But solidarity with Rohan, who had a special propensity for infuriating members of his own class, was by no means assured.

The *parlement* of Paris was not the only, or even the most obvious place to try a bishop of Strasbourg. Rohan was a prince of the Holy Roman Empire and a prince of the Catholic Church, and the king's attribution of the case to the *parlement* had the potential to enrage both Vienna and Rome. In the event the emperor acquiesced – after all, it was his own sister who had mooted a trial. The pope, however, was splenetic, though he directed most of his ire at the cardinal for agreeing to submit to a secular tribunal.

Rohan's defence was further assailed on 5 September when Jacques-Nicolas Blin and Alexis-Joseph Harger, the joint secretaries of the Bureau académique d'écriture, examined the queen's forged signature. They compared it to handwriting samples from Jeanne, Cagliostro, the baron de Planta, Jeanne's maid Rosalie Brissault and three of Jeanne's associates. From the obliquely crossed 't's, the loopy 'o's and the final 's's, the experts concluded that Planta was the closest match. Though they cautioned that the paucity of evidence made their attribution provisional, it nonetheless lent credence to the belief that Rohan had masterminded the theft of the necklace.

15

Witness Protection

O N 5 SEPTEMBER, letters patent, issued by the king at Saint-Cloud, officially transferred the case to the *parlement* of Paris. They trained their sights on Rohan, proclaiming that he,

> unknown to the queen, our very dear wife and companion, had said to them [the Boehmers] that he had been authorised by her to make the acquisition . . . We have not been able to regard the matter without a just indignation, that someone should have dared to appropriate an august name which is dear to us in so many regards and to violate with such extraordinary temerity the respect owed to royal majesty.

Jeanne received only a glancing mention – Rohan had claimed that 'he had been tricked by a woman named La Mothe de Valois'.

The crimes were to be investigated jointly by the Grand Chambre and the Tournelle – the highest civil and criminal courts in the *parlement* – deliberately excluding the hotheads and gadflies who populated the lower rungs of the magistracy. 'The matter required haste so that which might disappear with delay should not be allowed to be destroyed.' The *parlement* registered the case without any remonstrance on 6 September. This caused further perturbation to the Rohan, since the letters patent delimited the scope of the investigation: their propositions were taken as established fact, and were not themselves to be scrutinised. As they presumed that the cardinal had violated the respect due to the queen and appropriated her name, there seemed to be only one possible verdict at which the *parlement* could arrive – guilty.

The care the crown took to increase the chances of Rohan's conviction emerges from the drafting of the *plainte* (charge) by the *procureur-général* Guillaume-François-Louis Joly de Fleury. The *procureur-général* represented the king's interest before the *parlement* – in this matter, the king's interest was greater than in most. Tired, old and sickly, Joly de Fleury had a reputation as a drudge – Beugnot called him 'the most objectionable mediocrity ever seen . . . it is hard to understand how such a man could attain one of the most important offices of state' – who lived in the shadow of two brilliant brothers, one of whom served as *contrôleur-général*; the other, Omer Joly de Fleury, was an influential *parlementaire* and hungry for ministerial office.

A memo written by a member of Joly de Fleury's staff on 3 September stated that 'what must be alleged in the *plainte* is not the forgery of the document, but the supposition about the writing and the signature on the document and that which was done as a result regarding . . . the sale of the necklace'. The author must have realised that Rohan was indeed the victim of a swindle, otherwise the counterfeiting of the queen's hand would surely have been the newel around which the *plainte* was constructed. Having suspected that Rohan had been deceived, Joly de Fleury could no longer centre his case on the forgery, since Rohan would doubtless encourage the court to see Jeanne as guilty and himself as her dupe – and therefore acquit him. To forestall this, Joly de Fleury made a discernible attempt to mitigate Jeanne's involvement: a sentence in an early draft which stated 'it appears that a woman named la Mothe de Valois is one of the principal accomplices in the crime' appeared in the final version as 'it appears that a woman named la Mothe de Valois is implicated in the affair as having tricked the cardinal, according to the declaration he made'.

A shift of focus was needed to convict the cardinal. Joly de Fleury laid emphasis on the cardinal's insolence – the presumption that the queen was the kind of person who would commission a man she had not spoken to in years to assuage, without her husband's knowledge, her slakeless appetite for luxury. In this lay the crime of *lèse-majesté* – impugning the dignity of the king or queen. The notion of *lèse-majesté* incorporated any defilement of the king's majesty and authority: it was treasonous because the king embodied the nation; and sacrilegious because the king ruled by divine right.

The court appointed two *rapporteurs* (investigating magistrates) to oversee the collection of the *information* (evidence). They would not, for the time being, interview those in the Bastille, but question witnesses whose names had emerged during the police investigation or who had come forward. At the end of this stage, they would recommend which suspects should be detained further for interrogation. Jean-Baptiste-Maximilien Titon de Villotran and Dupuis de Marcé were chosen for the task. Titon was a libertine and man of overbearing character (he had once ordered the arrest of a lawyer for criticising him in a published defence of a client). He was regularly chosen as *rapporteur* in major cases and had great success at winning over his fellow magistrates. As important, from the crown's perspective, was his membership of the *parti ministériel*, and he had benefited from the king's largesse. An ex-soldier and milquetoast nonentity, Dupuis bent before his more forceful colleague. From the outset there was a concerted effort to conclude the case to the crown's satisfaction. There was a continual three-way correspondence between Titon, Joly de Fleury and d'Aligre, the *parlement*'s *premier président*, who had been on a royal retainer of 80,000 livres for a number of years and was, in Georgel's caustic assessment, 'known for his opulence, his greed and a special talent for acquiring money at the most advantageous rate . . . his principles were flexible and his morals even looser'.

Now that she was under parliamentary investigation, Jeanne was required to appoint a lawyer. Her first choice was her old friend Jacques Beugnot. But Beugnot was petrified that he would soon himself be arrested for perverting the course of justice by helping Jeanne burn her papers. He did not dare to leave Bar for days after Jeanne was arrested. When he returned to Paris, he was advised by friends to flee, and each morning woke up and braced himself for the knock at the door. He wandered frequently past the Bastille, imagining himself locked within its towers, so the horror would be softened when the time came. His trunk lay packed in his room 'like a friend placed as a sentinel'.

After the issue of the letters patent, Beugnot was summoned by de Crosne. He approached the lieutenant-general's office, shivering with trepidation, convinced he would be bundled into a carriage and driven to the dread citadel. Instead he found the chief of police in affable form:

> Monsieur, it is for Madame de La Motte that I speak . . . Madame de La Motte, whom I've just left, has chosen you as her counsel. Here is your entrance pass for the Bastille. I ask that you present yourself when it opens, from nine to ten o'clock. This poor woman has not seen a friendly face for two months [more like a month, but Beugnot's memoirs are frequently imprecise with datings] and I promised her that tomorrow without fail you would be there in the morning.

Beugnot refused outright to take the case. Its difficulty, he protested, far exceeded his experience. No matter, said de Crosne; Cagliostro's lawyer Thilorier was equally callow – here was an opportunity to forge a reputation. But Beugnot, convinced that one misstep would ruin his career, would not be swayed. Instead, Jeanne appointed Mâitre Doillot, an experienced lawyer, if not an especially acute one (Vergennes called him an 'imbecile'), who had been hauled out of semi-retirement because others were chary of touching the case.

Barely heard amid the rumpus over Rohan's disgrace was the reedy yet persistent wail of the Boehmers. They had neither their diamonds nor payment for them. Bassenge had told an acquaintance the day after the cardinal's arrest that he believed Rohan had acted honourably at all times. But good intentions would not disperse their creditors. They complained to officials in the king's household, who fobbed them off with nebulous promises of compensation. When they had heard nothing further, they wrote to the unfeeling Breteuil: 'We beg you, Your Excellency, to place again before the eyes of Their Majesties our worries and fears, undoubtedly well-founded fears about events that could make our misfortune irrevocable.'

The minister was as unresponsive as a wooden leg, so they turned to Vergennes. He suggested they bring a civil case in London against the jewellers who had bought the diamonds from Nicolas. Impossible, said Boehmer, who could be steely when necessary. 'Neither myself nor my associate have any documentation regarding this sale with Monsieur and Madame de la Motte. We cannot, for that reason, bring a case.' But the king was never going to pay for a necklace that he hadn't wanted, his wife hadn't wanted and which no longer even existed. On 3 November, he wrote a formal letter to the Boehmers telling them the necklace had been bought fraudulently and the case was being dealt with through legal channels – nothing they did not know already. The implication was clear: if you want your money, you will have to petition the *parlement*.

The difficulties facing Rohan's legal team were formidable to the point of hopelessness. Though public sympathy leant towards the cardinal, the full influence of the king and queen was being exerted against him (the sympathies that really mattered belonged to fifty or so judges who were as susceptible as anyone to royal attention). Rohan's case rested on little more than yelps of innocence. Great tracts of the story remained *terra incognita*. Crucial witnesses had disappeared. Who had written the signature on the bill of sale? What had happened to the necklace? Where was Nicolas de La Motte? And before whom had Rohan prostrated himself in the Bosquet de Venus?

While Target took charge of the legal strategy, the Abbé Georgel, Rohan's vicar-general, coordinated the gathering of intelligence that covertly paralleled the *parlement*'s, as well as managing the diocese of Strasbourg. This was an act of great magnanimity, since, after Rohan had fallen under Cagliostro's spell, Georgel had been excluded from his inner circle. He had grown so disillusioned with the cardinal's 'tone of imperious harshness' that he contemplated retirement (the only reason that he, too, had not been arrested was because his disfavour was widely known).

Georgel took up Rohan's business with renewed vigour. He visited the cardinal twice each day and slept for only three or four hours a night. He obtained copies of the depositions given by Boehmer, Bassenge and Sainte-James, which were supposedly for ministerial eyes only. In order to paint Jeanne as a hardened intriguer, he tried to discredit her claims of royal descent, grubbing about for stories from acquaintances who mocked her airs and graces, and discovering she had never received permission to call herself 'de Valois'. Castries and Calonne provided, on the quiet, information about her contained in the royal archives. The most useful source was Frémin, the clerk of the *parlement*, who transcribed all the interrogations conducted by Titon and Dupuis then passed on copies to Georgel (this may explain why, months later, he was replaced as stenographer – though the dilatory pace of his handwriting might also have had something to do with it).

Most pressing was the need to cement the Boehmers' goodwill. There was fear in Rohan's camp that if a settlement were not reached with them, their testimony would prove harmful to the cardinal's prospects. Rohan agreed that the necklace should be amortised, but finding the money amid ledgers reddened with debt was difficult. The jewellers refused to accept the annual revenue from the abbey of Saint Vaast, as the income would stop accruing to the Rohan family on his death. Generously, however, the king agreed to reserve the money for the Boehmers, even if Rohan died before the full amount had been repaid. Economies made up the shortfall: all but twelve of the cardinal's horses were sold off and arrangements were eventually reached with all creditors.

Not long after *parlement* accepted the case, Georgel was approached by an *abbé* called Joincaire who revealed that a crucial witness was lying low but prepared to talk – Père Nicolas Loth, Jeanne's confessor and factotum. Loth was secretary to the head of the Minim friary that backed onto Jeanne's house on the rue Neuve-Saint-Gilles. He styled himself grandly – and utterly unjustifiably, as was the habit of many of Jeanne's acquaintances – as *procureur-général* of the Provinces, though the only procuring he excelled in was of prostitutes for Nicolas. Loth was eager to leave holy orders and had once been picked up by the police at a ball for dressing in mufti. Jealous of Jeanne's closeness to Villette – his ear cleaved to the doors the pair locked behind them – he bustled about on Jeanne's behalf with pitiable and ingratiating efficiency. When the La Mottes abandoned Paris, they granted Loth power of attorney over their affairs.

Loth had told Joincaire that his conscience would not let him sleep at night (what actually kept him awake was fear of arrest). One evening, Loth arrived in disguise at Joincaire's house to meet Georgel and told him much – if not everything – of what he knew: the gifts from the Boehmers for finding a buyer for their necklace; the hillocks of diamonds, supposedly given by Marie Antoinette; the frantic preparations for departure in early August.

For the first time, Georgel discovered the identities of two people whose evidence would, if obtained, prove vital. Loth recalled Jeanne basting with compliments a young girl known as d'Oliva for her performance as the queen; and he revealed Villette as a co-conspirator of the La Mottes. Loth brought with him examples of Villette's correspondence and Georgel immediately noticed the similarities to the handwriting in letters that Rohan had received from Marie Antoinette.

Georgel suspected that Loth was holding something back, and asked Target to question him. Target warned that only complete cooperation would save the friar from the Bastille; Loth's reticence sprung open and the full story fluttered out. Jeanne had dictated to Villette the letters she sent to Rohan in Marie Antoinette's name; the money requested from Rohan by the queen streamed through the La Mottes' fingers; Nicolas had sold the diamonds from the necklace in London; both he and Villette had fled abroad. The only reason he had acquiesced to this criminality, Loth pleaded, was his bewitchment by Jeanne.

Rohan was especially heartened by one revelation in particular: Jeanne had burned all her correspondence. He no longer needed to fear that his unclerical intentions towards the queen would be unearthed. Target knew that Loth's testimony needed to be heard by the *rapporteurs*, but they had complete discretion over whom to interview. Joly de Fleury, aware that any evidence implicating Jeanne would necessarily exonerate Rohan, attempted to block the deposing of Loth, only acquiescing after the personal intervention of Miromesnil. The keeper of the seals was not the only minister to provide material to support Rohan's operations. Vergennes circulated Nicolas's description to French embassies around Europe:

He looks between twenty-eight and thirty years old; he is about 5'5"; he has well-proportioned legs, a spindly body, and slightly low-slung shoulders. He has a long face, an aquiline nose and a little pock mark on the tip of his nose. He is pale like a leper; his eyebrows and eyes are nearly black. The hair up to the beard is brown and his lower lip is a little thick. Taken in all, he does not cut an unattractive figure.

Georgel, now informed that the diamonds had been sold in England, sent Louis Ramond de Carbonnières, an aide-de-camp of the cardinal, to London.* Carbonnières, assisted by François Barthélemy, the deputy head of the French mission, tracked down Barthélemy Macdermott, the friar who had acted as Nicolas's guide earlier that year. Macdermott was initially reluctant to talk, but was convinced to provide a statement by Carbonnières's impassioned plea that only he could save Rohan – and a smattering of bluster that he might otherwise be arrested as an accomplice. The priest agreed to testify at Rohan's trial, though Carbonnières believed he was still concealing Nicolas's current hideaway. Gray and Jefferys, the two jewellers whom Nicolas had approached, were also deposed; both confirmed, after examining a sketch of the Boehmers' necklace, that the diamonds shown to them had been taken from it.

A crucial breakthrough came in the Austrian Netherlands. D'Oliva, living under the assumed name of Madame Genet, had been arrested in Brussels on 19 October along with her lover, Toussaint de Beausire. She had remained in Paris until the end of September, but fled the country after, Georgel suspected, Jeanne's lawyer had put the frighteners on her with grizzly stories of the Bastille's *cachots*. Vergennes's intelligence led him to believe that d'Oliva was in the Low Countries, and he had instructed Hirzinger, his chargé d'affaires in Brussels, to 'take secret measures and to consult with the magistrates of the Brussels police to try and discover the fugitives and have them arrested'. Yet securing their return from Brabant seemed nigh-on impossible – Brussels was a safe haven for fugitives, political and criminal, precisely because its privileges forbade extradition to France.

The only way that d'Oliva and Beausire could be repatriated, the foreign minister told Georgel, was by their own volition. They needed someone to gain their confidence and tease them out. With the Paris Police now effectively acting as Rohan's agents, Inspector Quidor, its specialist in delicate diplomatic operations, travelled to Brussels. On arrival, he discovered the couple desperate for release, and willing to risk rearrest in France. D'Oliva must have been

* In later life, Carbonnières would become a distinguished mountaineer, and an expert on the flora and geology of the Pyrenees.

comforted by the sight of the benevolent policeman, whom she knew as a bantering antagonist from her streetwalking days. Quidor genuinely took pity on her: 'I believe her more stupid than mischievous or wicked,' he wrote to Vergennes. But the copper's good word came to naught: by 4 November, d'Oliva and Beausire had joined Rohan, Jeanne and the Cagliostros in the Bastille.

16

Tired and Emotional

S EDULOUSLY, SINGLE-MINDEDLY AND exhaustingly, the magistrates
and the *procureur-général*'s office had laboured through the autumn
to substantiate the case against the detainees. 'The work is long and
tiring,' wrote Pierre Laurencel, Joly de Fleury's deputy, to his boss.
'I beg you, sir, not to refer to me any other matter.' Nicolas's banker
and the assorted goldsmiths, diamond brokers, clockmakers and
upholsterers who had done business with the La Mottes, along with
Madame du Barry herself – handed down from her carriage by the
senior magistrate Titon – were all deposed at the Palais de Justice.*

For the first time, the narrative Jeanne had presented to de Crosne
was subjected to exacting contradiction. Loth told Titon that a rash
of spending in the La Mottes' household broke out at the same time
as gifts were granted by Rohan in the late summer of 1784, and
again after the sale of the necklace. Jeanne had explained to the friar
that these were the golden fruits of the queen's orchard. He also
recalled that at the end of July, when Jeanne gave Rohan 30,000
livres to pay the interest on the necklace, she was scrabbling around
to raise exactly that sum of money. Laporte and Bassenge confirmed
Loth's testimony that Jeanne had boasted of the queen's friendship,
and a number of Parisian artisans reported that, during the first half
of 1785, Jeanne had offered to pay them with diamonds rather than
cash. Most significantly, d'Oliva's testimony substantiated Rohan's
seemingly fantastical story about meeting the queen in the gardens
of Versailles: she admitted to having been groomed by the comtesse
de La Motte to perform a favour for the queen, to being dressed

* Du Barry, now in retirement after the death of her lover, Louis XV, had once
received a petition from Jeanne.

up, led at night to the palace gardens and presenting a rose to an unknown man, to whom she said 'You know what this means.'

The slow erosion of Jeanne's credibility ought to have buoyed Rohan. Yet the mere fact that Jeanne may have deceived him did not absolve him from the sin of presumption, and suspicions that he had authored the fraud still adhered to him. His debts were motive enough; he was the last person seen with the necklace; and the testimony of a single distinguished witness threatened to suck the air out of Rohan's declamations of innocence.

Baudard de Sainte-James told Titon that, at the party where he and the cardinal discussed a loan to the queen, Rohan had 'assured [him] he had seen in the queen's own hands 700,000 livres in banknotes which she had wanted to give to him to hand over to Monsieur Boehmer as payment for the necklace'. The cardinal had added that 'he feared deeply that she would not keep the 700,000 livres and would not put them to the use that they had been intended'. Not only was the slur of spendthriftiness yet another example of Rohan's contempt for Marie Antoinette, but, for the first time, evidence was presented that Rohan had boasted of meeting the queen in private. If he had really spoken these words, then he appeared little different from Jeanne – a man who flaunted his connections with the queen to squeeze money out of the rich and desperate. Sainte-James's testimony inflicted a wound the sharks scented.

Though life at Versailles continued as though Rohan had already been swallowed by oblivion, he continued to fascinate and torment those connected to the case. 'Happy are they', wrote Vergennes to his ambassador in Rome, 'whose occupations shelter them from hearing from morning until evening arguments for and against the same matter, which makes everyone feel imprisoned, for no reason and no useful purpose.'

Louis was briefed regularly about the progress of the investigation and Vergennes's attempts to track down the suspects. But he wished to be reminded of the affair no more frequently than necessary. Soubise, who raged around the Court denouncing the cardinal's detention, was expelled from the council of state: 'His presence there pains me,' said Louis brusquely. The queen told her family that all memories of the cardinal and the necklace had been banished from her mind, now the *parlement* had jurisdiction over the case; in reality, she was unable to purge herself of barbed thoughts. She obtained a portrait of Jeanne and contemplated the woman who had stolen her identity and defaced it; whose crookedness she now, in the eyes of her traducers, owned. One of her *femmes de chambres* remarked that 'the affair is very painful for her and requires a lot of effort' – the effort to forget it, the effort to conceal the pain when she couldn't. The impropriety of forcefully defending her honour in public – when Madame Campan offered to testify, Louis refused her permission ('it would look as if you were sent by the Queen and that would not be right') – left her feeling impotent. She became a character in other people's stories, but her own went unreported. The leg-ironed speed at which the trial dragged on gave birth to fears that the immediate delight at Rohan's imprisonment entailed humiliations unappreciated at the time: 'From the moment the cardinal was arrested,' Marie Antoinette wrote to her brother Joseph II, 'I had counted on the fact that he would no longer be able to reappear at Court; but the proceedings which will last for seven months could have other consequences.'

At the beginning of November, Laurencel presented Joly de Fleury with an analysis of the case against the cardinal. Sainte-James and Bassenge's depositions excited the prosecution the most. Unlike Boehmer, whose memories were fragmentary, Bassenge had provided a very detailed account of events leading up to and beyond the purchase of the necklace. He remembered clearly the occasion when Rohan revealed he was negotiating on behalf of Marie Antoinette – a *prima facie* abuse of the queen's name. The testimony had already led Laurencel to conclude that 'the cardinal is much more guilty than Madame de la Mothe'. Where Jeanne's account clashed with Rohan's, Laurencel was invariably inclined to believe the former: for example, he accepted, without cavil, Jeanne's contention that Rohan dismembered the necklace and instructed Nicolas to sell it in London.

Laurencel displayed a carnivorous tenacity in picking over the evidence against Rohan. One can read him anticipating Target's lines of defence: that the cardinal never claimed to have received orders from the queen in person; that had his motivations been criminal, he would never have insisted that the jewellers thank the queen in writing. Laurencel was aware, too, of the political context of the trial:

> No one regards the cardinal with any esteem or respect, but they pity his family. They do not want to believe him guilty of a forgery, of an infamous swindle; they would rather like to believe he is crazy, misled by his ambition and the victim of seduction by a woman devoid of honour, with whom he did not blush to live.

Knowing that his superiors wanted to crush Rohan, Laurencel arranged the evidence in such a way that it spelt out 'fraudster' not 'fool'. Employing an obtuse logic, he argued that since Rohan admitted delivering the necklace to Jeanne, and Jeanne admitted that Nicolas sold diamonds given to her by Rohan, Rohan must therefore have instructed Jeanne to prise the diamonds from the necklace and dispose of them on his behalf. 'There are no grounds', the deputy wrote, 'for saying the cardinal de Rohan was led astray by Madame de La Motte . . . If Madame de La Motte counterfeited the signature of the queen, or had knowledge that the signature was assumed, she only participated in the manoeuvre at the instigation of the cardinal' (though Laurencel admitted there was no evidence to attribute the forgery to Rohan).

Laurencel had a specific intention in expanding Rohan's crimes from the simple but incontestable *lèse majesté* of passing off the signature of the queen, to the far more dramatic crime of theft. When the magistrates gathered to consider the evidence, he wanted the *parlement* to pass a *decret de prise de corps* – a ruling that remanded suspects under the most stringent conditions – against the cardinal. The more calculating Rohan appeared, the more likely the *decret de prise de corps* would be voted through. Though claiming to employ the 'principle of equity', vindictiveness was his motivation; the pro-Court faction wished to see Rohan suffer palpably during the trial. Laurencel told Rohan's relatives that 'they would have to accept that Rohan was a lost man'.

On 14 December, fifty-six magistrates, on the pews of the Grand Chambre of the Palais de Justice, listened for ten hours straight to Titon's report on the evidence. The peers of the realm, entitled to sit as members of the Grand Chambre, had recused themselves from proceedings involving one of their number. There was a popular expectation that now, once the witnesses had fleshed out the details, Jeanne's deception of Rohan would emerge and the case against him dropped. A snatch of satirical verse ran:

> The Pope made him red
> The king blackened him
> Madame de la Motte smeared him
> The *parlement* will doubtless clear him.

But doubts about his conduct evidently persisted. *Decrets de prise de corps* were passed against Rohan, Jeanne, d'Oliva, Cagliostro and, in absentia, Nicolas, which meant the first four would remain in detention, to be interrogated by the *rapporteurs* and placed in gladiatorial confrontations with witnesses and each other. The court's ruling was deeply worrying for Rohan, since it was the first test of the disposition of sympathies in the *parlement*. Forty-eight of the judges had voted for *prise de corps*; a handful of radical judges, whom Louis XVI had dubbed 'The Firestarters', argued for a more lenient form of remand. It was alleged that the baron de Breteuil had suborned the court, but such comprehensive malfeasance was unlikely: as Castries asked in his diary, 'how do you corrupt forty-eight people?'

The suspects had spent four months in the Bastille, while the evidence against them was assembled; four months in which they grew quieter, weaker, more friable emotionally and physically. Black thoughts stampeded; bodies dried out in stale silence. The daily constitutional around the fortress's crenellations was not sufficiently invigorating for Jeanne: 'For want of air, for want of exercise, deprived of the pleasing variety so essential to health, my countenance wore the sallow hue of languor, and my eyes were dimmed with weary watching.'

With the delusion of someone who is lord of four walls and a vassal to the lock and key, Jeanne convinced herself that the simplest means of escape was jemmying up the flagstones with a knife. She failed, like many before her, though she did discover that a distant relative of hers, Anne-Gédéon Lafitte, marquis de Pelleport, was locked in the cell below. Pelleport was a miscreant of notable ingenuity and durability, and he had already been incarcerated four or five times at the behest of his family for 'dishonourable atrocities'.

How Jeanne discovered her neighbour is unknown – a friendly turnkey may have made the introduction. At first they communicated by knocking on the floor, later passing letters to each other on a string through the bars in the window, until they were rumbled and Pelleport was transferred to a different tower. Jeanne's only other diversion was singing: an aria from *Richard Coeur de Lion*, Grétry's hit opera of the previous year, in which the imprisoned King Richard laments 'If the universe forgets me, / If I must pass my entire life here, / What use is my glory, my valour' was a favourite (there is an unhappy homophony between 'valeur' and 'Valois', and she substituted her own name into the song). The isolation was punishing: 'I communed with myself and was silent,' she wrote in her memoirs, paraphrasing the Psalmist. On one occasion, she was treated to a tantalising glimpse of her sister from the top of the fortress: her lawyer, Doillot, had positioned Marianne on the street in a line of sight from the Bastille. Dawdling behind her guard, Jeanne hurriedly flapped her handkerchief at the tiny figure below, but the brevity and distance only made her feel her loneliness more keenly. Early in September, Jeanne wrote to de Crosne asking that two letters be passed on to Nicolas – she had no idea where he was, though did not know that the police were equally clueless – begging him to visit and supplement her scrimped rations.

In October, Jeanne was told that her brother had died aboard his vessel in the East Indies. She had not seen him for years – her thoughts had turned to him only when expropriating his royal pension – but his passing seemed to confirm her abandonment by the world. 'I remained very pensive,' she wrote, 'combating a multitude of the most gloomy ideas that presented themselves in quick and painful succession.' That night she was seized by a delirium that was only calmed when an anodyne was forced down her gullet. Jeanne was not beyond simulating fits to attract attention, but her imprisonment had unquestionably riven her mental health – Cagliostro, too, suffered: when first admitted, he was placed on suicide watch – and her friendships with the few Bastille employees she encountered daily, such as her nurse and the prison chaplain, were poisoned by suspicions they were in the pay of Rohan (these were not, given attempts by Georgel to infiltrate other stages of the legal process, without grounds).

Rohan had an altogether comfier time: the king had authorised 120 livres – an enormous sum – to be spent on him each day. He was billeted in the quarters of the lieutenant of the Bastille, with a single sentinel – more in honour of his status than to guard against escape – before his unlocked door. The governor's garden was placed at his disposal, and he dispensed charity to the most wretched prisoners he encountered.

Visitors came so frequently that the Bastille's drawbridges were barely raised (at his dinner parties the guests feasted on oysters and champagne). On 29 August he was visited by the prince de Condé and the duc de Bourbon – two junior members of the royal family, allied by marriage to the House of Rohan – as well as a shining host of Rohan relatives: the comtesse de Brionne and her daughters, the princesse de Carignan, the prince and princesse de Vaudémont, his brothers the archbishop of Cambrai and the prince de Montbazon, the duke and duchesse de Montbazon, prince Camille de Rohan, prince Charles de Rohan, the comtesse de Marsan, the maréchal de Soubise, the duchesse de La Vauguyon and the vicomte de Pont. That was before Rohan met, on more practical business, with his squire the comte de La Tour, Carbonnières, Georgel and five other abbés, four lawyers, two accountants, two valets and his doctor.

But mental strife begat bodily weakness which no amount of company could cure. A severe attack of asthma at the onset of autumn prevented Rohan's daily stroll, and within two months his muscles had atrophied to such an extent that he could not walk without support. Gallstones subjected him to exquisite pain. Despite his ailments, he maintained a vigorous interest in legal minutiae: letters that survive from his time in prison show him demanding to read relevant papers, chivvying Georgel for news from abroad and elucidating contradictions in evidence. Displaying his analytical acuity was one way to recover his dignity.

Rohan also suffered from a smothering depression at his loss of liberty. His relatives and Georgel struggled to buoy him up, but only his furious wish for exoneration staved off complete despair. 'between ourselves', he wrote, 'that I begin to feel tired, but only makes me redouble my efforts, especially as I don't want my enemies to have any doubt of them. I want to be seen going down into the arena and wiping the blood off the tracks.'

In normal circumstances a *decret de prise de corps* should have led to the transfer of the prisoners to the *parlement*'s own facilities, and the immediate interrogation of the suspects. But Louis insisted that everyone charged should remain in the Bastille – a royal palace – even the comtesse de Cagliostro against whom a much weaker *decret* had been passed. It took three weeks of wrangling before the *parlement* acceded, three weeks in which rumours festered that the government had no intention of letting the investigation continue and would simply leave the accused to die in prison.

Georgel had been caught unawares by the severity of the *decret*. Rohan was now forbidden from seeing anyone apart from the staff of the Bastille and the *parlement* until after the interrogations; Georgel worried that the solitude might lead to a breakdown. No further communication would be allowed with his lawyers, and Target was acutely aware that Rohan needed continuous coaching to survive Titon's unforgiving scrutiny. Georgel, who had been entrusted with the running of Rohan's diocese and estates, pleaded with Breteuil for permission to write to Rohan on business matters – naturally, the governor of the Bastille would unseal and read all the letters. The minister was unable to find a reason to refuse. In the twenty-four hours before the cut-off point, Rohan and Georgel recycled a cipher they had used in Vienna, so they might discuss the case while appearing to speak only of recalcitrant tenants and troublesome priests. More detailed instructions were sent in letters written with invisible ink, smuggled in by a physician permitted to examine the cardinal.

17

Nicolas Abroad

A Picaresque

WHERE WAS NICOLAS de La Motte? One rumour placed him in Scotland. Another whispered that he had turned Turk in Istanbul and signed up with Barbary pirates. No one knew for sure whether he was dead or alive. At the end of August, the Paris Police sent a man to smoke him out in the Low Countries. Two months later, the foreign ministry heard that he was in Italy, set to embark for India. He was everywhere and nowhere.

Nicolas's travails were as strange and eventful as the rest of the Diamond Necklace Affair. He had not been arrested at the same time as Jeanne and, later, partisans of Rohan wondered whether the baron de Breteuil had deliberately allowed a crucial suspect to escape in order to undermine the cardinal's defence. But it is more likely that no warrant was issued for Nicolas simply because Rohan had not mentioned him in his slapdash confession to the king.

After Jeanne's apprehension, Nicolas wandered around Bar as though nothing out of the ordinary had happened. With his usual disdain for consistency, he told some people that Jeanne was in the country, others that she was at Versailles. He confided to Beugnot that Jeanne had been arrested, though insisted it was only a minor misunderstanding: 'Madame de la Motte has only left for three or four days at most; she is going to give the minister the explanations that are needed. I've worked out that she will be back on Wednesday or Thursday and we must meet her and return her in triumph to her house.'

Was Nicolas, Beugnot wondered, even more beef-headed than he had realised? He urged the comte to flee to England.

'What has Jeanne told you?' asked Nicolas suspiciously.

'Nothing, even more reason for a quick escape,' replied Beugnot, who could only imagine the outrages Nicolas was implicated in.

Nicolas shrugged nonchalantly as he left Beugnot's house, but as soon as he arrived home he prepared to leave. He made over his house to his sister and brother-in-law; he buried some of the diamonds, and left other valuables in the uncertain care of relatives, who were all too eager to look after them. Having told his servants he was taking advantage of his wife's absence to holiday in Europe, Nicolas departed for the Channel coast accompanied by his valet, 100 louis in cash, two packets of loose pearls and a satchel full of diamonds.

They reached Boulogne on 20 August and spent two nervy days in town – the wind was sitting unhelpfully – before setting sail. On arriving in London, the first thing Nicolas did was to retrieve the jewellery he had left with Gray during his visit in May, before settling in among the French expatriate community.

One evening, while leaving the Theatre Royal, Haymarket, Nicolas caught a cab to avoid the rain. It had barely moved off when he was thumped over the head. Groggy, he wondered whether the carriage had overturned, but as his vision regained focus, he noticed the back window had been smashed. Peering out, Nicolas saw someone hanging off a stanchion, holding what appeared to be a cane. With remarkable generosity of spirit for someone who had just been brained, Nicolas presumed that the man was simply trying to catch a free lift and had accidentally knocked out the glass – but no sooner had Nicolas settled down again in a corner than another thrust from the rear of the cab brushed his chest. The lamplight caught the sword's steel. Ringing the bell in a frenzy, Nicolas jumped out of the coach, windmilling his own stick, as the unknown assailant disappeared down the murky streets.

This story is retailed in Jeanne's *Mémoires Justificatifs*, published three years later, and Nicolas's own memoirs, compiled in old age. Nicolas speculated that the would-be assassin was commissioned by either the queen or the cardinal – but it is clear from surviving documents that neither camp knew his whereabouts. Both were more interested in repatriating him alive – to stand trial – than in a coffin. If Nicolas was actually attacked, it was probably an opportunistic attempted robbery of a showy foreigner.

Nicolas left London in mid-September, conscious that word of his arrival would soon snake into the ears of the French ambassador. His instincts were acute – only a few days after his departure, Barthélemy, the minister in the French embassy, discovered the hostel where he had been staying and applied to a magistrate for an arrest warrant.

Wearing chain mail under his clothes, armed with two pistols, a swordstick and a concealed dagger, his pockets filled with ash to blind any assailants, Nicolas travelled northwards to meet Macdermott, his fixer on his previous visit to England, in Manchester. Once appraised of events in France – or at least Nicolas's self-serving version of them – Macdermott advised him to adopt a false name and lie low in Ireland. Accompanied by his attentive if bibulous manservant, Nicolas set off for Holyhead.

In Wales, Nicolas, according to his memoirs, met a perky eighteen-year-old girl with whom he fell in love. He stayed with Miss Stuart and her aunt for two weeks, during which time she 'offered herself to [his] desires . . . with an innocence, a confidence, a candour that was most touching'. The aunt seemed eager the pair should marry; Nicolas did nothing to disillusion her, convincing himself, hard-heartedly, that Jeanne would commit suicide before the trial concluded – nothing shameful, then, in courting a young lady. Having promised to return once his 'business' in Ireland was complete, Nicolas sailed to Dublin.

By Christmas, he was well established there. He claimed, thanks to Macdermott's letters of introduction, to have mingled in the highest society, even discussing the arrest of the cardinal with the viceroy, the duke of Rutland – not the sort of behaviour you would expect of a mysterious Frenchman who wished to evade the attentions of the British authorities.

At the turn of the year, Nicolas lost all his appetite and fell ill, a condition he put down to excessive partying and his worry that the bloodhounds of Vergennes were catching up. His servant suggested they move to Scotland, where he could convalesce in the mountains, spend less money and hear no talk of Rohan. Telling his acquaintances that he was visiting Kilkenny and Cork, Nicolas headed in the opposite direction towards Drogheda, riding all the way on horseback in the hope that the exercise would do him good. It just made him feel worse – by the time he arrived at the coast, he could only keep down tea and eggs. When he reached Glasgow, Nicolas was in constipated agony, having spent eighteen successive days without moving his bowels. Two friendly doctors he had met on the voyage administered enemas without success, and they suggested he consult a distinguished doctor in Edinburgh. At first, this physician appeared confused by Nicolas's condition and changed his treatment daily, but soon the doctor's questions led Nicolas to surmise his suffering was not accidental. Poison was at work. Had he left matters a week longer, he would have been a dead man.

18

Questions, Questions

11 January 1786

A FREEZING ROOM in the Bastille. On one side of the table, Titon, still snivelling and tetchy from the cold that had delayed the interrogations. On the other, Rohan, outwardly defiant, inwardly a wormery of nerves. Frémin, the clerk, hunched over a pile of blank sheets of paper, was poised for dictation.

'What is your name, surname, age, rank and address?' asked the magistrate.

'I am Louis-Réné-Edouard, cardinal de Rohan, prince-bishop of Strasbourg, grand almoner of France, aged fifty-two, living in Paris, vieille rue du Temple, the Hôtel de Strasbourg.'

'On 24 January 1785, were you not at the house of Boehmer and Bassenge?'

Rohan did not answer the question. Instead, he raised objections to being tried by the *parlement*. As a priest, as a prince of the Holy Roman Emperor, as grand almoner and as a cardinal, he deserved a court of his peers. The choice presented to him by the king had been nothing but coercion, since he had already been deprived of his liberty and was unable to claim the rights of his offices. Having registered his objections, Rohan then began a lengthy disquisition, detailing his relationship with Jeanne from their introduction by Madame de Boulainvilliers. The strategy of reciting a statement had been devised by Target to prevent Rohan confusing facts. Throughout the rest of the interrogation, he would frequently refer back to his opening remarks rather than answering questions directly.

Titon may have suspected that Rohan would try such an improper manoeuvre: he had previously forbidden him from bringing a written chronology to crib off during the interrogation. Now, he evidently thought the smoothest way of securing Rohan's cooperation was to let him expound. Rohan's narrative was comprehensive – it lasted two full days – only omitting any reference to his written correspondence with the queen. He spoke of his charity to Jeanne – he could not believe that 'a person to whom I had only done good would want to trick me' – and her reciprocal kindness in earning for him Marie Antoinette's forgiveness; of the time he had seen 'a person whom I believed to be the queen in Versailles'; and of the acquisition of the necklace. Vulnerabilities were pre-emptively reinforced and explained: Rohan denied ever having seen the queen's handwriting, or 'if by chance some signature had passed beneath my eyes, I paid little attention to the shape of the letters'; forging the signature would have been an unnecessary jeopardy had he perpetrated the fraud, as the jewellers never requested an autographed bill of sale. Rohan himself had insisted on the signing, since 'the more the Boehmers put their confidence in me, the more I needed to show them that I was occupied in their interests'.

The other purpose of Rohan's justification was to prompt Titon to hear witnesses who had not yet been called. He showed himself well-informed about Jeanne's expenditure during the period he presumed her to be poor; about the plush furnishing of the house in Bar; about the jewellers she had commissioned; and about Nicolas's trip to London. 'I urge the court', he implored, 'to acquire through the legal proceedings knowledge of all these facts.'

So voluminous was Rohan's speech that it took Titon five days to absorb the information before returning to questioning. He found Rohan in a feisty mood. The cardinal expressed outrage when presented with the signed terms of sale: 'I am astonished to see . . . this item, which had not been entered into the investigation through [the normal procedure of] sealing. I declared its existence to the king out of my profound respect, and I handed it over to the minister for the king alone, and as evidence of the good faith with which I acted.' This line of reasoning had previously been engaged by one of the few pro-Rohan judges in the *parlement*: since the cardinal had voluntarily handed over the document as proof of his innocence, it could not be used against him. Such an argument involved a certain sleight of hand. Rohan's preservation of the terms of sale were intended to prove that he had not deliberately deceived the jewellers – had he been a fraudster, he would surely have destroyed it immediately – but it still served as evidence for the crime of *lèse-majesté*.

Like the *parlement*, Titon recognised the bombast here. He accused Rohan of using the bill to beguile the jewellers; he accused him of instructing the Boehmers to lie to the baron de Breteuil about the whereabouts of the necklace; and he built up to a corrosive indictment of Rohan's conduct and character:

> I put it to you that not having received any signs of the queen's patronage, you could not have flattered yourself that she chose you for a job she would only give to someone honoured with her personal confidence. You had not been allowed to believe that the queen might have wanted you to organise a deal such as this. Your condition, office and rank did not permit you to take upon yourself a deal of this kind without having taken the greatest precautions to make certain that you were not being tricked. It's unbelievable that you could have been deceived by the forged handwriting and forged signature of the queen. According to the defence you have presented, it is highly surprising that you should not have preserved the letters that were brought to you, containing the orders of the queen . . . It follows from the investigation that you wanted to persuade the jewellers and others that you dealt directly with the queen over the necklace. In keeping the bill of sale, which was by rights the jewellers', you rendered them powerless to take any steps to obtain their payment. It appears, all in all, that you sought to deceive Boehmer and Bassenge by using the august name of the queen.

For the first time, with terrifying clarity, Rohan saw that the prosecution was willing to shape every piece of evidence into a nail to crucify him. Rohan's response, in contrast, was dulcet and measured, confessing flaws of temperament but not crimes.

> However alarming the picture that has been presented might be, I hope that the explanations and evidence collected in the course of the investigation will dissipate every doubt, if they truly exist. The sign of favour that I believe I had received from the queen when, shamefully tricked, I believed that I had met the queen herself, gave me hope of no longer being in disgrace. The profound desire that I had for it made

me believe too easily, but after this illusion – the cause of my blindness – it appeared to me that not only could I believe without temerity that the queen gave me a sign of her kindness in honouring me with this task but, since every instruction from the queen is a favour, it ought to be seized eagerly. Certainly, without my blindness and illusions, I would not have acted as I had done.

The interrogation chamber did not cow Jeanne. 'She speaks to Monsieur Titon like she speaks to the police and public,' noted Target, after an evening talking shop with her lawyer. Jeanne began by telling her inquisitor her life story. She spoke of her adoption by the Boulainvilliers, her marriage to Nicolas, her first encounter with the cardinal, her patroness's death and her resort to Rohan: 'he assured me that if I was telling the truth about my titles, my affairs and my debts, he would make the effort to ease them'. Over a single six-month period, the cardinal subsidised her with 80,000 livres. On another occasion at the end of 1784 he gave Jeanne 15,000 livres, saying 'Invest this as you see fit. Since I know your affairs will become successful, regard this as something to tide you over.' When it was put to her that Rohan had only given her a few louis at a time, Jeanne answered with disdain that 'I was not made to accept such sums of money, nor was the cardinal made to offer them.'

'Is it not true,' asked Titon 'that you never stopped telling people you saw the queen and enjoyed great influence over her, and that you had her entire confidence?'

'I have not said this to anyone,' Jeanne replied, and explained how such a confusion might have arisen. 'Because of the wealth that I received from the princes and princesses of the Blood and the benefits that I received from the Cardinal . . . which ultimately came from the king' – Jeanne implied that the payments from Rohan came from the reserves of the grand almonership – 'I said insistently to those who congratulated me that the court wished that I be justly treated. Moreover, I never said that I had any access to the queen, because it was quite apparent at Versailles that I never went to the queen's apartments.' The suggestion she had shown people letters that had supposedly been written to her by Marie Antoinette was a 'horrific' absurdity.

Jeanne also denied duping Rohan into believing he had secretly met the queen. She knew d'Oliva, that was true, and had even taken her down to Versailles in the summer of 1784 (though 'for what purpose she was going, I did not know'). But dressing her up as Marie Antoinette and leading her to a secluded grove for Rohan to press a rose into her hand? 'What you suggest is fantasy.' Anyone who falls for such 'an unbelievable fable of stupidities' must be 'touched by madness' – 'the Académie Française ought never again be open to the cardinal, after having spoken, or got others to speak, such idiocies'. The accusations about her role 'make me indignant with so many lies and horrors'.

But Jeanne did not rely on exasperated outrage alone. More than the other defendants, she was aware that presenting a believable account was more important than presenting a true one. The eighteenth century had seen an unprecedented epidemic of such stories, which were winningly captivating while bearing only a limited relation to historical fact – they were called novels. Novels presented a complex dialectic between fiction and truth to their readers: often the title contained the word '*histoire*' or '*mémoire*' – Abbé Prévost's *Manon Lescaut*, one of the most popular books of the century, was entitled in full *L'Histoire du Chevalier des Grieux et de Manon Lescaut*. This language sought to secure the value of the novel, a form which had been frequently attacked as frivolous or immoral, by eliding it with more established genres. This antagonism was not merely rhetorical: novels were effectively banned in France from 1737 (though that is not to say they weren't read) until the appointment of the liberal Malesherbes as the country's chief censor in 1750.

Works of fiction were frequently accompanied with introductions or prefaces that purported to show that the book was not simply a figment of imagination. *Les Liaisons dangereuses* was supposedly arranged from a cache of letters entrusted to its editor; the first edition of *Gulliver's Travels* attributed authorship to Lemuel Gulliver himself. Readers were savvy enough to identify a novel when they met one, but the presence of such features attests to an anxiety about truthfulness among writers, as the novel sought to clothe itself in the trappings of non-fiction. Fascinated readers invested so much in some characters that they hoped they existed beyond the confines of the book's covers: Rousseau received fan mail asking him what happened to Saint-Preux after the end of *La Nouvelle Héloïse*.

Literate, cultured individuals – such as, say, you might find sitting on the benches of the *parlement* of Paris – had been attuned to the techniques through which a story might gain credibility without having a basis in proven fact. Classical aesthetic theory was founded on two related concepts: *vraisemblance* ('verisimilitude' or 'plausibility') and *bienséance* ('propriety'). Fictional narratives were judged successful if characters behaved as one might expect them to in a given situation, while the laws of propriety restricted people of certain social classes or nationalities to specific kinds of conduct. The seventeenth-century Jesuit rhetorician René Rapin wrote in his *Réflexions sur la poétique d'Aristote* that 'one must never make a warrior of an Asian, a faithful friend of an African, a Persian ungodly, a Greek honest, a general of a Thracian, a German cunning, a Spaniard modest, nor a boor of a Frenchman'.

As defenders of novels noted, this meant that history was usually stranger – and more immoral – than fiction. 'Bizarreness is a privilege of reality,' declared the writer Roger de Bussy-Rabutin. *Vraisemblance* is not the kissing cousin of true stories, but their enemy. Baculard d'Arnaud wrote in 1786 in a preface to his *Délassemens de l'homme sensible* that history was nothing more than a 'disgusting compilation of prostituted praise, calumniatory satires, false judgements, criminal lies, humanity everywhere insulted, everywhere suffering, trampled underfoot, vice everywhere heaped with eulogies, fawned upon, rewarded'. He objects, in part, to the failure of historical narratives to reward the just and punish evildoers; but alongside this sits distaste at the shapelessness of history, its gruesome extremes.

Legal narrative is torn between these two genres. Like history, it reconstructs past events through evidence. But, since these narratives are invariably contested, it must, like fiction, deal in likelihoods – and the more plausible an interpretation, the greater the chance of convincing a court. Jeanne was conscious throughout the trial that Rohan's case rested on the *parlement* believing that his mind had been rendered captive to strange delusions, so she repeatedly invoked psychological plausibility as the standard for judging Rohan's story:

would Rohan really have observed the handing over of the necklace concealed in an alcove? 'Surely he would have himself spoken to this man, and wouldn't he himself have handed over such a precious item, and would he have hidden himself at a time when he ought to have been taking the most stringent safeguards?' Suggestions she had accepted large sums of money after the alleged event were 'madder and madder', since who would hand over such amounts without demanding a receipt? Jeanne argued that Rohan's version of events should be rejected, precisely because it did not reach the standards of successful fiction.

The allegation of *lèse-majesté* checked the cardinal with a conundrum, as Jeanne was quick to seize upon: 'It was not possible that the cardinal might have imagined the queen would participate in such an extraordinary and deceitful performance [in the gardens of Versailles], and that the cardinal should blind himself to the point of not recognising the queen.' Rohan could only rebut it with a defence which, in admitting conduct unbecoming of his station, breached the bounds of narrative propriety. The verb *devoir* ('ought') contains a telling ambiguity. Take, for example, the sentence, 'The cardinal ought to respect the queen': it implies both obligation (the cardinal has a duty to respect the queen) and probability (the cardinal is likely to respect the queen). In real life – especially the life of a womanising prelate, a free-thinking churchman, a near-bankrupt almoner, a gullible *philosophe* – the one does not necessarily entail the other. Jeanne's indignation on Rohan's behalf – she could not believe he had acted in this shameful way, because his story appeared so unlikely – knifed the cardinal with a smile. Titon never asked her why, in that case, Rohan had made a series of humiliating admissions. Herein lay the canniness of Jeanne's approach – it was not her question to answer.

Jeanne was also aware that details, often superfluous, lent a colouring of reported truth – what Roland Barthes called the 'reality effect' – to every tale, a sensation of accuracy that might be taken for the real thing. Dates, times, and sums of money were arranged like trinkets in a drawing room. Jeanne admitted to walking on one occasion in the park at Versailles with d'Oliva, but the girl certainly did not have a *gaulle* on: instead she wore 'a dress in the English style of embroidered Indian chiffon, with a pink petticoat underneath, and with a calash of white gauze that she had borrowed because her own bonnet was very dirty'.

Jeanne made her case with vigour, even in the face of corroborated testimony to the contrary. She gave Titon the following account of her dealings with the jewellers: when Boehmer and Bassenge approached her to help find a home for their necklace, she replied that 'I'm very sorry not to be of use, but no one I know could possibly acquire such an object.'

'But can't the cardinal buy it on behalf of the king?' the jewellers were supposed to have asked.

'I don't meddle in such affairs,' Jeanne had said primly.

Only after the event did the Boehmers tell her Rohan had purchased the necklace.

'You are being very discreet,' she joshed her friend. 'You did not tell me that you had seen the jewellers and bought the necklace.'

'Aha! You are very curious,' said Rohan. 'And who do you think it is for?'

'I don't know,' replied Jeanne.

'It's for your sovereign – but it is top secret, because everything could go awry.'

Around the same time, Rohan asked Jeanne to help him sell some diamonds. Titon suggested she ought to have realised these were from the dismantled necklace. Jeanne replied:

> Had I known the diamonds came from the necklace, I would not have sold them and I would have warned the jewellers. My husband, seeing so many diamonds, said to me one day: 'What the devil! Where do they come from?' I asked the cardinal various questions about where the diamonds came from. He replied: 'They are from old pieces of jewellery that I no longer wear, now that I am an old man.'

This, she explained, was the reason she frequented so many diamond brokers, jewellers and clockmakers in the first few months of 1785, visits she itemised to the point of tedium.

While claiming she was uninformed about the cardinal's intentions, Jeanne insinuated that Cagliostro guided all his decisions – he must have led Rohan down the road to perfidy. The cardinal had told her: 'People don't know the fortune of this being, they do not know who he is, for he is a god. Look at his portrait, look at the eyes looking to heaven, he is an utterly extraordinary man.' Cagliostro had presided over a sabbath, the pungent incense of which had solemnised Nicolas's departure to England to sell diamonds there on Rohan's behalf.

Throughout, Jeanne played the innocent, oblivious of the jealousies of Court that made Rohan's position so awkward. 'I am astonished', she told Titon, 'that the cardinal claims to have needed me to set up a meeting with the queen.' Presented with the bill of sale, she denied having ever seen it but remarked that even she knew the queen did not sign her name 'Marie Antoinette de France'. When Rohan had entrusted her with jewels to sell, she reported him saying, 'Here are the diamonds; if you were intelligent . . . but no, your husband can tell me what they are worth.' Politicians like Rohan plot; beneficiaries of their kindness only simper with gratitude – this was Jeanne's *vraisemblance*.

Jeanne also threw elbows at any witnesses whose testimony threatened to contradict her own. Loth, her traitorous friend, was accused of pandering to Rohan because he hankered after an appointment; d'Oliva had slept with her husband and was still smarting from being dropped when Jeanne found out; she had heard that Cagliostro, who had no obvious source of income, was on the verge of buying a house for 50,000 écus cash. Their prejudices against her tainted their testimony.

Any variant tales the court might have heard about necklaces and forged signatures and prostitutes in fancy dress were 'stories devised between all those involved to give [them] more plausibility'. Titon, who found Jeanne's responses 'extraordinary', asked if she had 'witnesses to confirm for us this differing account'. She did not, replying emphatically that she spoke 'the most exact truth'. The only reason no documentation existed to prove her assertions was because Rohan had stripped her of her papers shortly before she went to Bar in August 1785. And, she riposted, if Titon continued to accuse her of passing letters between the cardinal and the queen, he should produce them.

Jeanne's slippery skill in constructing an alternate reality, which slalomed around the undeniable facts, is brilliantly demonstrated in her claustrophobic rendering of the affair's denouement:

It was the second of August. Having just arrived at my house at eleven o'clock in the morning, the cardinal said to me: 'I need your help and assistance. I have just done a stupid thing. You know the necklace which I've mentioned was for the queen? There was a documented arrangement, and I had the idiocy to say to Boehmer, who was tormenting me, "Dear God, present yourself to the queen", and to make him write a letter to the queen. They [the jewellers] have just told me that the queen does not understand what they are on about, and this was told to them by Madame Campan, one of the queen's *femmes de chambre*, who had gone to seek them out.'

At this point Rohan said, trembling, that he was about to be undone. He begged me to send immediately for Bassenge, to instruct him about rectifying the stupid thing he had made Boehmer do, and to tell him that he had been played for a fool by the queen, who had wanted to destroy him for a long time, and the Mesdames de Polignac, who had mended their differences with the baron de Breteuil, his greatest enemy, in order to deceive and destroy him the better.

When I asked the cardinal how he had been tricked and if he had seen the queen, he responded, 'Yes.' I replied, 'Do you have any of her letters?' He responded, 'I have never actually seen her write, but I have a large number of them.' He took out one, which he showed me, and he folded it over so I would not be shown the middle section. On it were the words: 'Send via the little countess a sum of money' – I can't remember how much – 'for these unfortunates. I am upset that they should be troubled.' I asked him, 'What is all that about?' He replied: 'It's for the interest [on the necklace].' I said, 'As you are not sure what the queen's handwriting actually looks like, you could obtain an example of it through your family, and ascertain whether your fears are real.' 'I dare not,' he said. 'They would not understand me.'

However, he then said, 'I'll try to get a sample – The devil! Could she have tricked me, this little countess?' And stalking round the room, he repeated over and over again, 'Could she have tricked me? Oh! No, I know Madame de Cagliostro too well, she is not capable of such a thing.' Seeing himself torn, he said to me: 'Come and see the great number of spies that are outside your door; they have not left mine for several days. I fear that there may not be enough time to set this right. Go, find Bassenge straight away, and tell him that I know he can hold his nerve – I value that. He should go to Versailles to speak to the minister in place of Boehmer, who has been summoned by him, and he should say that Boehmer was confused, and did not mean to speak to the queen of a necklace, but of earrings of a considerable price . . . which he told me had been made for the queen – in order to make it more plausible, he should bring them with him. Insist to him that I will pay him for them. They have trusted in me too much for me to let them become bankrupt over such a thing. And I have more than enough money at my house to calm their fears. But if he does not cooperate, I could act like the queen – and deny it.'

Jeanne went on to tell Titon that the cardinal had kept her prisoner in his home for a day and a half, unsuccessfully bullying her into fleeing abroad, lest she divulge what little she knew of his activities.

Careful plotting is at work here (note the delayed identification of the little comtesse). The incoherent elements of Jeanne's version – what exactly had Boehmer done wrong by writing to the queen? Why was she needed as an intermediary with Bassenge? – convey the impression of someone confused by machinations that have only been half-explained. Vagueness is the essence of the strategy – a means of spreading suspicion without having to fix it, proliferating potential criminals and so diluting the case against her. The nature of the Cagliostros' involvement is left unresolved, but compelling reasons to doubt the couple are suggested. They chime with Rohan's known weaknesses – his susceptibility to beautiful, fallen noblewomen, to mystagogues who promise him the world. They are foreigners whose wealth is unexplained and who threaten the realm with their malign, unchristian, democratic cult.

Rohan's sudden shifts of mood, from anxiety to relative confidence, from concern for the Boehmers to threats against them, are convincingly those of a man flailing under stress. Even Jeanne's failure to remember the exact sum of money written in the letter shown to her by Rohan is a gesture of authenticity, a sign that she is struggling to recollect rather than imagining afresh. Most riskily, Jeanne introduces the suggestion that the queen intrigued to destroy Rohan. This revelation is, of course, attributed to Rohan himself, and her interrogator is encouraged to wonder whether he invented it to explain away his own financial incompetence. But the risk is a calculated one, aimed at stretching the undeniable accusation of *lèse-majesté* against the cardinal, which until now was arguably unintentional, into more treacherous territory – that he considered the queen a base politician, a sovereign who did not look down benevolently upon all her subjects but enviously singled out rivals for destruction.

Cagliostro and d'Oliva were subjected to much briefer interrogations. Despite Jeanne's efforts to characterise him as Rohan's *éminence grise*, Cagliostro demonstrated that he had only arrived in Paris after the necklace had been purchased. He claimed to have been suspicious of the comtesse de La Motte from the beginning, but only at the end of July, when he saw the counterfeited signature of Marie Antoinette, did he realise the cardinal had been deceived.

Cagliostro was also required to defend the seance he had directed. He protested that it had been a jest, which he only agreed to perform after Rohan had pleaded with him to allay Jeanne's concerns about the queen's forthcoming labour – though he squirmed evasively over the details. There may have been thirty or so candles lit, but that was 'normal for a prince's house'; he could not remember whether he was decked out in fantastical crosses and sashes. But Cagliostro perfectly refuted Jeanne's insinuations that the woman who deceived Rohan was his own wife – the comtesse de Cagliostro could not have forged letters from the queen, since she was illiterate.

At the end of January, Rohan was recalled by Titon so that he could hear the accusations that Jeanne had made against him. The cardinal was by now exhausted and resentful of the finicky sifting of his recent past. His responses, in the most part variations of 'everything she says is false', sounded petulant and uncooperative. Sometimes he answered only with a curt 'no'. The fight in him had burned out; the effort of repelling Jeanne's inventions appeared too great. Titon wrung from him sad admiration for the craft with which Jeanne had trussed him up:

Madame de La Motte's conduct is not so thoughtless. She believed that she had me so wrapped up in her ploys that I would not dare say anything. And indeed, the twists had multiplied to such an extent that I would have certainly preferred to pay, to not reveal anything, and leave Madame de La Motte to enjoy the fruit of her intrigues.

19

Cheek to Cheek, Toe to Toe

THERE WAS A two-week break following the interrogations, as the *rapporteurs* prepared to brief the *parlement*. At this session, those under investigation had the opportunity to present a *requête*, an application to the court which argued for more lenient treatment or even a dismissal of their case. The lawyers were readmitted to the Bastille and huddled with their clients in preparation. Events in Rome did not augur well for Rohan. The college of cardinals, meeting on 13 February 1786, agreed with near unanimity that Rohan should be suspended from the cardinalate for six months, during which time he was required to justify his decision not to insist on a trial before an ecclesiastical court.

The reading of the interrogation report to the *parlement* was set for 15 February. There was a widespread belief that the king would choose this moment to suspend the case and punish Rohan in private but the date arrived with no word from Versailles. Target's *requête* repeated at length the contentions that Rohan had put forward during his interrogation: a secular court had no jurisdiction over him, and that his actions proved that he had been deceived by Jeanne. The court was unmoved. Titon successfully construed Rohan's description of his fellow bishops as a 'competent tribunal' into a slur on the *parlement*'s authority and abilities.

A *réglement à l'extraordinaire*, a judgement that placed the investigation on the most serious criminal footing, was passed against Rohan, Jeanne, d'Oliva and Cagliostro. The witnesses were to be summoned again for a *récolement*, where they would be read back their testimony and given the opportunity to amend anything that had been misrepresented the first time around. Two sets of confrontations would then take place: the accused would face relevant witnesses and respond to their allegations; then each of the accused would confront his or her fellow suspects, and transcripts of the interrogations would be quibbled over line by line.

The *parlement*'s *réglement à l'extraordinaire* deflated Rohan. He grimly reported to his lawyer a remark he had overheard: 'If the cardinal was tricked at first, he will end up by sharing in everything. The investigation is not running in his favour.' Georgel asked Target to 'slip off for half an hour to see the prince. He's morbid about the confrontations. He will not listen to my good sense.'

A more aggressive posture than had been displayed in the interrogations was now required. Target wrote:

> It is greatly to be desired that the cardinal does not wrap himself in the cloak of his innocence, as he has done far too often since the beginning of this affair. It is a battle in which it is not sufficient to have good reasons, good weapons and good troops. He must leap into combat, in order to fight with success. He must be persuasive, for both hot heads and cool characters are won round only by firm conviction, a belief presented with the appearance of confidence in those whom one wants to persuade. It is the cunning of the courtier that he needs to employ.

There was only a short window to prepare the cardinal, as he would again be forbidden visitors once the confrontations started. Target repeatedly stressed the importance of giving 'proactive answers' instead of brusque denials. Dates and locations needed to be precisely remembered. The cardinal needed to contest forcibly the evidence of Sainte-James and the Boehmers on the grounds that they were too financially involved in the fate of the necklace to offer impartial testimony. Only if ambushed by letters he had written to Marie Antoinette was he to affect memory loss.

Dupuis de Marcé, the junior investigating magistrate, was slated to oversee the confrontations. Target had hoped for someone less dopey, but admitted that it did not matter especially, since the questions were as formulaic as a 'catechism'. 'A good man, humane and no schemer', Dupuis was also 'very slow and let himself be led by impulse'. The absence of the self-confident and intellectually vigorous Titon presented Rohan with an opportunity to impose himself on the proceedings.

Other forces countermarched in anticipation. Breteuil strove to weaken Rohan, exiling Georgel, the cardinal's advisor, bottle-washer and morale booster, to Mortagne-au-Perche in Normandy. The proximate cause was a Lent sermon, inspired by Paul's Second Epistle to Timothy, that Georgel had written in Rohan's name, and nailed up in all churches under the grand almoner's purview. Paul wrote the letter while held captive by Nero in Rome: 'Be not thou therefore ashamed of the testimony of our Lord, nor of me his prisoner.'

It did not require a steeping in biblical hermeneutics to construe the allegory: Georgel was Timothy, Rohan Paul, and Louis Nero, the canonical example of an arbitrary, capricious tyrant. Georgel denied that he had any such implications in mind – 'if this terrible thought had occurred to me, I would hardly have had the brazenness and the confidence to nail this pastoral address under the eyes of the king in his own chapel'. Breteuil, who despised Georgel and had been looking for an opportunity to dispose of him, banished him from Paris with a *lettre de cachet*. On 11 March, Georgel wrote to Target: 'I must leave at six and will not have the consolation of embracing you . . . I will make myself worthy of my modest courage.'

One intriguing piece of circumstantial evidence points to Breteuil's meddling at this juncture. During the *récolement*, Bassenge was the only witness to make a significant change to his testimony, one that threatened to stove in Rohan's defence. The jeweller belatedly recalled the conversation with Rohan on 4 August – just after Jeanne told Rohan she had been banished by the queen – in which he questioned whether the cardinal had complete confidence in his intermediary:

'I ask you this because you informed me on a few occasions that there was an intermediary employed in this business.'

Rohan hesitated: 'If I pause before replying to you, it is only so that my answer should be completely prepared. I am only contemplating about whether to tell you everything . . . if I were to say that I dealt directly with the queen, would you relax?'

'Yes,' replied Bassenge.

'Well,' continued Rohan, 'I assure you that I dealt with her in person.' But he added threateningly: 'Never mention this conversation because

I will deny it. I can say many things to you which I can't tell your associate because he has a very weak head.'

Bassenge's addition was so poisonous because it accused Rohan of consciously appropriating the queen's name to smooth out his business arrangements. There is, however, something unnatural about Bassenge's language. Why did he need to gloss his mention of the intermediary with a reminder that Rohan had spoken of this person a number of times previously? The language rings of a mediocre playwright inexpertly crowbarring in backstory, of playing to the gallery. This version of the conversation is also contradicted by another witness – Philippe-Jacques Serpaud, a tax collector and friend of the Boehmers. Bassenge recounted this conversation to him a fortnight after he had spoken to Rohan. According to Serpaud, the cardinal made no mention of speaking directly with the queen – he simply swore that he had always spoken the truth.

In 1797, a dozen years after the affair, Georgel bumped into Bassenge in Basel. In his memoirs, the abbé records that the jeweller admitted his and Boehmer's depositions had been invigilated by Breteuil – 'they had not followed blindly all that he had desired, but they were obliged to be silent about things which he did not wish them to declare'. Georgel is highly partial and there is no other evidence that Bassenge was pressured by the queen's party to modify his testimony – but his initial deposition was the longest of all the witnesses, displaying a meticulous command of detail and describing at length his exchanges with the cardinal. It is almost unbelievable that he forgot such a significant conversation first time around. There were mutterings through the trial that ministers connived to fabricate evidence against Rohan – one can smell it, if not quite see it, in Bassenge's *récolement*.*

The confrontations were painstaking and relentless. Day after day, the witness statements and interrogations were unpicked line by line. Every claim could be challenged, countered, reinforced, dismissed,

---

* In this incident, Bassenge did not simply suppress information he should have divulged, but actively invented a conversation. But then, had he not been entirely honest during the trial, there is no reason to assume he would have been entirely honest to Georgel.

derided or tweaked. Constant vigilance was required through the draining hours in a cage with enemies who sought to tear you apart. Each morning that Rohan was required, he placed his red skullcap on his head, pulled on his red stockings, strung his medallions round his neck and was led by de Launay, the governor of the Bastille, to the *salle de conseil*, where he was handed over to Dupuis.

At first, Jeanne continued to play the untroubled innocent, as though expecting an acquittal. With Rohan she remained cheerful: 'she uses her strength', he wrote, 'to hide her troubles'. He told Target that she, unheard by the officials, admitted in a whisper to having lied. She bantered with Dupuis, trying to project 'the confidence of an innocent soul'. But the chafing of her isolation and vulnerability became increasingly obvious.

Jeanne broke down in tears in front of Nicolas's valet. She harangued Loth for doing the devil's work. Sometimes the guards had to drag her, wriggling defiantly, to the interrogation chamber. On other occasions she collapsed in fits, which may have been simulated to avoid answering awkward questions. The baron de Planta's obstinate responses brought on a swoon – after Jeanne had been revived with *eau de vie*, and was being returned to her cell, she clamped her teeth around her jailer's forearm. Once, the turnkey entered her cell to find her completely nude, and had to dress her forcibly. Jeanne believed everyone around her was conspiring to destroy her: the Bastille's confessor transmitted her confidences to Rohan; the court clerk, Frémin, refused to transcribe her responses accurately.

But she could still be savage and cunning in her own defence. Her ferocity whipped tears out of d'Oliva; she had believed d'Oliva 'an honest woman', until discovering that the girl had seduced her own husband. D'Oliva remained resolute in the face of the bullying, and Jeanne grew pale on hearing d'Oliva's deposition read out, surreptitiously gesturing that she should retract the mention of Marie Antoinette's letters.

D'Oliva responded: 'Madame, it's no good making signs at me. I will maintain all my days what I've declared to the judges.'

This enraged Jeanne: 'I make signs at you! Yes, I make signs at you that you are a monster, for having said the things you have said.'

'Alas, madame, it is you who are the great monster, for having made me do the things that, unfortunately, I have done, as the blind instrument of your intrigues.'

The cajoling realised minor triumphs with weaker witnesses. Jeanne's chambermaid, Rosalie Brissault, proved pliant, meekly deferring to her objections. But her aggression could make her cavalier: in one confrontation, Rohan expressed amazement that she had claimed the patronage of people who might easily be called to confound her, 'exposing herself by using lies, which she knew would be refuted'. More obdurate opponents were slathered with pitch. She insisted that Planta was entirely unreliable, since, one day in October 1784, he had cornered her in her husband's room and 'pressed her strongly to respond to his desires', while maniacally shaking his cane and promising to make her fortune.

Jeanne repeatedly argued that the unlikelihood of her own audacious actions was proof they never happened. How could she have shown d'Oliva letters from the queen, since discovery of such an outrage would have condemned both of them? How could she have boasted about her friendship with Marie Antoinette, for, had the queen found out, she would have been crushed? She refused to admit deceiving the cardinal by disguising d'Oliva as the queen: 'the whole story of the garden about which the witness [the baron de Planta] speaks is absolutely false'. Every accusation that she could not counter was explained by the amorphous conspiracy against her, and Jeanne warned that a guilty verdict against her would unleash a scandal of much greater magnitude: 'I certainly see that there is a plot formed to destroy me; but I will only perish while revealing the criminal mysteries that expose people of great standing still hidden behind smiles.'

Rohan began the confrontations with the witnesses in ailing health. His nose ran, his leg ached. Continuous medical attention, he wheedled, was required. Prolonged exposure to the Bastille had certainly debilitated the cardinal, though in this case he was hamming furiously; he needed a friendly doctor – whom the prison authorities eventually agreed to admit – to smuggle messages into prison once contact with the lawyers was again cut off. It turned out to be all too easy: 'I need a printing press for my correspondence,' he joked.

Rohan cultivated a calm, forensic demeanour, in contrast to Jeanne's hysteria: 'I am not responding to my interrogator in a manner that will pander to the *parlement*,' he wrote to Target. 'I prefer to fill [my defence] up to bursting with proofs that will demonstrate to everyone the falsehood of my adversaries.' He was energetic and forthright, only occasionally lapsing into the harrumphings of 'false, all false' that had marred his interrogations. A keen tactical awareness emerged in his confrontation with d'Oliva: both realised that their best chance of acquittal was in corroborating each other's accounts – d'Oliva had confused matters in her deposition by misdating her performance at Versailles by a number of months – so both admitted that they were so flustered with trepidation in the Bosquet de Venus that they could not remember clearly what was said and done. Like dancers, they sprang responsively to the other's steps: 'Were the letters that Madame de La Motte claimed to have come from the queen written on a paper with a blue pattern?' asked the cardinal. 'I believe they were,' replied d'Oliva compliantly.

The confrontation with Sainte-James was one of the most important. Here was the opportunity to convince the navy treasurer that he had not boasted of seeing 700,000 livres in the queen's own hands. The terrace on which they had snatched a conversation was noisy, Rohan argued, and Sainte-James must have misheard him. But Sainte-James remained resolute: 'I do not have any motive for imagining or making up such a conversation and maintain what I said.'

Bassenge also required challenging on the purported conversation he had suddenly remembered during the *récolement*, which Rohan vehemently denied ever took place. Target held the jeweller in contempt: 'The behaviour of this man is clearly shown', he wrote, 'in how he tries in his deposition to flatter the cardinal, and how he tries to fix the blame on him. We must pick this deposition to pieces to make it fail.' 'He will be hard and self-satisfied,' the cardinal told his lawyer, but 'he will not be stubborn.' In the event, the jeweller did not bend, and Rohan was forced to plead that, since Bassenge was a lone witness, his testimony should be ignored – yet still his allegation clung to him like thorns.

A major development occurred in Rohan's confrontation with Père Loth, when Loth was shown the document outlining the conditions of the necklace's sale. 'It appears to me', he told Dupuis, 'that the four "approuvés" and "Marie Antoinette de France" are similar to Villette's handwriting.' For the first time, a suspect for the forgeries had been identified. Loth admitted he had never actually seen Villette compose letters from the queen, but remembered once walking in on Villette and Jeanne at work, and noticing a note on blue-bordered paper – it was exactly the kind of paper on which Rohan received Marie Antoinette's letters and it was covered in Villette's writing.

20

An Extraordinary Rendition

GENEVA, A WARM evening in early spring. By the side of the square, a young man is strumming a guitar. For some reason – perhaps irritation at his strangulated playing, perhaps he is provoked – a brawl breaks out. The man is arrested and hauled before the magistrate where, it emerges, he is none other than Rétaux de Villette. He had been living since he fled Paris in a spa not far from Geneva under the name Marc Antoine, though the discipline required to remain incognito was clearly beyond him: his 'acts of libertinage' had already brought him to the attention of the stern Calvinist authorities, who had threatened him with expulsion.

Everyone in Europe had heard of the Diamond Necklace Affair, and French embassies and consulates had circulated a description of Villette to local law officers – the Genevois authorities knew something of the character of the man in their custody. Villette admitted to the magistrate that he was an acquaintance of Jeanne and had been asked by her to sell some diamonds. Then, the previous summer, he had been told by Jeanne that her business ventures had collapsed; she advised him to travel to Italy and provided a stipend for the purpose. Villette said that, having heard the news from Paris over the past months, he had been 'incapable of resting easy, since the queen had been compromised'. What he did not know, however, was that d'Oliva had also been arrested. When her name was mentioned, he stammered guiltily: 'It could only have been this girl who compromised me, because I am sure that Madame de La Motte would not talk about me. If this girl has spoken, I am a lost man.'

The Genevans, wishing to curry favour with the French, were willing either to keep Villette immured indefinitely or repatriate him – whichever was more amenable. On 19 March Vergennes wrote to the Syndics of Geneva asking them formally to arrest Villette, and Inspector Quidor of the Paris Police was sent to escort him home. Quidor had been ordered to treat Villette with 'all possible mildness' and 'establish trust' with him. On the journey back the captive choked up confessions like a half-drowned man: he admitted attending on Jeanne and d'Oliva during the garden scene, and implied that Jeanne had deceived the cardinal to obtain the necklace. Villette's effusions were not entirely unstudied – there was a certain degree of calculation aimed at deflecting suspicion that he had been at the heart of the plot.

Word of Villette's arrival at the Bastille on the 29 March percolated through the city. D'Oliva, who caught a glimpse of the new prisoner, recognised him immediately. The arrest was of such significance that the king himself demanded to see Villette's papers. Initially, Villette was interrogated as a witness. Retracting some of his confidences to Quidor, he admitted only that Jeanne had told him the crown jewellers were selling a very valuable necklace. A short while later, he had been asked by Jeanne to broker the sale of some diamonds. When presented with the terms of sale, he was unable, he said, to identify the forged handwriting. The *parlement* was unconvinced. On 6 April, they passed a *decret de prise de corps* against him, and he was immediately seated for interrogation by Titon.

Villette's answers were extremely circumspect and reflected his uncertainty of the extent of the court's knowledge about his and Jeanne's activities. He acknowledged little more than the questions themselves revealed: that he took dictation from Jeanne for a number of documents; that he met d'Oliva through the La Mottes, and went to Versailles with the three of them in July 1784. As they walked through the park he injured his heel and rested on a bench, so had no idea what occurred in the Bosquet de Venus.

But when Titon asked 'Do you know that the girl d'Oliva played the role of the queen?' Villette's pretence of ignorance became unsustainable: 'I learnt about it immediately afterwards; I certainly admit that I had the idiocy to regard this wrongdoing as a joke and I laughed a lot about it. Lengthy remorse has atoned for the moment of madness.' He had no idea, he added, why Jeanne had dressed up d'Oliva as the queen. What Villette did not know, and had no chance of knowing, was that Jeanne's defence relied on a complete denial of the garden scene ever having occurred.

Less oblivious betrayals of his co-conspirator surfaced as well. Villette said that Jeanne had told him she received the queen's favours; he had noticed, in the summer of 1785, that the La Mottes had an abundance of diamonds of unknown provenance. As he was prodded further about the sale of the necklace, he could offer no insight into the circumstance surrounding it, until he was asked directly: 'Do you recognise the handwriting of the words *approuvé* and the signature *Marie Antoinette de France*, and was it not you who wrote them?'

Something wilted within Villette, as he realised that a wispy evasion on this count would be swatted down by the court. Nonetheless, he maintained his denials, while proposing an ingenious legal argument in his defence:

> Suppose that as a result of being totally enamoured, I may have been made to commit a crime of this nature. It is easy to imagine how I would be afraid of confessing this. Admit, moreover, that things looked stacked against me; suppose, even, that false witnesses might have deposed that they had seen me write these words, it would then be a case of judging the action and myself as guilty.
>
> But, indeed, neither the handwriting nor the signature are the queen's. Not only has there been no copying of the queen's handwriting, in which case there has been no material forgery; and not only was there no use of the signature that the queen uses, so there has been neither forgery nor the crime of *lèse-majesté*, but even the signature that exists cannot be that of the queen, since it takes the form 'Marie Antoinette de France', who is an imaginary being in this kingdom. I ask therefore, what weight can be attributed to such a signature? Ought it not be treated in the way it was taken? First by the queen's jewellers, who conduct business with the queen, and especially by the cardinal, a man of the Court who, because of his position and rank, ought to recognise the handwriting here, and at least know how Her Majesty signs and that the name 'Marie Antoinette de France' could not be her signature. Note, furthermore, that this [the signature] is only a tiny thing that I could not have profited from. Note,

furthermore, that one can only object to this document, of which I am suspected of being the author, in so much as it was presented to the jewellers as being the true handwriting of the queen and convinced them to hand over the necklace. If the crime lay there, it could certainly not be imputed to me, since I know neither the cardinal nor the jewellers. If I claimed such connections I'd be laughed at and arrested. In a word, I made no use of the signature, and did not profit from it.

Titon was flummoxed by the argument, and made no objections during the interrogation. By the *récolement*, however, a response had been formulated. There was a very simple reason why the writing of the words 'Marie Antoinette de France' was a crime: they had been already deemed so by the king's letters patent. No further quibbling over the matter was possible.

For the time being, the ostensible success of his argument made Villette a little more cocksure.

'Did the cardinal know that the words *approuvé* and the signature . . . were not the handwriting and signature of the queen?' asked Titon.

'I don't have actual knowledge,' he replied. 'But, without being as enlightened as the cardinal, I think that I would not have been deceived had I been in his position.'

Perceptions that he had fled to escape arrest were misguided, Villette concluded – he had left Paris in August 1785 'to fulfil a longstanding wish of travelling to Italy'. Nothing could have been more innocent.

While Villette was being interrogated, Dupuis began to arrange confrontations between the accused. First came the face-off between Jeanne and Cagliostro, a brief, bursting flare, prologue to the lengthier sessions between Jeanne and Rohan. Jeanne scythed away at Cagliostro's character and breathed mephitic suggestions about his activities: he was a commoner who lied about his nobility, a fantasist who had imagined his exotic birth, 'an opportunist who wanted to live at the cardinal's expense'. Remaining vague about Cagliostro's involvement in the Diamond Necklace Affair to exacerbate the sense that his influence permeated it like a fog, Jeanne accused the comte of 'seeking to involve the cardinal in things in order to compromise him'.

Cagliostro responded in kind: Jeanne had told him that she

possessed a key to the queen's private apartments; that she visited them often; and that the queen had even called on her in her own home. Cagliostro's counter-attack enraged Jeanne so much she hurled a candlestick at him in frustration, though she managed only to burn her own eye.

The two incompatible narratives that had been presented to the investigating magistrates finally bore down on each other in the confrontations between Jeanne and Rohan. Jeanne sought to mire the cardinal in detail. The entirety of the first day – five hours long – was spent compiling all the payments she claimed to have received from Rohan. There were ten in 1782 alone, most of them worth thousands of livres, along with hampers crammed with game and wine. Rohan responded with a frustration that showed his difficulty in rebutting such falsehoods: 'You deliberately multiply the details in order to make things plausible,' half-admitting that the relative thinness of his own account weakened his case. The sums of money she spoke of, Rohan argued, amounted to almost all the funds available to the grand almoner. When her imaginary facts were coshed by reality, she responded with indignation: 'You should be ashamed of yourself for acting so badly today when you once did so much good.'

This was just one of a repertory of poses Jeanne struck. Sometimes, she spoke obliquely, hinting at a conspiracy to bury her. At other times her voice was serrated with menace. She could be angry or prolix or self-congratulatory. Even the shifts in her story could be summoned in her defence: 'to the public, one can say what one wants,' Jeanne told Rohan. 'But in the confrontations one must speak the truth.'

Rohan's allegations were reflected back onto him. It was the cardinal, she claimed, who had showed her letters from the queen which promised his elevation to chief minister; it was the cardinal who had guided her to a secret entrance to the queen's rooms through which he entered unseen. These fantasias were ornamented with comical embellishments. To disguise himself, Jeanne announced, Rohan used to wander around Versailles in a white *lévite* and a deep-bowled hat, burying his face in a handkerchief. To sneak into Trianon, he would scurry across a plank over a ditch – on one occasion he fell in, dislocating his thumb and tearing his skullcap.

Court intrigue, Jeanne suggested, explained everything. When the cardinal discovered that the signature was false,

> he told me that it was the Polignac woman who had dreamt up all this intrigue to destroy me. 'I will let go of that affair,' he told me. 'I am going to continue to go to Versailles, where I will seize the first opportunity that presents itself to speak to the king, and I will throw myself at his feet as I tell him about all my suffering. I know that everything will be all right. I can count on his kindness and I will not have to deal with the queen. Rather, I have many people that matter on my side, Monsieur de Vergennes, Monsieur de Maurepas and my family.'

The comte de Maurepas was certainly a formidable politician, but his influence had diminished precipitously since his death five years earlier.

Rohan responded by arguing that he and Jeanne ought to be held to different standards:

> My simple denial of Madame de La Motte's alleged suppositions ought to have the force of proof and not be treated as equivalent with Madame de La Motte's denials. For it has been demonstrated and will be shown again during the course of the investigation that at every event for which there are witnesses, they testify against her. Consequently my assertions have been proven true by the same testimony. I must be believed when I contradict her, since Madame de La Motte has spoken falsely at all times – anything she says without proof or witnesses, and which is denied by me, will be false again.

More succinctly he said: 'Everything that Madame de La Motte calls a fact is actually a story made up on the spot.'

Rohan admitted he had been 'guilty of too great a credulity and good faith – but that is my only wrong'. His too-generous heart had inhibited him from exposing Jeanne, even when his suspicions of her deceit were grounded:

> A fear seized me of harming Madame de La Motte, that she should fall much deeper into the pain that I had seen in her and about which she had expressed herself so movingly, at having fallen into the unhappy position of having displeased the queen. Had I added to these griefs, I could have harmed her irreparably.

Despite his fortification of the moral high ground, the cardinal could be nimble-footed on occasion. 'It is not a crime if I'm mistaken about a date,' Jeanne pleaded as she tried to mop up an inconsistency. 'It's not a crime', Rohan shot back, 'but it is a falsehood.' Yet he indulged in falsehoods of his own. Still worried that evidence of his correspondence to the queen might emerge, he set down for the record that he had left Jeanne on a number of occasions by herself in his study, where she would have had the opportunity to filch a stash of his notepaper. Who knows, he suggested, what letters might have been forged with his signature: 'I reject therefore all these writings on which there is only my signature and I reject equally letters that she might produce or which might concern the sale of the diamonds.'

Both Jeanne and Rohan were aware that, in their disputation, they needed to avoid replicating the crime of appropriating the queen's name each time they tried to explain themselves. It offered Rohan an excuse to fulminate by rote, when feeling exhausted. He felt 'the most cruel sorrow to see a name worthy of such respect impersonated in this way; the horror that these words cause me is the only response that I will permit myself'. Jeanne showed herself aggrieved at every mention of the queen: 'I am exposing all of the cardinal's lies and am suffering more than a person ought to be obliged to, for invoking the queen's name in my defence.'

Jeanne's attitude towards Rohan wavered throughout the confrontations. In some instances, she portrayed him as a satanic manipulator, who had bribed d'Oliva to support his invention of the garden scene. Witnesses Rohan cited in support were part of the 'cabal of the cardinal'. But she also expressed pity for him – 'he was not the only guilty party in this horrible affair: it was [Cagliostro's] advice to the cardinal that set him up to be the victim' – and offered to prove that Cagliostro was guilty of even 'blacker crimes' (evidence of which she never got round to providing).

Despite the misery Jeanne had inflicted upon him, Rohan could not suppress his respect for the faint gleams of integrity he discerned. After Jeanne had explained that the reason her husband had fled immediately after her arrest was to avoid divulging secrets told to him by the cardinal, Rohan wrote to Target: 'I cannot stop myself admiring the care which she took to absolve her husband.' In Jeanne's presence, he veered between admiring and abhorring her jusqu'auboutisme.

'You are right to have insulted my credulity. I render homage to all of your skill,' Rohan told his adversary.

'Surely, I am less skilful than a member of the Academy,' replied Jeanne, her gloating lathered in faux-humility.

'I have nothing', said Rohan, 'but contempt for you.'

On 9 April, Harger and Blin, the two graphologists who had originally examined the forged signature, examined it again, after having been shown a number of Villette's papers. Harger believed that there had been a deliberate effort by Villette to mask his handwriting. Confronted with the expert witnesses, Villette did not raise any objections since 'I myself had admitted that I was the writer of the *approuvés* and the signature' – in fact, he had not – but denied deliberate counterfeiting. This was the most significant development in the inquiry so far. Finally, the investigating magistrates knew for certain the identity of the signature's forger, and could link him to Jeanne de La Motte. Rohan's legal team had also made the connection. Loth had obtained from the director of the post office a letter Villette had written in January 1785. Target compared this with the letters from the queen which Georgel had secretly preserved, and pinned their authorship on Villette.

Jeanne was not eager to reacquaint herself with Villette. After news reached her of his arrest, she was discovered hiding under her bed, naked and drooling. In their first confrontation, Jeanne distanced herself from her partner in crime. He was not, as Loth had alleged, her *homme des affaires*, but a drinking buddy of Nicolas. She continued to feign ignorance of the garden scene. Even if she had organised such an escapade, Jeanne said, she would not have told Villette, an unrepentant gossipmonger, about it. (Unfortunately, d'Oliva had already testified that Jeanne 'did not keep anything secret from him [Villette] . . . she did nothing without warning him and consulting him'.)

Villette havered, speaking only in the most general terms, and refused to commit himself: 'I am obliged to respond to you on each article with care and precision according to the oath I made to tell the truth and the respect I have for justice.' He may have 'misunderstood' events of which he had no first-hand knowledge. Villette adapted his story to suit whoever was in front of him; despite his admission to Harger and Blin, he now maintained that 'I did not write the words . . . and the signature.' The only reason he had offered his counterfactual justification to his interrogator was 'because of my fear of a judgement against me'.

Weak and obviously terrified, Villette seemed ripe for manipulation by Jeanne. She grew emboldened, demanding that Villette reveal the identities of the letter-writers she had supposedly ordered him to impersonate. He remained silent.

Then, suddenly and without prompting, Jeanne discarded one of the primary crutches of her defence: she admitted disguising d'Oliva as the queen in the Bosquet de Venus to deceive the cardinal. A balletic justification followed. Rohan had sought her assistance in arranging a reconciliation with the queen. Having no connections in the queen's inner circle, she had been unable to oblige. When Rohan had angered her – Jeanne would not expand on the cause, but her gloss, 'which decency silences me from telling', suggests sexual betrayal – she took revenge by toying with the cardinal's most dearly held desires, convincing him the queen had forgiven all. In order for her plan to work, she laid claim temporarily to the queen's friendship, but she insisted the pretence was dropped immediately afterwards.

Jeanne must have realised that Villette, unlike the others who vouched for the garden scene, could not be discredited as a parasite of Rohan, and feared he was not far from breaking before Titon and Rohan. A complete realignment of her defence – even if it now left her open to the charge of *lèse-majesté* – was necessary. Villette saw safety in cloying piety: 'I would like nothing better than to say that I wasn't in the grounds [of Versailles] or in [Jeanne's] house that day, but my duty to the truth means that I have to say that I was there.'

By the time Villette was confronted by Rohan, however, he had stiffened his spine. Rohan was also livelier, reinvigorated by the capture of such an important witness. They sparred over the nature of Villette's friendship with the La Mottes: Rohan called them 'as close as a married couple'; Villette decried his attempts 'to make me responsible for the actions of Monsieur and Madame de La Motte, as if I had nothing more urgent than busying myself with their affairs'. The cardinal identified Villette as the man, supposedly a member of the queen's entourage, he had witnessed collecting the necklace from Jeanne's Versailles apartment. Villette replied to this 'infernal audacity' that Rohan's description of a pasty-faced, brown-haired, beetle-browed man bore no resemblance to him. 'Without wishing to accuse you of fraud,' said Rohan, sounding like an Englishman, 'it is possible that you could have blackened your eyebrows and whitened your face.'

Rohan did not manage to squeeze out from Villette an admission that he had actively participated in the stagecraft of the garden scene – though he suspected, correctly, that Villette was the person whose arrival had sent them scramming – but, pelting him with example after example, the cardinal forced him to concede that Jeanne had cozened acquaintances 'based on the belief that she had credit with the queen'. Yet still Villette denied any knowledge of the *collier d'esclavage*.

'It is unbelievable', said Rohan, whose own behaviour had not been especially believable, 'that Jeanne would not have spoken about the necklace to such an old friend.'

'Just because something appears unbelievable to you', Villette answered tartly, 'does not make it less true . . . Silence is the lover of success.'

This drew from Rohan a scalding peroration:

Monsieur de Villette was intimately connected with Madame de La Motte. Monsieur de Villette wrote for Madame de La Motte. It was in him that Madame de La Motte confided about d'Oliva's performance. The handwriting of Monsieur de Villette resembles the words '*approuvé*' and the signature, and the manner in which Monsieur de Villette excused the person who wrote the signature in question – all these point to the fact that he is the author of it.

Rohan was conscious that Jeanne, not Villette, was his ultimate adversary. After the harangue, the cardinal took a more conciliatory line. Perhaps Villette 'was tricked' as the cardinal himself had been. 'It's not that I want you to be proven guilty,' Rohan murmured, 'it's that I want the guilty party to be found.'

Villette was not yet tempted; Rohan's own conduct still exuded suspicion. Villette countered: 'In all of your testimony, one never sees clearly why you had so much trust in Madame de La Motte. Perhaps there exists a mysterious reason which you desire or fear seeing the light of day.'

'I fear no revelation,' said Rohan, striving to convince Villette that betrayal of Jeanne was no betrayal at all.

> But I beg you in your turn to consider you are held back in what you're prepared to admit by a misguided sentiment, which is the fear you have of compromising the single person who has compromised everyone, who has plunged me and you into unhappiness . . . in wanting not to compromise the single person who is guilty of everything, you push aside the benefit of a confession at the moment when a version of events, which is recognised as true, is supported by more than enough proofs that, even without your own admission, are sufficient to condemn you.

Villette acknowledged Rohan's kindred sympathy for his judicial persecution, but still held firm until the end of the confrontation: 'If I am guilty, the strength of evidence against me will necessarily lead to the person who set the plan in motion.'

Cagliostro's introduction to Villette took a more ludicrous turn. The Great Copt worked himself up to such a pitch that he started gabbling away in Italian, to the great annoyance of Dupuis. He then launched into a ninety-minute sermon on the 'duty of a man of honour, the power of providence and love of his fellow man'. According to Cagliostro's own account, he

> made [Villette] hope for the mercy of God and of the government . . . My discourse was so long and so forceful that I stopped without being able to speak further. The rapporteur was so touched and so moved, that he said to Villette that he must be a monster if he was not affected, since I had spoken to him as a father, as a man of

religion and of morality, and that all I had just said was a celestial discourse.

The stenographer, too, must have been equally rapt, as, alas, none of Cagliostro's wisdom was recorded for posterity.

21

The Truth Will Out

T HE EVIDENCE WRENCHED from Villette required Rohan and Jeanne to confront each other for a second time. They raked the same ground, furrowing the earth grown over with weeds which smothered the truth; discussions became absurdly involuted – one circled at great length around how much of Villette's face had been obscured by a handkerchief when, disguised as the queen's footman, he had collected the necklace.

The cardinal fenced more aggressively than before, no longer holding himself aloof in distaste. He bored through Jeanne's defence as though with a sharp, straight awl. On 24 April, Jeanne was compelled to admit to Rohan, as she had to Villette, that she had disguised d'Oliva as Marie Antoinette. It had never been her intention 'to deny that Mademoiselle d'Oliva was presented to the cardinal in the park as being the queen, and it was not by chance that they met'. She reluctantly admitted compromising the queen's dignity but believed that Rohan's crime in imagining 'that he could have such a meeting' was far worse. Her reticence up to this point had been to spare the cardinal more humiliation: 'If I delayed in revealing the truth, it was only because I did not want everyone to know the misdeeds of Rohan.'

Rohan immediately pounced, proclaiming that 'no credence should be lent to anything that Madame de La Motte might dream up from now on, because she has been convicted of falsehood in everything she has said'. And he decried Jeanne for suggesting they had once been lovers:

> I have hesitated up to this point from replying with a very natural repugnance to all the *doubles entendres* proposed by Madame de La

Motte about my relations with her . . . she has kept such an allegation on stand-by for a long time, a calumny that she has had prepared
to excuse her lies when she is forced into a position in which she
can no longer sustain her case.

The cardinal's forcefulness rattled Jeanne. In a snatched conversation
out of earshot of Dupuis, she told Rohan, 'if I admit a great deal
in anger, I will become cautious when I'm no longer in this state'.
Jeanne returned to Villette's betrayal, scratched it to make it disappear, pondered aloud how she could be revenged without slitting
her own throat along with his:

> if Villette had forged the document as he has been accused, his first
> priority would have been to keep quiet about the scene involving
> d'Oliva with which he has compromised me greatly [but], in con-
> fessing this, he would have feared that this admission would have
> provoked me in turn to reveal that he was the person who wrote
> the *approuvés* and the signature.

Once self-interest is summoned as proof of innocence, there are no
other places to hide.

Willing Jeanne over the brink, Rohan begged her

> not to keep holding things back and to admit the crimes that are
> not personally yours. You would prove by your admission that you
> were merely incriminated. This thing has gone on much longer than
> you thought it would. You did not have the intention of doing all
> this evil and causing the unhappiness you have caused. You should
> admit everything you have so stubbornly concealed, which has pushed
> you towards the abyss that is opening before you and which causes
> our current misfortune. Finally, you should make this admission
> because of honour, religion and humanity . . . I am more worried
> for you than for myself.

Not a criminal, merely incriminated – these were distinctions which
Rohan knew, and knew that Jeanne knew, would have no traction
with the court. Rohan's outburst does not reveal a man who has
happily entrusted himself to providence and the law: there is frustration
at Jeanne's unnecessary prolongation of the proceedings – everyone
else recognised that she would be found guilty – and despair at the
torment she had caused, and might still cause him when the verdict

was reached. (Target was clear-sighted about the consequences of Jeanne's obstinacy: 'Thus', he told Rohan, 'does the duck cut its own leg and wring its own neck.')

While Rohan and Jeanne scrapped, Titon worked over Villette again. The formidable magistrate did not permit the retractions and contradictions which the more lax Dupuis had previously let slide. Villette, feeling the breath of justice moist on his neck, had already written to Vergennes, begging for the king's mercy in exchange for illuminating 'certain details'. The foreign minister did not respond, but Titon harvested them anyway: Villette had replied, at Jeanne's dictation, to Rohan's letters addressed to Marie Antoinette, which betrayed an 'ambition [to become first minister] that was the cause of his blindness' and led the cardinal to be duped:

> It was sometime in January 1785 that Madame de La Motte showed me the terms of the sale for the necklace, which needed to be signed. I did so on the assurance given to me that it would never leave the cardinal's possession, that he would never put it to any other use apart from being shown to the jewellers.

He had suffered more than anyone: betrayed by 'Madame de La Motte [who] promised me she would retrieve the document in order to destroy it'; stiffed of his share of the proceeds ('I owe it to the truth to say that she had again promised me a great reward and she did not keep her word'); and exploited by a seductress who took advantage of 'my weakness and malleable character'. The reason for the near-complete confession was readily offered to Titon: 'I fear', said Villette, 'of being the only person against whom proof will be legally established' – and, therefore, of bearing the full brunt of the king's vengeance.

Like a pendulum that twists as it swings, strangling its own arc, Villette returned yet again to confront Jeanne and the cardinal. His second meeting with Jeanne on 5 May was painful for both parties. She felt far greater affinity with her amanuensis than with her husband. 'I would love it if you were not guilty, as I would myself,' Villette told her in sorrow, 'but unfortunately the crime has been demonstrated.'

Grimly, as even the judges called her a liar, Jeanne continued to reject their imputations, refusing even to accept Villette's confessions of his own involvement.

> If I had been in the situation of forcing Monsieur de Villette to make the document in question, Monsieur de Villette, who is more savvy than me, would have been in a better position than me to judge the consequences . . . and he would not have been so deprived of sense to manufacture a forgery and compromise the queen.

Villette, wishing to mitigate his former lover's punishment as best he could, pleaded with her that 'you understand your interests very badly'. An admission might not 'expiate [your lies] in the eyes of justice' but it would moderate the punishment. Jeanne's obstinacy was nothing more than 'ill-judged self-assurance', and continued denials 'will only add to your wrongs, not diminish them'.

Jeanne responded with the haunting tranquillity of someone embracing their fate:

> I understand more than anyone the self-interest I would have felt were I guilty and hoped that an admission would make the punishment less severe; but I am waiting calmly for my punishment, as I am not guilty, because up until now I have proven by my conduct that I am innocent, since I remain calm without trying to evade anything even when I have the chance.

Yet signs emerged that her conscience was shifting restlessly. Jeanne informed Titon that d'Oliva did not know that she was impersonating the queen; and she exonerated Cagliostro ('I never claimed that he did [play a part in the affair]', she told Rohan. 'The only accusation that I have against him is that he advised you to blame me.')

But she doughtily maintained her innocence as though her sanity might otherwise slip her grasp. In her last confrontation with Rohan, he implored her to reveal any confederates; instead

> she hid beneath her hat so that I would not see the tears flowing, but they were too much and after having let them run for a few moments, she demanded to have read back to her what had been said; but then her expressions of grief began again and she replied, sobbing, that she had nothing to say. After the commissioner had

remarked that after several opportunities she had not said anything, she said that she would answer to Providence alone, and she called on it as a source of strength, after a moment's silence.

The cardinal, in contrast, glowered with confidence. Since Villette had come clean, he no longer felt the need to play the sympathetic confessor to reel in the truth, and was determined that the *parlement* should look upon Villette as equally complicit as Jeanne. Aware that the conviction of his enemies would not necessarily entail his own absolution from the charge of *lèse-majesté*, Rohan spoke, as Jeanne had done, of a wider conspiracy to disgrace him. Now Villette and Jeanne had been discredited, he even denied ever writing to Marie Antoinette or pestering Jeanne to arrange an audience with her. The senior magistrates of the *parlement* would decide whether these late efforts to cut himself adrift from previously acknowledged misjudgements were credible.

The muscular bullying of Villette belied the state of Rohan's emotional and physical health. When the archbishop of Paris received special permission from the king to visit the cardinal in January 1786, he barely recognised him. Rohan was rattled by the fear that his secret communications with Target would be discovered. 'I do not dare send you the continuation of the confrontations until I have your word that you will only show them to M[onsieur] Target,' he wrote to Traverse, the compliant surgeon who attended on him, 'for, I'll say it again to you, if they get wind of it or suspect anything, there are all sorts of actions which might be taken.'

Every confrontation left him exhausted and depressed, because of their gruelling length and the 'unsupportable' uncertainty. He spoke to Dupuis de Marcé, who was sympathetic to his plight, of

the pain I feel in pressing arguments on guilty people who have yet to make an admission, and who seem to me not strong enough to defend themselves. I recognise this sentiment but I don't think I am in the wrong since . . . the new calumnies of my adversaries make me realise how my feelings towards them are far from what I ought to show them and so I become more forceful. Yet despite this I predict that if these same adversaries give way to the force of truth and appear to regret their crimes, they will have the same claims upon my sympathy.

Rohan's ailments gave him little pause for magnanimity. His stomach cramps were so severe that he suspected poison at work (the blame actually lay in a dodgy stew); his migraines were debilitating; his eyes leaked pus. The only visitor in his cell was God, to whom he turned more frequently than he had done in more carefree times. He had written, on the wall of his cell, the words of Psalm 119: '*It is good* for me that I have been afflicted; that I might learn thy statutes.' The embarrassment he had brought upon his family tortured him too: 'I embrace you from the bottom of my heart,' Rohan wrote to his brother, 'as I do all my relatives. At that word tears stream from my eyes and my cruellest torment is that which I cause them.'

There were justifiable worries that the magistrates, especially Titon, were no longer acting impartially. Their lines of questioning sought 'to join me in some fashion to their [Villette and Jeanne's] lot'. When facing yet another interrogation in the latter stages of the case, Rohan wrote in anguish that 'it will be very difficult for me to hide the pain . . . if I am forced to face Titon'. Fortunately, the magistrate had not pressed him over the contents of the letters to Marie Antoinette, where undoubtedly the worst examples of his *lèse-majesté* lay. And the cardinal could not shake the queen from his mind. 'Let me know', he wrote to Target on one occasion, 'if it is true that the queen is always sad?' On another he simply asked, 'Have you any news of the queen?', hoping only that her misery would not be added to his crimes.

Jeanne's increasing derangement had been the subject of much speculation, some of which, it appears, had been deliberately spread by Rohan's allies: she had leaped at the cardinal and scratched his face; she had beaten up Cagliostro; she had made a pass at the governor of the Bastille; her *femme de chambre*, overcome by remorse, had tried to drown herself. Her parlous legal position gave her great cause for agitation. The comte d'Artois expressed her prospects tersely: 'I fear that my dear cousin Valois may be hanged by her pretty neck.'

On 22 May, Titon began his report to sixty-four magistrates of the *parlement*, an unusually large tribunal since the roster had been swelled by honorary counsellors – legal grandees who turned out for high-profile cases. Despite the cardinal's Ciceronian performance during the confrontations, the Rohan had few reasons to be confident: the allegations of *lèse-majesté* appeared insurmountable; the court had been well managed for a number of years by the *premier président*, d'Aligre, whose pockets clinked with royal emoluments; the Rohan, and the cardinal particularly, were not held in great affection.

The abbé de Véri noted in his diary on 23 March 1786 that neither side conducted itself honestly:

> A widespread rumour is running wild which certainly is a terrible calumny but which is no less detrimental for that. They say that 4 million livres have been set aside to be distributed among the judges once the cardinal has been condemned. I am very far from believing such an imputation. I must, however, admit that several of the judges have given in to a too noticeable partiality. On the subject of the cardinal they get very heated, those for as much as those against. The number of those who are against now appear the stronger. The first president d'Aligre shows his colours with so little decency that the cardinal could demand his recusal.

According to Georgel, the queen herself had intervened, telling a group of judges that Rohan was 'the enemy of her rest and her reputation'. They knew which way to vote. In the streets and cafes of Paris, grisly punishments were conjured up: Jeanne would have her head chopped off, Villette his hand.

For eight days the voluminous transcripts of the interrogations and confrontations were read out, word for word. In the early hours of 30 May, the prisoners were transported to the Conciergerie, the prison annexe of the Palais de Justice where the *parlement* sat. They were due to be cross-examined by the entire court later that morning. Jeanne, d'Oliva and Villette were driven there shortly after midnight; Rohan and Cagliostro arrived at five o'clock in the morning. Was it a deliberate attempt by Joly de Fleury and Titon to exhaust them? Titon righteously insisted he only wanted to spare the cardinal the inconvenience of bunking down in a new cell. They were escorted by a troop of Bastille guards who remained on parliamentary premises, all the better, the conspiratorially minded thought, to snatch them away should the prosecution be thrown out. Security was twisted tight. The exits of the *parlement* were sealed; even lawyers were not allowed access.

Despite the precautions, a large crowd gathered to observe the suspects. Cagliostro strutted with ebullience but Rohan looked feeble: 'he leant on his cane a great deal, and seemed very lame from the swelling and inflammation that he has had for some weeks past in his right knee'. He limped through 'a vast concourse of people, who observed a profound silence, and seemed deeply affected, many of them being observed to be shedding tears'.

The court settled down at eight o'clock to question the suspects individually. All of them were forced to kneel on the *sellette*, the traditional low stool, in submission to the *parlement*'s authority. First they summoned Villette, clad all in black, who, with watery eyes, confessed his crimes. So eager was he to prove cooperative that lengthy answers spouted forth before the judges had even finished their questions.

Next came Jeanne, wearing a black hat trimmed with lace and ribbons, and a demure lavender-grey dress tied with a metal-studded belt. Though in her memoirs she recalled feeling terrified – 'my knees knocking together, and my whole frame trembling with agita- tion, unable to articulate a single syllable' – on the day she appeared to onlookers composed and articulate, if ultimately transparent. One wrote of her 'assurance . . . with the eye and face of a deceitful woman surprised at nothing', and her clubbable attitude towards the judges verged on impudence. 'That's a trick question,' Jeanne upbraided one judge, like a schoolmistress disappointed with a lazy answer. 'I know you, Monsieur l'Abbé. I expected that you would ask me that.' Even she, however, leapt back when shown the *sellette*, though she soon recovered her composure and reclined as though stretched out on 'a chair in her apartment'. Jeanne admitted nothing, apologised for nothing, held back nebulous secrets so as 'not to offend the queen', and declared the cardinal to be a great rogue who tutoyed Marie Antoinette in more than two hundred letters. Whenever she was contradicted, she scratched her head dismissively.

Rohan was summoned next. He was dressed in a violet soutane, the mourning garb for cardinals, a red skullcap and shoes with low, red heels. Across his chest, he proudly wore the sash of the Order of the Holy Spirit, to which the king had appointed him. He carried himself with dignity, 'dismayed but not humiliated, cool . . . respectful but noble, in short worthy of his birth and rank', and a number of judges stood as he entered. Pale and exhausted, he seemed so weak that the judges invited him to sit on a more comfortable chair rather than kneel – he compromised by perching on the edge of a bench. For two hours, he fielded questions, modestly, respectfully and to the point, never shirking a direct answer (the cynical alleged he referred repeatedly to a crib hidden in the fold of his robes). At the end he stood and saluted the bench, who returned the gesture. He left through a side gate – the guards had massed on the other side of the palace to mislead the crowds – and greeted courteously the few bystanders milling around. D'Oliva and Cagliostro were dealt with cursorily. Just over two weeks before d'Oliva had given birth in the Bastille and now looked bemused at her lost innocence – like the peasant girl in Greuze's *The Broken Pitcher*, according to one judge. She kept the court waiting to feed her child, then stuttered out monosyllabic replies between sobs. Cagliostro, who presented himself in a green suit braided with gold, amiably tattled in Arabic, Greek and Italian. The gaggle outside the court cheered as he emerged. He felt himself returning to life, like a parched flower in torrential rain.

22

In the Gossip Factory

'IT IS THE depth of opinion in this nation that, in the end, decides the great questions,' wrote Vergennes as the *parlement*'s investigation plugged away. Even this arch-conservative acknowledged a democratic imperative that had been growing in volume over the previous fifty years. Yet while practically everyone recognised the existence of public opinion, locating it was much harder.

'Does the public exist?' asked the Parisian journalist Louis-Sébastien Mercier. 'What is the public? Where is it? By which organ does it make its will known? . . . Say to a man who holds a position, *the public disapproves*; he will reply: *I also have my public, who approve, and I'll stick with that one*.'

The public sphere that emerged during the seventeenth and eighteenth centuries existed between the privacy of the home and the outer limits of the state's authority. It was oppositional, disputatious, rational. Through its institutions – the salon, the coffee house, the Masonic lodge, the scientific academy, the debating society, the efflorescence of journals, gazettes and news-sheets – culture and politics were subjected to robust consideration, and a political consciousness emerged among a class of people who had no role and little influence in government.

France was still a society cramped by censorship, and Paris a city infested with police informers. Though newspapers were widely read, the most influential were still published abroad – in Britain, in the Low Countries and in the Rhineland – to avoid being suppressed. The king's subjects needed to take care about their words and the publications they read, for fear of landing in the Bastille. There were few touchier topics of conversation than the Diamond Necklace Affair.

Breteuil's clarion blast to arrest the cardinal sounded across Europe.

As it faded, a babble of wonderment grew louder, speculations combining and splitting like petrol on water. Paris was a workshop of gossip: according to the *Correspondance Secrète*, 'there are no suppositions so criminal or absurd that they are unable to find partisans'. Had the queen wanted the necklace but the king forbidden it to her? Had Jeanne almost persuaded Rohan to buy the necklace for the queen, but instead he sold it in Denmark and squandered the proceeds? Had Cagliostro, Rohan and the Holy Roman Empire conspired to re-annex Lorraine, lost by the Habsburgs during the Thirty Years War? 'The people in general,' reported the duke of Dorset, the British ambassador, 'unaccustomed to events of so extraordinary a nature, have imagined there must be some intrigue of state at the bottom, and that very great personages are implicated in it.' No one knew any certainties, and many did not want to know – the latest rumour always trumps the truest one.

The variety of opinion was whittled down as members of the public chose which side to champion. Familiarity won nobody any friends. 'In the town, they accuse Madame de La Motte and the cardinal,' wrote the *Correspondance Secrète*, 'but at the Court they accuse the queen.' Many – not just enemies of the Rohan family – were willing to believe that Rohan had stolen the necklace to meet his towering debts. Even Vergennes, an ally of the Rohan, struggled to believe in the cardinal's innocence. 'It is rare that someone with so much wit could also have been so stupidly duped,' he wrote to the marquis de Noailles, the ambassador in Vienna.

Equally vociferous were those who presumed the queen wanted to hush up a failed plot to ruin the cardinal. The comte de Fersen heard a whisper that

> it was only a jest between the queen and the cardinal, that all was well between them, that she had indeed instructed him to buy the necklace, and that she pretended she could not stand him in order to disguise the jest, that the king, having been informed of it, had reproached her, that she had fallen ill and made herself seem pregnant.

Seasoned courtiers looked on helplessly at the gross mishandling of the affair. The clamour of Rohan's arrest, wrote the duc de Levis, was suited to a 'crime of state that was too imminent to brook the slightest delay', not for 'a minor intrigue of a charlatan and a knave, who had plotted to swindle money from a credulous, vain man . . . Wise men find the minister's conduct almost as blameworthy as the cardinal's . . . The name of the queen had been compromised [by Breteuil's actions] more than by all the libels published against her.'

Within a month of the scandal's outbreak, there was a clear majority who believed in Rohan's innocence of the theft of the necklace. They presumed the king must have reached the same conclusions and would halt the trial, exiling the cardinal temporarily, were punishment needed. Support for the cardinal among the higher echelons of society was particularly vigorous. After *parlement* took charge of the investigation, the Rohan family embarked on a campaign on his behalf. The Rohans were linked by marriage to the junior branches of the Bourbons, the Condés and the Contis, and soon princes of the blood were openly denouncing the queen. Even the Habsburg emperor reached a different conclusion from his sister over Rohan's actions. 'He is very capable of absent-mindedness and can't keep control of his finances,' he told the marquis de Noailles, 'but he's not someone who would immerse himself in actual criminality.' Nobles felt outrage at the brutal treatment of a member of their order, manhandled in front of the crowd like a pickpocket. A number of high-born ladies had less patriotic reasons for standing by Rohan – they were relieved that he had burnt his correspondence, so their billets doux would remain forever unread.

The affair left its imprint on fashion and consumer goods: straw hats bedecked with red ribbons – *chapeaux du cardinal sur paille* (hats of the cardinal on a straw pallet) – grew fashionable among his detractors. A faience plate from Vizelle in the south-west from the year of the trial depicts an approximation of the necklace's design with beads in ebony and amber to lend colour. Printers recycled etchings of participants in forgotten causes célèbres, captioning them 'comtesse de La Motte', 'Mademoiselle d'Oliva' or 'Rétaux de Villette', and sold them by the thousand. Pornographic mannequins of Jeanne in coitus with Rohan and Villette were also available. In London, a tavern in St James's Street charged five shillings just to see a portrait of Jeanne.

The longer Rohan was detained, the more sympathy he accrued. By mid-May 1786, Dorset reported that the 'whole of public opinion is greatly in [his] favour'. Ballads characterised Rohan as a moon-calf rather than a racketeer, playing up his gullibility to assure that 'a senate will soap him clean'. One ventriloquised Rohan instructing his supporters:

> My good friends, who run through the town
> To obtain my absolution
> I make this humble confession
> Tell everyone that I'm a clown.

The most important publications relating to the affair were *mémoires judiciaires* or *factums* – trial briefs issued by the lawyers of the accused – which in theory were directed at the judges, but were printed and distributed with the court's endorsement. The crafting of a *mémoire* was a barrister's primary responsibility in Ancien Régime France. As lawyers in criminal cases were prohibited from sitting in with their clients during interrogations or pleading directly before the judges, this was their most effective means of advocacy. The *mémoire* was one of the most popular genres of its day – high-profile cases regularly generated print runs of 10,000.

A hybrid of narrative and legal argumentation, the *mémoire* braided together a sympathetic biography of the defendant with analysis of evidence, and looked to literary models for inspiration.* Paris had never seen a case before with such a quantity of *factums* produced. So many were printed at the height of the investigation that pedlars cried out 'voilà du nouveau' with each new publication.

Jeanne's lawyer Doillot was the first to publish. He portrayed Jeanne as an ingénue, taken advantage of by a charismatic man protected by powerful interests and infatuated with Cagliostro, 'a false prophet' who led him to perdition. A confusing fuzziness hovers

---

* As Sarah Maza has shown, the melodramatic chiaroscuro of the *mémoires* normally drew inspiration from the bourgeois drama of Diderot, Mercier and Beaumarchais. The Diamond Necklace Affair was closer, she argues, to *opera buffa*, since it 'offered a complicated plot, disguises and mistaken identities, purloined letters, elegant settings, and luscious female characters. It had all the elegant shallowness of a light (and late) rococo comedy'.

over the *mémoire* – it is full of aspersion and half-accusations, but never clarifies who was to blame for the necklace's disappearance ('the countess is guilty of nothing,' wrote Doillot, 'but that does not necessarily mean the cardinal is guilty of everything'). Doillot accused Cagliostro of accumulating a huge fortune of hazy origin, but never explained his interest in the diamonds beyond 'imagin[ing] the multiplication of the necklace in a hundred ways'.

The vagueness was purposeful; it dramatised Jeanne's marginality, showed her shuttling in and out of a larger plot of which she only caught intermittent glimpses. But this had the perverse consequence of reinvigorating the *lèse-majesté*, for it became impossible for Doillot to argue definitively that the queen had not been involved. Marie Antoinette exists in the *mémoire* as a spectral presence, sensed through the curtain or in the wings – not unlike a discreet yet omniscient schemer, conscientiously covering her tracks as she works her mischief. In order to save herself, Jeanne drew on – and infused with new life – the image of the queen as an unwearying intriguer.

Four thousand copies of the *mémoire* were printed and distributed free, in order to muster support for Jeanne, and the Parisians practically laid siege to Doillot's house. A contemporary recorded:

> I was not ten steps from this house – the house of M Doillot, when a lawyer's clerk, quite winded, covered in perspiration, called out to me eagerly, 'Have you got it, sir? Have you got it?' . . . As I turned the corner of this accursed street, the carriage of a doctor, who was bursting his lungs by shrieking 'the one by Mâitre Doillot', almost ran me over . . . I swear in good faith I thought at this moment that, rather than distributing a *mémoire* about the case, they were giving away gold to every Frenchman who happened to want it.

Aficionados found the style and structure execrable, though its uncontested accusations still besmirched Rohan. The *Mémoires Secrets* adjudged that it was 'very badly written but implicated the cardinal exceedingly'. Its reviewer, alert to the tactical positioning of lawyers, noted 'at first it appears disgusting that Madame de La Motte, in admitting her infinite obligations to the cardinal, should implicate him so seriously – but her natural line of defence requires it'. The cardinal's friends were deeply worried. Georgel acknowledged that, irrespective of the *mémoire*'s truth, 'the public is interested in a young woman who says that she is victim of intrigue and lust'. He had touched on something significant. Readers, who regarded the *mémoires* as proto-novels, cared less about impeccable logic or sheaves of affidavits than a rollicking story.

A lull followed the appearance of Jeanne's *mémoire* until after 15 February, when a *mémoire* in defence of Cagliostro was published. Three thousand copies sold out within a day, and eight guards were stationed at the door of his lawyer's house to marshal the avid crowds. Wide-eyed stories of Cagliostro's wizardry had been batted about since his arrest in August. The *Correspondance Secrète* reported that, under questioning, he had 'remarked that he could think of no misdeed to account for his arrest, unless it might be the assassination of Pompey – although regarding that ancient crime, he had acted under the Pharaoh's orders'. The *Gazette de Cologne* contained further tales of the supernatural – Cagliostro and his wife had escaped from their cell in the form of a dove and a wood pigeon respectively, though had returned on the instructions of the Supreme Being, who assured them they would overcome, like Daniel in the lions' den.

Cagliostro struck a precarious balance in his *mémoire* – distancing himself from the more outlandish notions without discarding his mystique. He described himself simply as a doctor, one who cared altruistically for all mankind, irrespective of status. France was his 'adoptive homeland', before the Bastille consumed him.

Following this exordium, Cagliostro embarked on his life story. The mufti of Medina had raised him in his own palace. He did not know where he was born or who his parents were, though his tutor, the wise Althotas, reassured him they were 'noble and Christian'. In Medina, Acharat (as Cagliostro was then known) excelled in his studies and learned to 'love God, to love and serve those closest to him, and respect the religion and laws of every place', a creed that rendered him innocuous and palatable to enlightened audiences. Accompanied by Althotas on a kind of oriental grand tour, Acharat travelled through Asia and Africa. In Egypt he was initiated in the mysteries of the Pyramids. When Althotas died, Acharat adopted the title Count Cagliostro, went to Rome where he married, then travelled round Europe dispensing ageless wisdom and home-brew remedies.

To propitiate the wary, Cagliostro perfumed his story with a tang of Christianity; to those enamoured of his exoticism, he was a font of Eastern knowledge. His narrative draws sustenance from stories such as Samuel Johnson's *Rasselas* and Voltaire's *Zadig*, fables set in the Orient about the troubled quest for happiness. Cagliostro invited his readers to see his biography as a tale of moral instruction, in which the tribulations of an Arabian savant set an example of the life lived well. Voltaire's *conte* enabled Cagliostro to play the *comte* (the relationship was not lost on Doillot who, in a hurried response, mocked Cagliostro's *mémoire* for reading like a novel).

D'Oliva proved even more intriguing than the Great Copt. At Versailles, many continued to believe that 'His Eminence enjoyed in the park of Versailles the favours of Mademoiselle d'Oliva, believing he had obtained those of the princess whom she impersonated, and that rose is the emblem of this kindness.' Courtiers laid bets over who would bed her first on her release. An astonishing 20,000 copies of her *mémoire* were printed, so great was the demand, and each of these would have had multiple readers. Considering that Paris had a population of around 600,000 and literacy rates by the end of the eighteenth century were 47 per cent for men and 27 per cent for women, it is not impossible that nigh-on every literate Parisian dipped into her story which, according to the *Mémoires Secrets*, was like something out of the *Thousand and One Nights*.

D'Oliva milked sympathy from her age, gender and class. The gift of the title 'baronne d'Oliva' only showed that 'I was not a woman worthy enough of [Jeanne]'. 'My femininity, my youth, feeble, ignorant and timid, without knowledge of the way to do things', rendered her vulnerable to Jeanne and Nicolas, who easily took advantage of her 'credulous and docile being, without credit, without protection, without support'. Blondel, d'Oliva's lawyer, skilfully offered the titillation his readership wanted, while never admitting his client had strayed.

It has been argued that, in assimilating themselves with Marie Antoinette, Jeanne and d'Oliva, in their *mémoires*, also transmitted to the queen the stain of female deviousness through association. This requires some qualification. Lawyers could not help giving factual accounts of events to defend their clients, even though that meant they replayed the counterfeiting of the queen's appearance and handwriting – but there is little evidence to suggest that readers were incapable of distinguishing the true Marie Antoinette from the fake one.

But the *mémoires* enabled the expression of a radical politics in another way – by implicitly contrasting a justice firm and indifferent to rank, with the king's ineffectiveness and partiality. The Paris Bar had long incubated liberal sentiments – as in many other cases, the Diamond Necklace *factums* appealed to 'rights' and 'liberties' which trumped royal prerogatives. All the lawyers involved in the case, bar the aged Doillot, would take part in the Revolution.

There is a levelling impulse throughout Blondel's *mémoire*. D'Oliva orders Jeanne to 'descend from the heights of your family tree, from where you defy the laws . . . I am nothing but you are only my equal, when we are together at the feet of the justice of men, before which all names, all ranks, all illustriousness must disappear, as before eternal justice.' Within this coils a denial of the supremacy of kings, for it is the Valois name that 'must disappear'. Elsewhere, d'Oliva hugs Rohan tight: 'despite the enormous distance that separates us in the social order, this deplorable affair is, however, with regard to him as regard to me, a great and too memorable example of the danger of liaisons [du danger des liaisons]'. They had both been brought low, both barred in indistinguishable cells – all are victims, like the cast of Laclos's novel. The liaisons are not merely a local cause of disaster but a symptom of more profound change – the dated ideology of a hierarchical society cracking apart under the strain of social mobility. There could be no more potent allegory for this than a prostitute playing the queen in the latter's own back garden.

The cardinal's lawyers had hoped to release their *mémoire* in the window between the interrogations and the confrontations, when Rohan was allowed to consult them again. But Joly de Fleury blocked publication, demanding numerous revisions to run out the clock. When it finally appeared in mid-April, it had been gestating for a number of months – Target had read excerpts to a private audience in his own home as early as the beginning of February.

The delay was partially self-inflicted. The contents had to be approved by all four of the cardinal's lawyers, who did not always sing in harmony. Rohan, who considered himself to have as incisive a mind and fine a style as his counsel, insisted on being involved in discussions, immersing himself in the minutiae and adding new details gleaned from the confrontations. 'These words "difficult" and "terrible" are two terrible expressions,' he wrote to Target, the competition with his fellow *académicien* sizzling through.

As inevitably happens with documents bolted together by committee, the *mémoire* swelled in size. It was three times the length of any other published during the trial and stuffed further by the inclusion of an appendix of the depositions Carbonnières had taken down in England. Rohan was worried about its bulk, but ultimately proud of the achievement:

> I would really like to express my great and total satisfaction with the redaction. Well done, Target. Tell him, I beg you, that it is with complete confidence that I will remember him for this – it is a masterpiece – worthy of him. It is perfect to the highest possible degree. Go, I beg you, to tell him immediately.

Others differed in their estimation. Georgel thought the bloat muffled the *mémoire*'s impact: 'it was voluminous and didn't live up to the reputation of the author; one would have wanted more accuracy and dignity. The facts that needed to be stressed in order to have significant effect were lost in minute details that overshadowed the work.' The initial print run was a mere 1,100 – such was the eagerness to read it and the scarcity of exemplars that Rohan's secretaries cleaned up by selling copies at the inflated price of an écu.

Target's *mémoire* painstakingly demolished Doillot's. Where Jeanne's lawyer had relied on atmospherics and innuendo, Target built his case on dates and sums of money and nuggets of evidence mined by Georgel. Target's primary strategy was to convince his audience to see the theft of the necklace as the gravamen of the charge against Rohan, not the *lèse-majesté* incorporated in the letters patent: it was far easier to prove Rohan had been the victim of a swindle than to exonerate him of thought crimes. By causally linking the forged letters, the scene in the garden at Versailles and the theft of the necklace, Target hoped Rohan's innocence in the third matter would colour the judges' attitude towards the rest. In order to accomplish this, Target had to portray Rohan as a fool, effortlessly led on and stupid enough to believe a tarted-up prostitute was the queen herself (Rohan's pride resisted this characterisation, and he tried to tone down some of the language).

At the same time, Target also sought to depict Rohan as an altogether more substantial figure, a hero of classical tragedy whose fall offered pause for moral reflection:

> The revolutions that occur in the destiny of great men awaken suddenly among people all the passions at the same time: in some a barely concealed joy, circumspect grief in others, here worried and sorrowful pride, elsewhere the baseness that consoles itself in the sight of these reversals, in all an energetic curiosity, which goes about setting to right the truth and lies.

Rohan's monumentality held a grim fascination for lesser-souled men; his demolition transcends petty legal questions of right or wrong.

There was something fundamentally democratic in Target's approach – like Blondel's – which repeatedly invited the reader to envisage himself in Rohan's situation: 'Suppose that you had been tricked as him, that for a long time you had been in great error . . . a false image of the most desired truth. Don't say that you would have known to avoid the traps laid for his good faith; no one can fix the limits on illusion.' It must have been galling, for a Rohan of all people, to invite the common man to burrow into his mentality. Here was an ecumenical, humanist antidote of the devious transplantation of prostitute and princess surgically engineered by Jeanne. Justice, Target suggested, derives not from divine right or the sword of authority, but the empathetic imagination of right-thinking men.

The bluntest profanity the *mémoires* collectively committed against the crown did not ever need mentioning. What Mademoiselle de Mirecourt described as 'the fundamental law of this kingdom' was broken: 'that the public cannot suffer to see its princes lower themselves to the level of mere mortals'. Snagged in a narrative which they had not the power to steer, Louis and Marie Antoinette were, in the words of the queen's dressmaker Rose Bertin, 'transformed into simple individuals'. The *mémoires'* resemblance to novels thrust this descent into relief. The dumb loss of authority was nowhere more apparent than in the king and queen's appearance as characters in other people's stories. Ostensibly they were treated with respect, all parties agreeing that they were not implicated. Yet the persona of Marie Antoinette which Jeanne had mocked up was still subject to the lawyers' debates – in the squabbling over whether Rohan had seen in person the queen riffling through banknotes, in the quibbles over what exactly had been said by d'Oliva in the garden. The Diamond Necklace Affair brought to the surface a realisation which had been brewing for some time – the royal family no longer governed their own image. This *lèse-majesté* was of an exponentially greater magnitude than anything dreamt up by Jeanne.

23

Judgement Day

A T SIX O'CLOCK on the morning of 31 May, Joly de Fleury began to lay before the *parlement* the charges against the defendants. The case for the cardinal's conviction stood foremost. Rohan's great crime had been 'temerity': the temerity with which he had concluded that the bill of sale had been signed by the queen; the temerity with which, surmising that the king would disapprove of the acquisition, he had flouted the royal will; the temerity with which he had 'continued to lead the jewellers in the mistaken belief that the queen had knowledge of the transaction'; and the temerity with which he had knelt before a woman he presumed to be the queen in the gardens of Versailles.

Joly de Fleury then pressed further, arguing that Rohan knew it had not been Marie Antoinette who had ordered him to broker the necklace's acquisition. 'The cardinal's entire conduct', he thundered, 'displays only falsehoods and lies.' This allegation proved too much for a number of *parlementaires*. Extraordinarily Joly de Fleury's own deputy, the *avocat-général* Abbé Séguier, argued against his superior, not even bothering to disguise his contempt. 'You're on the verge of descending to the grave', he railed, 'and you wish to cover your ashes with ignominy and to make us magistrates share it.'

The court then heard the sentences Joly de Fleury was seeking. For Villette: whipping, branding, confiscation of possessions, lifetime service in the galleys. For Jeanne: whipping, branding, confiscation of possessions, imprisonment. For Rohan: an apology to the queen for his presumptuousness, resignation from all his positions, a ban on entering a royal palace when the king or queen were in residence, punitive damages. 'If it weren't for the dignity with which he has held himself and the considerations that are due to his family,' Joly de Fleury spat, 'I think that he would merit the same punishment as Rétaux de Villette.' The court was also requested to rule d'Oliva *hors du cour* – released only because the evidence for a conviction was inconclusive. Only Cagliostro was to be fully acquitted.

The *parlement* was not obliged to vote on Joly de Fleury's recommendations alone: any judge was permitted to suggest alternative punishments. Two magistrates proposed that Jeanne be executed, so the thirteen ordained judges recused themselves, clerics being forbidden from spilling blood. This was a boon for the cardinal, a man not held in much affection by his fellow churchmen – only two were known to side with him.

The significance of the case was not lost on the assembly. Lefèvre d'Ormesson, one of the court's *présidents*, said that he had never been involved in a case which required such delicate balancing between respect for the king and the principles of justice. The judges knew Joly de Fleury's recommendations epitomised the king's wishes, and any dilution would be taken by Louis as a snub. Pricked on by the sense of occasion, the zealots attacked the *procureur-général* as partial, illogical and overly harsh. The court would douse itself in moral turpitude should it convict Rohan, they claimed. One magistrate lectured:

> The cardinal was tricked, shamefully tricked. For what is our purpose, sirs, if it is not to seek out the deceiver and to punish them? We therefore pity the cardinal, we should untie the irons that bind him and regard ourselves as lucky in saving the honour of the innocent and, through that, cementing our own.

Robert de Saint-Vincent then stood to harangue his colleagues for their timidity. The craggy rock on which *parlementaire* opposition to the crown fastened, he accused the king's ministers – always a tactful way to avoid blaming the king – of wishing to make the *parlement* an instrument of their vengefulness:

> Since when have *ministerial* conclusions been admitted? Yes, I say *ministerial*. These have never been drawn up by the prosecutor. You will not find there conclusions reached by a magistrate. They are too opposed to the laws, to correct procedure, and never has *parlement* listened to something so distant from its principles.

REPRÉSENTATION EXACTE
DU GRAND COLLIER EN BRILLANTS DES Srs BOËHMER ET BASSENGE.
Gravé d'après la grandeur des Diamans.

The necklace of slavery: it was so heavy that the two streamers on the right and the left ran down the back of the wearer to stop her toppling over

La Reine en gaulle by Elisabeth Vigée-Lebrun: this unregal depiction of Marie Antoinette caused consternation when it was exhibited in 1783 among viewers who thought the queen was 'dressed like a serving-maid'

Nicole le Guay, dubbed the baronne d'Oliva: might not a brief glimpse on a dark night lead one to identify this woman, with her slender neck and prominent chin, as Marie Antoinette?

Jeanne de La Motte-Valois: she channelled her unfulfilled fantasies of life at the heart of the Court into more lucrative outlets. This image is the frontispiece of the judicial *mémoire* printed in her defence during the trial

A chaste child, under Cagliostro's direction, sees visions of the future within a vase of purified water

Love Letter by Jean-Honoré Fragonard from *The Progress of Love*

A seventeenth-century painting by Jeanne Cotelle the Younger of the Labyrinth, a planted maze at Versailles that would be pulled down to make way for the Grove of Venus, where the Cardinal de Rohan was convinced he met the queen

The Cardinal de Rohan, sketched by Philibert Louis Debucourt two years before
the Diamond Necklace Affair broke: though charming, witty and generous,
Rohan was brought low by his oceanic credulity and sense of entitlement

Guy-Jean-Baptiste Target: the moral conscience of the Parisian Bar and the mastermind of Rohan's defence, he refused to represent Louis XVI when he was put on trial by the National Convention during the Revolution

Bust of Cagliostro by Jean-Antoine Houdon: his gaze bore into people 'like a gimlet' and his voice sounded 'like a trumpet muted with a crepe veil'

'The Leap of the Royal Family from the Tuileries to Montmédy':
a print mocking the failed escape attempt by Louis and Marie Antoinette
in 1791. The diamond necklace descends from the queen's petticoats to
Jeanne and Rohan, who are looking up them

A fan depicting characters involved in the affair: plates decorated with
the necklace, straw hats with cardinal-red ribbons, even dolls of Jeanne
and Rohan coupling were also available

This was not just simulated outrage: the maréchal de Castries, himself a minister, noted in his diary that Joly de Fleury's conclusions had obviously been dictated by creatures of the queen.

Saint-Vincent's line of argument was propitious, since the *parlement*'s legitimacy derived from its perceived independence and willingness to defy the king. Even the court party had no wish to be viewed, in the public eye, as government lackeys, and d'Aligre, who for months had coordinated the prosecution with Joly de Fleury, could not bring himself to join with the *procureur-général*'s view that Rohan deliberately obtained the necklace by deception: it 'was impossible to conclude that he is an accomplice or had any knowledge of those things which he was involved in that led to this infamy'. In d'Aligre's view, Rohan should simply apologise to the queen for the offence caused. Hardly anyone rose in support of Joly de Fleury – one who did, the honorary counsellor Persan, spoke so softly that no one could hear him.

The mood throughout the day was sepulchral. The judges chewed their lunch, normally a convivial gathering, in silence. Every time a magistrate left the chamber, they were buttonholed by Rohan's stalwarts. After sixteen hours of debate, at ten o'clock in the evening, the court settled down to vote. Most of the judgements reached were uncontroversial. The forged *approuvés* and signature were to be ceremonially struck out. Jeanne was to be punished *ad omnia citra mortem*, to everything bar death: flailing; branding on each shoulder with 'v' for 'voleuse' (thief); imprisonment in the Salpêtrière, the women's poorhouse-cum-prostitutes' reformatory in the Faubourg Saint-Victor. D'Oliva was ruled *hors de cour* and Cagliostro acquitted. Villette, however, was spared the lash and instead banished in perpetuity. His show of contrition had convinced the court that he was simply 'a passive tool, led on by the La Mottes'.

The greatest uncertainty lay over the fate of Rohan. Over the course of the day it had become obvious that the punishment suggested by Joly de Fleury would not pass. But it was unclear until the end whether Rohan too would be ruled *hors de cour*, the taint of criminality still upon him. The *présidents à mortier*, the ten senior magistrates, a number of whom cherished ministerial ambitions, split five each way. As night closed in on that long, bitter day, twenty-three judges voted to rule Rohan *hors de cour*, twenty-six to absolve him completely.

Rohan left the Palais de Justice to applause and cries of 'Long live the *parlement*, long live the cardinal'. Lips kissed his hands and cassock. Fishwives, assuming the court had spoken in one voice, thrust bouquets of roses and jasmine into the hands of Titon, who brushed them aside testily: 'I am not on the side of the judgement that passed, and I don't deserve this applause.' So overwhelming was popular support for Rohan that one observer declared: 'I don't know where the *parlement* would have fled, if they had given an unjust judgement.'

The cardinal was not immediately released. Target breast-stroked through the crowd to reach his client only to be told by the governor of the Bastille that Breteuil had banned anyone from speaking to Rohan, and that he and Cagliostro had been ordered back to the prison. A near riot ensued as Rohan's carriage turned towards it, and the multitude was only assuaged when Rohan leant out of a window and assured them he was returning of his own volition. They followed him, yodelling triumphantly all the way.

The judgement was not inevitable; Rohan's conviction could well have been secured had it not been for two tactical failings by the king's law officers. The first was managerial: had Joly de Fleury dealt with Rohan separately, and the clerical counsellors remained in the court, it is likely that Rohan would have received a more equivocal verdict. The greater error, though, lay in the inept attempt to frame Rohan for the embezzlement of the necklace. If the charges against Rohan had been limited to *lèse-majesté*, they would have been impossible to refute; but the letters patent hemmed the prosecution in by presuming the cardinal guilty of embezzlement, and Joly de Fleury insisted on stressing this unproven allegation when he might have scudded over it in silence.

The judges were experienced and discriminating, so why did so many of them vote to acquit Rohan on all counts, when they knew he was culpable, at the very least, of *lèse-majesté*? In a report written shortly after the trial, Mercy-Argenteau explained the division entirely in terms of self-interest. The verdict had been rigged by Calonne, the finance minister and strong supporter of the Rohan, to whom a number of judges were in hock: one wanted help with buying a property, another wanted his tax bill written off, another, deeply in debt, hoped for a pension. Others had liaisons – romantic or political – with the Rohan family. Mercy-Argenteau was so determined to attribute support for Rohan entirely to greed that some of his explanations are ludicrously contrived. One judge, Boula de Montgodefroy, apparently cast his ballot for the cardinal because 'his nephew was threatened with having four horses that had been intended for him taken away, if his uncle voted against [him]'.

But Mercy-Argenteau overestimated the finance minister's influence over the *parlement*. Calonne had never been held in much esteem by the counsellors – greybeards remembered his efforts in the 1760s to suppress their fraternal *parlement* in Brittany. In the last months of 1785, he had tried to steer a large increase in government debt through the *parlement*, which had expressed to the king doubts about Calonne's integrity and financial acumen. Come May 1786, Calonne was in no position to sway the court to his will; Beugnot, in his interpretation of the verdict, argued that Calonne was viewed as a representative of the crown rather than an ally of Rohan. According to Beugnot, d'Aligre, in revenge for the ministry's bludgeoning through of the loan, refused to rally support for Joly de Fleury's conclusions. The Diamond Necklace trial marked the beginning of the end of the Court party.

It was, however, generally acknowledged that Rohan and his ministerial partisans on one side, and Breteuil on the other, intrigued with the judges for the desired verdict. Supporters of the queen believed some judges had been swayed by 'ladies who had performed a part not very commensurate with their principles'. Castries, a reliable analyst with no skin in the game, reported that Breteuil had tried to negotiate lenient punishments for Villette and Jeanne in exchange for Rohan's conviction. The Rohan were equally underhand. One contemporary ballad ran:

> If the Cardinal's ruling
> Appears completely askance,
> You ought to know that money
> Governs everything in France
> Eh bien,
> If you see where I'm going.

No one wanted to give Marie Antoinette, pregnant and fragile, the news from Paris. Eventually, the duchesse de Polignac told her. The queen was distraught and disinclined to believe in Rohan's innocence. For two days, she did not venture out. 'Condole me,' she asked Madame Campan:

> The intriguer who wished to ruin me, or make money by misusing my name, adopting my signature, has just been fully acquitted. But, as a Frenchwoman, let me pity you. Unfortunate indeed are a people who have for their supreme tribunal a set of men who consult only their passions, some of whom are capable of being corrupted, and others of whom have an audacity which they have expressed against authority.

To Polignac, a friend who, in truth, had not been wholeheartedly supportive during the trial, the queen wrote: 'Come and weep with me, come and console my soul, my dear Polignac. The verdict which has just been given is a terrible insult. I am bathed with tears of grief and despair. I can be satisfied with nothing when perversity seems to search for every means to torture my soul.'

The king was winded too, blaming himself for humiliating his wife by attributing the case to the *parlement*. In retrospect, said the baron de Fremilly, this outsourcing of justice was like 'throwing a match underneath a barrel of powder, and the barrel blew up with a terrible bang'. The journalist Rivarol wrote that 'Monsieur de Breteuil has taken the cardinal from the hands of Madame de La Motte and crushed him against the forehead of the queen, who will retain the mark.' Louis and Marie Antoinette could scarcely believe that the *parlement* had, in effect, ruled that the queen could be mistaken for the kind of woman who might arrange a midnight assignation, buy a ruinously expensive necklace without her husband's permission and correspond in secret to a known roué.

Louis offered a more indulgent explanation for the verdict, viewing the judges as deferential to caste rather than corrupt or insolent:

> The affair has been decided outrageously. However, it is easily accounted for . . . The *parlement* perceived in the cardinal only a prince of the church, a Rohan prince, a near-relation of a prince of the Blood. While what they ought to have seen was a man unworthy

of his ecclesiastical character, a great nobleman degraded by his shameful connections.

He, too, could still not comprehend that Rohan had been trussed and stuffed by Jeanne: the cardinal, he was sure, had bought the necklace and 'was not so silly as to believe that Madame de La Motte was received by the queen and deputed to carry out such a commission'.

On the evening of 1 June, Rohan was taken home from the Bastille by his brother, the prince de Montbazon. His entire family had assembled at his *hôtel* to greet him, along with numerous other well-wishers. (Cagliostro had to hack his way through even thicker crowds to reach his own door, before delivering an impromptu speech of thanks.) The realists in Rohan's family acknowledged that, even with his acquittal, the cardinal could not cling to his office and honours. They advised him to resign the grand almonership, but Rohan resisted and no decision was taken that evening. The following day, as Rohan prepared to return to the Palais de Justice to thank the judges, a revenant filled his doorway – Breteuil, who, suffering from gout, had been borne on a litter to the cardinal's house with, for the second time, a *lettre de cachet* from the king. Louis had felt that, for the crown's standing, the cardinal needed to be chastised, since the court had so perversely acquitted him. 'Indecent joy' lit the baron's sallow face as he hobbled through the *hôtel*. Rohan was not to leave his house nor receive any visitors for three days; he was then to travel to Chaise-Dieu, his monastery by the Loire in the Auvergne (where, the king wrote to Breteuil, 'I hope that he sees very few people') and await further instructions; and he was to step down immediately as grand almoner.

Both the nobility and much of the general citizenry were indignant at the cardinal's treatment by the king. In their eyes he was innocent, laundered clean of guilt by the *parlement* (though some looked on more sceptically: the cardinal's innocence shone 'like a turd underneath a lantern', according to one scabrous song). 'Tyranny' was yelled from street corners, in answer to the king's *lettre de cachet*. 'They pity him,' wrote the baron de Staël of Rohan, 'as they pity oppressed virtue, and they call what the royal court has done harshness, so that the public take the side of a man whom up till now has been covered in contempt.' Castries, looking back ruefully, identified in the popular reaction 'the seed of the Revolution that would happen three years later'. Up until this juncture Marie Antoinette alone had been the target of anti-royalist feeling; now, for the first time, the king's actions were also regarded as despotic.

Under French law, convicts were forbidden from learning the exact nature of their punishments until they were carried out. The *parlement* went into recess for Pentecost immediately after the trial, and no further action could be taken for three weeks. Villette and Jeanne knew that the court had found against them, but not how they would be dealt with. In the Conciergerie, Villette raised the spirits of the other inmates by playing the violin, but his sentence distressed his family. A pitiful letter survives among Joly de Fleury's papers from Villette's brother, begging the *procureur-général* to allow him to visit and make arrangements for the exile. It ends: 'I am going to throw myself at the feet of the throne, if the jailer of the Conciergerie again refuses to let me see him. For this is the last day that I can prolong a stay as sad as it is expensive, considering all that calls me back to my house.' Joly de Fleury did not bother replying and, as far as we know, the brothers were not granted a final reunion. Villette was led to a city gate with a halter around his neck and presented, as was customary on these occasions, with a loaf of stale bread. The executioner 'with great solemnity, turning the culprit's back upon Paris, gave him a smart kick in the breech, and bade him never to return!'

When Jeanne heard what her punishment was to be – in her autobiography, a snatch of conversation slides through her barred windows – she collapsed in her chair, as if stung by 'an electrical shock'. It was the first of a number of fits she suffered during this period of custody. On one occasion, she collapsed crying, 'Merciful heaven! What will become of me! – I am certainly destined for destruction.' Another time, she hurled her plate and cutlery up in the air, before trying to dash her brains out with a Dutch china mug (afterwards she was banned from the unsupervised use of crockery). But there was also comfort in the domestic rhythms of the Conciergerie, a far cry from the isolation of the Bastille: Jeanne dined each day with the concierge and his family, and played cards in the evening with the oldest child.

No one knew whether Jeanne's sentence would be carried out. Castries and Mercy-Argenteau had heard noises that she would be spared, but could not confirm them. Outside the prison, only one friend agitated for clemency – Doillot, her lawyer. He lent her money and implored Breteuil for at least a suspension of the sentence, only to be fobbed off. His fidelity to such a pariah seemed barely explicable – his brother concluded that 'it must be either that he has gone mad, or else that Madame de La Motte has enchanted him, as she enchanted the cardinal'.

Throughout her limbo, Jeanne was unable to see her lawyer. Early on the morning of 21 June, she was finally informed that they had permission to meet. Having walked through the Palais de Justice, Jeanne was confronted, not with Doillot, but a clerk of the court, who, without so much as a word of greeting, began to read out her sentence. She grew 'flustered with astonishment, rage, fear and despair, and this sent her into convulsions. She could not comprehend what was being read to her. She rolled on the ground, yelling wildly.' The judgement was read out twice, to make certain that Jeanne had understood. 'It is the blood of the Valois that you outrage,' she yelled and, imploring the crowd, asked: 'Will you suffer a descendant of your kings to be treated thus? Rescue me from these murderers.'

The flailing became more purposeful when the branding implements were drawn out. Jeanne grabbed the executioner by the neck and snapped at his hand with her teeth. It took four men to bring her under control, tie her hands behind her back, noose her neck with a rope and lug her to the gate of the Conciergerie. Her hair coiled wildly, her clothes were half peeled off, her body writhed as though in ecstasy, her mouth filled with curses at the judges, at Rohan, at the queen, and all the while the executioner 'talked to her like a tooth-drawer, assuring her most politely that it would all be over soon'. The *parlement* was eager for the punishment to be carried out before midday, to avoid a crush of spectators. In the event, a lacklustre straggle of fifty people had assembled. Some cried out that Jeanne was a scapegoat, a victim of court intrigue.

She refused to remove her blouse so they cut her dress open along the spine and laid her flat on her stomach. Someone screamed an obscenity at the sight of her naked thighs. The birch flagellated her back, which swirled with a mess of blood. Then the brand, heated to a ruddy gold, was applied. She grew more frantic, bucking like a ship anchored in a storm. The executioner only marked one shoulder; a second thrust, intended for the other, stamped her on the breast. Her bloodshot eyes looked like they would burst from their sockets, her lips contorted like a gargoyle's. The smell of roast meat curled skywards. She fell onto the shoulder of one of the guards, bit hard into it until she drew blood, and fainted. They placed her in the carriage and took her to the Salpêtrière, where she awoke, asked for a glass of water, and fainted again. Vinegar and eau de cologne were massaged into her face to revive her. An inventory was taken of her possessions: two handkerchiefs, a small gold-encrusted box, a purse containing 21 livres and six sols, and her gold earring, which she sold on spec to one of the doctors. She was then taken deeper into the penitentiary. Her hair was chopped into a round bonnet; she was dressed in a plain blouse. Anonymous as all the other inmates, broken and sore, she was no longer the woman who played the queen. She was left in her cell with a bowl of soup and a hunk of hard bread.

24

Catch Him if You Can

A Burlesque

IN THE SAME verdict that sentenced Villette and Jeanne, the court found Nicolas de La Motte guilty in absentia. Whipping, branding and perpetual service in the king's galleys awaited him – not that he planned on experiencing them any time soon, even though, by now, the French government knew exactly where he was. The story of how he was tailed and cornered is told by Nicolas himself in an insertion into Jeanne's memoirs, and appears one of the least credible aspects of a work that is, throughout, a jungle of fabrications. Yet the archives of the ministry of foreign affairs turn up documentary corroboration for nearly everything that Nicolas wrote.

While the Diamond Necklace suspects were being interrogated and confronted with each other, Nicolas spent three months convalescing in Scotland under the assumed name of Monsieur de Saint-Vincent. He had heard no news of his wife's plight and was down to his last few diamonds. As he regained his strength, Nicolas grew curious about events in Paris. Fortunately, his manservant Georges had encountered an Italian named Costa in a local tavern, who seemed well informed. Costa taught Italian and French in the households of grandees, and had a tinderbox temper: once, he told Georges, in a jealous rage he had soaked a mistress in nitric acid. Under the pretext of taking English lessons, Nicolas engaged Costa as a tutor in order to glean news from abroad.

Costa took Nicolas to a cafe that subscribed to the *Gazette de Leyde*, the most important of the French-language news-sheets. The newspaper carried precis of the lawyers' *mémoires* and gossip about the trial, and the first item that Nicolas glanced at was a rumour that he had been arrested and was being shipped back to the Bastille.

He also read of the mockery that Doillot's inept defence of Jeanne had been subjected to, and wrote to the lawyer, chiding his cack-handedness but also offering to return to Paris as long as guarantees were given that he would not be imprisoned in the Bastille.* The queen herself regarded this approach as yet another intrigue 'with the purpose of dragging [her] through the mud still further'. Nicolas was in no position to cut deals with the government, but he was horribly aware that it was only a matter of time before they caught up with him. He had narrowly avoided an awkward encounter at Mass – when accosted with a cry of 'You're the comte de La Motte-Valois, aren't you?' – by feigning a German accent. A show of willing, however insincere – there was no chance that the French authorities would let him return on bail – might help in any future plea-bargaining.

Nicolas needed someone reliable to deliver his letter in person. The only serviceable option was Costa. When Nicolas divulged his secret, Costa seemed 'petrified with astonishment', but immediately told him 'he hadn't felt for a long time feelings this agreeable, and he swore to me that I could count on him, life and death'. Costa accepted the mission, then immediately suggested his wife as a more discreet courier. Nicolas consented.

Madame Costa left for Paris in April 1786. Her disguise was unnecessarily elaborate. On arrival, Doillot thought that she was both a man and a spy, only admitting her after she had been anatomically inspected by his wife. The lawyer approached Joly de Fleury with Nicolas's offer, but the *procureur-général* would not be dictated to over the terms of surrender. It did not take long for others to hear of the emissary. Vergennes, the pro-Rohan foreign minister, and Breteuil, the queen's standard bearer in council, had their own interests in securing Nicolas's return. Madame Costa spent three days at His Majesty's pleasure in the Bastille, after Breteuil had ordered her arrest; then Vergennes had her briefly seized as she returned through Calais.

Nicolas, meanwhile, after his brush with detection, had decided

---

* A letter from Mercy-Argenteau to Prince Kaunitz confirms that the comte de La Motte indeed wrote to ministers, requesting permission to see his wife and plan their common defence.

it was too dangerous to remain in Scotland. He wanted to return to London, where it would be more convenient to intercept Madame Costa, but Costa convinced him to move to Newcastle, on the grounds that it was slightly closer to the capital than Edinburgh. If his logic seems spurious, it was because Costa was not the simple language teacher he purported to be – he was also in the pay of the French foreign minister. A number of letters survive in the ministry's archives from a freelance agent called François Benevent, who had Nicolas under surveillance and intercepted his post. Benevent was being run by d'Arragon, a secretary in the French Embassy. In exchange for 10,000 guineas for a deeply indebted 'friend', who had wormed himself close to Nicolas, Benevent offered to identify the wanted man and his whereabouts.

The treacherous friend was entirely imaginary – Benevent was Costa (one of the letters even refers to his wife as Madame de Costa de Benevent). The comte d'Adhémar, the French ambassador to the Court of St James and a close friend of the queen, bypassed normal diplomatic channels to transmit Benevent's proposition directly to Marie Antoinette, who informed her husband, who authorised payment. At first, Benevent suggested luring Nicolas to Hammersmith and kidnapping him, though this plan fell through and they looked, instead, north-east. Benevent was thoroughly unreliable and no patriot (not even, it seems, a French subject). Greed was his motivation, and almost immediately he began to cause problems for his handler, chivvying him for more money upfront, goading him with visions of Nicolas slipping through their hands.

At the beginning of May, Nicolas, pretending to be Costa's nephew, moved to Shields on Tyneside and took an isolated house close to the sea.* Almost immediately, Nicolas grew wary of his companion, a sense of unease exacerbated by the discovery of a poisoned dog outside his front door. They had not stayed there long when Madame Costa returned, having been released from prison, with a letter purportedly from Doillot. Short, vague, evasive but filled with encouragement to remain in Shields, it had, in fact, been dictated by Vergennes and only incited Nicolas's suspicions further.

---

* The sources do not specify whether this was North Shields or South Shields.

Later that evening, Nicolas determined to escape the Costas. He surreptitiously gathered his belongings and ordered a coach to wait for him at midnight. Then, pressing his ear to the couple's door, he overhead them whispering in English. He entered without knocking and saw, spread out over the furniture, a harvest of louis, booty that Madame Costa had bled from the French authorities in exchange for her cooperation. 'You are busy,' Nicolas apologised, and walked out with his decision ratified.

Costa now realised that Nicolas had fathomed him, and sought to rectify the situation. During a stroll with Nicolas later that evening, he admitted working for the ambassador, who had offered him 100,000 livres (a gross exaggeration) for securing Nicolas's testimony at the trial – not, he protested, to deliver him to the king's dungeons. Costa suggested a counterplot: they would scam the diplomats of the promised money and split it between them. Nicolas, always excited by the prospect of a fast buck, agreed, though he took the precaution of moving to the bustle of Newcastle. Costa wrote to his handler d'Arragon demanding 1,000 guineas immediately. They planned to take the money, then tell the diplomat that a 'kidnap in a port so full of people and so far from town is impractical' and suggest reverting to the previous plan of a snatch from a house by the Thames.*

Shortly afterwards, d'Arragon arrived in Newcastle with two undercover Paris cops in tow – Grandmaison and the ever-intrepid Quidor, the restitutor of Villette. Their scheme had been for a coal ship, manned by policemen disguised as sailors, to sail from Dunkirk to Shields, where Nicolas would be coshed, gagged and smuggled on board – a stratagem in flagrant breach of British sovereignty. Things, however, were not going entirely to plan. No boat had yet been requisitioned in Dunkirk, and the chosen men were not in

---

* In the section of Jeanne's *Mémoires Justificatifs* dictated by Nicolas, he explains that Benevent planned on giving him an enormously potent sleeping draught – enough to knock out twenty horses – trussing him up in a bag and dragging him onto the boat, from which 'without doubt [they would have hurled] him into the sea'. Though the diplomatic correspondence suggests that the French authorities may have preferred Nicolas permanently silenced, the only plan considered was one to seize him.

position. Grandmaison and Quidor's visit had begun equally haplessly: on arriving in London, they were told that d'Adhémar was in Bath, taking the waters. Once they had slogged over there, they learned he had left, a few hours earlier, for London.

The inspectors had not been briefed in Paris on the exact nature of their mission – their boss, de Crosne, had described it as 'intelligence-gathering'. When they finally caught up with d'Adhémar, and once he explained their role, they both expressed a 'great repugnance' for what was asked of them. Were they to be captured if the plot misfired, they risked hanging – in 1781, a French spy, François Henri de La Motte (no relation), had been strung up in London. In Versailles, Vergennes worried about the delays and his officials' competency. Rather than wait for a French ship to be prepared, he suggested, could not Benevent commission an English collier to transfer the 'prey' to France? At the same time, he sent another police officer, Inspector Subois, to Dunkirk to expedite matters.

Having cajoled the reluctant policemen into following him up north, d'Arragon discovered that Shields was not the somnolent village they had been promised, but a busy port in which every ship was kept under guard. A customs official inspected each vessel on arrival and departure and watchmen were stationed fifty paces apart at night. A surreptitious rendition stood no chance. When d'Arragon finally met Costa, the latter admitted that the target had embedded himself in the even more unpromising location of Newcastle. So cautious was Nicolas, Costa explained, that simply getting him to leave Edinburgh had been a struggle.

Costa offered a tempting alternative to rendition: Nicolas was ready to travel to London and negotiate, face to face with the ambassador, mutually satisfactory terms for handing himself in. 'He continues to insist that he is not guilty, but when he received the letter from his lawyer which advised him to return to Paris, he said to me that "it must be that this man thinks I'm an idiot".' D'Arragon agreed to pass on the offer to his superiors.

His superiors, meanwhile, were floundering their way through the rapidly disintegrating operation. D'Adhémar had ordered Inspector Subois to set sail from Dunkirk, without knowing whether

Quidor and Grandmaison were willing – or even able – to secure Nicolas. A pennant was affixed to the topmast so the policemen would recognise the boat. They, in turn, would signal with white handkerchiefs, like women waving off their husbands. Unfavourable winds meant that three more days were eaten up before the ship left Dunkirk; when it finally arrived in Shields, try as he might, Subois could see no white flecks fluttering on the shore. His colleagues had left five days earlier.

The ambassador was out of his depth. D'Adhémar asked Vergennes on 23 May if he should attempt the kidnap of Nicolas in London, or meet with Nicolas and try to broker a less violent solution? Nicolas's evidence might be crucial in the trial. But d'Adhémar refused to feign goodwill in order to tempt Nicolas into a deadfall: 'I would arrest Monsieur de La Motte myself,' continued d'Adhémar, 'if the law would order me to, but I do not want to be the instrument of betrayal, whether in drawing him to my house, or filling him with false confidence.' Vergennes was unimpressed by the emissary's scruples. 'I am more distressed than surprised by the changes that you have reported,' he wrote in response. 'It is quite clear that your man [Benevent] only wants easy profits . . . only seeks to prolong the negotiation in the hope of beguiling from you new benefits'. Vergennes refused to guarantee Nicolas safe conduct and ordered d'Adhémar to stay in touch with Benevent, but trust nothing he said.

Nicolas arrived in London towards the end of May. The spy-runner d'Arragon proposed denouncing Nicolas as a debtor, and bribing the bailiff to allow them to load him onto a French ship. Benevent refused to countenance such a risky manoeuvre. Before they devised an alternative, Nicolas took matters into his own hands. He wrote to d'Adhémar on 30 May, requesting safe conduct for a meeting, then turned up at the ambassador's residence, protected by two meaty Irish bodyguards, on the same day. While he was kicking his heels in the vestibule, d'Adhémar dashed off a dispatch to Vergennes: 'Our man is here . . . I'll inform you tomorrow of the meeting that I've had with him.' D'Adhémar, who had not yet received the foreign minister's admonitory response to his earlier letter, again urged Vergennes to make arrangements so that Nicolas's testimony could be heard, even asking that the judgement, now imminent, be delayed to accommodate it. 'I am certain', he wrote pointedly, 'that you will do that which is most agreeable to the queen.'

During two long conversations, Nicolas convinced d'Adhémar that he was a martyr unjustly pursued. 'He is a young man with an interesting turn of phrase,' wrote the ambassador in a dispatch, 'who has quite innocently been caught up in this unhappy affair.' Nicolas promised to serve time in prison – as long as it was not the Bastille – and return any remaining diamonds (it is hard to comprehend how d'Adhémar reconciled possession of the remnants of the necklace with Nicolas's self-proclaimed saintliness). The ambassador's eagerness to secure Nicolas's repatriation was fed directly from the top: 'Do not forget', he implored Vergennes, 'that the queen dearly desires that Monsieur de La Mothe should be interrogated before the judgement. Her Majesty did me the honour of telling me this most insistently before my departure.'

The differing attitudes of d'Adhémar and Vergennes reflect their loyalties at the climax of the Diamond Necklace trial. From Vergennes's perspective, as a supporter of Rohan, new evidence from Nicolas at this late stage could only have reinforced Jeanne's version of events – it was far safer to keep him offstage until judgement had been passed. Conversely, the queen's party, well informed about the progress of the trial, knew that Jeanne had been discredited as a witness. If they wanted to convict Rohan of criminal conspiracy, they needed corroborating evidence against him.

Vergennes stalled until the point of no return had been passed. Five days after the verdict, he wrote to the king with hypocritical fastidiousness:

> If Your Majesty agrees that Monsieur La Mothe surrender himself as he appears disposed, I beg you to authorise me to command the comte d'Adhémar to send him to any other minister apart from me. Nothing would disgust me more than be charged with receiving his deposition. The care that I had to distance myself from the affair has not stopped my silence several times being interpreted as a sign of partiality and prejudice.

Now the harrowing investigation had concluded, Vergennes knew Louis wished for nothing more than to forget the preceding nine months. As was disastrously proven during the Revolution, the king was endowed with a phlegmatism that enabled him to untether himself from troublesome events and drift along as though they had never happened. His reply shows he was blind, wilfully or otherwise, to his foreign minister's endeavours on behalf of the Rohan:

> Although you conducted yourself in this affair as you ought to have acted – as an honest man – I understand the disgust you would have at seeing La Mothe, and moreover that it would be useless. He has only one thing to do for himself, that is to return to justice to repent for his absence – it is for him to take on that responsibility. For me, now the judgement has happened, I am not bothered at all any more.

The king regarded the outlay on Benevent as 'money thrown into the river', but, he added, 'if he must be paid, it is better to do that than to hear all of the idiocies which this man will not miss the opportunity to spread in England'.

25

Farewell, My Country

O N THE SAME day that the *lettre de cachet* exiling Rohan was issued, Cagliostro received a similar document, ordering him to leave the kingdom within two weeks. On 13 June, he processed towards the coast to catch a boat bound for England. In Boulogne, he wrote, 'all the good people [were] by the shore! Their hands stretched out towards my boat, calling to me, crying out, heaping me with blessings, asking the same from me . . . thank[ing] me for the good I had done their brethren. They plied me with the most touching farewells.' As his ship sailed away, he 'cried out again and again as though they could hear me: "Farewell, Frenchmen! Farewell, my children; my country farewell!"'

Cagliostro still loved the people of France, but his forgiveness did not extend to its rulers. Shortly after his arrival in London, a *Letter to the French People* was published under his name (it was almost certainly ghostwritten); like other tracts written in the tremoring days before revolutions, this did not attack the king directly but lashed at his evil counsellors:

> I have been hunted from France. The king has been deceived. Kings are to be pitied for having such ministers. I mean to speak of the baron de Breteuil. What have I done to this man? Of what does he accuse me? Of being loved by the cardinal, and of not deserting him; of seeking the truth; of assisting suffering humanity, by my alms, my remedies, my counsels. Those are my crimes! . . . He cannot bear that a man in irons, a stranger under the bolts of the Bastille, in his power . . . should have raised his voice, as I have done, to make him known – him, and his principles, his agents, his creatures.

The *Letter* proceeded to indict the whole system of justice, which was open to abuse by officials who slip directives for imprisonment and confiscation of goods among the papers which the king hurriedly signs each day. All men risked internment on the basis of 'unknown complaints, obscure evidence that is never communicated, sometimes even on simple rumours, on scurrilous talk, sown by hatred and received by envy'.

The Bastille was a shrine to government's most vindictive tendencies – 'cynical impudence, odious falsehood, sham pity, bitter irony, relentless cruelty, injustice and death' – which nullified all of the king's pretensions to benevolence. Cagliostro remembered:

> For six months I was within fifteen feet of my wife without knowing it. Others have been buried there for thirty years, are reputed dead, are unhappy in not being dead, having, like Milton's damned souls, only so much light in their abyss as to perceive the impenetrable darkness that enwraps them. I said it in captivity, and I repeat it as a free man: there is no crime but is amply expiated by six months in the Bastille . . . Someone asked me whether I should return to France supposing the prohibitions laid on me were removed? Assuredly, I replied, provided that the Bastille became a public promenade.

Cagliostro also sought more tangible recompense for his suffering. Safe in England, he accused de Launay, the governor of the Bastille, and Chénon, a senior police officer, of having destroyed or sequestered at the time of his arrest 100,000 livres-worth of goods, including diamonds and other jewels, 'balms, drugs, elixirs', rolls of banknotes, gold coins and important documents. He also sought damages for the humiliating manner of his arrest. Chénon, in return, denounced Cagliostro as a combustible insurrectionary: 'We remember the terrible effect his *mémoire* had on the public . . . The retailing of it brought sedition nearer.'

Loath to hear the events of the Diamond Necklace Affair turned over again in a public court, the king appointed a special committee of state counsellors to investigate the case (a decision viewed as a stitch-up by Cagliostro's supporters). Cagliostro was offered a safe-conduct for the duration of the hearing by Breteuil, but refused to trust the man he had so recently denounced. Inevitably, the panel found that de Launay and Chénon had no case to answer. In London the verdict was condemned as a conspiracy to ruin Cagliostro and destroy Masonry. Even before crossing the Channel, Cagliostro had been feted by the English: his translated trial brief was described by *The Times* as 'perhaps the most extraordinary publication that ever engaged a body of people'. On his arrival, the king's sons paid court to the thaumaturge, and Whig dignitaries such as Richard Brinsley Sheridan and Georgiana, duchess of Devonshire clustered about him.

Cagliostro soon latched on to a new patron who provided him with a house in Knightsbridge, furnished with Indian mahogany, Italian porcelain and Persian carpets. Samuel Swinton was the founder of the *Courier de l'Europe*, a leading French-language newspaper edited in London and distributed across France. Swinton, a hard-bitten businessman and not someone who swelled with enthusiasm for alchemy, or sympathy for a downtrodden vagrant, spied the potential for profit in Cagliostro's celebrity.

Through Swinton, Cagliostro met Charles Théveneau de Morande, the editor of the *Courier*, and the first of two swaggering figures who discomfited Cagliostro's sojourn in England. In 1770, Morande had fled Paris and his gambling debts for London. A year later he published *The Armour-Plated Gazetteer*, a compendium of lewd anecdotes about noblemen, politicians and clergy, along with obscene stories about Louis XV and his mistress Madame du Barry. On completion, three years later, of a second work devoted exclusively to du Barry's cornucopian sexual techniques, Morande wrote to the French Court asking to be bought off. Beaumarchais was sent to negotiate a pay-off and supervised the burning of the entire print run one night in April 1774 (the noxious smoke that wafted across the Channel was said to have poisoned Louis XV, who died shortly afterwards). To earn his living, Morande became a prolific French spy, feeding three different departments with his reports – after he became editor of the *Courier* in 1784, he encoded intelligence into the newspaper's pages. At first, Morande looked favourably upon Cagliostro, lauding his compassion for the sick and poor.

Cagliostro also found himself in the protective embrace of Lord George Gordon, a man of peppery temperament and extreme politics. Known as 'Lord George Flame' or 'Lord George Riot', on account of the anti-Catholic disturbances he instigated in 1780, he was a virulent Francophobe, who saw in Cagliostro's resurrection the eventual downfall of the Bourbons. He managed a press campaign which accused the sinister – and entirely fictional – 'queen's Bastille party' of attempting to kidnap and re-imprison the count. He also became the Cagliostros' gatekeeper, aggressively interrogating each visitor as though he was potentially a French spy. Their home became a new prison, oppressively constricting the man who for months had dreamed of liberty. 'If I had not that dear creature, my wife', Cagliostro said, 'I should go and live with the wild beasts of the jungle, certain of finding friends among them.' Eventually Gordon extended himself too far in his jeremiads and was convicted of criminal libel against Marie Antoinette. Since Gordon had long been ostracised from polite company, Cagliostro lost most of his society friends through their association.

Meanwhile Morande, whose support required the regular lubrication of coin, turned against the unforthcoming Cagliostro. The *Courier* expended great energy in debunking his self-mythologising; among the feats mocked was Cagliostro's boast of foddering livestock on arsenic, when living in Arabia, in order to slay predators. In response, Cagliostro issued Morande in the *Public Advertiser* with a challenge to a singular duel:

> Of all the pretty tales you tell of me, the finest is surely that of the pig fattened with arsenic, who poisoned the lions, tigers and leopards in the forests of Medina. I am going, mister jester, to make a joke at your expense. In matters of physics and chemistry, arguments prove very little, persiflage proves nothing; experiment is everything. Allow me, then, to propose a little experiment that will entertain the public, at either your expense or at mine. I invite you to eat with me on November 9, at 9 o'clock in the morning. You will provide the wine and all the accessories; I will furnish only a dish done in my way; it will be a little sucking piglet, fattened according to my method. Two hours before dinner, I will present it to you alive and well, you will be responsible for killing and preparing it and I will not come near it until the moment when it is served on the table. You will cut it into four equal parts, you may serve me the part that you judge to be suitable. The day after this dinner, one of four things

will happen: either we will both be dead, or neither of us will be dead; or I will be dead and you will not; or you will be dead and I will not. Of these four chances I will give you three and bet you 5,000 guineas that the day after the meal you will be dead and I will be well. You must either accept this challenge, or acknowledge that you are an ignorant fellow, and that you have foolishly ridiculed a thing which is totally out of your knowledge.

Morande cavilled – his conscience, he claimed, would not bear Cagliostro's death. Instead, he suggested 'what carnivorous animal you think proper' should fight on their behalf, since he was 'unwilling . . . to submit to that degradation of assimilating myself to a Cagliostro'. The mealy reply was treated contemptuously: 'It is not your representative', said Cagliostro, 'but it is you that I wish to dispatch.' He never received satisfaction; Morande continued to scourge him in print and sought his imprisonment for debt.

For a time, Cagliostro found a measure of sanctuary with Philippe-Jacques de Loutherbourg, a fashionable Alsatian painter and set designer with occult interests, who provided a laboratory and a library filled with alchemical texts. The pair planned to found a new lodge, with a view to the eventual annexation of British Masonry. But when Cagliostro paid a comradely visit to a lodge in Bloomsbury, he was treated as a buffoon. His authority was further undermined when Morande reported that in one seance, instead of summoning angels, he had raised 'a fearful horde of orang-utangs whose grimaces, insults, and unworthy promiscuity the chaste idealists had to endure all evening'. In April 1787, pilloried beyond endurance, the Cagliostros left London for good.

Rohan's retreat from Court was more sedate. On 5 June 1786, he set out for Chaise-Dieu, accompanied by his brother Ferdinand and a train of seven carriages. He travelled with some trepidation, having fruitlessly asked Louis if he could reside in a more temperate region, so that his arthritic knee might escape the pinch of the Auvergnian winter (not that the journey was without comforts – two hundred labourers paved the last stretch of road for the cardinal's smooth passage).

The resident monks bore little affection for Rohan, who for years had valued the abbey only for its income. Yet they found him so modest and amiable, so eager to join the community – when a fire ravaged the town in July, he stood on the front line, pail in hand – that their loathing soon turned to respect. Rohan stayed for only four months, before moving to the more clement surroundings of the Benedictine abbey of Marmoutiers, near Tours, where he rested, meditated in prayer and immersed himself in provincial society. At the beginning of 1787, Rohan was restored to the cardinalate. He remained in touch with Target, to whom he confided about the transformations wrought on him: 'It seems to me, sir, that sorrows make still more sensitive the souls that injustice has not been able to harden. I confess that mine has retained that delicious source of happiness.' His servant Joseph Diss noted that, though the cardinal retained his 'irresistible charisma that worked on all who approached him . . . [he] never shook off the terrible ordeal of the affair of the necklace which aged him in several ways, emotionally as well as physically' (he still wore an eye patch and walked with a cane).

On 24 December 1788, the order for Rohan's exile was suppressed by the king. He made a victor's progress through Alsace, a double rank of infantry lining the route, the crowds fizzing around his coach, demanding to bear him themselves along the road. At his palace in Mutzig, he was greeted by dragoons with their sabres unsheathed, local dignitaries, clergymen and the community of two hundred Jews whose rabbi preached a sermon of welcome. An ode was composed for the occasion, entitled 'Apollo Recalled from Exile'. Two cardboard *arcs de triomphe* were erected in Saverne, alongside two obelisks showing the sun emerging from a cloud.

At home at last, Rohan grew introspective and read a great deal of verse – Homer, Horace and Virgil, as well as Tasso, Dante, Corneille and Racine. It was said that he had been working for many years on a work of literature, though it never amounted to anything. He continued to experiment, especially with electricity, and he predicted, on looking at his shotgun, that one day something similarly propulsive would enable people to 'cross space, to delve in the mysteries of the stars and the planets and communicate from one end of the world to the other'. The cardinal hoped to preserve Alsace's tranquillity from the political ructions undulating through the rest of France, though he realised that doing so was beyond his power. One evening, looking upon the ruined castle of Hohbarr, he declared: 'A voice seems to speak to me here that one day my palace down there will be like the rubble here. How can I prevent that? I would like to see raised an impassable wall between Alsace and France.'

Alsace could no more insulate itself from the crisis in the rest of the country than it could float down the Rhine and the Danube to hide itself in an obscure corner of the Balkans. Financial crisis could no longer be staved off and the king instructed the Estates-General, which brought together representatives of the nation's three estates – the clergy, the nobility and the commoners – to gather, for the first time since 1614, on 1 May 1789, in order to negotiate a solution. Rohan was elected as a deputy of the clergy of Haguenau. He hoped, amid the turbulence of allegiances, to win a measure of grace through steadfast loyalty to the king as democracy shivered the kingdom.

In the event, royalists suspected him of conspiring with the opportunist duc d'Orléans, and he was unable to take up his place when the king addressed the three estates on 5 May. He was still excluded by royal decree from Versailles and its environs. While it is unclear whether Rohan was himself eager to attend the Estates-General, or reluctantly accepted the responsibility thrust upon him by his admiring electors, liberals viewed Rohan's continued punishment as an example of vengeful despotism and campaigned for his admission. It took until 24 July for the election to be ratified; but Rohan could not fill his post immediately. He was temporarily in Ettenheim, in the transpontine half of his principality, having been flushed out of Alsace by anti-aristocratic rioting – part of the 'Great Fear' which blazed across the country that summer like forest fire. Only in September did the cardinal take up his seat in what had become the National Assembly. By then, the government's monopoly on power had sundered and the events we now refer to as the French Revolution careered onwards, ineluctable and unbridled.

On 17 June, the commoners, resisting procedural attempts to marginalise their voice, had declared themselves the National Assembly. Three days later, they found their meeting room locked.

Believing this to be an attempt to silence them, they trooped to a tennis court close by and swore to remain united as a body until 'the constitution of the realm and public regeneration are established and assured'. An impasse had been reached between the king and the National Assembly, who were further alienated when Louis attempted to impose his own conservative vision for constitutional reform. As increasing numbers of clergy and nobility drifted into the Assembly, the king was forced to acknowledge its legitimacy. His actions, however, suggested discontent. The dismissal of conciliatory ministers, scarcity of bread and the advance of 20,000 troops on Paris sparked panic and revolution – it was hard to distinguish between the two – in the capital. Ransacking and arson broke out. On 14 July, the Bastille was taken by a crowd high on fear and freedom. The marquis de Launay, the custodian of all the accused during the Diamond Necklace Affair, was decapitated. The upheaval cracked apart the king's authority and radical deputies sought to exploit it. From 4 to 11 August the National Assembly, giddy with destruction, sliced through the feudal ligatures of the Bourbon polity: seigneurial dues and rights, tithes, the sale of offices and serfdom were abolished. On 26 August, the Declaration of the Rights of Man and the Citizen was passed: sovereignty now inhered in the nation, not the monarch.

This unravelling of the kingdom went far beyond whatever gentle liberalising improvements Rohan had envisaged. The abolition of feudalism uniquely impinged upon Alsace, since the Treaty of Westphalia, through which Alsace had been incorporated into France, guaranteed that the feudal customs of the Holy Roman Empire would continue to be respected. The cardinal's income dwindled further in November, when church property was nationalised – Rohan's schedule for debt repayments relied predominantly on revenue from his abbeys and diocese.

Rohan relinquished any hope of diverting the course, at least locally, of the Revolution. In April 1790, his request to return to Alsace was accepted by the National Assembly. With the abolition of noble titles and a ban on displaying coats-of-arms, passed on 19 June, Rohan resolved to become an emigré. He left Saverne on 13 July, accompanied by twenty of his men, provocatively dressed in their liveries. The assembly had endorsed the day before the Civil Constitution of the Clergy, through which the state effectively kidnapped the church from Rome (a change to which the cardinal would never consent). A few days after his departure, the gardens of Saverne were uprooted by the rejoicing citizenry.

26

Down and Out in Paris and London

Primarily a hospital for the indigent, the Salpêtrière also detained criminal, licentious and unruly women. Its *maison de force* was divided into four sections: the *commun* housed prostitutes and women of 'evil conduct, life and manners'; the *correction*, rebellious women of good families, constrained by *lettres de cachet*; those with limited sentences were housed in the *prison*, and those with life sentences in the *grande force*. It was to this last that Jeanne, swollen tongue lolling out of her swollen mouth, was brought after her branding.

She was given a bed in a dormitory, under the glare of a cross-shaped window, but was soon transferred to her own cell. Not that she now lived in cushioned comfort; her room was furnished only with a straw mattress and a glassless window bolted dark with wooden shutters. It was cold and damp in all seasons. The prospect of endless years in this hole grieved Jeanne beyond consolation – 'a slow and prolonged death', she called it. In her first weeks she was an aspergillum of tears and the staff treated her stonily. One of the sisters told her that 'the cardinal is blessed in this house where he has done a lot of good. I advise you to keep your silence if you want to live in peace here.' Another warned 'If you fight with your companions, I warn you that no one will come to separate you. When there is a ruckus here, the doors are closed. If the prisoners injure themselves, they are bandaged. If they kill themselves, they are buried.'

Yet the public were still fascinated by Jeanne's plight, and sympathy at the severity of her punishment flooded towards her. Those who believed the queen had a hand in the Diamond Necklace Affair accused her of having 'abandoned Madame de La Motte to the horror of her fate'. The Court could not shrug Jeanne off: the comte d'Artois quipped to his brother, 'Think, sire, how much bother it will be to marry off the dauphin when it is known that one of his relatives is in the Hospital.' Rumours that a close confidante of the queen – perhaps the princesse de Lamballe, perhaps the duchesse de Polignac – had called on Jeanne heated suspicions of a cover-up. (The princesse de Lamballe had, in fact, visited the hospital on other business and expressed a passing interest to the superintendent in seeing Jeanne; the superintendent replied, 'Madame, the unfortunate comtesse has not been punished with an audience with you.')

Engravings were sold of Jeanne dressed in her scrubs – rough worsted clothes in grey and brown, clogs and a cap. Newspapers reported every shred of hearsay. 'She is stretched out on a bed of pain', wrote the *Gazette d'Utrecht*, 'which is steeped in her tears.' She was portrayed as a martyr, chosen by the Lord to live among the fallen and sinful.

> Her complexion is yellow. She has become extremely thin. She is mixed up with a crowd of women, the scum of nature and society, branded like herself, who yet have some consideration for the unhappy woman whom they call 'the countess' and whom they endeavour to console . . . Her food is black bread; on Sundays an ounce of meat, on Fridays a piece of cheese, on other days some beans or lentils soaked in plenty of water.

Like the other inmates, Jeanne earned her keep with needlework. Many came to visit her, but she shrank away, shutting her door or merging, wraith-like, into the grey-clad crowds.

One of Jeanne's fellow prisoners volunteered as her chambermaid, preparing soup and boiling coffee. Well-wishers sent her money and the duc d'Orléans, to spite the queen, organised a subscription on her behalf. Her situation was considerably improved when she cultivated the attention of Mathieu Tillet, one of the hospital's administrators, who obtained for Jeanne unlimited eggs, as well as wine, jam and sweets. He provided her with a bedstead, table and chairs, and fixed on the wall a print of the Magdalen and an ivory carving of Christ. Tillet visited Jeanne every day – a concealed staircase led directly to her cloister – and some suspected that prayer was not their only busi-ness (Jeanne's own memoir, at pains to present herself as a penitent, still admits that Tillet 'caressed me as much as if I had been his daughter').

Misery bred godliness – or at least a well-simulated version of it. The *Gazette de Leyde* reported that 'Madame de La Motte is becoming more and more stoical and resigned to her fate. For the greater part of the day, she employs herself in reading the ascetic book, *The Imitation of Christ*.' The archbishop of Paris found her 'sublime in the picture of suffering she draws, and in the piety and resignation she gives expression to'. Jeanne's behaviour, however, did not convey resignation. Less than a month after her arrival, an escape attempt went awry. 'She had already made a hole through which her head would go,' wrote the *Gazette d'Utrecht*, but 'she stuck in this opening, so that she could go neither forward nor backwards. Fright seized her; she struggled in vain, and her cries summoned the warders, who found her in that position. Her attempt has only increased the rigour of her confinement.'

But there were hidden figures, with power and money and silent purpose, who wished Jeanne released. At the end of November 1786, Jeanne's maidservant, Angelique, was informed by one of the guards that a plot was in motion to spring her. A letter arrived, delivered in the quiet of night, which stated 'PEOPLE are now intent on changing your condition'. According to the improbable scenario laid out by Jeanne in her autobiography, she was instructed to examine the key hanging from the belt of the jailer and draw it accurately enough for a replica to be made (Jeanne did not explain why she, rather than the compliant and well-placed guard, was chosen for this task). Somehow she managed to jigsaw together enough glances to sketch the key and it was duly cut, delivered and secreted.

The attempted evasion was delayed when Angelique was un-expectedly released and another girl, Marianne, appointed in her place. Eventually, the date for the escape was set for 5 June 1787. A rose was brought to Jeanne to signal that the prospect was fair (did Jeanne think of another rose, pressed into d'Oliva's hand nearly three years earlier?). Dressed in a rich blue frock coat, a black shirt, breeches, a hat and leather gloves, and prodding the ground with a cane, she wandered out of the prison (as with Jeanne's other

escapades, literary precedent may have embellished her account –
Manon Lescaut also escaped gaol dressed as a man).

What happened next is disputed. Jeanne claimed that she and
Marianne opened the locked doors with their key, then simply
hopped into a boat waiting where the Seine ran beside the hospital
and were rowed upstream to Charenton; the diarist Siméon-Prosper
Hardy recorded, less romantically, that the pair were picked up by
a coach waiting at the main gate. In either event, news of the
breakout quickly spread: the celebrity escapee was supposedly
glimpsed across the city, a flash of muslin leaping up carriage steps.
There were rumours that she had dug herself out or clambered over
the wall with the aid of a ladder.

At Provins, Jeanne was nearly unmasked. 'I see what is happening,'
a soldier ribbed her. 'You're a young lady running away from the
convent, and going to join the happy man who has your heart.'
Disconcerted, Jeanne drowned her disguise in a brook and transformed
herself into a bonny country wench, with frothy pastel petticoats and
a basket of butter and eggs swinging from her wrist. She and Marianne
hitched lifts with friendly carters and slept in forest glades. Jeanne
camped out in the quarries of Crottières, near Bar, and sent her maid
to alert her friends and in-laws. They were more generous with
sympathy than tangible aid.

From Bar, with sweaty brows and callousing feet, Jeanne marched
through Nancy, Lunéville, Metz, Thoinville, to relative safety in
Hollerich, across the border in the Grand Duchy of Luxembourg.
There she waited nervously until 27 July – fearful she would be
exposed and returned to prison – when she was intercepted by an
associate of Nicolas. They travelled swiftly through the Netherlands
to Ostend and caught the packet to Dover. At four o'clock on 4
August 1787, Jeanne saw her husband for the first time in nearly
two years.

Who were the guardian angels who uncaged Jeanne? It was clear
to all observers that she had received outside assistance. Did Jeanne's
confessor Tillet, who had shown himself zealous in her cause, lend
a hand? One of the investigating police officers wondered if 'she
might have been able to rely on some assistance from those in charge of
her'. The public's suspicion immediately fell on the queen's circle.

Madame de Polignac had travelled to England in May 1787, ostensibly to take the waters at Bath. But politic minds questioned whether the trip was not connected by a series of threats emanating from Nicolas. Already by August 1786, Nicolas had plans to publish a libel. The *Morning Star* of 13 December reported that 'nothing can stop the comte de La Motte from lifting the veil which covers this mysterious intrigue'.

D'Adhémar, the ambassador to Britain, believed that Nicolas's menaces should be ignored: 'If the government enters into negotiations of any sort whatsoever, we would be flooded with libels . . . To endure and show contempt, that is the sole course I believe reasonable.' He told the police chief de Crosne that 'nothing is more foolish than according significance to libels . . . Her Majesty would be very indignant that you should presume that such horrors might affect her in any way.' 'I endure their bellowing', he ruefully concluded of the *libellistes*, 'like I hear the cries of dogs in the street.' D'Adhémar was simply reiterating the policy the French government had pursued since 1783, when they realised that muckrakers were never truly bought off – they often tried to print the same material under a different title – and folding to blackmail only encouraged *les autres*. Yet this case was different. Whereas the majority of libels in the late 1770s and 1780s had portrayed figures long dead or socially irrelevant, such as Louis XV and Madame du Barry, Nicolas's hypothetical exposé aimed deep into the Court, scorching the queen and those closest to her, and potentially reigniting a scandal now in cinders. There is no proof the duchesse de Polignac was on anything more than a spa holiday, but it was widely presumed that the true purpose of her visit was to barter Jeanne's freedom for Nicolas's silence (Nicolas's own memoir, though hugely unreliable, speaks of a meeting with the duchesse).

This perception was strengthened by the slackness of the investigation. The head warder only contacted the public prosecutor five hours after Jeanne's disappearance, and the police on the following day. Collectively, they reached the limp conclusion that they could find 'nothing which would be able to indicate to us the means which were used for their escape' and suggested she may have floated down an aqueduct. (Inventive minds conjured up more colourful details: a British paper reported that Jeanne passed through seven doors – like some initiate in the Eleusinian mysteries – pressing gold into the guard's palm at each stage. It was said that she left hugging a birdcage containing a favoured canary.)

The La Mottes' reunion was not a joyous one. Nicolas had not remained faithful during their two years apart and found his new wife – always headstrong – touched by her tribulations. 'I quickly perceived that the great misfortunes she had suffered had much embittered her temper, and that tact and caution were needed to keep her in good humour.' Nicolas had thus far displayed the tact of a thundercloud and the caution of a drunk. 'In spite of all my patience,' he recalls in his memoirs, 'I could not help saying one day that her woes were all caused by her own waywardness and extrava-gances' (this from a man who stuccoed himself with diamonds at the earliest opportunity).

> I had no sooner uttered the words than she flung herself on a dagger she happened to be holding in her hand and, despite my promptness in running to her, along with the other people who were in the house, we could not prevent her from striking herself below the breast, and we saw her fall helpless to the floor.

Jeanne was not seriously wounded. The marriage endured despite each taking lovers, and, judging by the affectionate tone of their letters, mellowed into a kind of friendship. They were poor, but still tried to live grandly on credit. They worked their way into the French community in London, one that was treacherous, venal and sometimes deadly – but never dull. (There had been a sizeable contingent of Frenchmen in the capital since 1685, when the Revocation of the Edict of Nantes by Louis XIV had ended the toleration of Protestants and driven pious Huguenots abroad; and since the middle of the century they had been joined by a motley of political renegades, bankrupts, spies, blackmailers and deserters.)

Jeanne's most powerful patron was the former finance minister, the comte de Calonne, who had crossed the Channel after his resignation in 1787, fearing his enemies might prosecute him for fraud during his time at the Treasury. Jeanne needed money: the most obvious source was a 'justificatory memoir'. It would either sell in enormous numbers or she would be bought off by timorous ministers who had already shown their weakness in the arrangement struck with Nicolas. Calonne was ambitious to regain a seat in government. How better to prove his loyalty than by suppressing this treasonous publication?

The La Mottes reeled in Calonne with a go-between: Antoine Joseph Serres de La Tour, a man at the heart of the literary demi-monde, who agreed to ghostwrite Jeanne's memoirs. La Tour had been the founding editor of the *Courier*; after being ousted in 1783, he lived by hawking *Dragées de la Mecque*, sugar-coated pills for stomach complaints. When he informed Calonne of his employment, adding casually that the La Mottes were in parallel talks with Calonne's enemy the baron de Breteuil about disappearing the manuscript, the comte acted quickly. He wrote to the queen with an offer to snuff out the libel. The reply he received stated 'both their majesties believe that one should forget all about this writing'. Calonne was not deterred. His recent marriage to his immensely wealthy mistress had increased his annual income by 230,000 livres, and so desperate was he to re-ingratiate himself that he offered to suppress the libel with his own money and pay the La Mottes to retire to America. His willingness was again rebuffed. Yet he had been drawn in so far that he had already emended the manuscript in his own hand, deleting elements 'so crude and obscene, even as an intermediary, to send this document to the queen' – it was counterproductive, he felt, to show Rohan calling the queen a 'whore' and taking her from behind. Towards the end of 1788, the relationship turned sour. La Tour complained that Calonne's protracted haggling had lost the La Mottes the opportunity to cut a deal with Breteuil, and sued Calonne for compensation.

It seems that Calonne was played as Rohan had been, but other evidence suggests he may have had a directorial role. It was widely known that Calonne and Jeanne had been lovers.* Though neither

---

* Their affair ended when, during a game of piquet, Calonne declared, 'Madame, you have been marked', referring to Jeanne's cards. Jeanne took this as an allusion to her branding. She upended the table and leapt at him, tearing his face with her nails.

Madame Campan nor Nicolas de La Motte are especially reliable witnesses, both agree, as does the neutral marquis de Bombelles, that Calonne made substantial changes. Even had Calonne intervened only in the places he himself acknowledged, he let pass numerous other insinuations of adultery between Rohan and Marie Antoinette. Calonne might have been policing the boundaries of decency, but he still needed to preserve enough smut to make the memoirs worth burying. His interests were not solely the queen's. As Morande said, 'it is certain that the libel would never have appeared if Monsieur de Calonne had not involved himself in a negotiation that did not concern him'.

27

Confessions of a Justified Sinner

WHEN THE DEPUTIES arrived at the Estates-General, they brought with them *cahiers de doléances*, registers of grievances they wished the king to redress. Jeanne's own *cahier de doléances* was smuggled into France in the spring of 1789. On 15 May, Siméon-Prosper Hardy noted in his diary that 1,500 copies of the *Mémoires Justificatifs* had entered the country. Since booksellers distributed such treasonous material surreptitiously, it is difficult to quantify precisely the extent of the memoir's dissemination. But it has been estimated that over 10,000 copies, including pirate versions, circulated, a significant proportion among expatriate communities in London and the Low Countries. Its readership would have been much larger, as volumes were passed along, once imbibed, to others impatient to read of misbehaviour at Court.

The *Mémoires Justificatifs* were nourished by the Rousseauean sentimentality so popular in the eighteenth century. Jeanne presented herself as an ingénue transfixed and then destroyed by a 'monster of virtue'. The crime was compounded by the high rank of her persecutors, who should have treated her as an equal, not a dispensable pawn. The book's publication needed justification, too. Her survival in an impoverished state, Jeanne wrote, was a sign from God that she must sell her memoirs to replenish her confiscated wealth and roast the guilty. At liberty in England, far from the 'oppressive tyranny of France', she could finally speak the truth.

In the briefs published during the trial, Jeanne had denied ever knowing the queen. Now she confessed to not merely being an acquaintance, but to usurping Madame de Polignac as her closest confidante (and, she all but says, bedmate). There is a sexual shimmer to Jeanne's ambivalent language. 'Remember those moments of intoxication that I scarcely dare recount,' she addresses the queen. 'You lowered yourself to me.' According to Jeanne, Rohan was scorned by Marie Antoinette after she rejected his advances during his time as ambassador in Vienna.* The queen appeared receptive to Jeanne's suggestion they should be reconciled. This, however, was merely a ruse: she had sworn to ruin the cardinal but required him for the time being, intending to elevate Rohan to the ministry in order to subvert the kingdom to Austrian interests. Jeanne's story gave body and colour to the misty allegations made by revolutionary journalists that France was entirely in Austria's pocket. The existence of an Austrian Committee was a commonplace of the radical pamphleteering of the Revolution, and the vagueness of such accusations made them all the more sinister and irrefutable. These were bolstered by Jeanne's 'evidence' of a long-standing, treasonous intent. To readers willing to believe, the *Mémoires Justificatifs* offered a precursor of the plot now in motion.

Jeanne wished to show the queen and Rohan in thrall to desire, as well as political ambition. Accordingly, they become lovers, and the first third of the *Mémoire* is structured around their purported correspondence, in which rhapsody counterpoints with strategy. Marie Antoinette, worried that Rohan is gossiping about her letters, asks Jeanne to direct the garden scene in order to 'see him without seeing him' and judge his suitability for an official audience. At the height of his infatuation with the queen, Rohan negotiates the purchase of the necklace. Jeanne contradicts herself about the reasons for its purchase. Did the queen covet it specifically because the king denied it her? Did Rohan need to clear his debts before Louis would agree to appoint him chief minister? Did he therefore intend to sell the diamonds? How, then, did he expect to succeed? None of these questions are satisfactorily answered.

The queen is angered by the clumsy handling of the transaction, but drops a thumping hint to Jeanne to counterfeit her signature. This was Jeanne's first admission of forgery. Her narrative did not require such a divulgence: she could easily have attributed the

---

* This was a bald factual error, since Marie Antoinette had married Louis before Rohan's embassy.

handiwork to Rohan or Cagliostro, whom she had disparaged during the trial. But Jeanne was eager for her readers to understand that she was the ultimate cause of Rohan's fall and the public denigration of the queen. Perversely, forgery satisfied her yearning to realise her nobility through service at the queen's side – to become, figuratively, the queen's hand. And it also offered a formal justification for her literary project in aligning the *écriture* on the document and the more voluminous *écriture* of the *Mémoires Justificatifs*. It was by writing that Jeanne suffered, and it was through writing that she would redeem herself and punish those who abandoned her.

The necklace is not simply a McGuffin; it embodies all that is dysfunctional at Court. The word '*chaîne*' occurs frequently. The queen is chained by the searching eyes of the Polignacs; favour is 'chained' at her waistband; her life is a 'chain of imprudences'; she, in turn, seeks to 'chain the lion' – that is, the king. Networks of patronage, taken by courtiers as essential to advancement, are twisted into a fetter, as restrictive as the *collier d'esclavage*. The ties that bind bite at the wrists. Jeanne writes of her own 'chain of misfortunes' and compares her suffering to a 'dismemberment' – the fate which befell the necklace. Ironically, Marie Antoinette vainly asserts her independence by seeking to acquire the necklace, another chain – one that furthers her dependency and encumbers her with deceit. The only escape – after Breteuil, in Jeanne's telling, badgers the jewellers to reveal all – is through brutally cutting adrift her abettors, a denial which clamps the shackles of the Bastille around Jeanne and Rohan.

By braiding the necklace into a wider discourse of bondage, at a time when the liberties of Frenchmen were a matter of fierce debate, Jeanne re-conceived the Diamond Necklace Affair as a parable of freedom and its invisible – though still insidious – restraint by the inbreeding knot of families which leeched off the country's riches. Despite all she endured, Jeanne refrained from blaming Rohan and Marie Antoinette outright. He was a generous prince to whom Jeanne owed gratitude for his largesse; she a queen, for all her faults, who Jeanne admired. Jeanne's ordeals were caused by the 'evil clash of their terrible interests' – they, as much as Jeanne, were prisoners of the system.

The historian has no harder task than determining the impression of a book on the heart and mind of the average reader. Scholarship has developed the pornographic interpretation of the French Revolution, initially offered by Robert Darnton, who argued that Grub Street hacks, excluded from advancement in literary circles, turned on the Establishment and, by heaping obscenities upon the royal family, denuded the French monarchy of all respect. We now know that writers of *libelles* had a variety of motives; that the French government did an adequate job of suppressing the obscenities in the pre-revolutionary years; that the circulation of those works which were published was limited; and that Louis XVI and Marie Antoinette themselves rarely featured in *libelles*. In this light, the *Mémoires Justificatifs* become all the more potent. Simon Burrows, a leading revisionist of the pornographic interpretation, calls them a – if not the – 'foundational text'.

Unlike previous libels, Jeanne's memoirs were not an anonymous gazette of dirty stories, stitched together or reworked from earlier anthologies. It's hard to imagine that most readers actually believed these anecdotes; they were entertained, rather, by their insolence. *Les Amours de Charlot et Toinette*, for example, describes in verse an afternoon of passion involving a barely disguised Marie Antoinette and her brother-in-law, the comte d'Artois. Though it brings the reader up close to Marie Antoinette, draped naked over a bergère, it is recognisably a fantasy – even if Artois were actually her lover, would he really speak to her in quatrains? Accounts of the bedroom antics of the Most Christian King and Glorious Queen reduced them to sex dolls. In a country where the prevailing ideology still glued status to behaviour – French nobles, for example, could be stripped of their titles for engaging in unbecoming activities, such as commerce – whatever desacralisation occurred was the result of imagining the royals as lusty, bestial, spurred on by base appetites. The actual credence given to the gossip was largely irrelevant.

The *Mémoires Justificatifs* novelly adapted the genre. They report from the inside, meticulously tracing the seed of corruption. Though royal partisans then and readers now immediately alight upon the sexual impropriety, for the most part the book is remarkably restrained, often tedious. Jeanne is not afraid of being boring: her memoirs are, after all, 'justificatory', so every meeting and conversation is expounded at remorseless length; every hostile witness, however minor, rebutted with devotion. These features glaze the book with a verisimilitude which other libels do not even attempt to attain. Even the lesbian trysts and Marie Antoinette's infidelities are veiled in deliberately ambiguous terms, which a forgiving reader might interpret only as signs of girlish affection. This was far removed from the 'buggering' and 'fucking' found in cruder compositions.

But *Mémoires Justificatifs* also performed more insidious work – not just ridiculing the Bourbons, but providing plausible grounds to receptive minds that the queen had committed treason against the nation and her husband. The timing of publication augmented the book's effect (the French authorities, awakening to the peril late in the day, tried – and failed – to buy up the entire London print run). Four months later, the stormers of the Bastille discovered a library of the political pornography that ministers had sealed – forever, they had thought – in darkness. Now the French public glutted itself on improbable tales of Marie Antoinette's extravagant sex life; its receptivity to these stories was primed by the less graphic but seemingly well-evidenced accusations of Jeanne's memoirs.

The publication of the *Mémoires Justificatifs* prompted a familiar voice to re-enter the lists. The *Mémoire Historique des Intrigues de la Cour* was published in Venice in 1790. Its author was Rétaux de Villette, about whom nothing had been heard since he had been expelled from Paris in 1786. He had been victimised more than any of the participants, he mewled – 'used by all and abandoned by all'. The work is an unimaginative piece of political pornography – of Rohan's first encounter with Jeanne he wrote: 'Never was there a courtesan who had a boudoir more delicious, more voluptuous than that into which she was introduced . . . he placed his hands on her, his eyes gleaming with lust, and Madame de La Motte, gazing at him tenderly, made him know that he could dare all' – and a limp defence of his own actions. After this flare-up, he was never heard of again.

On 24 June 1789, Nicole (no longer the baronne d'Oliva) died. She had shone briefly as a celebrity after her release from prison – even moving in for a short while with her lawyer, Blondel – but her constitution had been shredded by the Bastille and childbirth. Doctors prescribed a period of recuperation in the countryside, and she lived for a while with her guardian in Passy. In April 1787, she married her on–off lover, and the father of her child, Toussaint de Beausire, a decision she would regret. She told a court in 1789 that

> I was barely married before I experienced shocking treatment at the hands of my husband. He ill-used me, and beat me several times. He is leading the most scandalous life, passing his nights in gambling hells and going with other women. And all this time I am confined to the house, in absolute poverty. We live under the same roof, but lodge separately – he in a fine front room; I in a poky little box behind . . . And now he wants me to go away, to retire into a convent, but will not give me the means of my subsistence.

Nicole eventually entered the convent at Fontenay sous Bois, where she died soon afterwards, a woman whose little happiness had been snatched from her by those more brutal and devious. Beausire did not waste much time grieving: he was at the head of the phalanx that overwhelmed the Bastille less than two weeks later.

The flux of 1789 presented Jeanne with an opportunity she had never anticipated. Might she not return to Paris and add the *parlement*'s verdict to the bonfire of absolutism? Radicals encouraged her homecoming; some influential Parisians, from across the political spectrum, believed she was hiding among them and fruitlessly sought her. But Louis was still on the throne and Jeanne was disinclined to expose herself while he still wielded power, especially since she had so recently baited him with the *Mémoires Justificatifs*.* Nicolas, more carefree (and also, perhaps, eager to rid himself of his wife's growing paranoia), insisted on moving back to Paris in August 1789 to campaign for a fresh hearing of the Diamond Necklace case. Soon he was bedded down with an English mistress, Madame Seymour, and was 'telling the most shameful tales' about Jeanne.

In Nicolas's absence, Jeanne struck up a correspondence with her sister, Marianne, whom she had not heard from since her prison days. The women were more fractious than familial. Marianne's

---

* Jeanne may have been in Paris, briefly and in secret, in November 1790, only to return to England because of the dangers.

activities during the intervening years had been morally equivocal: she had repeatedly petitioned the king to make over to her Jeanne's confiscated property. Whether she was attempting to secure it for herself or intended to recover it on her sister's behalf is not clear, but Jeanne certainly believed Marianne coveted her riches: she referred to her as a '*moisonneuse*' (a 'grasper') in a letter to Nicolas, and decried her as a 'monster' who 'has not had the heart to come to her sister's help'. Yet she yearned, at times, for Marianne's company – called her 'my consolation' – and pitied her, convincing herself that her sister had been led astray by a malignant lover.

Marianne had been horrified by the *Mémoires Justificatifs* and urged repentant silence as the only virtuous course. Why didn't they live together, she suggested, modestly and anonymously in 'Switzerland or Italy, or . . . some German principality' where the only diamonds and queens were in a pack of cards? Jeanne would not hear of this 'nonsense': she had smelted her justifications into biography. She truly believed she had befriended the queen, that she was a victim, not a criminal. Even in her letters to Nicolas, there is no conspiratorial backslapping – just outrage at their mistreatment. The falsehoods fermented in her mind into memories. 'Sorrow has not stopped pressing down on me until now, reducing me to a skeleton . . . I am very ill, my love, the bile is torturing me and sorrow eating my heart out; but courage still keeps me alive, the hope of conquering my enemies still sustains me.'

The many factions spun into existence by the Revolution trailed Jeanne, wishing either to silence her or ventriloquise her. The duc d'Orléans, his eye enviously fixed on the throne, sent emissaries to London to woo her, while Nicolas's frantic petitioning – of the mayor of Paris, of ministers, of the National Assembly – to revoke his sentence caught the attention of figures of all political stripes, from the king's reactionary brother, Provence, to the Jacobin Robespierre. The comte de Mirabeau, the taurine, pox-damaged, fire-preaching, debt-sunken revolutionary leader who secretly worked for the royal family, was convinced Nicolas's agitation for a retrial formed the keystone of a plot to overthrow the monarchy by casting doubt on the chastity of Louis's marriage and the legitimacy of his heirs.

A number of pseudepigraphal works appeared under Jeanne's name, which professed to reveal truths hitherto unmentionable. Another *Mémoire Justificatif* was published – indisputably inauthentic, not least because the material about Jeanne's early life derives from the *Histoire Véritable de Jeanne de Saint-Remi*, a pamphlet published at the time of the trial for the purpose of discrediting its subject – which accused Marie Antoinette of 'twice attempting to set alight and to submerge in blood an entire empire . . . who meditated on the death of her husband at the very moment in which she tired him with her perfidious caresses'. In a scenario ludicrous even by the standards of the Diamond Necklace Affair, Jeanne is cast aside by the queen when she refuses to poison Vergennes's hot chocolate. Another concoction, *La Reine dévoillée ou Supplement au Mémoire de Mde La Comtesse de Valois de La Motte*, was inspired by the epistolary libel which Jeanne pioneered in the appendix to her memoir. Taking the form of a portfolio of revealing letters from the Court's most powerful figures, *La Reine dévoillée* begins with discussions between the queen and the duchesse de Polignac about destroying Rohan, but broadens into an entire counterfactual history of the late 1780s, exposing the queen as the fons et origo of all government directives. It is a clear example of how the breach made by Jeanne in the reputation of court politics was prised open to allow a rangier critique of corruption and despotism.

Yet Jeanne was not a republican. As someone who valued her royal heritage deeply, she took no pleasure in the demolition of the Ancien Régime. Her ambiguous position emerges in two editions of *Père Duchesne*, an earthy paper written for the sans-culottes, though edited by a down-at-heel bourgeois, Jacques-René Hébert. Hébert's avatar was a salty, pipe-chuffing old codger whose woodcut appeared at the head of each issue above the caption, 'I'm the true Père Duchesne, for fuck's sake'. Père Duchesne calls on Jeanne, and receives a reciprocal visit after he injures himself falling down her stairs. In these pendant stories Jeanne is game and ingenuous, of 'sensitive character', wanting no vengeance against the queen, just a certification of her innocence; but she is mocked for her residual affection for Rohan, her class solidarity contrasted with Duchesne's 'good sense'. Duchesne flips from sympathising at her treatment to condemning her as an aristocrat (a recently coined and pejorative term). However useful Jeanne might prove as a totem for revolutionary factions, she would remain one of 'them' – a wannabe noble with rotten aspirations who saw the doors that she wished had been opened to her smashed in by more brutal hands.

28

The Fall of the Houses of Valois and Bourbon

JEANNE'S ANIMOSITY TOWARDS Marie Antoinette had sharpened after the publication of the *Mémoires Justificatifs*. 'On my life, for all the crowns in the world, I shall not disavow what I have said of her, and if she can only be cleansed by me, she will remain all her life as black as a chimney.' She planned an autobiography, telling her life from birth, which promised more revelations of royal misdeeds. Jacques Marivaux, the head of the king's secret police, had managed to inveigle his way onto Nicolas's legal team and manipulated the comte de La Motte into pleading with his wife not to publish. Having failed to convince her to back down or return to Paris – 'Why is my presence in Paris so much desired?', Jeanne wrote suspiciously. 'The Salpêtrière has not been destroyed, consequently they might throw me again into their loathsome holes' – Marivaux enlisted the aid of the general-administrator of the post office, Dubu de Longchamp, a fleeting acquaintance of the La Mottes.

In June 1791, Longchamp sent an associate called Bertrand to London to trail Jeanne and thwart any approaches by other factions. The mission was of the utmost secrecy – Bertrand never even mentioned Jeanne's name in his dispatches. On reaching London, he discovered a calamity had occurred. A Mr Mackenzie, an upholsterer to whom Jeanne owed money, had finally lost patience and sent the bailiffs round. Jeanne temporised, offering them a glass of wine; but a fear of arrest had been graven into her soul and, as her would-be captors drank, she escaped into a nearby house. Jeanne locked herself in a high room and improvised a barricade. The bailiffs gave chase and crashed through the door to see Jeanne hurling herself through the window. Her thigh cracked as she smashed into the street, her knee snapped, her eye spurted from its socket, 'the blood issued with a violence from her wounds, that for a while resisted every effort to stop its course'.

Jeanne was tended by a perfumer named Mr Warren, a friend and sometime landlord who lived on Lambeth Street near Westminster Bridge. Bertrand called on Jeanne on the day of his arrival:

> When I entered the room, she began to play on my feelings. She lifted the bedclothes so that I might see her injuries. There was never seen a sight so horrible. Her thigh is broken about the middle, one leg is broken at the knee and both are in splints. Deposits of pus are forming and the surgeon is obliged to make incisions to allow suppuration. Her whole body is a dark yellow in colour, from head to foot.

Four days later, Bertrand reported that her condition had deteriorated:

> A whitish spot has appeared on the thigh. After the administration of a poultice, a considerable swelling formed, which burst and flooded her thigh with pus, the odour of which was rather cadaverous, and the product was so abundant that five saucerfuls of it were thrown away. When I went in, the smell was unendurable, though a lot of brown paper had been burnt and all the windows were open.

Initially sympathetic, Warren soon felt the strain of supporting Jeanne. He grew irritated when she dirtied the linen, refused to subsidise a nurse and suggested that the inquisitive Frenchman might stump up for her care.

Despite Jeanne's battered state, Bertrand persisted in his mission. He offered Jeanne financial incentives to withdraw authorisation for her autobiography's release. Exhausted and in agony, she relented. But when the money was not instantly forthcoming, her mind boiled with despair and mistrust. Bertrand wrote to Longchamp:

> She told me that she was quite convinced I had only come to London to make her perish in the most outrageous manner; that it was in order to seize her hard-earned crust by delaying the publication of her work, which was her only means of subsistence; that she would have gladly pardoned me if I had plunged a knife into her heart; that all that was left to her, after revenging herself on you and me, was to end her unhappy existence as promptly as possible. I believe that if her strength had permitted, she would have carried out this cruel design.

At eleven o'clock in the evening on 23 August 1791, Jeanne died. Though her condition had been improving for a number of days, a surfeit of mulberries brought on a spasm of vomiting which choked her. She was buried three days later at St Mary's, Lambeth. 'She had a horse, mourning coach, etc.', wrote Warren to Nicolas, angling for assistance with the funeral expenses, 'and a few friends attended'. Many found it hard to believe that Jeanne's injuries had been sustained merely for the sake of a paltry debt. The timing seemed too pertinent, and a lattice of mythology quickly wired itself around the accident: Georgel said that she had been accidentally defenestrated during an orgy; Nicolas claimed that her pursuers were in fact agents of the duc d'Orléans sent to snatch her.

The Life of Jane de St Remy de Valois was published shortly afterwards. It was a baggier thing than the *Mémoires Justificatifs*, armoured with boilerplate about despotic abuses. Yet its literary quality – Carlyle dubbed her style the 'bastard heroic' – was admired to the extent that Laclos was mooted as its ghostwriter (not so implausible, since he worked as an operative for the duc d'Orléans). It was – due, probably, to the influence of her amanuensis – more political than her earlier book and spiked with reformist rhetoric. Life at Court was 'a prostitution, a mercenary employment, to me infinitely more intolerable than my infant wretchedness'; a paean to workers concludes, 'I have always respected the labourer and the peasant'; and the peroration envisaged in France 'an august Senate dispensing freedom and happiness to a renovated Empire'. The desacralisation operates more subtly here – the queen is not a lusty harpy but all too human, susceptible to the common vices of jealousy, hatred and greed. And if her failings were run-of-the-mill, the book implicitly asked, why did she deserve to be queen?

Louis was sufficiently perturbed by the publication of a French edition to buy up, after a tip-off-cum-blackmail attempt by Nicolas, the entire print run (the queen herself believed such efforts were inevitably futile). They were stored in the room of Laporte, a royal functionary, before being transported on 26 May 1792 to the Sèvres porcelain factory for incineration. It took five hours to burn the lot. Or almost all of it. The man tasked with the job behaved so operatically, loudly forbidding workers from coming near the ovens, that suspicions were aroused.

Radicals in the Assembly agitated for an investigation: it was suggested that the crown had destroyed evidence of the queen's dealings with Austria, or banknotes forged to fund counter-revolution. Laporte's house was searched and a single copy of the book found; the Assembly ordered its reprinting. The preface to the new edition declared that 'the lengths to which the Court has gone to prevent the publication of this work clearly prove how greatly the monarchy feared its publication, how many facts it contains which the royalist party would have preferred to keep from public knowledge'.

Jeanne's death spurred Nicolas into activity: he was now a torchbearer for a victim of despotism. He wrote to the keeper of the seals demanding a retrial – with, naturally, a more sympathetic bench than the one corrupted by Vergennes, as he put it, in the original case: 'the French people will choose judges who would blush to let themselves be led, step by step, into the labyrinth of Themis by an insolent and ferocious vizier'. On 4 January 1792, Nicolas was imprisoned in the Conciergerie. This was exactly what he wanted: the contumacy verdict against him for his earlier failure to appear before the *parlement* needed serving out before the judgement could be revoked. According to Nicolas's memoirs, a fire broke out on the following night. Robespierre himself rushed to the prison to ensure Nicolas's safety, and there were rumblings that royalists had tried to burn Nicolas alive.

A new court was convened and on 20 July 1792 Nicolas was absolved of all his crimes – but only through a technicality, 'in view of the fact that the indictment submitted by the *procureur-général* to the *parlement* of Paris (as was) on 7 September 1785 was signed only at the end and not on each and every sheet, which is contrary to the law'. Nonetheless, because of the severity of the charges under consideration, Nicolas remained in custody. On his eventual release later that year, he wound up in Bar where, for the second time, he married a local girl, with whom he had a son.

The Diamond Necklace Affair brought with it a transformation in the queen's political role. Previously she had been ineffectual or uninterested in matters of state; now her influence was felt and she began to attend council regularly. On Vergennes's death in 1787, she manoeuvred her own favourite, Loménie de Brienne, into office. Her interventions were motivated by patriotism – to her adopted country, not her native one. She refused to act as an unthinking instrument of Austrian policy, the role for which her mother had groomed her. It was unacceptable, she told Mercy-Argenteau, that the 'Court of Vienna should nominate the ministers of the Court of France'. Though she would be repeatedly maligned as a traitor until her death, the queen strove, even in the most precarious circumstances, to reconcile her actions with the national interest as she saw it.

She had little respite from the public bruising she had endured. Her daughter, Sophie, died in 1787; the dauphin less than two years later. Her husband fell into a depression which he never shook off. Despite retrenchments in the Court's expenditure, she became known as 'Madame Deficit'. She waxed fat; her looks were consumed by it; her hair turned white. After the storming of the Bastille, she was abandoned by her closest friends, the Polignacs and her brother-in-law Artois, who fled the country. From then on, the Revolution became a parade of humiliations, an erosion of the grandeur and deference to which she had become accustomed.

On 6 October 1789, Versailles was invaded by a rabblement of working-class women, goaded by hunger and inebriated with rumours of orgies spiced with counter-revolutionary sweet-nothings. They dismembered two of her *garde du corps* and violated her bed with the points of their pikes. The king, the queen and their children were frogmarched back to Paris, as the crowd sere-naded them as the 'baker, the baker's wife and the baker's boy', and the impaled heads of the dead soldiers bobbed about them. Even at this early stage, Marie Antoinette predicted the course of events: 'my duty is to die at the feet of the king'. The royal family installed themselves in the Tuileries, a disconsolate palace that had long been used as a dormitory for royal attendants. The king made a show of gladly embracing the new dispensation, but everyone knew the National Guardsmen who protected them impounded them too.

Currents of feeling about the queen that had been diverted underground spurted forth in great gouts. Samizdat libels with tiny circulations were now published in multiple illustrated editions and freely sold. She was compared to murderous, profligate and promiscuous queens from history – Fredegund, Agrippina, Messalina, Catherine de' Medici – and portrayed as sexually monstrous, insatiable, devouring both men and women. There were concatenated couplings in multiple orifices; it was said she disguised herself as a streetwalker to masturbate men in public. In *The Public Bordello* she declares that 'if all the cocks that have been in my cunt were laid end to end, they would stretch all the way from Paris to Versailles'. Some of the libels listed her supposed lovers; Jeanne and Rohan were usually included. But the orgies were not ends in themselves – they were occasions for planning the torture and obliteration of her enemies, even regicide. There were no limits to the depravities that might be imagined and the royal family, quailing and with their power leaching away, proved incapable of a sustained refutation.

Kennelled in Paris, the queen re-emerged as an important political actor – it is possible that she may have even resorted to forgery when the king was morose and paralysed with indecision. She was busy in the organisation of the royal family's escape in the summer of 1791. The plan was to head north-east to Lorraine and rally their supporters, hoping that their subjects in *La France profonde* would prove more loyal than the obstreperous Parisians. If that failed, they might hop over the border to freedom. The royal party slipped out of Paris on 20 June in a custom-made berlin, disguised as the household of a minor noble.

A combination of poor planning, rashness and a stolid inability to improvise led to the coach being stopped in Varennes; commissioners were sent by the National Assembly to retrieve the absconded Bourbons. An anonymous print of the time shows Marie Antoinette floating out of the Tuileries with her family clinging on to her. A necklace descends from the enormous balloon-like canopy of her dress, like a rope or glittering turds. Jeanne, her décolletage revealing almost everything, hangs on to the lowered diamonds with Rohan by her side. It offers an eccentric version of the much-chewed-over theme of royal extravagance – the queen shitting diamonds in her hurry to escape – and a telling instance of historical compression: the Affair is the original cause of the queen's incarceration – Marie

Antoinette can never escape it, just as she fails to escape the palace. The necklace will always haul her down.

A fiction was cooked up with the connivance of the National Assembly that the royal family had been abducted, but what political influence Louis had previously held disintegrated. That autumn he accepted under compulsion a new constitution that provided him with much diminished powers. The beginning of the end arrived the following summer, when France was invaded by a Prussian-Austrian alliance. Inevitably, Marie Antoinette was barracked with accusations of abetting the enemy. The monitions of the Brunswick Manifesto, issued by the commander-in-chief of the Allied forces, against harming the king and queen only served to incite the Parisian street. On 10 August 1792, with the Tuileries surrounded, Louis and his family sought sanctuary with the Assembly. Republicans pounced on the king's abjection and, on 21 September, the monarchy in France was abolished. The quondam king, who had been compulsively reading about Charles I, knew how his own story would end.

That Christmastide, Louis Capet, as he was now known, was indicted for treason before the country's new representative body, the National Convention. His conviction was inevitable, though not the sentence – but the Convention voted, by a small majority, for death, and Louis was guillotined on 21 January 1793. He had promised to visit his wife that morning but he never came.

After the execution, grief could be read on Marie Antoinette's body. She grew pallid, skeletal and sullen (it did not help that her toilette was no longer as all-masking as in her heyday). She was afflicted by debilitating bleedings, caused perhaps by incipient cancer of the womb. All that nourished her now was pious adherence to the old faith. It seemed as if the queen would not suffer the same fate as her husband; the talk was of exile or repatriation to Austria. But after a series of military reversals and a royalist revolt in the Vendée on the Atlantic coast, the Convention's fears were trained on her.

In July, with roars and tears, she was separated from her son, whose preservation had directed all her activities over the four preceding years. She was transported to the Conciergerie, where Jeanne had spent a couple of anxious weeks after *parlement* had ruled against her. And, like Jeanne in the Salpêtrière, she became an attraction – a tigress captured, declawed, tentatively prodded. The instinct for survival had left her and she showed little interest in the crackpot schemes for escape proposed by her adherents. On 14 October 1793, Marie Antoinette was brought before the hanging judges.

According to the comte de La Marck, 'it is in the malice and lies which were spread between 1785 and 1788 by the Court against the queen that one must look for the pretext for the accusations of the Revolutionary Tribunal'. These accusations ranged from great crimes such as plundering the nation of gold to, on one occasion, casting a 'vindictive' stare at a member of the National Guard. The Diamond Necklace Affair was directly invoked as an example of her pitiless destruction of the 'agents of her criminal intrigues'.

'Did you not', asked Fouquier-Tinville, the prosecutor, 'make the acquaintance of the woman La Motte for the first time at Petit-Trianon?'

'I never saw her there,' the queen answered.

'Was she not your victim in the famous affair of the necklace?'

'She could not have been, since then I did not know her.'

'You persist to deny what you know.'

'My intention is not denial. It is the truth that I have spoken, and I will continue to speak it.'

The most vicious charge, which provided the darkest shading in the cartoon of the queen's inexhaustible depravity, alleged that Marie Antoinette had sexually abused her son. Hébert himself presented the 'evidence' to the court. 'Nature herself refuses to respond to such a charge laid against a mother,' she replied. Her dignity and nimble parrying counted for naught. She was found guilty of high treason and sentenced to death.

On 16 October 1793, the day of execution, her hair was cropped and her hands bound. She had dressed all in white, the solitary despondent gesture the black ribbon about her bonnet. She wrote to her sister-in-law with words of fortitude for her two children, before being placed in a cart and driven to the Place de la Revolution. The howls of the crowd did not discompose her. The Jacobin artist David sketched her with thinning hair tasselling her cap, her straight back the only means of defiance, her eyes lowered and jaw fixed as though setting her face into its own death mask. At the scaffold she apologised to Sanson, the executioner, for treading on his foot and exasperatedly dismissed a priest who urged 'courage': 'Courage! One needs it much more to live than to die.' Then she placed her head in the guillotine and waited for the exhale of the falling blade.

29

Madness, Sadness, Poverty

CAGLIOSTRO, THE MAN who prophesied the fall of the Bastille, found himself struck down by its debris. After leaving London, his peregrinations took him to Switzerland, where he lived, bankrolled by his followers, in a tiny chateau near Bienne. But a fusillade of exposés, including two plays by Catherine the Great, *The Trickster* and *The Tricked*, eroded his supporters' confidence and Cagliostro's mounting paranoia did little to conciliate them. He left the country in 1788, accusing his closest allies of conspiring to poison him.

He and Seraphina travelled to Savoy, then down through Italy, harried as they went by Bourbon emissaries. Seraphina wished dearly to live again with her family; with support from sympathetic clerics, she convinced Cagliostro that the Pope might be willing to incorporate Freemasonry into orthodox Catholicism. He dutifully began to attend confession and practised his catechism. The couple arrived in Rome in May 1789, on the eve of the French Revolution, having been given indications that their entry into the Papal States would be nodded through. There was fervid interest in their arrival and, though Cagliostro took care not to fraternise in public with known Masons, he still conducted a seance for the cream of Roman society in which he turned water into wine 'rather similar to Orvieto white'.

Despite assurances that he would not be troubled if he renounced his activities, Cagliostro was arrested by officials of the Inquisition on 27 December 1789, just as he had sent a petition to the National Assembly for readmittance to France. Who was the Judas? It turned out to be his wife. As the troop of soldiers prepared to apprehend him, Cagliostro smelt betrayal. He aimed his pistol at Seraphina, but it failed to fire. She had, for months, found her husband's rages and lunatic episodes – most likely the effects of tertiary syphilis

– unbearable. On one occasion, she had soaped the stairs to their house in the hope Cagliostro would slip and break his neck. Seraphina believed that a conviction for impiety would lead to a dissolution of their marriage; she provoked Cagliostro's blasphemous impulses with constant prayer and genuflection and encouraged the servants to report his outrages. The plan worked: 'What saints, what Virgin? That's a load of rubbish; you'll find all the saints you want up my arse.'

Other allegations included exposing himself, demanding worship of his cock as a relic, encouragement to fornication, prostitution of his wife, failure to observe fast days, disparaging Jesus, Mary, the Apostles, saints, cardinals and priests (whom he called nancy boys and cuckolds), destroying holy objects, forbidding prayer, denying Christ's divinity, god's omnipotence and the existence of Purgatory, idolatry, heresy, fraud, forgery, slander, incitement to rebellion and rejoicing at news of revolution in France.

Seraphina was detained in the convent of Sant'Apollonia, for further examination; Cagliostro in the Castel Sant'Angelo. Despite his wife's treachery, he was inconsolable without her and begged the guards to allow them to share a cell. Meanwhile, searches of the Cagliostros' house uncovered a number of suspicious objects 'including a doll in the shape of a flexible and yielding woman, a bed, a sofa, a mirror, two crossed swords, several rings of fire, apparatus of fumigation, tripods and many instruments of lechery'.

Forty-three witnesses were deposed over the course of the fifteen-month investigation. Emissaries fanned out across Europe to gather evidence and Cagliostro's powders were subjected to chemical analysis. So important was the case that Pope Pius VI sat in on the interrogations. Suspicion of Cagliostro was bound up with fears about events in France, and he was accused of having instigated the Revolution in revenge for his treatment by the Bourbons. His presence in Rome, the Inquisition suggested, was to foment revolt, raise a fleet and establish a republic in the Papal States – a document was found among Cagliostro's papers that predicted Pius would be the last incumbent of the throne of St Peter.

Cagliostro tried to argue that the tenets of the Egyptian rite were entirely compatible with Catholic dogma. But his gab had gone. 'I don't understand all your word-games. I don't even understand myself any more. I don't know what to say. I weep for my sad condition, I only seek help for my soul. I am in error a hundred thousand times with regard to religion.' He offered to make a public retraction, to turn missionary and convince his followers to suckle from the bosom of the Church. 'All I desire is the salvation of my soul. I am ready, indeed anxious, to undergo the most severe public correction.' Then he collapsed and tried to recant, screaming he had been tortured. Little had been achieved in softening the inquisitors' final verdict, and they rejected his last-minute plea of insanity: 'The defendant is a sceptic, an atheist, an animal, a despicable and very wicked man, held by many to be an impostor, a rascal, a source of false religion, fierce and brutish, a charlatan, fanatic, scoundrel, heretic, deist and most depraved and ignorant in religious matters.'

They sentenced him to death but, as he knelt with the black hood stifling his breath, mitigated the punishment to life imprisonment 'without possibility of pardon'. He was not allowed pen or paper; his shaving implements were confiscated, lest he slash his own throat. Seraphina, too, had unwittingly prepared her own demise. The court were unwilling to release someone so long contaminated by Cagliostro, and she was remanded in perpetuity in the convent.

In April 1791, Cagliostro was transferred to San Leon in the duchy of Urbino and placed in the care of the papal duke, Cardinal Doria. Erected at the peak of a cliff 700 metres above a valley with a sheer drop on all sides, the castle looks like an axe-head knapped out of the rock against the sky. Machiavelli judged it the 'strongest fortress in Europe'. Cagliostro was lodged at the top of one of the towers – mist slithered in through the bars and hung in droplets on the walls. Generally, he was treated well – the Pope did not want the death of the most famous man in Europe on his hands – though subjected to daily religious instructions by priests intent on his salvation. Worried that Cagliostro might be liberated by a squadron of hot-air balloonists, his jailers moved him to a more secure cell hewn into the cliff face.

With great ingenuity, he managed to fashion a pen from a straw in his mattress; he compounded snuff and piss and blood for ink. A minuscule almanac was found in which he had written: 'Pius VI in

order to comply with the desires of the Queen has caused my suffer-
ings . . . Woe betide France, Rome, and her followers.' He manifested
signs of insanity, feigned or genuine it was hard to tell: crying out to
his wife as though she were nearby, alternating between self-starvation
and gorging, wailing from his window, rattling the bars, upending
chamber pots over his captors, secreting fish so the rotting stench would
choke the priests who came to reason with him. A peephole was
drilled in the door to keep him under constant surveillance; his cell
was regularly searched; yet even after he'd been shackled to the wall,
sharpened screws and rods, sown to ambush his guards, were
discovered.

On the morning of 26 August 1795 he collapsed with a stroke.
Syphilis had etched itself through his brain. Weakening, he refused
the last rite. He died that evening at the age of fifty-two, a scrawny,
wispy-bearded ghostly thing, without his panacea, without gold,
without plump diamonds, without the beholden audience which
had acclaimed him the most fascinating man in Europe.

Rohan observed the Revolution's murderous spiral from the safety
of his crow's nest in Ettenheim, in the German part of his diocese,
and he devoted his much diminished resources to supporting his
fellow exiles. Yet revanchists distrusted the cardinal for his involvement in the National Assembly, and the princelings of the Holy
Roman Empire regarded his remaining territory as so much carrion.
He was a dangling man, trusting no one, reinforced by no one,
impotently threatening the Alsatians with hellfire if they joined in
with the spoliation of his belongings.

Wistfully dreaming of the reconquest of Alsace, Rohan encouraged
the vicomte de Mirabeau – the comte's reactionary brother – to
decamp to Ettenheim along with his raggle-taggle army. Mirabeau
was so rotund he was known as Mirabeau-Tonneau – Mirabeau the
barrel – and it was said of the preponderance of untested aristocrats
in his crew that 'each soldier has two captains, two lieutenants and,
to flee, two legs'. They scoured the Rhine valley for recruits, but
local potentates, fearful of a French backlash, withheld their support.
Rohan, by contrast, threw himself into planning and personally
designed the uniforms of black and yellow, with piratical armbands

embroidered with a skull and the motto 'Victory or Death'. Mirabeau's well-dressed troops crossed the Rhine on 13 May 1791; they were surprised at the natives' refusal to acknowledge them as liberators. As soon as a militia began to muster in Strasbourg, Rohan's army fled back into German territory. For weeks after, Mirabeau would row into the middle of the river and broadcast insults at the French soldiers on the far bank. Meanwhile, his men behaved as unoccupied soldiers are prone to do – gambling, whoring and drunkenly splashing in fountains to the annoyance of the locals.

The execution of Marie Antoinette struck Rohan like a fever – he did not eat or sleep for several days after hearing the news. On 21 October 1793, still pale and weak, he sat in the church at Ettenheim to hear a requiem Mass for the late queen. As the Dies Irae played, Rohan stood up, raised a palm up to silence the organist, steadied himself against his throne. He lifted his hands to the sky and exclaimed in a voice which to the congregation sounded like death itself, 'Domine, miserere mei et exaudi vocem meam' – 'Lord, have pity on me and hearken to my voice' – before collapsing and being stretchered into the sacristy. Had he been overcome by his complicity in the queen's fate? Was he mortified that the opportunity for forgiveness had passed?

Rohan recovered from the trauma. For the next few years he lived like a country parson, preaching and hunting and benevolently regarding his flock. On one occasion, his sedate existence was disturbed by a revenant. Returning from stalking of an evening, Rohan and his huntsman stumbled upon a peasant who provided them with a light, then disappeared into the dusk like smoke. They searched for him and came to the foot of an old oak tree, where Rohan dashed out the embers of his pipe; a glint in the same spot caught his eye and he extracted a nugget which, on examination, turned out to be gold. A few days later, word trickled in from Rome that Cagliostro had died. Rohan asked his huntsman if he could identify the phantom peasant from a selection of miniatures; the retainer alighted upon the Great Copt, whom he had never met. It may simply have been a series of coincidences – a rustic with a rough Sicilian fizzog, a shiny clod – but Cagliostro's hold over the cardinal had never slipped. The phantom only confirmed to Rohan the persistence of the comte's miraculous powers.

In July 1796, the thrust by French armies into the Austrian Empire drove Rohan to Switzerland, where he was granted asylum until the Austrians restored him at the end of the year. After the election of royalists in Alsace, Rohan was encouraged to return to Saverne; he refused, not wishing to look upon the palace he had so lavishly repaired in ruins once more. Frightened by an anti-royalist coup in France in 1797, Rohan fled again, this time to Bavaria. As Napoleon rose to power and conflict broke out once more between France and the other continental powers, Rohan retreated deeper into Austria. Only with the Treaty of Lunéville in February 1801, in which peace was declared between France and the Holy Roman Empire, did Rohan feel safe to return to Ettenheim. He continued to be harried even there. The Concordat concluded between Napoleon and the Papacy officially stripped him of the Alsatian part of his diocese. In the last sermon addressed to his French flock, made all the more poignant because he was unable to deliver it in person, he wrote: 'Tell them that even in ceasing to be their bishop, I will never be capable of losing the feeling that unites me with them. Remind them that, raised among them in my tenderest youth, I will always be as one among them, even when circumstances appear to have separated us.'

Political usurpation snapped at the heels of his spiritual divestment. In the shredding and patching of German principalities which followed the eddies of great power politics, the margrave of Baden was granted the remaining lands of the one-time prince-bishop of Strasbourg. There was no one left to appeal to. On 27 September 1802, while the cardinal was out hunting, the Badeners entered Ettenheim. Rohan returned home to find himself sovereign of only his game bag. He was permitted to remain in his residence but his health, never robust especially since his Bastille days, began to fail; on 17 February 1803, at the age of sixty-eight, Rohan died. The duc d'Enghien, grandson of the prince de Condé and secret husband of Rohan's niece, reported that 'the cardinal finished things beautifully and truly edified us. He was with gangrene in the lungs for two days, and therefore without any hope, and had no inkling of the state he was in, even believing that he was improving.' On the eve of his death, he told his gathered servants that he felt like a 'feather in the breeze'. And he drifted, painless and untroubled, towards his grave.

Weaselling through danger and improvidence, Nicolas outlasted them all. Little is recorded about his life between 1794 and 1815. There were rumours he spent time in Turkey and converted to Islam, but most likely he moved between Bar and Paris, perhaps dabbling in some light anti-Napoleonic agitation. When Louis XVI's brother – formerly the comte de Provence, now Louis XVIII – was permanently reinstalled on the French throne after Waterloo, he appointed Jeanne's old mucker Beugnot as a minister. Beugnot managed to wangle a position for Nicolas as director of the theatre at Porte-Saint-Martin on a salary of 3,000 francs a year. His notoriety was sufficient to grant him a cameo in Victor Hugo's *Les Misérables* as one of the 'weather-cocks' of the royalist salon frequented by Marius's grandfather, Monsieur Gillenormand: 'It was whispered . . . in somewhat awed tones: "You know who he is? He's the Lamothe of the Necklace Affair."' Hugo wrote that

> there was nothing remarkable about the Comte de Lamothe-Valois, an old man of seventy-five in 1815 [he was, in fact, sixty-five], except his taciturn, portentous bearing, his cold, angular countenance, flawless manners, coat buttoned to his stock and the long legs encased in trousers the colour of burnt sienna which he invariably crossed when seated. His face was the same colour. Nevertheless he counted for something in that salon because of his 'celebrity' and also, strangely enough, because of the name of Valois.

Despite the harm he had worked, he was welcomed as an authentic part of the nostalgists' Eden – there were other adversaries now.

Nicolas must have lost his grip on this sinecure because he emerges in the less salubrious role as a police nark, under the easily penetrable cover of 'Delmotte'. Ironically, his work involved tracing illegally published and libellous books. Louis XVIII, piqued to learn that such an infamous individual was now an employee of the state, asked Nicolas to compile his memoirs. Nicolas began enthusiastically but then told the king that he would not finish them 'unless he were assured of a pension on the civil list'. Louis had no inclination to reward the man who had scourged his brother and sister-in-law, and the project was filed in a drawer. The contretemps must have led the police to dispense with Nicolas's services, for he next emerges, impoverished and bereaved of his second wife, purveying the kind of texts he had previously helped suppress. After the accession of Charles X (the former comte d'Artois) to the throne on his brother's death in 1824, Nicolas returned to his memoirs in the hope that the new king might be more perturbed than his predecessor by the literary disinterment of his relatives, and willing to buy him off.

He produced an account that intermittently chronicles his life until the early years of Napoleon. It is a tale strung with reversals – at each stage, contentment and sanctuary seem close at hand only for fate to upend everything. Nicolas conceives of himself as Ulysses, a man perpetually thwarted by history from sailing back to the epoch in which he flourished. He appears at historical milestones, thrust centre stage with ersatz reluctance. There he is, hoisted onto the shoulders of the fishwives as they march on Versailles to haul the royal family back to Paris. Now he is initiated into the king and queen's secret plans to flee the capital. Inevitably, his cell in the Conciergerie is the one in which Marie Antoinette will be locked. Marooned on the far side of the Napoleonic era, he was at liberty to recast his fortuitous endurance as the trials of a hero.

Nicolas told the police he would prefer to 'strike a deal' for suppressing the memoirs in exchange for a small pension: 'in this unhappy state I am expecting to succumb every day, owing to the awful pain I am suffering and my constant falls. The government or persons with whom I have been negotiating will not have me long as an annuitant.' They agreed to provide a small stipend, and the money allowed Nicolas to live with a measure of dignity. He lodged with his niece; in September 1829 he was glimpsed in a park, walking 'with stumbling footsteps as he shuffled along heavily on his two crutches. His elegant and immaculate appearance, his perfectly polished manners, his eminent way of greeting all spoke in his favour.' But the cheer had been snuffed out – Nicolas made a number of suicide attempts in his final years. A natural death came on 11 October 1831. The announcement of his passing in the *Journal de Paris* was clotted with a lifetime's accrual of pseudonyms and sham titles: 'Mr Mustophragasis, Count of Valois, knight of St Louis and of the Crown, nobleman of Angoulême, has just died in Paris, at an advanced age and in poverty. He was the husband of the famous Madame de La Motte-Valois. He was generally known by the name of Valois-Collier.' He clung to the necklace to the very end.

The undead weight of the diamonds hung around even longer. The nationalisation during the Revolution of Rohan's church lands, which should have financed the necklace's repayment, bankrupted the Boehmers. Boehmer himself died in Stuttgart in 1794, while seeking the grand duke of Baden's help in obtaining compensation from Rohan's German properties. Bassenge's estate continued the struggle: in 1843, a Paris court was still considering a claim against the heir of Rohan's heir. The entirety of the debt was finally paid off in the 1890s, the Rohan regarding its clearance as a matter of familial honour, completing the cardinal's work of repentance.

30

Flashes in the Crystal

A Conclusion

JEANNE HAD TOO lively a spirit to remain long in the grave. Was her 'accident', as some believed, just a ruse to hide her disappearance? In 1825, an early historian of the affair met an Armenian potter who told a garbled story of the 'comtesse Gachet, *a former queen of France*, who had stolen a necklace . . . When she died, and was undressed to wash her body, two letters were found branded on her shoulder.' The baronesse de Bode remembered this comtesse speaking 'refined French, animatedly and with charm . . . She had known Cagliostro, never gave up talking of the Court of Louis XVI and led us to understand that she had a great mystery in her life.'

Miracles of resurrection did not cease. During the July Monarchy, a bishop, returned from abroad, had introduced to Parisian society a venerable noblewoman known only as comtesse Jeanne. A benefactor granted her a wing in his house where she entertained with whist and chit-chat of the Ancien Régime. When she died, her room was found filled with charred papers. The Paris newspapers declared the deceased to be Madame de La Motte.

She lived on, too, in literary works, though the dizzying melodrama of the Diamond Necklace Affair could not easily be confined within fictional frames. Alexandre Dumas's novel *The Queen's Necklace* is a farrago of lurching motivations and breezy coincidence. D'Oliva resembles Marie Antoinette so precisely that she is frequently taken for the queen in Parisian society, leading to unjust rumours about the latter's conduct; Cagliostro is an omniscient and near-omnipotent force of anarchy, manoeuvring each character undetected to perform his bidding, as he seeks to upend the French monarchy; the garden scene is played through a number of times, not just with d'Oliva, but with Marie Antoinette and her would-be lover. Dumas, who takes Marie

Antoinette's infidelity for granted, is at his most perceptive when describing the queen's powerlessness, the vulnerability of her reputation and her complete dependence on her husband's favour. Again and again, she shrilly protests her innocence only for no one to believe her – a dry run for her appearance before the revolutionary tribunal.

Goethe, repelled yet fascinated by Cagliostro, tracked down his family when he visited Palermo in 1787, pretending to be an Englishman with news from London of the great man. Three generations lived poverty-stricken in one large room, 'a single window lighted the great walls, which once had been painted, and on which, all around, hung dark pictures of saints in golden frames'. Cagliostro's teenage nephew told Goethe that 'it would be our happiness, if he were to come here someday and agree to take care of us. But . . . we hear that he disowns us everywhere and poses as a man of noble birth.' Four years later, Goethe's play about the Diamond Necklace Affair was performed in Weimar. Initially intended as an opera, *The Great Copt* is a slight work whose anonymous characters are easily identified with historical protagonists. The Cardinal (Rohan) is duped by both the Marquise (Jeanne) and the Count (Cagliostro), who establishes a cult of universal brotherhood to serve his own greed. Goethe primarily intended to ridicule Cagliostro, though he was aware of the episode's more disturbing ramifications: 'the story of the necklace seems to me as frightening as the head of the Medusa' – it irrevocably 'destroyed royal dignity'.

Thomas Carlyle's 1837 essay 'The Diamond Necklace' is the most exhilarating nineteenth-century treatment of the scandal. Having come to the subject through his interest in Cagliostro, Carlyle caught a glimpse of 'Romance', of history fuelled by 'passion' – passions which were becoming trussed up by modern life's imperative for respectability and mind-deadening drudge work. Here was a story which, in its vitality, in Rohan and Jeanne's refusal to accept the political and social limitations placed on them, shows itself to be a sliver of Universal History – the chaotic spirit-web that runs through time but which we are often blind to. Jeanne is a 'spark of life'; Rohan is filled with 'radical vigour and fire' even though he allows them 'to stagnate and ferment . . . [like a] Mud-Volcano, gurgling and sluttishly simmering'.

Carlyle constantly emphasises how history's tendrils wind beyond the consciousness of the participants. He gives a bravura speculative biography of the diamonds, from 'the uncounted ages and aeons [they lay] silently imbedded in the rock'. The Diamond Necklace Affair is played out during an epochal moment: the transition between 'the age of Chivalry . . . and that of Bankruptcy'. Carlyle uses these terms when writing of Louis's refusal to buy the necklace because of his straitened finances, but they are more broadly applicable to the case. Rohan's courtliness, the value he places on breeding, his wooing of Marie Antoinette like an infatuated troubadour are mercilessly exploited by Jeanne, a speculator out for quick money with no deference towards institutions. She is the Revolution in microcosm, an avatar of modernity, the power of which Carlyle cannot help admiring, even though he despises many of its consequences.

The episode also had a complex personal significance for Carlyle. He griped that history had now 'degenerated into empty invoice-lists of Pitched Battles and Changes of Ministry'. At one point in the essay, he urges the reader to place '*aesthetic* feeling' above 'insatiable scientific curiosity'. The affair was as much an allegory of the parching of his profession by desiccated antiquarians, just as the live-wire Jeanne is restrained and bolted in the Bastille. Carlyle had written about Cagliostro at great length elsewhere and he condemns him in 'The Diamond Necklace' as an 'arch-quack'. Yet, almost in spite of himself, Carlyle cannot help lighting upon points of similarity between them. He is normally careful to distinguish his characters' voices from his default glutinous style; but it is noticeable how much Cagliostro, whose address to his 'fellow scoundrels' concludes the essay, sounds like his creator at full pelt. History's impossible task was, for Carlyle, to convey 'the ever-living, ever-working Chaos of Being' without traducing it into plodding linearity. Cagliostro, as the apostle of chaos, falsity, imposture, is more alive than anyone else to history's impurity. In granting the 'King of Liars' the prescience to see France consumed in a 'Fire-sea', Carlyle shows how closely the historian's insight presses against the mountebank's. 'Are not intrigues', Rohan asks earlier in the essay, 'the industry of this our Universe; nay is not the Universe itself, at bottom, properly an intrigue?' If so, the Diamond Necklace Affair reveals the fabric of history to the blinkered world.

A number of historians have refused to believe that Rohan was simply a dupe and the queen entirely uninvolved in the purchase of the necklace. The profusion of voices, the 'whole illimitable dim Chaos of Lies', as Carlyle put it, has led some to hear the grind of a conspiracy amid the cacophony. Munro Price, a leading authority on pre-revolutionary France, has written that 'I at least suspect that the Cardinal may have been an accomplice of la Motte's in her scheme to steal the necklace'. Yet if this was the case, why did Rohan retain the bill of the sale – the evidence which nearly damned him – and why did he insist the jewellers thank the queen, a gesture that would arouse suspicions? Louis Hastier, author of the very scholarly *The Truth about the Affair of the Necklace* (1954), believed that Jeanne was acquainted with the queen, who even looked on as Rohan knelt before d'Oliva. Michelet, the great historian of France, thought the same, though the only evidence he could adduce in his favour was Marie Antoinette's fondness for performing plays by Beaumarchais. He believed Rohan and the queen had collaborated in obtaining the necklace, pinning Jeanne with the blame when their unseemly activities threatened to flower into public scandal.

The purpose of this book is to establish that the most likely explanation of the facts is Rohan's innocence, Jeanne's guilt and Marie Antoinette's lack of involvement – a purpose complicated, though not obviated, by the characters' strange behaviour. Dissenting historians have frequently argued that it is unbelievable Rohan should not have recognised the queen's signature or doubted her appearance in the garden. But to read motivations back into events, we need to assume a consistent standard of rationality, one that we rarely live up to ourselves. Enthusiasm is as much an engine of history as calculation.

At the same time, I hope this book has revealed the extent to which the Diamond Necklace Affair is stitched into the fabric of the Revolution. This was a perception shared by a number of those involved, irrespective of which side of the verdict they fell. Nicolas de La Motte declared that 'the sentence by which we were condemned was the signal for the astonishing revolution which was brought about with so much ease by the corruption of the Court, the disorder of the finances, and the tyranny of those who shared in public power' – all significant factors which the Affair accreted, justly or otherwise, into readily comprehensible symbols of the country's malaise.

The queen's confidante, the princesse de Lamballe, writing from an entirely different perspective, believed that the Affair marked the moment when the French stopped regarding Marie Antoinette as 'a beneficent deity'. Lamballe may have been unduly rosy-eyed about the early years of the queen's reign, but she acutely notes that Marie Antoinette's own reaction intensified the contempt of her subjects:

> Public opinion began to vacillate, and the private enemies of the princess stimulated the discontent . . . No one told the queen that the coldness the crowd manifested towards her might have fatal results, and far from seeking to destroy it, she took offence. Her features, hitherto so sweet and caressing, expressed in public nothing but haughtiness and disdain for the opinion of those whom she never dreamt of regarding as able to dispose of her destiny and that of her family.

There are more subtle ways in which the Diamond Necklace Affair made its presence felt during the Revolution and the Terror. Jeanne's actions brutally dramatised what had been known for a long time – that the Bourbons were no longer the uniquely glorious individuals prescribed by royal ideology. Their signatures, even their corporeal forms could be replicated. While Jeanne was in prison, a certain Madame Equant was accused of a similar offence – forging the signature of the king's brother Provence to obtain goods on credit from merchants. This may simply have been a copycat crime or symptomatic of something deeper: the prevalence of a belief that the worth of a king or queen or prince was in the amount they spent or the leverage that might be extracted if they fell into one's debt. They had become commodities, they had a value – the Boehmers knew it, so did Rohan – and, like all economic goods, their value might rise and fall. So when the economy collapsed and the price of bread rose, it was easy for the country to ask if they could afford an absolute monarchy.

The affair also educated the French public in ways of interpreting their rulers' actions that would fundamentally guide the dynamics of the Revolution. The historian Lynn Hunt has noted that 'the obsession with conspiracy became the central organizing principle of French Revolutionary rhetoric'. Periodic bloodlettings were prompted by fear of traitors bringing down the country from within. The Diamond Necklace Affair was the defining opportunity presented to the French public in the pre-revolutionary years to learn to read conspiratorially. During the trial, and on the subsequent publication of Jeanne's memoirs, they were, it seemed, offered backstage access to the royal Court and invited to judge for themselves whether the conduct of their betters was hypocritical. In adjudicating over competing versions of evidence, Frenchmen developed similar sensitivities – paranoically so, in some cases – to the pronouncements and decisions of the men in charge. This was, of course, not the only classroom in which they learnt to read politics; but the affair offered a richer opportunity, full of reportorial detail, to speculate on royal misbehaviour than any of the vaporous slanders then wafting through the kingdom. The vigour with which members of all political factions attempted to track Jeanne down after the outbreak of Revolution is testament to a pervasive view that her story – irrespective of its veracity – was taken as an exemplary instance of royal despotism.

The object that chained Rohan and Jeanne and Marie Antoinette radiated a terrible glow. The suggestiveness of diamonds, the ballast of the scandal, gave weight to the calumnies against the queen – extant prejudices were electrified simply by the mention of the necklace in conjunction with her. Diamonds congeal wealth to its densest form. They induce disgust – Georges Bataille thought jewellery akin to excrement – because, however finely cut or polished, the admiration they provoke is a direct function of their value, beauty a tangential concept at best. Diamonds display a fortune efficiently – they incarnate profligacy. Had not Madame Deficit, in her untrammelled expenditure, shown herself bereft of a sense of economy, of lacking the awareness that self-restraint was a national priority? If you cut open Marie Antoinette, did you not expect to find a diamond for a heart? It is understandable why some Frenchmen found it so hard to disentangle her from the necklace.

Gems also secrete sexual connotations – Diderot's *Les Bijoux indiscrets* (*The Indiscreet Jewels*) were prating genitals. A stolen necklace was an apt symbol for the lost virtue of Marie Antoinette, orbited by rumours of infidelity. Diamonds draw the eye but also distract it; their flash in the light fascinates, but they hold the gaze on the surface and are impenetrable to the core. They betoken a secret world, in which conspiracy may flourish, in which enemies are crushed in the clench of a fist, in which the Austrian plenipotentiary might guide the queen's hand across the engine of government. In the flare of the diamond, one meets the lure of the dangerous, enigmatic female.

Retrospectively, it was particularly poignant that they were strung together in a necklace, laid around the most vulnerable juncture of the body, the indestructible crystal against the lacerable skin and cartilage and vein. It does not take much force to make a choker choke. And, as the French discovered, the quickest way to kill a queen was to slice straight through her throat.

And what of the diamonds themselves? Unfortunately, the records of Daniel Eliason, the broker who bought most of those Nicolas sold to the London jeweller William Gray, no longer survive, so following a paper trail is impossible. Two grand English dynasties – the Sackvilles and the Leveson-Gowers – have claimed that stones from the necklace were set into family heirlooms, a tasselled diadem and a 22-stone *sautoir* respectively. Vita Sackville-West wrote to *The Times* on 1 January 1959 with evidence she had found in the archives at Knole – a receipt from 1790 for a necklace from Jefferys of Piccadilly. But Nicolas sold the stones five years earlier and Jefferys, dubious about their provenance, had refused to buy them. The genealogy is probably apocryphal, most likely arising from the service of two forebears – John Sackville, 3rd duke of Dorset, and George Leveson-Gower, later 1st Duke of Sutherland – as successive ambassadors to the French Court between 1784 and 1792. But diamonds are hardy things, and history does not scar them. Somewhere, anonymously, in a Swiss safe or around a neck, reconfigured into earrings or brooches or a mortuary statuette of a beloved Dobermann, they sit, unperturbed by the anguish they caused.

Acknowledgements

This book has been nearly six years in the making and would not have been completed without the abundant support and encouragement I received. I'm grateful to Lisa Hilton, Michael Holroyd, Alan Jenkins, Candia McWilliam and Boyd Tonkin for the award of a Society of Authors Grant that substantially funded my research in Paris; and to Robert Macfarlane, Claire Armitstead and Tristram Hunt for a Royal Society of Literature/Jerwood Award in 2010, which provided an invigorating fillip during a particularly overwhelming period of research.

The staff of the London Library, the British Library, the Bodleian Library, the Archives de la Bastille, the Archives des affaires étrangères at La Corneuve, the Archives nationales in Paris, the Bibliothèque historique de la ville de Paris and especially the Bibliothèque nationale – who allowed me to examine documents normally available only on microfilm – were helpful and attentive throughout.

In Paris, I was hosted in palatial accommodation, first by Jean-Marie Besset, then by Koukla and Christopher MacLehose. Richard, Jane and Edmund Gordon and Tom Fleming generously provided me with idyllic rural retreats where I could concentrate solely on my work.

My colleagues at *Literary Review* – Alex Blasdel, Frank Brinkley, David Gelber, Tom Fleming, Nancy Sladek and Tom Williams – have not merely tolerated my extracurricular activities but have been remarkably enthusiastic and accommodating towards them. I'm particularly grateful to Nancy for her generosity in allowing me five months' leave to research and write this book.

Tim Blanning, Tom Fleming, Wil James, Charlotte Mardon-Heath, Andy Miller, Kate Prentice, Leo Robson and Naomi Wood all read this book in various states of disrepair. Their comments have improved it immeasurably and their excitement at the story kept mine burning. Any mistakes that remain are naturally my own.

Sarah Day worked exceptionally hard in helping me get to grips with the hundreds of pages of trial documents. Fleur Macdonald and Susannah Robinson also provided vital research assistance.

I'm thankful for the companionship, encouragement, advice and help offered by Daniel Beckman, Joshua and Gila Beckman, Christopher de Bellaigue, K. Biswas, Mark Bostridge, Nina Bowden, Michael Burleigh, Ambrogio Caiani, Hermione Calvacoressi, Irving David, Jon Day, Samantha Ellis, Charlotte Faircloth, Nicholas Gill, Eveleen Habib, John Hardman, Susanna Hislop, Lydia Garnett, Philip Goodman, Louise Greenberg, Molly Guinness, Paula Johnson, Ivan Juritz, Jeremy Lewis, Laura Keeling, Philip Mansel, Tom Marks, Tim Martin, John Pemble, Alfie Spencer, Tom Stammers and Nicki Stoddart, as well as many of those previously mentioned.

Simon Trewin, my agent, has enthusiastically championed this book throughout its long gestation. His assistants Ariella Feiner, Liv Shean, Sophie Lobl and Matilda Forbes-Watson have been models of professionalism.

I will always be thankful to Nicholas Pearson at Fourth Estate for taking a punt on an unproven writer bearing a proposal riddled with typos. John Murray, my new home, has welcomed me warmly. I'm grateful to everyone there, especially Nick Davies, for sanctioning the transfer, Sara Marafini, for the wonderful cover, Caroline Westmore, Lyndsey Ng, Bea Long, Ben Gutcher, Jason Bartholomew, my copy-editor Martin Bryant, my proofreader Nick de Somogyi and Douglas Matthews for the index.

My editor Mark Richards spotted the potential in the Diamond Necklace Affair before anyone else and has held my hand, patted my back and shaped this into a far better book than it would otherwise have been.

Finally, my father, without whose manifold support – emotional, intellectual, financial, nutritional – I would have given up long ago. There are not words to express my love, admiration and gratitude.

Illustration Credits

Notes

Abbreviations

AAE: Archives des affaires étrangères

AN: Archives nationales

Bastille: Archives de la Bastille

BHVP: Bibliothèque historique de la Ville de Paris

BN: Bibliothèque nationale

Campardon: *Marie-Antoinette et le procès du collier* (the transcripts of the investigating magistrates' interrogations of the suspects are printed as an appendix)

Castries: Journal de Maréchal de Castries

CMA: *Correspondance de Marie-Antoinette (1770–1793)*, edited by Evelyne Lever

Compte Rendu: *Compte Rendu de ce qui s'est passé au Parlement rélativement à l'affaire de M le cardinal de Rohan*

D'Arneth and Flammermont: *Correspondance Secrète du Comte de Mercy-Argenteau avec L'Empereur Joseph II et Le Prince de Kaunitz*, edited by Alfred d'Arneth and Jules Flammermont

D'Arneth and Geffroy: *Marie-Antoinette, Correspondance Secrète entre Marie-Thérèse et le Comte de Mercy-Argenteau*, edited by Alfred d'Arneth and M. A. Geffroy

Georgel: *Mémoires*, Abbé Georgel

Hardy: 'Mes Loisirs', Siméon-Prosper Hardy

HVJSR: *Histoire Véritable de Jeanne de S.-Remi, ou Les Aventures de la Comtesse de La Motte*

JdF: Fond Joly de Fleury

LJSRV I: *The Life of Jane de St Remy de Valois, Heretofore Countess De La Motte*, Volume I

LJSRV II: *The Life of Jane de St Remy de Valois, Heretofore Countess De La Motte*, Volume II

MCB: *Mémoires du Comte Beugnot, 1779–1815*

Mémoire Cagliostro: *Mémoire pour le Comte de Cagliostro, accusé; contre M le Procureur-Général, accusateur*

Mémoire Jeanne: *Mémoire pour Dame Jeanne de Saint-Remy de Valois, Epouse de Comte de La Motte*

Mémoire Rohan: *Mémoire pour Louis-René-Edouard de Rohan, Cardinal de La Sainte Eglise Romaine, Evéque & Prince de Strasbourg, Landgrave d'Alsace, Prince-État d'Empire, Grand Aumônier de France, Commandeur de l'Ordre du Saint-Esprit, Proviseur de Sorbonne, &c, Accusé, contre M Le Procureur-Général*

MGO I: *Mémoire pour la Demoiselle Le Guay D'Oliva Fille Mineure, emancipée d'age, accusée*

MGO II: *Second Mémoire pour la Demoiselle Le Guay D'Oliva Fille Mineure, emancipée d'age, accusée*

MHV: *Mémoire Historique des Intrigues de la Cour*, Rétaux de Villette

MJ I: *Mémoires Justificatifs de la Comtesse de Valois de La Motte*, Volume I

MJ II: *Mémoires Justificatifs de la Comtesse de Valois de La Motte*, Volume II

NLM: *Mémoires Inédits du Comte de Lamotte-Valois*

PLMA: *The Private Life of Marie-Antoinette*, Jeanne Louis Henriette Campan

Requête Rohan: *Requête au Parlement, Les Chambres Assemblées, par le Cardinal de Rohan*

Prologue: Before the Law

1   Before Paris awoke: see *Tableau de Paris* by Louis-Sébastien Mercier, ed. Jeanne-Claude Bonnet (Mercure de France, 1994), 'Les heures du jour', vol. 1, pp. 873–81.

1   the wrong one: Hardy, 31 May 1786.

4   'rock the throne of France': quoted in *The Queen's Necklace* by Frances Mossiker (Phoenix, 2004), p.ix.

4   'the Diamond Necklace trial': ibid.

4   actions of their betters: see, for example, the work of Robert Darnton, Simon Burrows, Lynn Hunt and Sarah Maza.

5   'Changes of Ministry': 'The Diamond Necklace' by Thomas Carlyle in *Critical and Miscellaneous Essays*, vol. 5 (Chapman and Hall, 1869), p.5.

1. Princess in Rags

7   lowlier, adoptive one: see 'Family Romances' in *The Standard Edition of the Complete Works of Sigmund Freud*, vol. 9, pp. 237–41; for the application of 'Family Romances' and Freud's work more generally to the late eighteenth-century France, see *The Family Romance of the French Revolution* by Lynn Hunt.

7   'source of all belief': op. cit., p.237.

7   'the west of Troyes': the account of Jeanne's early life predominantly draws on her two memoirs, *Mémoires Justificatifs de la Comtesse de Valois de La Motte* and *The Life of Jane de St Remy de Valois, Heretofore Countess De La Motte*, the memoirs of Beugnot and the anonymous *Histoire Véritable de Jeanne de S.-Remi*.

8   less than a century: *Aristocracy and Its Enemies in the Age of Revolution* by William Doyle, p.15.

8   illegally minting coins: PLMA, p.15.

8   famines which afflicted France: see 'The Famine Plot Persuasion in Eighteenth-Century France' by Stephen Kaplan, *Transactions of the American Philosophical Society* (1982), vol. 72, no. 3.

8   less than 1,000 livres a year: *The French Nobility in the Eighteenth Century: From Feudalism to Enlightenment* by Guy Chaussinaud-Nogaret, p.62.

9   'the natural whiteness of her skin': LJSRV I, p.5.

9   'amounted to nothing': HVJSR, p.4.

9   for a share: NLM, p.17.

9   herd the cows: BHVP MS691/150.

9   'like savages': MCB, p.16.

10 pummelled his wife: MJ I, p.7; HVJSR, p.vi; LJSRV I, p.13.

10 native Parisians: *Paris: Biography of a City* by Colin Jones, p.237.

10 prostitution and theft: see *The Poor of Eighteenth-Century France 1750–1789* by Olwen Hufton, pp. 69–106.

10 'King of France': LJSRV I, p.14.

10 Abbé Henocque: the name is confirmed in *Description de la Généralité de Paris* by Philippe Hernandez.

11 'welcome our approach': LJSRV I, p.16.

11 tremors through the living: see *Paris*, Jones, p.238.

11 'such a mother!': LJSRV I, p.18.

11 'such degradation': op. cit., p.22.

12 no more than ten: Hufton, pp. 38–40.

12   buy her dinner: HVJSR, pp. 7–12.

13   one account: HVJSR, pp. 8–9.

13   Jeanne's own account: LJSRV I, p.37ff.

13   'history of the kingdom': entry for BOULAINVILLIERS (Henri, Comte de) in *Le Siècle de Louis XIV* by Voltaire.

14   'by chance on the road': quoted in *Les Bâtards de la Maison de France* by the marquis de Belleval, p.46.

14   their title deeds: *Mémoires de Mademoiselle Bertin sur la Reine Marie Antoinette* (Paris, 1824), pp. 96–7.

14   'particularly in writing': LJSRV I, p.44.

14   'ironing, housekeeping, nursing': op. cit., pp. 46–7.

14   'person of my condition': op. cit., p.53.

15   '*servant to a servant*!': ibid.

16   'unreasonable to remonstrate': op. cit., p.68.

16   'perhaps might offer': op. cit., p.66.

17   'unbending in his judgements': MCB, p.18.

17   Brest in April 1776: MJ I, p.9, HVJSR, p.31.

17   'trifling': LJSRV I, p.92.

17   gambling debts: *La Cour de France* by Jean–François Solnon, p.493.

17   'passing in my breast': LJSRV I, p.108.

17   fermented gases unobtrusively: op. cit., p.110; Hardy, 8 December 1776, 21 December 1776 and 2 January 1777.

18   than their religious calling: *Histoire de l'Abbaye Royale de Longchamp* by Gaston Duchesne, pp. 92–4.

18   'not a decent one': MCB, p.16.

18   the druids had done: see *Histoire de Bar-sur-Aube* by L. Chevalier.

18   'for a long time': *Essais historiques de la ville de Bar-sur-Aube, publiés d'apres un manuscrit inédit portant la date de 1785* par J.F.G., p.15.

19   demure and winsome: MCB, p.20.

19   look too closely: op. cit., p.21.

19   'society of this demon [Jeanne]': op. cit., p.22.

20   'the women in the town': ibid.

20   live with his mother: Nicolas's family history is found in NLM, p.6ff.

20   'friendly and sweet': MCB, p.22.

20   'excelled in the metropolis': LJSRV I, p.154.

21   'counts, barons, and viscounts': quoted in *The Institutions of France* by Roland Mousnier, vol. 1, p.138.

21   titles were genuine: see *Les Nobles et Les Villains du Temps Passé* by Alphonse Chasset, p.208.

22   'up to all pleasures': BHVP MS691/151

22   'to good use': MCB, p.24.

22   'his wife's first years': MCB, p.25.

23   'enter business' . . . 'mad directives' . . . 'natural debt': op. cit., p.26.

23   'powerful friends and money': op. cit., p.27.

2. The Man Who Never Grew Up

24   cataract of disdain: the account of Rohan's life before his involvement with Jeanne de La Motte draws on *Les Rohans: 'roi ne puis, duc ne daigne, Rohan suis'* by Alain Boulaire, *Le Siècle de Rohan: une dynastie de cardinaux en Alsace au XVIIIe siècle* by Claude Muller, *Louis de Rohan: le cardinal 'collier'* by Eric de Haynin and *Mémoires* by Abbé Georgel.

24   'their most elevated rank': quoted in Haynin, p.15.

25   'brat in red heels': quoted in Haynin, p.29.

25   'that one might encounter': quoted in Boulaire, p.186.

26   'his tastes and his friendships': *Mémoires (inedits) de l'Abbé Morellet*, vol. 1, p.26.

26   'Bite'em': Letter from Voltaire to Marmontel, 10 October 1777.

26   'as it's possible to be': quoted in Haynin, p.32.

27   'comparable to his': *Mémoires de Marmontel* (Paris, 1857), p.237.

27   'arms against religion': quoted in Haynin, p.131.

27   'never against my adversary': quoted in *The Republic of Letters: A Cultural History of the French Enlightenment* by Dena Goodman, p.109.

28   'a dashing rogue': quoted in Haynin, p.44.

28   petals before her: The description of Marie Antoinette's entrance into Strasbourg is taken from *Mémoires de la Baronne d'Oberkirch sur la cour de Louis XVI et la société française avant 1789* (Mercure de France, 2000), p.43ff.

28   'than a coadjutor': CMA, Marie Antoinette to Maria Theresa, 21 June 1771.

29   'as odd as it is improper': D'Arneth and Geffroy, Mercy-Argenteau to Maria Theresa, 24 July 1771.

30   four undersecretaries: Georgel, vol. 1, pp. 218–19.

30   'other countries': quoted in *Vienna: Legend and Reality* by Ilsa Barea, p.63.

30 'rebounded onto my daughter': D'Arneth and Geffroy, Maria Theresa to Mercy-Argenteau, 8 July 1771.

31 'I will never forget . . . air of composure . . . attentiveness and respect': op. cit., Maria Theresa to Mercy-Argenteau, 10 February 1772.

31 'presumption and flippancy': op. cit., Maria Theresa to Mercy-Argenteau, 1 March 1772.

31 'without morals': op. cit., Maria Theresa to Mercy-Argenteau, 18 March 1772.

31 'this wicked genius': op. cit., Maria Theresa to Mercy-Argenteau, 1 September 1772.

32 'scrupulous decency': Georgel, vol. 1, pp. 229–30.

32 'in the imperial vault': quoted in *Maria Theresa* by Edward Crankshaw, p.298.

33 'of Monsieur Durand': 'Correspondance entre le duc d'Aiguillon et le prince-coadjuteur Louis de Rohan', *Revue d'Alsace*, vols 54–58 (1903–7), Rohan to d'Aiguillon, 6 February 1772.

33 'steadfastness nor money': quoted in Muller, p.329.

33 'warm towards the Poles': Rohan to d'Aiguillon, 6 February 1772.

33 'any rumour that spreads': quoted in Haynin, p.62.

33 'the fate of Poland': d'Aiguillon to Rohan, 27 April 1772.

33 'sudden turn of events': quoted in Muller, p.330.

34 'third partitioning power': Georgel, vol. 1, p.254.

34 'to persecute me!': D'Arneth and Geffroy, Mercy-Argenteau to Maria Theresa, 9 January 1774.

35 'swarthy and swollen': the duc de Croÿ, quoted in *Louis XV* by Michel Antoine, pp. 991–2.

35 'for some time now': D'Arneth and Geffroy, Maria Theresa to Mercy-Argenteau, 16 July 1774.

35 'abbey in compensation': op. cit., Mercy-Argenteau to Maria Theresa, 15 August 1774.

35 'no longer speaks to him': ibid.

36 'succeed with her': *Mémoires du Baron Besenval sur la cour de France* (Paris, 1987), p.377.

37 'with regret': Georgel, vol. 2, p.19.

37 sacrifice to the Lord: quoted in Boulaire, p.205.

38 collection of Chinese porcelain: see *Le goût chinois du cardinal Louis de Rohan*, edited by Étienne Martin.

3. Faith, Hope and Charity

39   a more suitable person than Rohan: This chapter draws on the memoirs used in the first chapter, Georgel's memoir and the trial records, which are found in AN X2B/1417.

40   'my support, my life': LJSRV I, p.194.

40   'raze the written troubles in her brain': op. cit., p.197.

41   sounded comfortable: for *chambres garnies*, see the chapter on the subject in Mercier, vol. 1, pp. 129–31.

41   hived off in the chateau: the description of Versailles draws on, among other works, *The Culture of Power and the Power of Culture: Old Regime Europe 1660–1789* by Tim Blanning, *Daily Life at Versailles in the Seventeenth and Eighteenth Centuries* and *Versailles, Ville Royale*, both by Jacques Levron, *Derrière la façade: vivre au château de Versailles au XVIIIe siècle* by William Ritchey Newton, *Quand les rois régenait a Versailles* by Daniel Meyer and *Versailles: A Biography of a Palace* by Tony Spawforth.

41   'an architectural monster . . . a large head': quoted in Spawforth, p.12.

42   'This inner disorganization' . . . 'his own person': quoted in *Daily Life at Versailles*, Levron, p.199.

42   'as soon as possible': quoted in *The Culture of Power*, Blanning, p.417.

43   'and is tasteless': quoted in Solnon, p.451.

43   horse and carriage: see op. cit., p.449.

43   'and of ministers': see 'La Galerie de Versailles' in Mercier, vol. 1, pp. 945–52.

43   'in a particular manner': LJSRV I, p.225.

43   'she had not sought': MJ I, p.16.

44   'and in a carriage': MCB, p.28.

44   The Hôtel: the description of the Hôtel de Rohan-Strasbourg is taken from *Les Hôtels de Soubise et de Rohan-Strasbourg* by Philippe Béchu and Christian Taillard.

45   'striking beauty' . . . 'on her lips': Georgel, vol. 2, p.35.

46   'dare all': MHV, p.11.

46   'one does with a lawyer': MCB, p.30.

47   'passions was frightening': op. cit., p.49.

47   still taken an interest: AN X2B/1417/10/Planta.

47   haunch of venison: AN X2B/1417/86/10.

47   80,000 livres: 'Interrogation with Jeanne', Campardon, p.276.

47 when Jeanne defaulted: 'Interrogation with Rohan', Campardon, p.245; Requête Rohan, pp. 23–44; Mémoire Rohan, pp. 9, 12.

47 explanation for his actions: AN X2B/1417/86/7.

47 regular weekly stipend: AN X2B/1417/54/Loth. Madame Colson, who lived with the La Mottes and was Loth's avowed source, contradicted the claim in her own testimony (AN X2B/1417/54/Colson).

48 down the stairs: Mémoire Rohan, p.14.

48 'people for burning': 'Le Marais', Mercier, vol, 1, p.220.

48 Jeanne regularly pawned . . . curtains in pawn: BHVP MS691/152–3

48 'sleeping on straw': quoted in *The Diamond Necklace* by Frantz Funck-Brentano, p.110.

49 October 1783 found them . . . lentils and haricot beans: Mémoire Rohan, p. 11; BHVP MS691/152.

49 'was bled five times': BHVP MS691/153.

49 'visit Madame': ibid.

49 nearly 800 livres: MJ I, p.14.

50 'and footmen': LJSRV I, p.259.

4. Antoinette against Versailles

51 royal dynasty's magnificence: This chapter is based on *Louis XVI* by John Hardman, *Marie Antoinette* by Antonia Fraser, *Louis XVI* by Evelyne Lever and *Marie Antoinette: la dernière reine* by Evelyne Lever.

51 'I am frightened of her': quoted in *Marie Antoinette*, Fraser, p.21.

51 'affability': quoted in op. cit., p.30.

51 'at her own Court': quoted in op. cit., p.112.

52–3 'mind of an accountant' . . . 'eight in the evening': *Louis XVI* by John Hardman, p.22.

53 'I do not need you': quoted in *Louis and Antoinette* by Vincent Cronin, p.77.

53 'vainly to hold together': quoted in *Preserving the Monarchy: The Comte de Vergennes, 1774–1787* by Munro Price, p.13.

54 'fall on me': quoted in *Louis and Antoinette*, Cronin, p.70.

54 'that's a bother': see *Louis XVI*, Hardman, p.75.

54 'hunting and his metal-working': quoted in *Marie Antoinette*, Fraser, p.129.

55 'redoubled caresses': quoted in op. cit., p.80.

55 'and bids goodnight': quoted in op. cit., p.144.

55 'prudish': quoted in op. cit., p.102.

56 'repugnance for the whole subject': quoted in op. cit., p.117.

56 'towering rage' . . . 'away from the queen': the abbé de Veri, quoted in *Louis XVI*, Hardman, p.69.

56 'and a little childish': quoted in *Marie Antoinette*, Fraser, p.61.

56 'at Versailles today': quoted in *Marie Antoinette*, Fraser, p.91.

57 'tumbled off a donkey': quoted in *Louis and Antoinette*, Cronin, p.159.

57 'for their happiness': quoted in *Marie Antoinette*, Fraser, p.124.

59 'avidity or egotism': the comte de Tilly, quoted in *Marie Antoinette*, Fraser, p.120.

60 'people with such ease': quoted in *Marie Antoinette*, Fraser, p.97.

5. In My Lady's Chamber

62 like a felled sapling: BHVP MS691/153.

62 did not deter her: Rohan's testimony about the initial stages of Jeanne's deception is found in Campardon, p.207ff; other accounts are found in Georgel, vol. 2, p.39ff, HVJSR, p.52ff and MCB, p.48ff.

62 for 9,000 livres: BHVP MS691/160.

62 'vain': 'Interrogation with Villette', Campardon, p.408.

63 for voicing doubts: BHVP MS691/217.

63 'from doing evil': quoted in *The Diamond Necklace*, Funck-Brentano, p.123.

63 'before her mother and father': HVJSR, p.49.

63 'smooth and insinuating': MCB, p.35.

64 'his most beautiful days': Georgel, vol. 2, p.37.

64 Grand Duke Paul . . . her displeasure known: PLMA, p.176.

66 'with mirrors and panelling': the comte d'Hézecques, quoted in *Versailles aux dix-huitième siecle* by Pierre Nolhac, p.304.

66 'examining their worthiness': quoted in *La Vérité sur l'affaire du collier* by Louis Hastier, p.57.

66 'My cousin, the comtesse de Valois': Mémoire Rohan, p.28.

67 worth thousands of livres: AN X2B/1417/10/Regnier; BHVP MS691/159.

67 45,000 livres from the king: BHVP MS691/64.

67 to pay the landlord: ibid.

67 stepped off the coach: BHVP MS691/152.

67 sinecure for a friend: BHVP MS691/129.

68 'hear about every day . . . visibly altered': Georgel, vol. 2, p.40.

68 'Be discreet': op. cit, p.41.

68 nearby rue Saint-Anastase: BHVP MS691/156.

69 forging letters of recommendation: BN JdF 2088/79.

69 a repeat offender: for the story of Madame Cahouet de Villiers see MCB, p.33 and PLMA, p.130. There is a good account in *La Vérité sur l'affaire du collier*, Hastier, p.105ff.

69–70 'most familiar style' . . . 'regularity in the letters': PLMA, p.130.

70 rapprochement with the queen: for Madame Goupil, see PLMA, p.130.

71 'monster': Mémoire Rohan, p.18.

71 She predicted to Rohan . . . queen's valet: Georgel, vol. 2, pp. 63–4.

6. Notes on a Scandal

72 built on letters: see *The Structural Transformation of the Public Sphere* by Jurgen Habermas, p.48. Habermas claims that the eighteenth century was the 'century of the letter'. The sending and receiving of letters was an integral part in the creation of the private sphere, and therefore the cleavage between public and private through which modernity emerged.

74 'the outcomes that I desire': MJ 'Pièces Justificatives', Letter IX, p.26.

74 'on the earth's surface': op. cit, Letter XVIII, p.41.

74 'chained the lion . . . that I want to do': ibid.

74 'happiest of his life': op. cit., Letter II, p.8.

74 would not finish: MCB, p.170.

75 'guarantee its authenticity': *Les Liaisons Dangereuses* by Choderlos de Laclos (Penguin: London, 1961), p.17.

76 'dazzling': quoted in *Choderlos de Laclos* by Ronald C. Rosbottom, p.46.

76 'without morality': quoted in *Laclos ou le paradoxe* by René Pomeau, p.68.

76 'horrors and infamies': quoted in op. cit., p.4.

76 'feared, admired, celebrated': quoted ibid.

78 'her tyrant or her slave': *Les Liaisons Dangereuses*, Laclos, p.334.

79 'slightest resemblance to you': op. cit., p.177.

79 'joyful, at rest': op. cit, Letter 150, p.352.

79   'he will be pleased to hear': op. cit., p.252.

80   'your very humble servant': op. cit., Letter 121, p.287.

80   'I should be embarrassed': op. cit., p.160.

81   'some way of sustaining it': op. cit., Letter 67, p.145.

81   'lock away whatever I wish': op. cit., Letter 1, p.23.

81   'never writing letters': op. cit., Letter 81, p.186.

7. To Play the Queen

83   the gardens of the Palais-Royal: This chapter primarily draws on d'Oliva's depositions during the trial and her two trial briefs.

83   morality was tossed aside: See 'Palais-Royal' in Mercier, vol. 1, pp. 381–3.

84   'woo her': MGO I, p.12.

84   hard-working but poor family: For d'Oliva's early years, see MGO I, 9 and MGO II, p.51ff.

84   'satisfaction and joy' . . . 'at Court': MGO I: pp. 12–13

84–5 'You might be a bit surprised' . . . 'of the queen herself': op. cit., pp. 14–16.

86   'lively impatience' . . . 'smallest thing in the world': op. cit., p.17.

86   'you will meet there': op. cit., p.19.

87   'You will hand over the rose' . . . 'there you are': op. cit., pp. 19–20

87   'I foresee for you': Mémoire Rohan, p.19.

88   'her protection and benevolence': ibid.

88   'the past will be forgotten': ibid.

88   'quick, quick, go': MGO I, p.22.

88–9 'has just been done' . . . 'carry around with you': op. cit., pp. 22–3.

89   near anagram of 'Valois': see, for example, *The Diamond Necklace*, Funck-Brentano, p.147 and 'The Diamond Necklace Affair Revisited (1785–1786): The Case of the Missing Queen' by Sarah Maza in *Marie-Antoinette: Writings on the Body of the Queen*, edited by Dena Goodman, p.87.

89   unthinkingly thrown together: I am indebted to Caroline Weber's *Queen of Fashion* for the discussion about the semiotics of the *gaulle*.

90   'dressed like a serving-maid' . . . 'a chambermaid's dust-cloth': quoted in *Queen of Fashion*, Weber, p.161.

90   'most indecent position': quoted in *Versailles, côté jardins* by William Ritchey Newton, p.196.

90–1 'lot of criticism in Paris': D'Arneth and Geffroy, Mercy-Argenteau to Maria Theresa, 15 September 1779.

91 'in a bad novel': *Mémoires de Mademoiselle Bertin sur la Reine Marie Antoinette*, p.98.

92 'respected in a government': quoted in *Beaumarchais: A Biography* by Maurice Lever, pp. 209–10.

94 'The letter Malvolio finds': see *Twelfth Night*, Act II, Scene v.

8. Diamonds and Best Friends

96 'formal and grave': MGO I, p.24.

96 'drunk with joy': BHVP MS691/218; Mémoire Rohan, p.23.

97 'decisiveness and industry': quoted in Haynin, p.140.

97 'such a bankruptcy': quoted in op. cit., p.136.

97 'with great kindness': Castries, p.302.

98 sprucer than normal: BHVP MS691/159; AN X2B/1417/10/Regnier.

98 'You boasted' . . . 'to no one': BHVP MS691/161.

98 A consortium . . . in the scheme: BHVP MS691/154, 163.

99 On 8 September . . . returned to Paris: MCB, pp. 36–42.

99 'service in peacetime': op. cit., p.47.

100 'idle lawyers [and] tradesmen': HVJSR, p.49.

100 'easy for me' . . . 'social conventions': MCB, p.47.

100 Jeanne reacted . . . well-aimed book: NLM, p.87.

101 'sparkle of the stones': *Journal* by Marquis de Bombelles, 8 February 1783.

101 Madame du Barry: *Correspondance Secrète*, 24 August 1785.

101 'fan barnacled with rocks': PLMA, p.102.

102 'ships than jewels': op. cit., p.196.

102 'Madame I am ruined' . . . 'way again. Go': ibid.

103 Bassenge hoped that a friend of his: The account draws primarily on Rohan's testimony to the investigating magistrates, his trial brief, the depositions of Boehmer, Bassenge, Achet and Laporte, and two statements the jewellers gave to the queen before and after the cardinal was arrested. The jewellers' statements are recorded in Appendix VI of the Compte Rendu and the entry for 16 September 1785 in the diary of Siméon-Prosper Hardy respectively.

103 'such a heavy burden' . . . 'these sort of affairs': Hardy, 16 September 1785.

103 'to be useful': ibid.

104 'secret negotiation': Georgel, vol. 2, p.58.

104 de Planta was horrified: see AN X2B/1417/54/Planta.

105 'heartwarming news': AN X2B/1417/8/Achet.

105 'distinguished nobleman': Hardy, 16 September 1785.

105 offered to reward . . . mentioned together: ibid. and AN X2B/1417/54/Bassenge.

105 'item of great importance': AN X2B/1417/54/Boehmer.

105–6 'unique specimen' . . . 'arrangement of stones' . . . 'much is it?': AN X2B/1417/54/Bassenge.

106 'act of folly' . . . 'madness' . . . 'appear glamorous': ibid., but see also 'Interrogation with Rohan', Campardon, p.233, in which Rohan protests that his language was less forceful.

107 would be left unpaid: see AN X2B/1417/54/Valbonne and Grenier.

107 'will pay shortly': 'Interrogation with Rohan', Campardon, p.212.

107 'Monsieurs Boehmer and Bassenge': Réquete Rohan, p.8.

108 'her intentions to me': 'Interrogation with Rohan', Campardon, p.213.

108 'someone from the queen': op. cit., p.214.

109 'you thanked the queen?': op. cit., p.215.

109 'to deserve a gift': AN X2B/1417/8/Laporte.

110 'a portrait medallion': BHVP MS691/155.

9. The Greatest Man in Europe: An Interlude

111 a Jesuit agent: The details of Cagliostro's life come primarily from *The Seven Ordeals of Count Calgiostro* by Iain McCalman and *Cagliostro: A Biography* by Roberto Gervaso.

114 'Negro trumpeter': see *The Origins of Freemasonry* by Margaret C. Jacob, p.18.

114 'a couple of painters': *The Seven Ordeals*, McCalman, p.37.

114 'who ever lived': quoted in op. cit, p.57.

115 'pure cult of natural religion': *Cagliostro*, Gervaso, p.72.

115 'arch of steel': quoted in *The Seven Ordeals*, McCalman, p.42.

115 'with a crepe veil': the Baronne d'Oberkirch in her *Mémoires*, p.117.

116 'distilled water': *The Seven Ordeals*, McCalman, p.86.

117 'to extend life': *Bad Medicine* by David Wootton, pp. 2–4.

118 'nor I of him': quoted in *Cagliostro*, Gervaso, p.116.

118 'religious awe' . . . 'worthy of mine' . . . 'his compass': quoted in *The Seven Ordeals*, McCalman, pp. 113–14.

118 'prolong life': AN F7 4445/2–4550/2, 'Interrogation with Cagliostro', 6–7.

119 Franz Anton Mesmer: for Mesmer, see *Mesmerism and the End of the Enlightenment in France* by Robert Darnton.

120 'and subjugated them': Georgel, vol. 2, p.45.

120 'now in Paris': quoted in *Cagliostro*, Gervaso, p.127.

120 'hand in glove': MCB, p.52.

120 'obscurity of one': quoted in *The Diamond Necklace*, Funck-Brentano, p.89.

120 'the size of Paris': MCB, p.54.

121 'you will see nothing': Mémoire Cagliostro, p.26.

122 'any demons' . . . 'Kiss it hard': 'Interrogation with Jeanne', Campardon, p.314. Jeanne is a partial source, but it is noticeable how, when the account is put to Cagliostro, he responded with squirm and bluster.

10. Follow the Money

123 On 8 February . . . refused to buy them: AN X2B/1417/54/Paris.

123 'What is your name?' . . . 'none of your business': AN X2B/1417/68/Vidal-Lainé.

123–4 'If you're not doing' . . . closed the case: AN X2B/1417/10/Bruginères.

124 70,000 livres-worth . . . forty-nine brilliants: Mémoire Rohan, pp. 46–7; BHVP MS691/168.

124 In the middle of April: the account of Nicolas's activities in London derives primarily from Mémoire Rohan and Requête Rohan.

124 6,000 livres: see AN X2B/1417/54/Perregaux.

124 'a most brilliant' . . . 'any other city': Jean-André Rouquet, quoted in *Brilliant Effects* by Marcia Pointon, p.29.

125 two French ministers: see BN JdF 2088/266.

126 one of Jeanne's friends: BHVP MS691/65.

126 jewellery case alone: Requête Rohan p.16.

126 200,000 livres each year: see *The French Nobility in the Eighteenth Century*, Chaussinand-Nogaret, p.57.

126 dour and peeling: 'Interrogation with Rohan', Campardon, p.219.

127 'position you deserve': Georgel, vol. 2, p.76.

127 as a man: 'Interrogation with Rohan', Campardon, p.263.

127–8 On 10 July . . . The jewellers grudgingly agreed: see op. cit., p.220 and AN X2B/1417/54/Bassenge.

128 'write it now': 'Interrogation with Rohan', Campardon, p.221.

128 'and our respect': BHVP MS691/302

128 'best of queens': Requête Rohan, p.11.

129 'mental aberration' . . . 'Saint-Cloud': PLMA, p.197.

129 'at your calmness': AN X2B/1417/54/Bassenge.

129 A second sickening flinch: 'Interrogation with Rohan', Campardon, p.221.

130 Sainte-James's business: this biographical sketch draws on *Claude Baudard de Sainte-James* by Denise Ozanam.

130 'payment of the necklace' . . . 'to serve': AN X2B/1417/54/ Sainte-James.

130 Rohan told the queen: the account of Rohan's activities and dealings with Jeanne from here until his arrest is primarily reconstructed from Requête Rohan, Mémoire Rohan and his interrogations.

131 Breteuil was a: details of Breteuil's life come from *The Fall of the French Monarchy: Louis XVI, Marie Antoinette and the Baron de Breteuil* by Munro Price.

131 'of my authority': Georgel, vol. 1, p.419.

132 'worry and despair': BHVP MS691/216; see also Mémoire Rohan, p.69.

133 more sinister interpretation: see Georgel, vol. 2, p.87ff.

133 'Are you sure'. . . 'someone tricked you?': op. cit., p.91.

133 during that month: see Bibliothèque municipale d'Orléans MS1421–3, 'Memoirs of Lenoir'.

11. Days of Reckoning

134 'has the necklace': 'Interrogation with Rohan', Campardon, p.221.

134 'I'm tricked': op. cit., p.222.

134–5 'The queen does not' . . . 'do it for you': 'Interrogation with Cagliostro', Campardon, p.342.

135 'of your suspicions': Georgel, vol. 2, p.92.

135 Jeanne scrabbled . . . nest eggs: AN X2B/1417/54/Loth; BHVP MS691/55.

136 Rohan had known . . . another two months: AN X2B/1417/10/ Boehmer; AN X2B/1417/54/Bassenge.

136 The cardinal's confrontation . . . had arrived: Mémoire Rohan, p.73ff; BHVP MS691/65 and 157.

136–7 Jeanne asked Bassenge . . . 'He can pay you': AN X2B/1417/8/Bassenge; AN X2B/1417/54/Bassenge.

137–8 'But the answer' . . . 'or the minister': PMLA, pp. 197–8

139 'in her name': Castries, p.296.

140 and the queen: AN X2B/1417/54/Serpaud.

140 Rohan himself . . . granted the chance: 'Interrogation with Rohan', Campardon, p.272.

141 'to me like this?': Georgel, vol. 2, p.97.

142 'expedite the rest': Mémoire Cagliostro, p.29.

142 'Don't worry' . . . 'not completely true': AN X2B/1417/54/Serpaud.

12. 'I Will Pay for Everything'

143 Only Nicolas . . . unknown party: AN X2B/1417/54/Bassenge.

143 'will not see him': PLMA, p.198.

143 about her debt: AN X2B/1417/54/Sainte-James.

144 'It was of' . . . 'lent Boehmer money': PLMA, p.198.

144 'lost some diamonds': BHVP MS691/33.

144 'business to light': PLMA, p.199; see also Castries, p.296, who confirms this encounter.

145 'shall know it': PLMA, p.199.

145 a written statement: see Compte Rendu, 'Pièces Justificatives', p.18ff.

145 found at home . . . Rohan's culpability: see Castries, p.297.

145 'Have you seen' . . . 'What's it to you?': Mercier, 'La Galerie de Versailles', vol. 1, p.945.

146–8 'It is true, sire'. . . 'arrest the cardinal': This exchange is reconstructed from the four sources mentioned above: Castries, pp. 297–8; de Crosne's account is found in *Mémoires tirés des archives de la police de Paris* by Jacques Peuchet, vol. 3, pp. 158–61; Rivière's account is in the Archives d'Aube, EE 1623; Holstein's account is in *Corréspondance diplomatique du Baron de Staël-Holstein et du Baron Brinkman*, edited by L. Leouzon le Duc (Paris, 1881), pp. 21–3.

13. Arresting Developments

149 to Bar-sur-Aube: see AN X2B/1417/68/Texier. The account of Jeanne's time in Bar draws primarily on MCB, p.60ff. The description

of Jeanne's house is based on the inventory of her assets taken by the authorities after her arrest and found in AN X2B/1417/111.

150 'out of the window': MCB, p.61.

150–2 'princess of the church' . . . burnt paper and wax: op. cit., pp. 68–72.

153 'Take me to her room': AAE MDF 1399/182.

153 Once the baron: the account of Rohan's actions until he is taken to the Bastille are drawn from Georgel, vol. 2, p.101ff and Hardy, 17 August 1785.

154 'other this evening' . . . 'his enemy' . . . 'a serene countenance': Georgel, vol. 2, p.108.

154 'I must arrest him': op. cit., p.110.

154 ministerial committee: see Castries, p.298ff.

155 'is excessive proof' . . . 'yet seen': *Louis XVI and the comte de Vergennes: correspondence 1774–1787*, edited by John Hardman and Munro Price, Louis XVI to Vergennes, 16 August 1785.

155 still cheerful: see *Mémoires Secrets*, 17 August 1785.

155 'horrors of tyranny': quoted in *Lettres de Cachet and Social Control* by Brian E. Strayer, p.xii.

155 'greatest part of the nation': *Des Lettres de cachet et des prisons d'état* by the marquis de Mirabeau (Hamburg, 1782), p.208.

156 of the Enlightenment: the picture of the Bastille is based on *The Bastille: A History of a Symbol of Despotism and Freedom* by Hans-Jürgen Lüsebrink & Rolf Reichardt and *Citizens* by Simon Schama.

156 'best Moka coffee': quoted in *Citizens*, Schama, p.392.

157 'more cruel than death': *Mémoires sur le Bastille et sur le détention de M Linguet, écrit par lui-même* (London, 1783), p.67.

157 'you an order': *Mémoires Secrets*, 1 September 1785.

157 'as friends': Castries, p.301ff. The rest of the interview with Vergennes and Castries is taken from this source.

14. Hotel Bastille

159 'we will take' . . . 'distinguish them': LJSRV I, p.398.

159 The pair interrogated: the transcript of Jeanne's Interrogation is contained in AN K162/14/2.

159 'reaching the courts': AN K162/14/2/5.

159–60 'great man' . . . 'god' . . . 'to have done': AN K162/14/2/7-9.

160 'appeared suspect': Bastille MS12457/27.

160 'through medicine': AN F7/4445/2–4550/2, 'Interrogation with Cagliostro', 1.

160 age of eighteen: AN F7/4445/2–4550/2, 'Interrogation with Cagliostro', 7. The initial set of interrogations with witnesses are contained in AN F7/4445/2–4550/2.

161 'eyes of everyone': D'Arneth and Flammermont, vol. 1, Marie Antoinette to Joseph II, 22 August 1785.

161 'in her hand': ibid.

161 'I am accused': the account of this meeting is taken from Castries, pp. 303–4.

162 'confound that woman': ibid.

162 'rebuke her': Georgel, vol. 2, p.122.

164 'mercy of the king': op. cit., p.126.

164 'justice and goodwill': BN JdF 2088/36.

164 'being discovered': D'Arneth and Flammermont, vol. 1, Marie Antoinette to Joseph II, 19 September 1785.

164 'one of his subjects': Georgel, vol. 2, p.129.

166 to a secular tribunal: for the papal reaction to the arrest see AAE CP Rome/901–3.

166 theft of the necklace: Harger and Biln's report is found in BHVP MS713/143–7.

15. Witness Protection

167 'unknown to the queen' . . . 'La Mothe de Valois': Compte Rendu, 'Pieces Justificatives', pp. 3–5.

167 'to be destroyed': ibid.

167 on 6 September: BN JdF 2088/42.

168 'offices of state': MCB, p.45.

168 'sale of the necklace': BN JdF 2088/12.

168 'accomplices in the crime' . . . 'declaration he made': for the changing versions, see BN JdF 2088/15–30.

169 the king's largesse: on Titon, see La Prostitution et La Police des Moeurs au XVIIIe Siecle by Erica-Marie Benabou, p.387.

169 'morals even looser': Georgel, vol. 2, p.131.

169 'as a sentinel': the account of Beugnot's worries and de Crosne's attempt to recruit him for Jeanne's lawyer derives from MCB, pp. 76–81.

170 'imbecile': AAE CP Angleterre 556/163.

170–1 'Neither myself . . . bring a case': BHVP MS691/31–2.

171 On 3 November: BHVP MS691/45.

171 'imperious harshness': Georgel, vol. 2, p.115.

171 renewed vigour: on Georgel's endeavours, see Georgel, vol. 2, p.116ff. Much of his work is confirmed by the Dossier Target (BHVP MS691).

171 'de Valois': BHVP MS691/150.

172 passed on copies to Georgel: BHVP MS691/187.

172 Most pressing . . . all creditors: Georgel, vol. 2, p.143ff.

172 Not long after: on Loth and Georgel, see op. cit., p.148ff.

172 Loth was . . . dressing in mufti: on Loth, see AN X2B 1417/54/Loth and MCB, p.53. On his extracurricular activities see BN JdF 2088/371.

173 'an unattractive figure': AAE CP Autriche 350/289.

174 Georgel, now informed: on Carbonnières in London, see Georgel, vol. 2, pp. 167–8, AAE CP Angleterre 554/158, 170 and 333, and AAE MDF 1399/248.

174 A crucial breakthrough: on d'Oliva's capture, see AAE MDF 1399/228–89.

174 'take secret measures . . . have them arrested': quoted in *L'affaire du collier*, Lever, p.177.

175 'mischievous or wicked': AAE MDF 1399/278.

16. Tired and Emotional

176 'other matter': BN JdF 2088/204.

176 at the Palais de Justice: testimonies are recorded in AN X2B/1417/54 and AN X2B/1417/68.

176 that sum of money: Loth's testimony is AN X2B/1417/54/Loth.

176 rather than cash: see AN X2B/1417/54/Laporte and AN X2B/1417/54/Bassenge.

177 'what this means': AN X2B/1417/54/D'Oliva.

177 'assured [him] he' . . . 'had been intended': AN X2B/1417/54/Sainte-James.

177 'no useful purpose': AAE CP Rome 901/373.

177 'pains me': Castries, p.309.

178 She obtained a portrait: PLMA, p.203.

178 'a lot of effort': BN JdF 2088/196.

178 'would not be right': PLMA, p.203.

178 'have other consequences': d'Arneth and Flammermont, Marie Antoinette to Joseph II, 27 December 1785.

178 Laurencel was invariably: Laurencel's memorandum, from which all these quotations are taken, is found in BN JdF 2088/66–9.

179 'lost man': Georgel, vol. 2, pp. 151–2.

179 On 14 December: AN X2B/1417/69; Hardy, 14 December 1785.

180 'doubtless clear him': BHVP MS691/294–5.

180 *Decrets de prise de corps*: AN X2B/1417/62; Hardy, 15 December 1785.

180 'forty-eight people?': Castries, p.309.

180 'with weary watching': LJSRV I, p.412.

180 in the cell below: see AN X2B/1417/10/Planta. On Pelleport, see *The Devil in the Holy Water, or the Art of Slander from Louis XIV to Napoleon* by Robert Darnton, pp.167–76.

181 'my glory, my valour': AN X2B/1417/17/6; LJSRV I, p.446.

181 'and was silent': LJSRV I, p.412.

181 On one occasion: op. cit., p.442.

181 'and painful succession': op. cit., p.435ff.

181 on suicide watch: Bastille, MS12457/12.

182 each day: Castries, p.321. The account of Rohan in the Bastille derives primarily from Georgel, vol. 2, p.134ff.

182 oysters and champagne: see *The Diamond Necklace*, Funck-Brentano, p.244.

182 and his doctor: Bastille MS12457/59.

182 A severe attack of asthma . . . exquisite pain: see Hardy, 12 October 1785, 4 November 1785, 24 November 1785 and BHVP MS691/4–5.

182 contradictions in evidence: see BHVP MS691/3–29.

182 smothering depression: BHVP MS691/184.

183 'blood off the tracks': BHVP MS691/6.

183 In normal circumstances . . . die in prison BN JdF 2088/46; AN X2B/1417/82; Hardy, 1 January 1786.

183 Georgel had been: Georgel, vol. 2, p.179.

17. Nicolas Abroad: A Picaresque

184 him in Scotland: Hardy, 4 December 1785.

184 with Barbary pirates: HVJSR, p.67.

184 in the Low Countries: AAE MDF 1399/139.

184 embark for India: CP Autriche 350/248.

184 the cardinal's defence: see Georgel, vol. 2, p.208.

184 With his usual: see HJSRV, p.66 and Mémoire Rohan, p.17.

184–5 'Madame de La Motte' . . . 'for a quick escape': MCB, p.172.

185 He made over . . . look after them: AAE MDF 1399/182; BN Jdf 2088/102.

185 Having told his servants: the only accounts of Nicolas's spell in Britain are his own, which are to be found in NLM, p.67ff and MJ II, p.91ff.

186 an arrest warrant: AAE CP Angleterre 554/171.

186 'was most touching' . . . 'business': NLM, p.81.

18. Questions, Questions

188 delayed the interrogations: Hardy, 1 January 1786.

188 'What is your name' . . . 'Boehmer and Bassenge?': 'Interrogation with Rohan', Campardon, p.206. The full transcripts of all the suspects' interrogations are given in the 'Pièces Justificatives' to *Marie-Antoinette et le procès de collier* by Emile Campardon.

189 during the interrogation: BN JdF 2088/72–3.

189 'want to trick me': 'Interrogation with Rohan', Campardon, p.208.

189 'be the queen in Versailles': op. cit., p.209.

189 'the shape of the letters': op. cit., p.208.

189 'in their interests': op. cit., pp. 212–13.

189 'all these facts': op. cit., p.209.

189 'with which I acted': op. cit., p.22.

190 'the august name of the queen': op. cit., pp. 240–1.

191 'as I had done': op. cit., pp. 241–2.

191 'police and the public': BHVP MS691/187.

191 'to ease them': 'Interrogation with Jeanne de La Motte', Campardon, p.274.

191 'tide you over': op. cit., p.276.

191 'made to offer them': op. cit., p.279.

191 'Is it not true' . . . 'horrific': op. cit., pp. 277–8.

192 'I did not know': op. cit., p.283.

192 'What you suggest is fantasy' . . . 'with so many lies and horrors': op. cit., p.289.

193 'boor of a Frenchman': quoted in 'Vraisemblance et Motivation' in *Figures II* by Gérard Genette, p.73. The discussion here draws on

Genette's essay and 'Prose Fiction: France' by English Showalter in *The Cambridge History of Literary Criticism: Volume IV – The Eighteenth Century*, edited by H. B. Nisbet and Claude Rawson.

193 'a privilege of reality': quoted in *Figures II*, Genette, p.74.

193 'fawned upon, rewarded': quoted in 'Prose Fiction: France', Showalter, p.225.

194 'most stringent safeguards': 'Interrogation with Jeanne de La Motte', Campardon, p.304.

194 'madder and madder': op. cit., p.292.

194 'of not recognising the queen': op. cit., p.290.

194 'reality effect': see 'The Reality Effect' in *The Rustle of Language* by Roland Barthes, pp. 141–8.

195 'was very dirty': 'Interrogation with Jeanne de La Motte', Campardon, p.288.

195 'I'm very sorry' . . . 'such affairs': op. cit., p.296.

195 'You are being' . . . 'could go awry': op. cit., p.301.

195 'I am an old man': op. cit., p.321.

196 'utterly extraordinary man': op. cit., p.313.

196 'a meeting with the queen': op. cit., p.280.

196 'Marie Antoinette de France': op. cit., p.302.

196 'what they are worth': op. cit., p.307.

196 Loth, her traitorous . . . 50,000 écus cash: op. cit., pp. 285–6; op. cit., p.321.

196 'extraordinary' . . . 'exact truth': op. cit., p.318.

197–8 'It was the second of August' . . . 'deny it': op. cit., pp. 326–7.

199 'normal for a prince's house': 'Interrogation with Cagliostro', Campardon, p.344.

200 'fruit of her intrigues': 'Interrogation with Rohan', Campardon, p.270.

19. Cheek to Cheek, Toe to Toe

201 before an ecclesiastical court: AAE CP Rome 902/104.

201 'competent tribunal': Compte Rendu, p.52ff. The Compte Rendu, though clearly favourable to Rohan, gives an exhaustive account of the judges' deliberations.

202 'in his favour': BHVP MS691/134.

202 'my good sense': BHVP MS691/192.

202 'needs to employ': BHVP MS691/125–6.

202 'proactive answers': ibid.

202 'catechism' . . . 'led by impulse': ibid.

203 Montagne-au-Perche in Normandy: on Georgel's exile see Georgel, vol. 2, p.189ff and Hardy, 13 March 1786.

203 'of me his prisoner': King James Bible, 2 Timothy, 1:8.

203 'king in his own chapel': BHVP MS691/125–6.

203 'my modest courage': BHVP MS691/201.

203–4 'I ask you' . . . 'very weak head': AN X2B/1417/8/Bassenge.

204 'them to declare': Georgel, vol. 2, p.67.

204 The confrontations were: the account of the confrontations derives in the main from the transcripts in the trial dossier in the Archives nationales. Jeanne's confrontations with the witnesses are in X2B/1417/10 and with the accused in X2B/1417/86. Rohan's confrontations with the witnesses are X2B/1417/84 and with Jeanne in X2B/1417/17.

205 handed over to Dupuis: *Mémoires Secrets*, 20 March 1786.

205 'hide her troubles': BHVP MS691/230.

205 'of an innocent soul': Georgel, vol. 2, p.186.

205 of Nicolas's valet: Mémoire Rohan, p.50.

205 She harangued . . . dress her forcibly: Georgel, vol. 2, p.186ff; *Gazette de Leyde*, 14 April 1786; Hardy, 26 March 1786.

205 tears out of d'Oliva: Georgel, vol. 2, p.187.

205–6 'an honest woman' . . . 'of your intrigues': MGO II, p.15.

206 to her objections: AN X2B/1417/10/Jeanne's confrontation with Rosalie Brissault.

206 'would be refuted': AN X2B/1417/17/44.

206 'respond to his desires': AN X2B/1417/10/Jeanne's confrontation with the baron de Planta.

206 'absolutely false': ibid.

206 'hidden behind smiles': Georgel, vol. 2, p.188.

206 in ailing health: Bastille: MS12457/67–8.

206 'for my correspondence': BHVP MS691/26.

207 'falsehood of my adversaries': BHVP MS691/221–4.

207 'Were the letters' . . . 'believe they were': AN X2B/1417/84/Rohan's confrontation with d'Oliva.

207 'maintain what I said': AN X2B/1417/84/Rohan's confrontation with Sainte-James.

207 'make it fail': quoted in *The Diamond Necklace*, Funck-Brentano, pp. 337–8.

207 'he will not be stubborn': BHVP MS691/197.

208 'similar to Villette's handwriting': AN X2B/1417/84/Rohan's confrontation with Loth.

20. An Extraordinary Rendition

209 Geneva, a warm evening: the account of Villette's arrest derives from the ambassadorial reports in AAE CP Genève/95.

209 'acts of libertinage': AAE CP Genève/95/394.

209 'incapable of resting' . . . 'a lost man': AAE CP Genève/95/408.

210 'establish trust': AAE CP Genève/95/405.

210 choked up confessions: see AN X2B/1417/68/Quidor.

210 through the city: Hardy, 3 April 1786.

210 as a witness: see AN X2B/1417/68/Villette.

210 interrogation by Titon: AN X2B/1417/20; BN JdF 2089/13.

210–11 'Do you know' . . . 'moment of madness': 'Interrogation with Villette', Campardon, p.363.

211–12 'Do you recognise' . . . 'profit from it': op. cit., pp. 368–9.

212 the matter was possible: AN X2B/1417/9/Recollement of Villette.

212 'Did the cardinal' . . . 'in his position': 'Interrogation with Villette', Campardon, p.375.

212 'travelling to Italy': op. cit., p.380.

212 'an opportunist' . . . 'compromise him': AN X2B/1417/14/ Confrontation between Cagliostro and Jeanne.

213 her own eye: MJ II, p.87.

213 'make things plausible': AN X2B/1417/86/8.

213 'did so much good': AN X2B/1417/86/9.

213 'one must speak the truth': BHVP MS691/265.

214 'Maurepas and my family': quoted in *L'affaire du collier* by Evelyne Lever, p.246.

214 'will be false again': AN X2B/1417/17/5.

214 'on the spot': AN X2B/1417/86/35.

214 'my only wrong': AN X2B/1417/17/5.

214 'harmed her irreparably': AN X2B/1417/86/40.

215 'It's not' . . . 'is a falsehood': AN X2B/1417/86/25.

215 'sale of the diamonds': quoted in *L'affaire du collier*, Lever, p.243.

215 'the most cruel' . . . 'in my defence': AN X2B/1417/86/32.

215 'cabal of the cardinal' . . . 'blacker crimes': AN X2B/1417/86/15.

216 'absolve her husband': BHVP MS691/236.

216 'You are right' . . . 'contempt for you': AN X2B/1417/86/46.

216 mask his handwriting: AN X2B/1417/93.

216 'and the signature': AN X2B/1417/92.

216 naked and drooling: see *Despatches from Paris, 1784–1790*, edited by Oscar Browning, vol. 1, p.107.

216 'and consulting him': AN X2B/1417/18/4.

217 'I am obliged' . . . 'misunderstood' . . . 'I did not' . . . 'against me': AN X2B/1417/86/49.

217 'me from telling': ibid.

217 'to say that I was there': AN X2B/1417/18/3.

218 'a married couple': AN X2B/1417/17/9.

218 'their affairs': AN X2B/1417/17/23.

218 'infernal audacity': AN X2B/1417/97/2.

218 'whitened your face': AN X2B/1417/17/16.

218 'with the queen': AN X2B/1417/17/11.

218 'It is unbelievable' . . . 'lover of success': AN X2B/1417/17/13.

218–19 'author of it' . . . 'was tricked': ibid.

219 'to be found': AN X2B/1417/17/25.

219 'In all of your testimony' . . . 'plan in motion': AN X2B/1417/97/4.

219–20 'duty of man' . . . 'celestial discourse': BHVP MS691/240.

21. The Truth Will Out

221 'that they met': AN X2B/1417/17/36.

221 'such a meeting': AN X2B/1417/17/37.

221 'misdeeds of Rohan': AN X2B/1417/17/38.

221 'she has said': AN X2B/1417/17/36.

222 'sustain her case': AN X2B/1417/17/42.

222 'in this state': BHVP MS691/235.

222 'and the signature': AN X2B/1417/17/56.

222 'than for myself': AN X2B/1417/17/64.

223 'its own neck': BHVP MS691/228.

223 'certain details': Compte Rendu, p.101.

223 'cause of his blindness' . . . 'legally established': 'Interrogation with Villette', Campardon, pp. 383–8.

223 'has been demonstrated': AN X2B/1417/86/55.

224 'compromise the queen': AN X2B/1417/86/53.

224 'you understand' . . . 'diminish them': AN X2B/1417/86/52.

224 'have the chance': AN X2B/1417/86/56.

224 'to blame me': AN X2B/1417/17/97.

225 'a moment's silence': BHVP MS691/236.

225 barely recognised him: *Mémoires Secrets*, 16 January 1786.

225 'might be taken': BHVP MS691/5.

225 'unsupportable': BHVP MS691/228.

225 'upon my sympathy': BHVP MS691/225.

226 His stomach cramps . . . eye leaked pus: Georgel, vol. 2, p.195.

226 'which I cause them': BN JdF 2088/84.

226 'to their [Villette and Jeanne's] lot': BHVP MS691/228.

226 'to face Titon': BHVP MS691/232.

226 'always sad?': BHVP MS691/231.

226 'of the queen?': BHVP MS691/230.

226 drown herself: *Mémoires Secrets*, 30 April 1786.

226 'her pretty neck': *Correspondance Secrète*, 8 May 1786.

226 On 22 May: the account of the hearing draws primarily on the Compte Rendu, p.68ff, the diary entries of Siméon-Prosper Hardy for the period and precis of private deliberations of the judges which were smuggled to Rohan's legal team and are preserved in the Dossier Target.

227 'demand his recusal': quoted in *La Vérité sur l'affaire du collier*, Hastier, p.244.

227 'and her reputation': Georgel, vol. 2, p.175.

228 'he leant on his cane' . . . 'shedding tears': anonymous manuscript account in the British Library, Folio 707.g.26.

228 finished their questions: BHVP MS691/260.

228 'a single syllable': LJSRV II, p.98.

228 'surprised at nothing': BHVP MS691/261.

228 'ask me that': AAE MDF 1400/213.

228 'chair in her apartment': *Mémoires Secrets*, 17 June 1786.

228 'not to offend the queen': quoted in *The Diamond Necklace*, Funck-Brentano, p.303.

229 'his birth and rank': Compte Rendu, p.117.

229 as he entered: British Library, Folio 707.g.26.

229 returned the gesture: AAE MDF 1400/213.

229 according to one judge: see *The Diamond Necklace*, Funck-Brentano, p.305.

229 Greek and Italian: AAE MDF 1400/214.

22. In the Gossip Factory

230 'the great questions': AAE CP Rome 901/210.

230 *with that one*': 'Monsieur le Public' in Mercier, vol. 1, pp. 1473–4.

230 The public sphere: the discussion here inevitably takes as its starting point *The Structural Transformation of the Public Sphere* by Jurgen Habermas, and also draws on work by Robert Darnton and Sarah Maza on the relationship between literary production and public opinion; and *Lawyers and Citizens: The Making of a Political Elite in Old Régime France* by David A. Bell on the development of an ideology of liberty within the Parisian Bar.

230 Breteuil's clarion blast: the account of ebb and flow of rumour draws on the diaries of Siméon-Prosper Hardy and news-sheets, such as the *Gazette de Leyde*, the *Mémoires Secrets* and the *Correspondance Secrète*.

231 'to find partisans': *Correspondance Secrète*, 31 August 1785.

231 squandered the proceeds?: Hardy, 17 August 1785.

231 Thirty Years War?: op. cit., 24 August 1785.

231 'implicated in it': quoted in *Despatches from Paris*, Browning, vol. 1, p.71.

231 'accuse the queen': quoted in *The Diamond Necklace*, Funck-Brentano, p.247.

231 'so stupidly duped': AAE CP Autriche 350/120.

231 'herself seem pregnant': quoted in *L'affaire du collier*, Lever, p.158.

232 'published against her': *Souvenirs et Portraits* by the duc de Lévis (1815), pp. 157–8.

232 denouncing the queen: PMLA, p.202; Hardy, 10 September 1785.

232 'in actual criminality': AAE CP Autriche 350/252.

232 among his detractors: see *The Queen of Fashion*, Weber, p.159.

232 to lend colour: see *Brilliant Effects*, Pointon, p.152.

232 were also available: see *The Queen's Necklace*, Mossiker, p.439.

232 portrait of Jeanne: *General Evening Post*, 30 May 1786.

233 'greatly in [his] favour': quoted in *Despatches from Paris*, Browning, vol. 1, p.113.

233 'soap him clean' BHVP MS691/295.

233 'I'm a clown': BHVP MS691/297.

233 'false prophet': Mémoire Jeanne, p.4.

234 'rococo comedy': *Private Lives and Public Affairs*, Maza, p.204

234 'guilty of everything': ibid.

234 'in a hundred ways': op. cit., p.28.

234 'happened to want it': *Les Observations de P Tranquille sur le 1er mémoire de Mme la Comtesse de La Motte* (La Mecque, 1786), p.35, quoted in *The Diamond Necklace*, Funck-Brentano, p.274.

234 'the cardinal exceedingly': *Mémoires Secrets*, 28 November 1785.

234 'defence requires it': op. cit., 2 December 1785.

235 'intrigue and lust': Georgel, vol. 2, p.136.

235 avid crowds: *Mémoires Secrets*, 20 February 1786.

235 'under the Pharaoh's orders': *Correspondance Secrète*, 24 February 1786.

235 in the lions' den: quote in *L'affaire du collier*, Lever, p.190.

235 in his *mémoire*: see Mémoire Cagliostro, passim.

236 'emblem of this kindness': *Correspondance Secrète*, 17 April 1786.

236 on her release: *Mémoires Secrets*, 27 March 1786.

236 multiple readers: see *Private Lives and Public Affairs: The Causes Célèbres of Prerevolutionary France* by Sarah Maza, p.190.

236 *Thousand and One Nights*: *Mémoires Secrets*, 23 March 1786.

236 'enough of [Jeanne]': MGO I, p.7.

236 'to do things': op. cit., p.3.

236 'without support': op. cit., p.7.

237 'before eternal justice.': op. cit., p.38.

237 'danger of liaisons': op. cit., p.46.

237 run out the clock: Hardy, 3 March 1786.

237 in his own home: *Mémoires Secrets*, 2 February 1786.

238 'two terrible expressions': BHVP MS691/9.

238 'tell him immediately': BHVP MS691/23.

238 'overshadowed the work': Georgel, vol. 2, p.160.

239 'truth and lies': Mémoire Rohan, p.5.

239 'limits on illusion': op. cit., p.65.

239 'of mere mortals': quoted in *Queen of Fashion*, Weber, p.161.

239 'into simple individuals': *Mémoires de Mademoiselle Bertin sur la Reine Marie Antoinette*, p.131.

23. Judgement Day

241 At six o'clock: the Compte Rendu gives a very detailed account of the judicial debates about sentencing. Siméon-Prosper Hardy describes the aftermath.

241 'knowledge of the transaction': Compte Rendu, p.113.

241 'only falsehoods and lies': BN JdF 2088/26.

241 'magistrates share it': quoted in *The Diamond Necklace*, Funck-Brentano, pp. 301–2.

241 punitive damages: for Joly's conclusions, see AN X2B/1417/78.

242 'as Rétaux de Villette': BN JdF 2088/26.

242 cementing our own: Compte Rendu, p.130.

242 'from its principles': op. cit., p.131.

243 creatures of the queen: Castries, p.320.

243 'to this infamy': BN JdF 2089/36.

243 'led on by the La Mottes': Compte Rendu, p.120.

244 'Long live the *parlement*' . . . 'deserve this applause': Compte Rendu, p.154.

244 'an unjust judgement': quoted in *The Diamond Necklace*, Funck-Brentano, p.313.

245 'voted against [him]': d'Arneth and Flammermont, Mercy-Argenteau to Joseph II, 12 July 1786, 'Note sur l'arrêt du parlement de Paris'.

245 of the Court party: p.83.

245 'with their principles': PLMA, p.204.

245 for Rohan's conviction: Castries, p.320.

245 'where I'm going': quoted in *The Diamond Necklace*, Funck-Brentano, p.321.

246 'against authority': PLMA, p.204.

246 'torture my soul': quoted in *The Diamond Necklace*, Funck-Brentano, p.316.

246 'a terrible bang': quoted in *La Vérité sur l'affaire du collier*, Hastier, p.242.

246 'retain the mark': quoted in *The Diamond Necklace*, Funck-Brentano, p.240.

246–7 'The affair has' . . . 'such a commission': PLMA, p.204.

247 The following day: see Castries, p.321.

247 'Indecent joy': Georgel, vol. 2, p.207.

247 'very few people': AAE MDF 1400/217.

247 'underneath a lantern': *Mémoires Secrets*, 9 June 1786.

248 'covered in contempt': quoted in *L'affaire du collier*, Lever, p.290.

248 'three years later': Castries, p.322.

248 'to my house': BN JdF 2089/165.

248 'never to return!': *Morning Chronicle and London Advertiser*, 7 July 1786.

248 'an electrical shock': LJSRV II, p.121.

248 'destined for destruction': op. cit., p.124.

249 Doillot, her lawyer: see AN X2B/1417/122.

249 'enchanted the cardinal': Hardy, 21 June 1786.

249 'yelling wildly': HVJSR, p.72. The account of Jeanne's punishment comes from *Gazette d'un parisien sous la Révolution* by Nicholas Ruault, letter dated 31 June, Hardy, 21 June 1786 and the *Mémoires du Baron Besenval*, p.385.

249 'from these murderers': quoted in *The Diamond Necklace*, Funck-Brentano, p.334.

249 'be over soon': William Eden, quoted in *The Queen's Necklace*, Mossiker, p.484.

24. Catch Him if You Can: A Burlesque

251 guilty in absentia: the account of Nicolas's adventures derives from NLM, p.93ff, MJ I, p.102ff, and the papers contained in the Archives des affaires étrangères, series MDF 1400 and CP Angleterre 905.

252 'mud still further': quoted in *L'affaire du collier*, Lever, p.274.

252 'aren't you?': NLM, p.100.

252 'life and death': op. cit., p.104.

253 'friend': AAE MDF 1400/75.

254 'You are busy': MJ II, p.6.

254 'town is impractical': op. cit., p.8.

254 '[they would have hurled] him into the sea': MJ II, p.9.

255 'intelligence-gathering': AAE MDF 1400/159.

255 'great repugnance': AAE CP Angleterre 556/149.

255 'prey': AAE CP Angleterre 556/162.

255 'I'm an idiot': AAE MDF 1400/227.

256 'with false confidence': AAE CP Angleterre 556/227.

256 'you new benefits': AAE CP Angleterre 556/273.

256–7 'Our man is here' . . . 'to the queen': AAE CP Angleterre 556/275.

257 'He is a young man' . . . 'my departure': AAE CP Angleterre 556/283.

257 'partiality and prejudice': *Louis XVI and the comte de Vergennes: correspondence 1774–1787*, Hardman and Price, Vergennes to Louis XVI, 4 June 1786.

258 'Although you conducted' . . . 'spread in England': op. cit., Louis XVI to Vergennes, 4 June 1786.

25. Farewell, My Country

259 On the same day: the account of Cagliostro's subsequent career draws on *Cagliostro and Company* by Frantz Funck-Brentano, *Cagliostro: A Biography* by Roberto Gervaso, *The Seven Ordeals of Count Cagliostro* by Iain McCalman and *A King's Ransom: The Life of Charles Théveneau de Morande, Blackmailers, Scandalmonger and Master-Spy* by Simon Burrows.

259 'my country farewell!': 'Lettre au Peuple de France' (London, 1786), pp. 1–2

259 'his agents, his creatures': op. cit., p.2.

260 'received by envy': op. cit., pp. 3–4.

260 'injustice and death': op. cit., p.4.

260 'a public promenade': op. cit., pp. 4–5.

260 'balms, drugs, elixirs': quoted in *Cagliostro and Company*, Funck-Brentano, p.15.

260 'brought sedition nearer': quoted in op. cit., p.21.

261 'body of people': quoted in *The Seven Ordeals*, McCalman, p.143.

262 'queen's Bastille party': quoted in *A King's Ransom*, Burrows, p.162.

262 'friends among them': quoted in *The Seven Ordeals*, McCalman, p.158.

263 'out of your knowledge': quoted in *A King's Ransom*, Burrows, p.165.

263 'to a Cagliostro': quoted in op. cit., p.166.

263 'I wish to dispatch': quoted in *The Seven Ordeals*, McCalman, p.160.

263 'endure all evening': quoted in *A King's Ransom*, Burrows, pp. 166–7.

263 Rohan's retreat from: the account of Rohan's life after his acquittal draws primarily on *Les Rohans: 'roi ne puis, duc ne daigne, Rohan suis'* by Alain Boulaire, *Le Siècle de Rohan: une dynastie de cardinaux en Alsace au XVIIIe siècle* by Claude Muller, *Louis de Rohan: le cardinal 'collier'* by Eric de Haynin and *Cagliostro and Company* by Frantz Funck-Brentano.

264 'source of happiness': quoted in *Cagliostro and Company*, Funck-Brentano, pp. 231–2.

264 'as well as physically': quoted in *Le Siècle de Rohan*, Muller, p.412.

264 'to the other': quoted in op. cit., p.283.

265 'Alsace and France': quoted in *Louis de Rohan*, Haynin, p.270.

265 Alsace could no more: the account of the events in the French Revolution draws primarily on *The Great Nation* by Colin Jones and *The Oxford History of the French Revolution* by William Doyle.

266 'established and assured': quoted in *Oxford History*, Doyle, p.105.

26. Down and Out in Paris and London

268 after her branding: the account of Jeanne's life after her sentence is drawn from her two memoirs, *L'Evasion de madame de La Motte: un episode de l'affaire du collier* by Henry Légier Desgranges, *Cagliostro and Company* by Frantz Funck-Brentano, the relevant papers in the CP Angleterre series of the Archives des affaires étrangères and her personal papers held in the Archives nationales F7/4445/2–4550/2.

268 'slow and prolonged death': LJSRV II, p.154.

268 'live in peace here': quoted in *L'Evasion de madame de La Motte*, Légier Desgranges, p.117.

268 'they are buried': quoted in op. cit., p.118.

268 'horror of her fate': *Mémoires* of the princesse de Lamballe, quoted in *Cagliostro and Company*, Funck-Brentano, p.95.

269 'in the Hospital': quoted in *L'Evasion de madame de La Motte*, Légier Desgranges, p.88.

269 'an audience with you': *Morning Chronicle and London Advertiser*, 26 August 1786.

269 'in her tears': quoted in *Cagliostro and Company*, Funck-Brentano, p.97.

269 'in plenty of water': quoted in op. cit., pp. 97–8.

270 'had been his daughter': LJSRV II, p.149.

270 '*The Imitation of Christ*': quoted in *Cagliostro and Company*, Funck-Brentano, p.99.

270 'gives expression to': quoted in op. cit., p.98.

270 'of her confinement': quoted in *Cagliostro and Company*, Funck-Brentano, pp. 101–2.

270 'changing your condition': LJSRV II, p.189.

271 'has your heart': quoted in *Cagliostro and Company*, Funck-Brentano, p.110.

271 'in charge of her': BN JdF 2089/210.

272 'this mysterious intrigue': *Morning Star*, 13 December 1786.

272 'I believe reasonable': AAE CP Angleterre 559/22.

272 'nothing is more foolish'. . . 'in the street': AAE CP Angleterre 559/166–7.

272 'for their escape': BN JdF 2089/205–6.

273 'in good humour': quoted in *Cagliostro and Company*, Funck-Brentano, pp. 115–16.

273 'helpless to the floor': quoted in op. cit., p.116.

274 'about this writing': quoted in *Blackmail, Scandal, and Revolution: London's French Libellistes, 1758–92* by Simon Burrows, p.134.

274 'to the queen': quoted in *Calonne: financier, réformateur, contre-révolutionnaire, 1734–1802* by Robert Lacour-Gayet, p.265

274 'you have been marked': *Julie philosophe, ou le bon patriot*, vol. 2, p.19.

275 'did not concern him': AAE CP Angleterre 567/364.

27. Confessions of a Justified Sinner

276 'monster of virtue': MJ I, p.1.

276 'tyranny of France': op. cit., p.ii.

277 'yourself to me': op. cit., p.27.

277 'without seeing him': op. cit., p.57.

278 'chained': op. cit., p.20.

278 'chain of imprudences': op. cit., p.70.

278 'chain the lion': op. cit., p.78.

278 'chain of misfortunes': op. cit., p.14.

278 'dismemberment': op. cit., p.ii.

278 'evil clash of their terrible interests': op. cit., p.4.

279 of all respect: see *The Literary Underground of the Old Regime* by Robert Darnton.

279 'foundational text': *Blackmail, Scandal, and Revolution*, Burrows, p.152.

280 'and abandoned by all': MHV, p.4.

280 'could dare all': op. cit., p.11.

281 'of my subsistence': quoted in *Cagliostro and Company*, Funck-Brentano, pp. 77–8.

281 'most shameful tales': quoted in op. cit., pp. 129–30.

282 '*moisonneuse*': quoted in op. cit., p.136.

282 'monster' . . . 'her sister's help': quoted in op. cit., p.139.

282 'consolation': quoted in op. cit., p.134.

282 'some German principality': AN F7/4445/2–4550/2/13.

282 'nonsense': quoted in *Cagliostro and Company*, Funck-Brentano, p.137.

282 'still sustains me': quoted in op. cit., p.143.

283 'her perfidious caresses': *Second Mémoire Justificatif de la Comtesse de Valois de la Motte*, p.27.

283 'sensitive character': *Grande Visite de Madame de Lamotte au Père Duchesne Malade*, p.1.

283 'good sense': *Grand Visite du Père Duchesne à Madame Lamotte*, p.5.

28. The Fall of the Houses of Valois and Bourbon

285 'as a chimney': quoted in *Cagliostro and Company*, Funck-Brentano, p.146.

285 'loathsome holes': quoted in op. cit., p.163.

286 'stop its course': LJSRV II, 'Supplement', p.61.

286 'from head to foot': quoted in *Cagliostro and Company*, Funck-Brentano, pp. 166–7.

286 'the windows were open': quoted in op. cit., pp. 167–8.

286 'this cruel design': AN F7/4445/2–4550/2/49.

287 'few friends attended': AN F7/4445/2–4550/2/29.

287 'bastard heroic': 'The Diamond Necklace', Carlyle, p.78.

287 'infant wretchedness': LJSRV I, p.319.

287 'a renovated Empire': LJSRV I, p.vii.

288 'from public knowledge': quoted in *Blackmail, Scandal, and Revolution*, Burrows, p.137.

288 Nicolas into activity: the details of Nicolas's life after Jeanne derive from his own memoir and *Cagliostro and Company* by Frantz Funck-Brentano.

288 'and ferocious vizier': AN F7/4445/2–4550/2/11.

288 'contrary to the law': quoted in *Cagliostro and Company*, Funck-Brentano, p.183.

288 the queen's political role: the account of Marie Antoinette's life until her execution draws on the biographies by Antonia Fraser and Evelyne Lever.

289 'the Court of France': quoted in *Marie Antoinette*, Fraser, p.231.

289 'and the baker's boy': quoted in op. cit., p.281.

289 'feet of the king', quoted in op. cit., p.287.

290 'Paris to Versailles': quoted in *The Wicked Queen: The Origins of the Myth of Marie Antoinette* by Chantal Thomas, p.113. Other works consulted on the libelling of Marie Antoinette are *Marie-Antoinette et les pamphlets royalistes et révolutionnaires* by Henri d'Alméras and *Les Pamphlets Libertins contre Marie-Antoinette* by Hector Fleischmann.

292 'Revolutionary Tribunal': *Correspondance entre le comte de Mirabeau et le comte de La Marck*, vol. 1, p.60.

292 'vindictive': quoted in *Marie Antoinette*, Fraser, p.403.

292 'her criminal intrigues': quoted in *La Vérité sur l'affaire du collier*, Hastier, p.316.

292 'Did you not' . . . 'to speak it': quoted ibid.

292 'against a mother': quoted in *Marie Antoinette*, Fraser, p.402.

293 'than to die': quoted in *Marie-Antoinette et les pamphlets royalistes et révolutionnaires*, d'Alméras, p.390.

29. Madness, Sadness, Poverty

294 'to Orvieto white': quoted in *Cagliostro*, Gervaso, p.204.

295 'up my arse': quoted in op. cit., p.211.

295 'instruments of lechery': quoted in op. cit., p.207.

296 'regard to religion': quoted in op. cit., p.213.

296 'severe public correction': quoted in op. cit., p.216.

296 'in religious matters': quoted in op. cit., p.218.

296 'possibility of pardon': quoted in *The Seven Ordeals*, McCalman, p.207.

296 'fortress in Europe': quoted in op. cit., p.213.

297 'and her followers': quoted in op. cit., p.221.

297 'to flee, two legs': quoted in *Louis de Rohan*, Haynin, p.302.

298 'exaudi vocem meam': quoted in op. cit., p.316.

299 'have separated us': quoted in op. cit., p.324.

299 'he was improving': quoted in op. cit., p.329.

300 'feather in the breeze': quoted in op. cit., p.330.

300 'weather-cocks' . . . 'name of Valois': *Les Misérables* by Victor Hugo (Penguin, 1976), pp. 523–4.

300 'on the civil list': quoted in *Cagliostro and Company*, Funck-Brentano, p.247.

301 'strike a deal' . . . 'as an annuitant': quoted in op. cit., pp. 263–4.

301 'in his favour': quoted in op. cit., pp. 275–6.

302 'name of Valois-Collier': quoted in *The Queen's Necklace*, Mossiker, p.590.

30. Flashes in the Crystal: A Conclusion

303 'on her shoulder': quoted in *Cagliostro and Company*, Funck-Brentano, p.281.

303 'in her life': quoted in op. cit., pp. 282–3.

304 'in golden frames': *Italian Journey* in *Goethe: The Collected Works*, vol. 6 (Princeton, 1994), p.208.

304 'of noble birth': op. cit., p.211.

304 'the story of' . . . 'destroyed royal dignity': *Théatre complet: Goethe* (Gallimard, 1998), p.1662.

304 'Romance' . . . 'passion': 'The Diamond Necklace', Carlyle, p.1.

304 'spark of life': op. cit., p.42.

304 'radical vigour' . . . 'sluttishly simmering': op. cit., p.23.

305 'in the rock': op. cit., p.13.

305 'that of Bankruptcy': op. cit., p.18.

305 '*aesthetic* feeling' . . . 'scientific curiosity': op. cit., p.44.

305 'arch-quack': op. cit., p.84.

305 'fellow scoundrels': ibid.

305 'Chaos of Being': see 'On History' by Thomas Carlyle.

305 'Fire-sea': 'The Diamond Necklace', Carlyle, p.92.

305–6 'properly an intrigue?': op. cit., p.21.

306 'Chaos of Lies': op. cit., p.15.

306 'steal the necklace': review by Munro Price of *Private Lives and Public Affairs: The Causes Célèbres of Prerevolutionary France* by Sarah Maza in *Journal of Modern History* (Vol 67, December 1995), p.939.

307 'in public power': quoted in *Cagliostro and Company*, Funck-Brentano, p.181.

307 'beneficent deity' . . . 'that of her family': quoted in op. cit., pp. 95–6.

307 credit from merchants: see *General Evening Post*, 30 November 1786–2 December 1786.

308 'French Revolutionary rhetoric': *Politics, Culture and Class in the French Revolution*, Lynn Hunt, p.39.

308 akin to excrement: see 'The Notion of Expenditure' in *Visions of Excess: Selected Writings, 1927–39* by Georges Bataille, p.119.

309 22-stone *sautoir* respectively: see *The Queen's Necklace*, Mossiker, p.584.

Note on the Sources

I first came across the story of the Diamond Necklace Affair in an eight-page scherzo in *Citizens*, Simon Schama's history of the French Revolution, and was mesmerised by the involuted and precipitous tableau he presented. After some investigation, I discovered that there had not been a work published in English which made full use of the available sources since a cack-handed translation of Frantz Funck-Brentano's excellent *L'affaire du Collier* in 1902. The available printed sources – memoirs by Jeanne, Nicolas, Villette, Georgel and Beugnot; and trial briefs on behalf of all the accused – are self-evidently partial, vitiating the approach of Frances Mossiker in *The Queen's Necklace* (1961), which anthologised these texts with lavender-scented connective tissue to form a decide-for-yourself whodunnit. Thankfully, a number of other manuscript sources exist to triage the conflicting accounts of the protagonists. The interrogations of the main suspects were printed as an appendix to Emile Campardon's *Marie-Antoinette et le procès du collier* (1863). The trial dossier in the Archives nationales (once Rohan's townhouse) contains, additionally, interviews with witnesses and transcripts of the confrontations staged between them and the accused and among the accused themselves. The Archives nationales also contains the manuscript journal of the maréchal de Castries, minister of the navy, who maintained good relations with ministers sympathetic to both sides of the case. The Bibliothèque historique de la ville de Paris contains the Dossier Target, a collection of Target's research and correspondence during the trial. The view from the other side is found in the Bibliothèque nationale in the Fond Joly de Fleury, which contains the *procureur-général*'s notes and briefing papers. The journal of Siméon-Prosper Hardy, a Parisian bookseller who kept a diary of public events, is also kept here and provides a valuable insight into shifts in public opinion during the trial and rumours about the accused. The Archives des affaires étrangères holds information about the French government's attempts to extradite Nicolas and Jeanne from England, after their respective escapes. The Archives nationales also contains a number of documents pertaining to the La Mottes in England and France, just before and during the Revolution, the most significant of which are Jeanne's letters to Nicolas and her sister Marianne (the other side of the correspondences do not survive). Sadly, the letters at the centre of this strange episode – those which Rohan believed he was exchanging with Marie Antoinette – were destroyed, though I attempt in Chapter 8 to reconstruct as much of their content and tone as possible.

Bibliography

MANUSCRIPT SOURCES

Archives de l'Aube

EE 1623

Archives de la Bastille

MS 12457
MS 12517

Archives des affaires étrangères, La Corneuve

Correspondance Politique, Angleterre 328, 554–69
Correspondance Politique, Autriche 350–1
Correspondance Politique, Genève 95
Correspondance Politique, Pays-bas 174–5
Correspondance Politique, Rome 901–3
Mémoires et Documents, France 1399–1405

Archives nationales

AP 306/17 – Journal of the maréchal de Castries
F7 4445/2–4550/2
K 162
K 163
X2 B1417 – Trial dossier

Bibliothèque historique de la ville de Paris

MS 690
MS 691 – Dossier Target
MS 713

Bibliothèque municipale d'Orléans

MS 1423

Bibliothèque nationale

BN Nouv. acq. fr 6575–8
MSS France 6685 – Siméon-Prosper Hardy's Journal
MS Joly de Fleury 2088–9

British Library

Add 8760
Folio 707.g.26

PRIMARY PRINTED SOURCES

Adhémar, Gabrielle-Pauline, comtesse d', *Ma reine infortunée: souvenirs* (Paris: Plon, 2006)

Addresse de la comtesse de La Motte-Valois a l'Assemblée nationale pour être déclarée citoyenne active (London, 1791) (spurious)

Almanach de Versailles

Arneth, Alfred von (ed.), *Marie Antoinette, Joseph II und Leopold II: Ihr Briefwechsel* (Leipzig, Paris & Wein, 1866)

Arneth, Alfred d' & Flammermont, Jules (ed.), *Correspondance secrète du comte de Mercy-Argenteau avec L'empereur Joseph II et le prince de Kaunitz* (Paris, 1889–91)

Arneth, Alfred d' & Geffroy, Mathieu Auguste (ed.), *Correspondance secrète entre Marie-Thérèse et le comte de Mercy-Argenteau* (Paris: Mesnil, 1874)

Arrêt du parlement, la grand'chambre assemblée, du 31 mai 1786 (Paris, 1786)

Auckland, William Eden, Lord, *The Journals and Correspondence of William, Lord Auckland* (London, 1860–2)

Augeard, Jacques Mathieu, *Mémoires Secrets* (Paris, 1866)

Bégis, Alfred (ed.), *Le registre d'écrou de la Bastille de 1782 à 1789* (Paris, 1880)

Bernier, Olivier (ed.), *Imperial Mother, Royal Daughter: The Correspondence of Marie Antoinette and Maria Theresa* (London: Sidgwick & Jackson, 1986)

Bertin, Marie-Jeanne, *Mémoires* (Paris, 1824)

Besenval, Pierre Victor, baron de, *Mémoires* (Paris: Mercure de France, 1987)

Bette d'Étienville, Jean Charles Vincent de, *Défense à une accusation d'escroquerie* (Paris, 1786)

——, *Mémoire pour le sieur Bette d'Etienville, servant de réponse à celui de M de Fages* (Paris, 1786)

——, *Second mémoire à consulter* (Paris, 1786)

——, *Supplement et suite aux mémoires du sieur de Bette d'Etienville* (Paris, 1786)

Beugnot, Jacques Claude, *Life and Adventures of Count Beugnot* (London, Hurst and Blackett, 1871)

——, *Mémoires du comte Beugnot, 1779–1815* (Paris, 1959)

Boigne, Louise-Eléonore-Charlotte-Adélaide d'Osmond, comtesse de, *Mémoires* (Paris: Champion, 2007)

Bombelles, Marc, marquis de, *Journal* (Genève: Librairie Droz, 1977—)

Bordel Patriotique (Paris, 1791)

Boutaric, Edgard Paul (ed.) *Correspondance secrète inédite de Louis XV* (Paris, 1866)

Browning, Oscar (ed.), *Despatches from Paris, 1784–90* (London: Royal Historical Society 1909–10)

Cagliostro, Alessandro, comte de, *Mémoire pour le Comte de Cagliostro contre Maître Chesnon fils et le Sieur de Launay* (Paris & London, 1786)

——, *Mémoire pour le Comte Cagliostro, accusé* (Paris, 1786)

——, *Requête à joindre au mémoire du comte de Cagliostro* (Paris, 1786)

——, *Requête au Roi pour le comte de Cagliostro contre le sieur Chesnon fils et le sieur de Launay*

——, *Traduction d'un lettre écrite par M. le comte de Cagliostro à M* (London, 1786)

Campan, Jeanne Louise Henriette, *Mémoires* (Paris: Ramsay, 1979)

——, *The Private Life of Marie Antoinette* (Stroud: History Press, 2008)

Le Capitaine Tempête à Jeanne de La Motte (Paris, 1790?)

Compte Rendu de ce qui s'est passé au parlement relativement à l'affaire de Monseigneur le cardinal de Rohan (Paris, 1786)

Conférence entre Mme de Polignac et Mme de La Motte au parc Saint-James (Paris, 1791)

Correspondance entre le comte de Mirabeau et le comte de La Marck (Paris, 1851)

'Correspondance entre le duc d'Aiguillon et le prince-coadjuteur Louis de Rohan', *Revue d'Alsace* (1903–7), vols 54–8

Correspondance Secrète

La dernière pièce du fameux Collier (Paris, 1786)

Fages-Chaulnes, baron de, *Mémoire pour M le baron de Fages-Chaulnes* (Paris, 1786)

Fars-Fausselandry, vicomtesse de, *Mémoires* (Paris, 1830)

Feuillet de Conches, baron Félix Sebastian, *Louis XVI, Marie-Antoinette et Madame Elisabeth: lettres et documents inédits* (Paris, 1864–73)

Flammermont, Jules (ed.), *Les Correspondences des agents diplomatiques étrangers en France avant la Révolution* (Paris, 1896)

Gazette de Leyde

Gazette d'Utrecht

General Evening Post

Georgel, Jean François, *Mémoires* (Paris, 1820)

Goethe, Johann Wolfgang von, *Italian Journey* (Princeton: Princeton University Press, 1994)

——, *Théâtre Complet* (Paris: Gallimard, 1994)

Hébert, Jacques, *Grande Visite de Madame de Lamotte au Père Duchesne Malade* (Paris, 1791)

——, *Grand Visite du Père Duchesne à Madame Lamotte* (Paris, 1791)

Histoire véritable de Jeanne de Saint-Rémi, ou les aventures de la comtesse de La Motte (Paris?, 1786)

Jugement rendu par le parlement de Paris sur l'affaire du Collier de diamant (Paris, 1786)

Julie philosphe, ou le bon patriot (Paris?, 1791)

La Motte, Jeanne de, *An Address to the Public Explaining the Motives which Have hitherto Delayed the Publication of the Memoirs of the Countess de Valois de La Motte* (London, 1789)

——, *Lettre de comtesse de Valois de la Mothe à la reine de France* (Oxford, 1789)

——, *The Life of Jane de St.-Remy de Valois* (London, 1791)

——, *Mémoire pour dame Jeanne de Saint-Rémy de Valois* (Paris, 1785)

——, *Mémoires justificatifs de la comtesse de Valois de La Motte* (London, 1789)

——, *Memoirs of the Countess de Valois de La Motte* (London, 1789)

——, *Réponse pour la Comtesse de Valois-Lamotte au Mémoire du Comte Cagliostro* (Paris, 1786)

——, *Sommaire pour la Comtesse de Valois-Lamotte, accusée* (Paris, 1786)

——, *Supplique à la Nation* (Paris, 1790)

——, *Vie de Jeanne de Saint-Rémy de Valois* (Paris, 1792)

La Motte, Marc Antoine Nicolas de, *Mémoires inédits du comte de Lamotte-Valois* (Paris, 1858)

Leouzon le Duc, L., (ed.) *Corréspondance diplomatique du Baron de Staël-Holstein et du Baron Brinkman* (Paris, 1881)

Lettre de Madame de La Motte au François au sujet de son ami Calonne (London, 1789) (spurious)

Lettre à l'occasion de la detention du S E M cardinal de Rohan à la Bastille (Paris, 1785)

Lettre d'un Garde-du-Roi pour servir de suite aux mémoires sur Cagliostro (Paris, 1786)

Les lettres de cachet presque ressuscitées, ou l'enlèvement nocturne de Mme de la Mothe (Paris, 1790?)

Lévis, Pierre-Marc-Gaston, duc de, *Souvenirs-Portraits* (Paris: Mercure de France, 1993)

Ligne, Charles Joseph, prince de, *Mémoires, lettres et pensées* (Paris: François Bourin, 1990)

Linguet, Simon-Nicolas-Henri, *Mémoires sur le Bastille et sur le détention de M Linguet, écrit par lui-même* (London, 1783)

London Chronicle

Manuel, Louis Pierre, *La Bastille dévoillé* (Paris, 1789)

Marmontel, Jean-François, *Mémoires* (Paris, 1804)

Mémoires authentiques pour servir à l'histoire du comte de Cagliostro (1786) (spurious)

Mémoires Secrets (London: John Adamson, 1780–9)

Mercier, Louis-Sébastien, *Tableau de Paris* (Paris: Mercure de France, 1994)

Mirabeau, Honoré Gabriel Riqueti, comte de, *Des Lettres de cachet et des prisons d'état* (Hamburg, 1782)

Moleville, Antoine François Bertrand de, *Mémoires particuliers* (Paris, 1816)

Monbarey, Alexandre Maire Léonore de Saint-Mauris, prince de, *Mémoires* (Paris, 1826–7)

Morellet, André, abbé, *Mémoires (inédits) de l'abbé Morellet* (Paris, 1820)

Morning Chronicle and London Advertiser

Mulot, François-Valentin, *Mémoire à consulter et consultation pour frère François-Valentin Mulot* (Paris, 1786)

Nougaret, Pierre Jeanne Baptiste, *Anecdotes secrètes du dix-huitième siècle* (Paris, 1808)

Oberkirch, Henriette-Louise, baronne d', *Mémoires* (Paris: Mercure de France, 1989)

Observations de P Tranquille sur le 1er mémoire de Mme la comtesse de La Motte (Paris, 1786)

Oliva, Marie Nicole Leguay d', *Mémoire pour la demoiselle le Guay d'Oliva* (Paris, 1786)

——, *Second mémoire et pieces justificatives pour Mademoiselle le Guay d'Oliva* (Paris, 1786)

Peuchet, Jacques, *Mémoires tirés des archives de la police de Paris* (1838)

Précourt, François Duhamel, comte de, *Réponse de M le comte de Précourt aux mémoires des sieurs d'Etienville, Vaucher et Loque* (Paris, 1786)

The Public Advertiser

Recueil de pièces authetiques, secrètes et intéressantes pour servir d'éclaircissement à l'affaire concernant le cardinal-prince de Rohan (Paris, 1786)

Recueil de pieces entre M le Cardinal de Rohan, madame de la Motte, etc (Paris, 1785)

La Reine dévoilée ou Supplément au Mémoire de Mde la comtesse de Valois de La Motte (London, 1789) (spurious)

La Résurrection du Collier (Paris, 1791)

Rohan, Cardinal Louis de, *Mémoire pour Louis-René-Edouard de Rohan, cardinal* (Paris, 1786)

——, *Pièces justicatives pour M le Cardinal de Rohan* (Paris, 1786)

——, *Réflexions rapides pour M le Cardinal de Rohan sur le sommaire de la dame de La Motte* (Paris, 1786)

——, *Requête au parlement, les chambres assemblées, par M le Cardinal de Rohan* (Paris, 1786)

Ruault, Nicolas, *Gazette d'un parisien sous la Révolution: lettres à son frère, 1783–96* (Paris: Librairie Académique Perrin, 1976)

Sabran, Eléonore, *Le lit bleu: correspondance, 1777–1785* (Paris: Tallandier, 2009)

——, *La promesse: correspondance, 1786–1787* (Paris: Tallandier, 2010)

Soulavie, Jean Louis Giraud, *Mémoires Historiques et Politiques du règne de Louis XVI* (Paris, 1802)

Second Mémoire justicatif de la comtesse de Valois de la Motte (London, 1790)

Suite des observations de Motus sur le mémoire de Mlle d'Oliva (Paris, 1786)

Villette, Marc-Antoine Rétaux, *Mémoire Historique des Intrigues de la Cour* (Venice, 1790)

——, *Requête pour le sieur Marc-Antoine Rétaux de Villette, ancien gendarme, accusé* (Paris, 1786)

The World

Zorn du Bulach, Antoine Joseph, baron, *L'ambassade de prince Louis de Rohan à la cour de Vienne, 1771–1774* (Strasbourg, 1901)

SECONDARY SOURCES

The Ageless Diamond (London: Christies, 1955)

Alary, Eric, *L'Histoire de la gendarmerie de la Renaissance au IIIème millénaire* (Paris: Calman-Levy, 2000)

Alméras, Henri d', *Marie-Antoinette et les pamphlets royalistes et révolutionnaires* (Paris, 1907)

Andrews, Richard Mowery, *Law, Magistracy and Crime in Old Regime Paris, 1735–1789* (Cambridge: CUP, 1994)

Anselme, Père, *Histoire généalogique et chronologique de la maison royale de France* (Paris, 1726–33)

Antoine, Michel, *Le Conseil du Roi sous le règne de Louis XV* (Genève: Librairie Droz, 1970)

——, *Louis XV* (Paris: Fayard, 1989)

Aravamudan, Srinivas, *Enlightenment Orientalism: Resisting the Rise of the Novel* (Chicago: University of Chicago Press, 2012)

Babelon, Jean Pierre, *Le Palais de justice* (Paris, 1966)

Baker, Keith Michael (ed.), *Inventing the French Revolution. Essays on French Political Culture in the Eighteenth Century* (Cambridge: CUP, 1990)

——, *The Political Culture of the Old Regime* (Oxford: Pergamon, 1987)

Bardin, Etienne Alexandre, baron, *Dictionaire de l'armée de terre* (Paris, 1841–51)

Barea, Ilsa, *Vienna: Legend and Reality* (London: Pimlico, 1992)

Barthes, Roland, *The Rustle of Language* (New York: Hill and Wang, 1986)

Baruch, Daniel, *Simon-Nicolas-Henri Linguet, ou l'Irrécupérable* (Paris: François Bourin, 1991)

Bast, Louis Amédée de, *Les Galeries de Palais de justice de Paris: Moeurs, usages, coutumes et traditions judiciaires* (Paris, 1851)

Bataille, Georges, *Visions of Excess: Selected Writings, 1927–39* (Manchester: Manchester University Press, 1985)

Baumgartner, Frederic J., *Henry II, King of France 1547–1559* (Durham, NC: Duke University Press, 1988)

Beales, Derek, *Joseph II* (Cambridge: CUP, 1987–2009)

Beaumarchais, Pierre-Augustin Caron de, *The Figaro Triology* (Oxford: Oxford World Classics, 2008)

Béchu, Philippe & Taillard, Christian, *Les hôtels de Soubise et de Rohan-Strasbourg* (Paris: Centre historique des Archives nationales, 2004)

Behrens, C. B. A., *The Ancien Régime* (London: Thames & Hudson, 1965)

Bell, David A., *Lawyers and Citizens: The Making of a Political Elite in Old Regime France* (Oxford: OUP, 1994)

Belleval, René de, *Les Bâtards de la Maison de France* (Paris, 1901)

Benabou, Erica-Marie, *La prostitution et la police des moeurs au XVIIIe siècle* (Paris: Perrin, 1987)

Berg, Maxine & Clifford, Helen (ed.), *Consumers and Luxury: Consumer Culture in Europe, 1650–1850* (Manchester: Manchester University Press, 1999)

Bernier, Olivier, *Louis the Beloved: The Life of Louis XV* (London: Weidenfeld & Nicolson, 1984)

Blampignon, E. A., *Bar-Sur-Aube* (Paris, 1900)

Blanning, Tim *The Culture of Power and the Power of Culture: Old Regime Europe 1660–1789* (Oxford: OUP, 2001)

——, *The Eighteenth Century: Europe 1688–1815* (Oxford: OUP, 2000)

——, *The Pursuit of Glory: Europe 1648–1815* (London: Penguin, 2008)

Bluche, François, *Les magistrats du parlement de Paris au XVIIIème Siecle, 1715–1771* (Paris, 1960)

——, *La vie quotidienne de la noblesse française au XVIIIeme siècle* (Paris, Libraire Hachette, 1973)

——, *La vie quotidienne de temps de Louis XV* (Paris: Hachette, 1974)

Bompard, Raoul, *Le Crime de lèse-majesté* (Paris, 1888)

Bosher, J. F., *French Finances 1770–1795: From Business to Bureaucracy* (Cambridge: CUP, 1979)

Boulaire, Alain, *Les Rohans: 'roi ne puis, duc ne daigne, Rohan suis* (Paris: Editions France-Empire, 2001)

Boyer, Marie-France, *The Private Realm of Marie Antoinette* (London: Thames & Hudson, 1996)

Brewer, John & Porter, Roy (eds.), *Consumption and the World of Goods* (London: Routledge, 1993)

Brooks, Peter, *The Novel of Worldliness: Crébillon, Marivaux, Laclos, Stendhal* (Princeton: Princeton University Press, 1969)

Browne, Rory, 'Court and crown: rivalry at the court of Louis XVI and its importance in the formation of a pre-revolutionary opposition' (unpublished PhD, Oxford 1991)

——, 'The Diamond Necklace Affair Revisited: the Rohan family and court politics', *Renaissance and Modern Studies* (vol. 33, 1989)

Burrows, Simon, *Blackmail, Scandal, and Revolution: London's French libellistes, 1758–92* (Manchester: Manchester University Press, 2009)

——, *A King's Ransom: The Life of Charles Théveneau de Morande, Blackmailer, Scandalmonger and Master-Spy* (London: Continuum, 2010)

Campardon, Emile, *Marie-Antoinette et le procès du collier* (Paris, 1863)

Campbell, Peter, Kaiser, Thomas E. & Linton, Marisa (eds.), *Conspiracy in the French Revolution* (Manchester: Manchester University Press, 2010)

Campbell, Peter (ed.), *The Origins of the French Revolution* (Basingstoke: Palgrave Macmillan, 2006)

Carlyle, Thomas, 'The Diamond Necklace' in *Critical and Miscellaneous Essays* (London: Chapman and Hall, 1869)

Carrez, Jean-Pierre, *Femmes opprimées à la Salpêtrière de Paris (1656–1791)* (Paris: Connaissances et Savoirs, 2005)

Castelot, André, *Marie-Antoinette* (Paris, 1958)

Castiglione, Dario & Sharpe, Lesley (eds.), *Shifting the Boundaries: Transformations of the Languages of Public and Private in the Eighteenth Century* (Exeter: University of Exeter Press, 1995)

Censer, Jack R., *The French Press in the Age of Enlightenment* (London: Routledge, 1994)

——, and Popkin, Jeremy D. (eds.), *Press and Politics in Pre-Revolutionary France* (Berkeley: University of California Press, 1994)

Chartier, Roger, *The Cultural Origins of the French Revolution* (Durham, NC: Duke University Press, 1991)

Chasset, Alphonse, *Les nobles et les vilains du temps passé* (Paris, 1857)

Chaussinand-Nogaret, Guy, *The French Nobility in the Eighteenth Century: From Feudalism to Enlightenment* (Cambridge: CUP, 1985)

——, *Mirabeau* (Paris: Editions de Seuil, 1982)

Chevalier, L., *Histoire de Bar-sur-Aube* (Bar-sur-Aube, 1851)

Cobban, Alfred, *A History of Modern France: Volume I, 1715–1799* (London: Penguin, 1972)

Cottret, Monique, *La Bastille à prendre: histoire et mythe de la forteresse royale* (Paris: Presses universitaires de France, 1986)

Courcelles, Jean Baptiste Pierre Julien, *Dictionnaire universelle de la noblesse de la France* (Paris, 1820–2)

Crankshaw, Edward, *Maria Theresa* (London: Constable, 1983)

Cronin, Vincent, *Louis and Antoinette* (London: Harvill, 1989)

Crowston, Claire Haru, *Fabricating Women: The Seamstresses of Old Régime France, 1675–1791* (Durham, NC: Duke University Press, 2001)

Cumming, Mark (ed.), *The Carlyle Encyclopedia* (Madison, NJ: Farleigh Dickinson University Press, 2004)

Cuzin, Jean Pierre, *Jean-Honoré Fragonard: vie et oeuvre – catalogue complet des peintures* (Fribourg: Suisse, 1987)

Darnton, Robert, *The Devil in the Holy Water, or The Art of Slander from Louis XIV to Napoleon* (Philadelphia: University of Pennsylvania Press, 2010)

——, *The Forbidden Best-Sellers of Pre-Revolutionary France* (London: HarperCollins, 1996)

——, *The Great Cat Massacre and Other Episodes in French Cultural History* (New York: Basic Books, 1984)

——, *The Literary Underground of the Old Regime* (Cambridge, Mass: HUP, 1982)

——, 'The memoirs of Lenoir, lieutenant de police de Paris, 1774–1785', *English Historical Review* (vol. 85, 1970)

——, *Mesmerism and the End of the Enlightenment in France* (Cambridge, Mass: HUP, 1968)

——, & Roche, Daniel (eds.), *Revolution in Print: The Press in France, 1775–1800* (Berkeley: University of California Press, 1989)

Docker, John & Fischer, Gerhard (eds.), *Adventures of Identity: European Multicultural Experiences and Perspectives* (Tübingen: Stauffenburg, 2001)

Doyle, William, *Aristocracy and Its Enemies in the Age of Revolution* (Oxford: OUP, 2009)

——, *Officers, Nobles and Revolutionaries: Essays on Eighteenth-Century France* (London: Hambledon Press, 1995)

—— (ed.), *The Old European Order 1660–1800* (Oxford: OUP, 1992)

—— (ed.), *Old Régime France* (Oxford: OUP, 2001)

——, *Origins of the French Revolution* (Oxford: OUP, 1999)

——, *The Oxford History of the French Revolution* (Oxford: OUP, 2003)

——, *Venality: The Sale of Offices in Eighteenth-Century France* (Oxford: Clarendon Press, 1996)

Duchesne, Henri Gaston, *Histoire de l'abbaye royale de Longchamp* (Paris, 1906)

Dumas, Alexandre, *The Queen's Necklace* (London, 1894)

Dunlop, Ian, *Marie-Antoinette: A Portrait* (London: Phoenix, 1998)

Egret, Jeanne *The French Pre-Revolution, 1787–8* (Chicago: University of Chicago Press, 1977)

Espezel, Pierre, *Le Palais de justice de Paris, château royale* (Paris, 1938)

Farge, Arlette, *Subversive Words: Public Opinion in Eighteenth-Century France* (University Park, Pa: Pennsylvania State University Press, 1995)

Farr, Evelyn, *Before the Deluge: Parisian society in the reign of Louis XVI* (London: Peter Owen, 1994)

——, *Marie-Antoinette and Count Axel Fersen: The Untold Love Story* (London: Peter Owen, 1995)

Félix, Joel, *Les Magistrats du parlement de Paris, 1771–90* (Paris: Sedepols, 1990)

Ferrière, Claude Joseph de, *Dictionnaire de droit et de pratique* (Paris, 1787)

Fierro, Alfred, *Histoire et Dictionnaire de Paris* (Paris: R. Laffont, 1996)

Fitzsimmons, Michael P., *The Parisian Order of Barristers and the French Revolution* (Cambridge, Mass: HUP, 1987)

Fleischmann, Hector, *Les pamphlets libertins contre Marie-Antoinette* (Paris, 1908)

Fosseyeux, Marcel, *L'Hotel-Dieu de Paris au XVII et au XVIIIe siècle* (Paris, 1912)

Fraser, Antonia, *Marie-Antoinette* (London: Weidenfeld & Nicolson, 2001)

Freud, Sigmund, *The Standard Edition of the Complete Words of Sigmund Freud* (London: Hogarth Press, 1953–74)

Funck-Brentano, Frantz, *Cagliostro and Company* (London: John Macqueen, 1902)

——, *The Diamond Necklace* (London: John Macqueen, 1901)

Furet, François, *Revolutionary France 1770–1880* (Oxford: Blackwell, 1992)

Gady, Alexandre, *Le Marais: guide historique et architectural* (Paris: Editions Carré, 1994)

Garrioch, David, *Neighbourhood and Community in Eighteenth-Century Paris* (Cambridge: CUP, 1986)

Gaxotte, Pierre, *Paris au XVIIIe siècle* (Paris: Arthaud, 1982)

Gay, Peter, *The Enlightenment: An Interpretation* (New York: Norton, 1977)

Genette, Gérard, *Figures II: Essais* (Paris: Editions du Seuil, 1969)

Gervaso, Roberto, *Cagliostro: A Biography* (London: Gollancz, 1974)

Goodman, Dena, *Becoming a Woman in the Age of Letters* (Ithaca: Cornell University Press, 2009)

—— (ed.), *Marie Antoinette: Writings on the Body of the Queen* (New York: Routledge, 2003)

——, *The Republic of Letters: A Cultural History of the French Enlightenment* (Ithaca: Cornell University Press, 1994)

Gruder, Vivian, 'The Question of Marie-Antoinette: The Queen and Public Opinion Before the Revolution', *French History* (vol. 16, 2002)

Gunn, J. A. W., *Queen of the World: Opinion in the Public Life of France from the Renaissance to the Revolution* (Oxford: SVEC, 1995)

Habermas, Jürgen, *The Structural Transformation of the Public Sphere: An Inquiry into a Category of Bourgeois Society* (Cambridge: Polity, 1989)

Halevi, Ran, *Les loges maçonniques dans la France d'ancien régime aux origines de la sociabilité démocratique* (Paris: Librairie Armand Colin, 1984)

Hardman, John, *French Politics, 1774–1789: From the Accession of Louis XVI to the Fall of the Bastille* (London: Longman, 1995)

——, *Louis XVI* (New Haven: Yale University Press, 1993)

Haslip, Joan, *Madame du Barry: The Wages of Beauty* (London: Weidenfeld & Nicolson, 1991)

Hastier, Louis, *La vérité sur l'affaire du collier* (Mulhouse: Editions Recontre, 1970)

Haynin, Eric de, *Louis de Rohan: le cardinal 'collier'* (Paris: Perrin, 1997)

Hernandez, Philippe, *Description de la généralité de Paris* (Paris, 1759)

Hillairet, Jacques, *Dictionnaire historique des rues de Paris* (Paris: Editions de Minuit, 1963)

——, *Evocation de vieux Paris* (Paris, 1953–58)

Hosford, Desmond & Wojtkowksi, Chong J. (eds.), *French Orientalism: Culture, Politics, and the Imagined Other* (Newcastle upon Tyne: Cambridge Scholars Publishing, 2010)

Hufton, Olwen, *The Poor of Eighteenth-Century France, 1750–1789* (Oxford: Clarendon Press, 1974)

Hughes, Peter, *Eighteenth-Century France and the East* (London: The Wallace Collection, 1981)

Hugo, Victor, *Les Misérables* (London: Penguin, 1980)

Hunt, Lynn (ed.), *Eroticism and the Body Politic* (Baltimore: Johns Hopkins Press, 1991)

——, *The Family Romance of the French Revolution* (London: Routledge, 1992)

——, *Politics, Culture and Class in the French Revolution* (Berkeley: University of California Press, 1984)

Hussey, Andrew, *Paris: The Secret History* (London: Viking, 2006)

Jacob, Margaret C., *Living the Enlightenment: Freemasonry and Politics in Eighteenth-Century Europe* (New York: OUP, 1991)

——, *The Origin of Freemasonry: Facts and Fictions* (Philadelphia: University of Pennsylvania Press, 2006)

Jacobs, Eva (ed.), *Women and Society in Eighteenth-Century France* (London: Athlone Press, 1979)

J. F. G., *Essais historiques sur la ville de Bar-sur-Aube* (Troyes, 1838)

Jones, Colin, *The Great Nation: France from Louis XV to Napoleon, 1715–99* (London: Allen Lane, 2002)

——, *Paris: Biography of a City* (London: Penguin, 2006)

Jones, Peter, *Reform and Revolution in France: The Politics of Transition, 1774–91* (Cambridge: CUP, 1995)

Kaiser, Thomas E. & Van Kley, Dale K. (eds.), *From Deficit to Deluge: The Origins of the French Revolution* (Stanford: Stanford University Press, 2011)

Kaiser, Thomas E., 'Who's afraid of Marie-Antoinette? Diplomacy, Austrophobia and the queen', *French History* (vol. 14, 2000)

Kaplan, Stephen, 'The Famine Plot Persuasion in Eighteenth-Century France', *Transactions of the American Philosophical Society* (vol. 72, 1982)

Kelly, G. A., 'From Lèse-Majesté to Lèse-Nation: Treason in Eighteenth-Century France', *Journal of the History of Ideas* (vol. 42, 1981)

Labourdette, Jean-François, *Vergennes, ministre principal de Louis XVI* (Paris: Editions Desjonquères, 1990)

La Chenaye-Desbois, François-Alexandre Aubert de, *Dictionnaire de la Noblesse* (Paris: 1770–86)

Laclos, Choderlos de, *Les Liaisons Dangereuses* (Penguin: London, 1961)

Lacour-Gayet, Robert, *Calonne: financier, réformateur, contre-révolutionnaire 1734–1802* (Paris, 1963)

La Croix Castries, René de, *Le Maréchal de Castries* (Paris: Editions Albatros, 1979)

La Fontaine, Jean de la, *The Complete Fables of Jean de La Fontaine* (Urbana: University of Illinois Press, 2007)

Landes, Joan, *Women and the Public Sphere in the Age of the French Revolution* (Ithaca: Cornell University Press, 1988)

La Place, Pierre Antoine, *Le théâtre anglois* (London, 1746–9)

Laugier, Lucien, *Le duc d'Aiguillon* (Paris: Albatros, 1984)

Legier-Desgranges, *L'évasion de Madame de La Motte* (Paris, 1949)

Le Roy Ladurie, Emmanuel, *The Ancien Régime: A History of France, 1610–1774* (Oxford: Blackwell, 1996)

Le Tourneur, Pierre (ed.), *Shakespeare traduit de l'anglois* (Paris, 1776–83)

Lever, Evelyne, *L'affaire du collier* (Paris: Fayard, 2004)

——, *Louis XVI* (Paris: Fayard, 1985)

——, *Marie-Antoinette* (Paris: Fayard, 1991)

Lever, Maurice, *Beaumarchais: A Biography* (New York: Farrar, Straus and Giroux, 2009)

Levron, Jacques, *Daily Life at Versailles in the Seventeenth and Eighteenth Centuries* (London: Allen & Unwin, 1968)

——, *Versailles, ville royale* (Paris, 1964)

Levy, Darline Gay, *The Ideas and Careers of Simon-Nicolas-Henri Linguet* (Urbana: University of Illinois Press, 1980)

Longueil, Charles-Henri, marquis de, *L'orphelin anglais* (Paris, 1769)

Lüsebrink, Hans-Jürgen & Reichardt, Rolf, *The Bastille: A History of a Symbol of Despotism and Freedom* (Durham, NC: Duke University Press, 1997)

McCalman, Iain, 'Mad Lord George and Madame La Motte: Riot and Sexuality in the Genesis of Burke's Reflections on the Revolution in France', *Journal of British Studies* (vol. 35, 1996)

——, *The Seven Ordeals of Count Cagliostro* (London: Century, 2003)

McMahon, Darrin M., *Enemies of the Enlightenment: The French Counter-Enlightenment and the Making of Modernity* (Oxford: OUP 2001)

Mansel, Philip, *The Court of France, 1789–1830* (Cambridge: CUP, 1988)

Marraud, Matthieu, *La noblesse de Paris au XVIIIe siècle* (Paris: Edition de Seuil, 2000)

Martin, Etienne (de), *Le goût chinois du cardinal Louis de Rohan* (Strasbourg: Musée de la Ville de Strasbourg, 2008)

Mason, Hayden T., *The Darnton Debate: Books and Revolution in the Eighteenth Century* (Oxford: SVEC, 1998)

Maza, Sarah, *Private Lives and Public Affairs: The Causes Célèbres of Pre-revolutionary France* (Berkeley: University of California Press, 1993)

Merrick, Jeffrey W., *The Desacralization of the French Monarchy in the Eighteenth Century* (Baton Rouge: Louisiana State University Press, 1990)

Meyer, Daniel, *Quand les rois régenait a Versailles* (Paris: Fayard, 1982)

Michaud, Louis Gabriel (ed), *Biographie universelle ancienne et moderne* (Paris, 1843–65)

Michelet, Jules, *Histoire de France* (Paris, 1879)

Miles, Jonathan, *Medusa: The Shipwreck, the Scandal, the Masterpiece* (London: Jonathan Cape, 2007)

Montbas, Hugues de, *La Police parisienne sous Louis XVI* (Paris, 1949)

Morel, Bernard, *Les joyaux de la couronne de France* (Anvers: Fonds Mercator, 1988)

Mossiker, Frances, *The Queen's Necklace* (London: Phoenix, 2002)

Mousnier, Roland, *The Institutions of France under Absolute Monarchy* (Chicago: University of Chicago Press, 1979–1984)

Muchembled, Robert, *Les Ripoux des Lumières: Corruption policière et Révolution* (Paris: Seuil, 2011)

Muller, Claude, *Le siècle de Rohan: une dynastie de cardinaux en Alsace au XVIIIe siècle* (Strasbourg: Nuée bleue, 2006)

Murphy, Orville T., *Charles Gravier, Comte de Vergennes: French Diplomacy in the Age of Revolution, 1719–1787* (Albany: State University Press of New York, 1982)

Nathans, Benjamin, 'Habermas's "Public Sphere" in the era of the French Revolution', *French Historical Studies* (vol. 16, 1990)

Newton, William Ritchey, *Derrière la façade: vivre au château de Versailles au XVIIIe siècle* (Paris: Perrin, 2008)

——, *L'espace du roi: la cour de France au château de Versailles, 1682–1789* (Paris: Fayard, 2000)

——, *La petite cour: service et serviteurs à la cour de Versailles au XVIIIe siècle* (Paris: Fayard, 2006)

——, *Versailles, coté jardins: splendeurs et misères de Louis XIV à la Révolution* (Paris: Tallandier, 2011)

Nicolardot, Louis, *Journal de Louis XVI* (Paris, 1873)

Nisbet, H. B., & Rawson, Claude (eds.), *The Cambridge History of Literary Criticism: Volume IV – The Eighteenth Century* (Cambridge: CUP, 1999)

Nolhac, Pierre, *Le château de Versailles au temps de Marie Antoinette* (Paris, 1889)

——, *Le château de Versailles sous Louis Quinze* (Paris, 1898)

——, *Histoire du château de Versailles* (Paris, 1918)

——, *Le Trianon de Marie-Antoinette* (Paris, 1914)

——, *Versailles aux dix-huitième siècle* (Paris, 1926)

——, *Versailles et la cour de France* (Paris, 1925–30)

——, *Versailles inconnu* (Paris, 1925)

——, *Versailles, les extérieurs et les jardins* (Paris, 1923)

O'Connell, Lisa & Cryle, Peter (eds.), *Libertine Enlightenment: Sex, Liberty and License in the Eighteenth Century* (Basingstoke: Palgrave Macmillan, 2004)

Ozanam, Denise, *Claude Baudard de Sainte-James* (Genève: Librairie Droz, 1969)

Ozanam, Yves, *Palais de justice* (Paris: Action artistique de la Ville de Paris, 2002)

Paskoff, Benjamin, *Linguet: Eighteenth-Century Intellectual Heretic of France* (Smithtown: Exposition Press, 1983)

Péju, Sylvie, *Palais de justice* (Paris: Seuil, 1987)

Pemble, John, *Shakespeare Goes to Paris: How the Bard Conquered France* (London: Hambledon and London, 2005)

Pimodan, Claude, comte de, *Le comte F. C. de Mercy-Argenteau, ambassadeur impérial à Paris sous Louis XV et sous Louis XVI* (Paris, 1911)

Pincas, Stéphane, *Versailles: The History of the Gardens and their Sculpture* (London: Thames & Hudson, 1996)

Pointon, Marcia, *Brilliant Effects: A Cultural History of Gem Stones and Jewellery* (New Haven: Yale University Press, 2009)

Pomeau, René, *Laclos ou le paradoxe* (Paris: Hatier, 1975)

Pottet, Eugène, *Histoire de la Conciergerie du palais du Paris, depuis ses origines jusqu'a nos jours* (Paris, 1922)

Poulet, Anne L., *Jean-Antoine Houdon: Sculptor of the Enlightenment* (National Gallery of Art, Washington DC/University of Chicago Press, 2003)

Prevost, Michel (ed.), *Dictionnaire de biographie française*

Price, Munro, *The Fall of the French Monarchy: Louis XVI, Marie Antoinette and the Baron de Breteuil* (London: Pan, 2003)

——, *Preserving the Monarchy: The Comte de Vergennes, 1774–87* (Cambridge: CUP, 1995)

——, & Hardman, John (ed.), *Louis XVI and the Comte de Vergennes: Correspondence, 1774–87* (Oxford: Voltaire Foundation, 1998)

Quérard, Joseph Marie, *Les Supercheries littéraires dévoilées* (Paris, 1869)

Quétel, Claude, *La Bastille: histoire vraie d'un prison légendaire* (Paris: Laffont, 1989)

Ravel, Jeffrey S., *The Contested Parterre: Public Theater and French Political Culture, 1680–1791* (Ithaca: Cornell University Press, 1999)

Ribeiro, Aileen, *The Art of Dress: Fashion in England and France 1750–1820* (New Haven: Yale University Press, 1995)

——, *Dress in Eighteenth-Century Europe 1715–1789* (London: Batsford, 1984)

——, *Fashion in the French Revolution* (London: Batsford, 1988)

Ridley, Jasper, *The Freemasons* (London: Constable, 1999)

Roche, Daniel, *The Culture of Clothing: Dress and Fashion in the Ancien Régime* (New York: CUP, 1994)

——, *France in the Enlightenment* (Cambridge, Mass: HUP, 1998)

——, *A History of Everyday Things: The Birth of Consumption in France, 1600–1800* (Cambridge: CUP, 2000)

——, *The People of Paris: An Essay in Popular Culture in the Eighteenth Century* (Leamington Spa: Berg, 1987)

—— (ed.), *La ville promise: mobilité et accueil à Paris (fin XVIIe siècle–début XIXe siècle)* (Paris: Fayard, 2000)

Roman, Christian, 'Le Monde de Pauvres à Paris au XVIIIe Siècle', *Annales. Histoire, Sciences Sociales* (vol. 37, 1982)

Rosbottom, Ronald C., *Choderlos de Laclos* (Boston: Twayne Publishers, 1978)

Sargentson, Carolyn, *Merchants and Luxury Markets: The Marchands Merciers of Eighteenth-Century Paris* (London: Victoria & Albert Museum, 1996)

Schama, Simon, *Citizens: A Chronicle of the French Revolution* (London: Penguin, 1989)

Schwarz, Robert M., *Policing the Poor in Eighteenth-Century France* (Chapel Hill: University of North Carolina Press, 1988)

See, Henri, *La France economique et sociale au XVIIIe siècle* (Paris, 1952)

Sgard, Jean (ed.), *Dictionnaire des journalistes, 1600–1789* (Universitaires Grenoble, 1976)

——, *Dictionnaire des journaux, 1600–1789* (Paris: Universitas, 1991)

Sheehan, J. H., *The Parlement of Paris* (Bodmin: Sutton, 1998)

Socard, Emile, 'Tablettes Généalogiques de la Maison de Valois de St-Rémy', *Mémoires de la Société académique d'agriculture, des sciences, arts et belles-lettres du département de l'Aube* (vol. 31, 1868)

Solnon, Jean-François, *La Cour de France* (Paris: Fayard, 1987)

Spawforth, Tony, *Versailles: A Biography of a Palace* (New York: St Martin's Press, 2010)

Stone, Bailey, *The French Parlements and the Crisis of the Old Regime* (Chapel Hill, NC: University of North Carolina Press, 1986)

——, *The Parlement of Paris, 1774–1789* (Chapel Hill, NC: University of North Carolina Press, 1981)

Strayer, Brian E., *Lettres de Cachets and Social Control in the Ancien Régime, 1659–1789* (New York: Peter Lang, 1992)

Swann, Julian, *Politics and the Parlement of Paris under Louis XV, 1754–1774* (Cambridge: CUP, 1995)

Szabo, Franz, *Kaunitz and Enlightened Absolutism, 1753–1780* (Cambridge: CUP, 1994)

Szerb, Antal, *The Queen's Necklace* (London: Pushkin Press, 2009)

Tackett, Timothy, *Becoming a Revolutionary: The Deputies of the French National Assembly and the Emergence of a Revolutionary Culture (1789–1790)* (University Park, PA: Pennsylvania State University Press, 1996)

——, 'Conspiracy obsession in a time of revolution: French elites and the origins of the Terror, 1789–1792', *American Historical Review* (vol. 105, 2000)

Thomas, Chantal, *The Wicked Queen: The Origins of the Myth of Marie-Antoinette* (New York: Zone Books, 1999)

Voltaire, *Le siècle de Louis XIV* (Paris: Nouvelle Librairie de France, 1985)

Wahl, Roger, *La folie Saint-James* (Neuilly-sur-Seine: l'Auteur, 1955)

Weber, Caroline, *Queen of Fashion: What Marie Antoinette Wore to the Revolution* (London: Aurum, 2007)

Weil, Françoise, *Livres interdits, livres persécutés 1720–1770* (Oxford: Voltaire Foundation, 1999)

Welch, Ellen R., *A Taste for the Foreign: Worldly Knowledge and Literary Pleasure in Early Modern French Fiction* (Newark: University of Delaware Press, 2011)

Williams, Alan, *The Police of Paris, 1718–89* (Baton Rouge: Louisiana State University Press, 1979)

Wootton, David, *Bad Medicine: Doctors Doing Harm Since Hippocrates* (Oxford: OUP, 2006)

Yogev, Gedalia, *Diamonds and Coral: Anglo-Dutch Jews and Eighteenth-Century Trade* (Leicester: Leicester University Press, 1978)

Index